WORKS ISSUED BY
THE HAKLUYT SOCIETY

———————

THE THIRD VOYAGE
OF MARTIN FROBISHER TO BAFFIN ISLAND
1578

THIRD SERIES
NO. 6

Plate I: Martin Frobisher: portrait by Cornelius Kettel, 1577.
This likeness, painted during the early months of 1577, sets the context of his imagined achievement. Behind Frobisher's left elbow stands a globe, though too indistinctly seen to portray his discoveries; he is comprehensively armed, perhaps a hint to potential interlopers, whilst around his neck, a whistle somewhat prematurely denotes high command at sea.
By permission of the Bodleian Library, Oxford

THE THIRD VOYAGE OF
MARTIN FROBISHER
TO BAFFIN ISLAND
1578

Edited by
JAMES McDERMOTT

THE HAKLUYT SOCIETY
LONDON
2001

Published by The Hakluyt Society
c/o Map Library
British Library, 96 Euston Road,
London NW1 2DB

SERIES EDITORS
W. F. RYAN
ROBIN LAW

ISBN 0 904180 69 7
ISSN 0072 9396

British Library Cataloguing-in-Publication Data
A catalogue record for this book is
available from the British Library

Typeset by Waveney Typesetters, Wymondham, Norfolk
Printed in Great Britain at
The Bath Press, Bath

CONTENTS

ILLUSTRATIONS AND MAPS

EDITOR'S NOTES

On sources

Sources for Frobisher's 1578 voyage are relatively abundant; an indication of a fairly widespread contemporary English interest in, if not necessarily enthusiasm for, its goals. Christopher Hall's log for the ship *Thomas Allen* and, on the return passage, the *Ayde* (BL Harleian MS 167/42, ff. 184r–200r), is reproduced for the first time in the present work. Hall was the chief pilot of the expedition, and his log contains much critical material that is not available elsewhere. Approximately half of the log and journal of Edward Fenton, captain of the ship *Judith* and Frobisher's lieutenant-general (Magdelene College Library, Cambridge: Pepys MS 2133 (paginated); pp. 17–75) has been transcribed previously and presented by W. A. Kenyon in his article 'The Canadian Arctic Journal of Capt. Edward Fenton', *Archivaria*, 2, 1980–81, pp. 171–203. Fenton is hereafter reproduced in full. Also from the same manuscript bundle is presented Fenton's schedule for provisioning the proposed colony, and a previously unpublished curiosity: an English prayer for the succour of voyagers to new lands, possibly to be attributed to Reverend Wolfall, a West Country preacher who accompanied the expedition and was intended to have remained with the colony. Another journal, usually attributed to Charles Jackman, master of the *Judith* (BL Harleian MS 167/41, ff. 181r–182v), is no more than a fragment; the remainder may have been stolen during a burglary of John Dee's home – possibly by, or at the instigation of, John Davis – sometime between 1583 and 1589.[1] This is reproduced for the first time in the present work. The narrative of Edward Selman, a merchant who sailed in the *Ayde* (BL Harleian MS 167/40, ff. 166r–180r), has been published previously in Admiral Collinson's 1867 Hakluyt Society volume, *Three Voyages of Martin Frobisher* and reproduced verbatim by V. Stefansson and E. McCaskill, in their (1938) *The Three Voyages of Martin Frobisher*. The transcription utilized in these works is incomplete, however, omitting substantial marginalia, and a new version is therefore presented in the present work. In mid-1579, Michael Lok, former treasurer of the ephemeral 'Company of Cathay', set down a damning indictment of Frobisher's record during the life of the enterprise, entitled 'The doynges of Captayne Furbusher amongst the Companyes Busynes' (BL Lansdowne MSS 100/1, ff. 1r–14v). Though extremely partial (often delightfully so), this has been reproduced here for the first time to balance the laudatory tenor of Best and Ellis, and to provide detail on events not discussed elsewhere.

---

[1] For this episode, see W. Sherman, 'John Dee's Role in Martin Frobisher's North-west Enterprise', in Symons, *Meta Incognita*, I, pp. 293–4. Both the ship's log of Christopher Hall and Edward Selman's narrative are fair copies, in Dee's hand, of original manuscripts which came into his possession soon after the collapse of the northwest enterprise.

Immediately following the return of the voyage, the London publisher Henry Bynnyman produced George Best's *A true discourse of the late voyages of discoverie for finding of a passage to Cathaya, by the North-West, under the conduct of Martin Frobisher, General* (1578); this was later reproduced by Hakluyt in the second edition of *Principal Navigations*. Best, an obviously well-educated gentleman who enjoyed the patronage of Christopher Hatton, had travelled previously in Muscovy. In 1577, he sailed with Frobisher as a volunteer, among several 'soldiers' intended to protect the expedition from anticipated Inuit aggression, and again in 1578, as captain of the *Anne Frances*, one of six vessels hired by the adventurers to transport ore mined in the new lands. His *True Discourse*, dedicated to Hatton, has been reproduced previously by Collinson, and, subsequently, by Stefansson and E. McCaskill. However, these works are long out of print, and as the editor will have frequent occasion to refer to the *True Discourse*, the part thereof which refers to the 1578 voyage is reproduced once more in the present volume. Another contemporaneously published account was Thomas Ellis's *A true report of the third and last voyage into Meta Incognita, achieved by the worthie Capteine, M. Martine Frobisher, Esquire, anno 1578* (London, Thomas Dawson, 1578). Ellis was one of the gentlemen-volunteers who sailed in the *Ayde* in 1578; his account, which previously has been reproduced by Stefansson and McCaskill, is relatively brief and adds little to that of Best. However, as occasional reference will be made to this work, the editor has considered it worthwhile, for the sake of completeness, to reproduce it once more in the present volume (several poems of questionable artistic merit, included by Ellis to laud Frobisher's achievement, have been omitted, as has an over-long and inapposite preface which rightly begs the reader's indulgence regarding its author's abilities).

By mid-1578, the Spanish court had been made aware of much of the detail of the enterprise by Bernadino de Mendoza, Philip II's indefatigable ambassador in London. Mendoza secured the connivance of a member of the 1578 expedition – possibly the English assayer, Robert Denham, or one of his assistants – and received a detailed report on the voyage following its return to England. His correspondence to Philip II, reiterating this information, is included in the present work. Finally, many references will be made to Michael Lok's financial accounts for the north-west enterprise (PRO Exchequer King's Remembrancer, E164/35, 36; HM715). Comprising some seven hundred pages of transactions entered into on the north-west adventurers' behalf, they are an invaluable and detailed source of data on the financing and outfitting of an English sixteenth-century voyage. Where necessary, these accounts will be quoted and individual pages reproduced, but it is not within the editor's brief to present such information in full.

On presentation

In keeping with the house style of The Hakluyt Society, the editor has expanded all elisions and shown them *thus*. Modern usage of v, u, i and j has been adopted; thus *divers*, not *diuers*, *used*, not *vsed*, *Cathay*, not *Cathaj*. Otherwise, capitalization, punctuation, spelling and grammar follow the original texts. As a general rule, the narratives have been presented with their original marginalia carried to the footnotes. In the case of the Fenton and Hall documents, which follow the ship's log format and note their respective ships' way in the sea by each watch, and whose form is therefore of intrinsic historical interest, the editor has maintained the original structure, with marginal annotations and sketches *in situ*.

INTRODUCTION

1. BACKGROUND TO THE 1578 VOYAGE

At eight o'clock on the morning of 31 May 1578, fifteen ships weighed anchor off Harwich Naze and set a course southwards towards the English Channel. Most of these vessels had been hired by the group of adventurers who had financed and set out the voyage; four were 'company' ships, owned as part of their common stock in the enterprise. Their flagship, the *Ayde*, a once and future naval vessel, had been contributed by the Queen, the most substantial investor.[1] The *Ayde*'s captain, the admiral of this fleet, was Martin Frobisher – previously a much-imprisoned privateer, ambiguous consort of Irish traitors and now, fleetingly, a putative English Columbus. In the previous two years, he had made Atlantic crossings to the south-eastern shores of the latter-day Baffin Island; this he had claimed by right of possession on behalf of his sovereign, who, with some style and wit, had named it Meta Incognita, the Unknown Limits. The coming voyage was to return there, to secure a bounty – it was fervently hoped – to rival that of the Spanish American empire. Expectations were high, but founded upon the shakiest premises.

In November 1574, Frobisher had approached and, subsequently, collaborated with Michael Lok – a London mercer, merchant adventurer and active propagandist for the expansion of English economic interests – in promoting a scheme to find and exploit a north-west route to the entrepôts of the Far East, far to the north of the known routes that were jealously guarded by their Spanish and Portuguese exploiters.[2] Since c.1561, contemporary maps had begun to depict the 'Strait of Anian', a broad east-west body of water separating the continents of America (to the south) and Asia (to the north).[3]

---

[1] Laid down at Deptford in 1560 and commissioned in 1562, the *Ayde* was first employed in the Channel in 1563 against privateers, and in the winter months of the same year against the French. The declared accounts of the navy show that she was at sea in 1567 and 1568, on the latter occasion possibly in a squadron commanded by Sir William Winter. Her rebuilding in 1580/1 suggests either that her design was by then outmoded, or that the experience of the 1577/8 voyages was a harsh one upon her fabric. Commanded by Edward Winter (son of Sir William), she later served in the 1585/6 West Indies Raid, and thereafter became something of the personal fiefdom of William Fenner, who commanded her in the Armada campaign, in the 1588/9 Narrow Seas squadron (under Sir Henry Palmer and Frobisher) and in the 1589 Portugal expedition. She took no part in subsequent major naval operations, and was condemned in 1599 (Oppenheim, *Administration of the Royal Navy*, p. 120, n. 9; Bodleian Library, Rawlinson MS A200, f. 30; PRO E351/2219, 2200, 2203, 2204, 2235; SP/12/215, 64, 76; 12/223, 76).

[2] For Lok's earlier career, see McDermott, 'Michael Lok', in Symons, *Meta Incognita*, I, pp. 119–31.

[3] The geographical feature preceded its nomenclature by some decades. The precise circumstances in which it developed in contemporary understanding remains obscure, though certain influences are clear. Venetian cartographers, uncritically accepting the 'data' of the apocryphal 15th-century Zeno voyage (as portrayed in the 1558 Zeno chart), attempted to reconcile the supposed discovery of the northern Atlantic islands of 'Estotiland', 'Friesland' and 'Icaria', and the Zeno chart's extreme northerly placement of Greenland, with existing intelligence. Previously, a number of cartographers – Rosselli (1532), Frisius (1544),

In 1566, Humphrey Gilbert had stood before the Privy Council and argued for the potential of this route against Anthony Jenkinson, the great proponent of a north-eastern route. Gilbert's arguments, set out in his *Discourse* of that year, had failed to persuade the Russia Company to relinquish its own, exclusive rights to find and exploit any northern route to the East, at which Gilbert set aside his proposed scheme to find the supposed strait.[1] Now, in 1574, Frobisher and Lok faced the same obstacle; but Frobisher's appeal to the Privy Council for assistance in 'persuading' the company, and Lok's assiduous efforts to achieve the same from within (he was the Russia Company's London agent, and a member of the company's council that had convened to consider Frobisher's proposal), swiftly undermined the resistance that previously had confounded Gilbert. In January 1575, having paid the sum of one pound to have a clerk write out their new licence, Frobisher and Lok secured the company's former right to exploit all discoveries to the north-west.[2]

Several senior members of the Russia Company, frustrated by the continuing failure to open up a trade route to the Far East via Muscovy, or indeed to realise a sustainable profit from trade with the Tsar's possessions, immediately subscribed to the project, as did a number of Lok's colleagues from the Mercers' Company. More august support came from the Privy Council: the Dudley brothers, earls of Warwick and Leicester, promised to subscribe, as did the earl of Sussex, Lord Burghley and Sir Francis Walsingham. In total, eighteen investors pledged some £875 to finance the proposed voyage.[3] This was not sufficient to set out a voyage as envisaged. Failure to increase their promised funding subsequently, and continuing doubts regarding Frobisher's fitness to command the expedition (several acts of piracy with which he had been linked previously had been directed against the cargoes of English merchants), resulted in the suspension of the project in mid-1575.[4]

Gastaldi (1546) and Salamanca (1550) – had speculated upon a broad body of water separating the western coast of America from a great, indistinct Arctic continent. To the east, this feature gradually narrowed, until the two landmasses touched to prevent – or almost prevent – egress into the Atlantic Ocean. Transposing upon this the Zeno data, the supposed Arctic continent was now assumed to be Greenland; but, with its southern extremity much further to the north than had been assumed previously, it seemed now that the expanse of water to the north of America might remain broad and open from the Atlantic to the 'Mare de Sur' (for north-west passage propagandists, the Zeno evidence was adduced in denying the possibility of a north-eastern passage, as it assumed Greenland to sweep north and eastwards to connect to the Scandinavian landmass). The first cartographer explicitly to name the Strait of Anian appears to have been Gastaldi (1561), though in the event he repeated the near closure of its eastern extremity. However, Ortelius (1564) and Cammocio (1567) opened up this easternmost feature, and in 1569, Mercator's vastly influential world map definitively 'confirmed' the wide expanse of the strait throughout its imagined course. For the sequence of maps, see Shirley, *Mapping of the World*, pp. 76, 93, 96–7, 105, 113, 124–5, 130–31, 138, 140–41; for the history of interest in the 'strait', see R. I. Ruggles, 'The Cartographical Lure of the North-west Passage', in Symons, *Meta Incognita*, I, pp. 179–256.

[1] *The discourse of syr Humfrie Gilbert knight, to prooue a passage by the North-west to Cathaya, and the East Indies*. This was published eventually in London in 1576, ostensibly to promote Frobisher's first north-west voyage.

[2] PRO EKR E164/35, p. 24 (the EKR material is incompletely foliated; all references are therefore to the pagination inserted by Craven Ord, Secondary of the King's Remembrancer Office at King's Mews, Charing Cross, c. 1821–4).

[3] Ibid., p. 3.

[4] For Frobisher's apparent unfitness to command the voyage, we have only the evidence of Lok himself (PRO SP/12/129, 44 (i)).

Early the following year, Frobisher and Lok approached their prospective adventurers once more, and received precisely the same offers of support. Lok, whose better judgement had become impaired by excessive enthusiasm for the project, committed himself – in addition to his own proposed venture of £100 – to lending the balance of funds necessary to set out a small expedition. Even so, the scale and aims of the voyage had to be revised to meet the modest budget. Two small barks – the *Gabriel* and *Michael*, of some 25–30 tons burden – and a seven-ton pinnace were purchased (the *Gabriel* and pinnace were newly built for the adventurers by Matthew Baker, one of the leading English shipwrights of the period).[1] Their outfitting, manning and victualling consumed most of the adventurers' remaining funds. Once through the anticipated passage, the original intention had been for the ships to pass on to 'Cathay' and initiate trade with the competent authorities there; whilst this remained the adventurer's primary goal, it was now tempered by the certainty that the quantity of merchandise allowed by the adventurers' budget would not be sufficient to realise a profit in 1576. Whether this understanding was the principal reason for the organization of the project as a non-terminable, joint-stock venture (rather than on the lines of the terminable models that had characterized early English voyages to the Barbary and Guinea coasts) is hard to assess – equally, the near-identical corporate structure of the Russia Company may have been influential – but it is clear that any new trade with the east was not expected to be immediately profitable.

The *Gabriel* and *Michael* departed from the Thames on 12 June 1576.[2] Despite contrary winds, mid-Atlantic gales, a brief diversion to the southern tip of Greenland (mistakenly identified as 'Friesland', courtesy of the Zeno map and subsequent promulgations of its data), a near-disastrous storm in the Davis Strait (in which the pinnace and her four hands were lost) and the defection and return to England of the *Michael* thereafter, Frobisher and his eighteen remaining mariners made a definite sighting of land to the westwards on 28 June, at approximately 62°30′N. Several days later, after sailing northeastwards across the entrance to what appeared to be a large bay or strait, and having made a brief but fateful examination of a small island at its northernmost extremity, Frobisher took the *Gabriel* into mouth of this potential passage to the east.

His reconnaissance was not successful. At a distance of no more than ten miles from the head of what would become known as Frobisher Bay, he called an end to their search, and the *Gabriel* returned to England. Her crew had lost a further five men to an Inuit ambush on 20 July; with only thirteen mariners remaining, Frobisher sought their opinion and agreed with the predictable consensus: that to pass on to the western exit of his 'strait' and from thence to Cathay was utterly impractical. Furthermore, the brief Arctic summer was almost over, and snow had begun to fall heavily upon the *Gabriel*. Even so, she might yet have sailed on for a few days more, to definitely prove or disprove the passage; but Frobisher seems to have weighed the chances of securing

---

[1] PRO EKR E164/305, p. 9.

[2] Extant contemporary accounts of the 1576 voyage are those of Christopher Hall (first reproduced in a heavily-censored form in Hakluyt, *PN* 1589, pp. 615–22) and Michael Lok (BL Cotton MSS Otho E VIII, ff. 47v–54r). George Best's narrative of the voyage in his 1578 *True Discourse* was probably compiled using these sources.

backing for a further expedition if he returned to England to report an outright failure, and decided to leave open the question of its existence in that location.[1]

The safe return of the *Gabriel* generated considerable excitement in England, even though the ostensible aims of the voyage had not been achieved. To the adventurers, it appeared that Frobisher had indeed found the passage – or perhaps, *a* passage – into the Southern Ocean, and the prospects for establishing a trade route to rival those of the Spanish and Portuguese empires seemed strong. Frobisher himself strongly argued that he had in fact found the true passage before a commission established to assess the need for, and scale of, a second voyage.[2] Nevertheless, his failure to bring home a more valuable token of his discoveries than an Inuk male captive undoubtedly contributed to the relatively modest number of potential new investors who now came forward. Prior to the end of March 1577, only forty-five subscribers (including the original adventurers) set their names to a provisional list, with a total stock of slightly more than £3,000;[3] a somewhat muted response to this potentially vast commercial opportunity.

However, in the intervening months, Michael Lok and others had been busy upon a secret matter that was about to render the question of a new eastern trade irrelevant. The Inuk captive had not been the only token of the new discoveries to be brought back to England. A piece of black ore, later described by Lok as of the size of a 'halfe pennye loafe',[4] had been picked up from the surface of Hall's island during a brief reconnaissance led by its discoverer, Christopher Hall, master of the *Gabriel*. Upon their return to England, Frobisher, apparently fulfilling an earlier promise, gave this to Lok as a momento, the first object discovered in the new land. Lok took it away, and having almost immediately decided that its shimmering surface hinted at quantities of precious metals therein, proceeded to pass samples to London assayers to have them confirm his optimistic diagnosis. Several of these, including William Williams and George Needham (assay masters, respectively, of the Mint and of the Mines Royal) duly tested the rock and informed Lok that the ore was worthless, but he persisted. An Italian assayer resident in London, Jean Baptista Agnello, took a further sample and declared it to contain both gold and silver, at which Lok began a supposedly discreet correspondence with Francis Walsingham, the Queen's principal secretary of state, to obtain a licence to secure sole rights to transport and work the ore. However, Sir William Winter, Controller of the Queen's Ships, had learned every detail of Agnello's

---

[1] McDermott, 'A right Heroicall Heart', in Symons, *Meta Incognita*, I, pp. 71–3.

[2] Document 5, p. 72: '… he vowched to them absolutlye w(i)th vehement wordes, speches and Oathes; that he had founde and discoverid the Straights, and open passadge by sea into the South Sea called Mar de Sur w(hi)ch goethe to Cathaj / and by the waye had founde divers good ports and harbors for passage of all the navye of her Ma(ies)ties Shipps, and affirmed the same by divers arguments of the depthe and culler of the water, the sight of the heade landes one boathe the sides of the Straightes at the west end thereof openinge into the broade Sea, called Mar de Sur, and the setting of the tydes w(i)th a fludd frome the west owt of the sayde sowthe sea / and by divers other arguments by demonstrac(i)on in the Cartes and Mappes, w(hi)ch things the Commissioners beleved to be trewe vppon his vehement speches, and oathes of affirmac(i)on …'. This evidence was decisive; the new commissioners wrote to the Privy Council on the 30 March 1577, concluding: '… uppon dyvers and sundry other matters whiche wee have perused and weyed, that the supposed Straight whiche *Master* Furbusher doth sett out is so farr fourth as we can gather and judge a trueth …' (PRO SP/12/111, 48).

[3] PRO SP/12/111, 48 (ii); reproduced in Collinson, pp. 108–9.

[4] Document 5, p. 72.

assays from a Saxon metallurgist, Jonas Schutz (introduced to Agnello by Sir John Berkeley and Sir William Morgan, Schutz had assisted in several assays during January 1577 unbeknown to Lok). Winter, in fact, knew much more about the business than Lok himself. Whilst Agnello had been offering Lok a fee of £30 for every ton of ore he might secure, he claimed elsewhere to have proved gold within the ore to a value, refined, of some £240 per ton (Schutz himself appears to have verified, or at least accepted, this assessment). On 29 March, the day after the inaugural meeting of the commission established to prepare the coming voyage, Winter confronted the unsuspecting Lok with his own findings. From that moment, word of the ore and its supposed properties circulated throughout London.[1]

Frobisher had taken no part in these byzantine manoeuvres. When, during dinner at Lok's house in January 1577, he had asked of the ore, he had been told that all the assays thereon had shown it to be worthless, and Lok himself subsequently admitted that he had only told the truth to his partner after 20 March, having been ordered to do so by Walsingham.[2] However, once news of the ore's supposed value became widespread, Frobisher immediately understood its significance to his own role within the enterprise. Examined once more by the commissioners for the forthcoming voyage, his claims for the ore's abundance in Hall's Island were as vehement and optimistic as those he had previously made for the north-west passage.[3] With these assurances, the commissioners and their masters on the Privy Council effectively abandoned the intention to follow up the previous year's attempt to reach Cathay, and concentrated instead on preparations to exploit this new and seemingly fabulous resource.

An unanticipated corollary of Lok's 'doble-dealings' (as he termed them) was the death of his hopes for the incorporation of a Company of Cathay. Several times during the early months of 1577, even as he struggled to prove some value in the ore, he had addressed requests to the Queen and Council, asking that articles be granted to formalize the legal identity of the enterprise (with himself as the first governor of the new entity).[4] The Queen had not refused any of these approaches; she had simply ignored them. With a potentially vast – and, if uncontrolled, a depreciatory – new source of income in prospect, she was not minded to allow any hand but hers to direct its means of acquisition and distribution. With the establishment of the commission, directly reporting to and receiving orders from the Privy Council, the functions of what had been intended as a private joint-stock company were henceforth exercised entirely under royal authority.

---

[1] The principal source for the early assays is Lok: PRO SP/12/112, 25; Agnello's seven letters to Lok (in Italian), are held in SP/12/112, 25 (i–ii); all have been reproduced previously by Collinson and Stefansson & McCaskill.

[2] PRO SP/12/112, 25.

[3] Document 5, p. 73: 'And therew(i)thall C. Furbysher vowched to the Com(m)issioners, w(i)th great speches & oathes, that there was Inoughe of yt to be had in that Countrye, too lade all the Queenes Shipps and sayd that as they sayled alongest in the straights he sawe the lyke thereof afarr of one that Iland, and one Loks lande alongest the shore, by the water lyenge lyke redd sande, glisteringe and one the rocks syddes of the shore, and at Gabriells Iland ynoughe of yt, w(i)th that Ewre of hawlls Ilande, w(hi)ch the com(m)yssioners did credyt and so certyfyed of their honors ...'.

[4] PRO SP/12/110, 21, 22; SP/12/111, 49.

The redirection of the aims of the enterprise secured a total of fifty-eight investors, new and old (though, surprisingly, several prospective adventurers withdrew at news of the ore and the corresponding, altered intentions for the coming voyage).[1] As in the previous year, the reality of what could be secured from their pockets required initial plans to be scale downwards; in this case, from a proposed fleet of two ships (of some 140 and 120 tons burden) and two barks, to a more modest scheme, whereby the Queen's ship *Ayde*, 'sold' to the enterprise as part of her venture therein, would be accompanied by the *Gabriel* and *Michael*.[2] All three vessels were to load ore in the new land, unless it was clearly proved to be worthless on site (a highly unlikely eventuality, given current expectations of the ore and the profound technical shortcomings of the small furnaces carried by the expedition). Should this be the case, the *Ayde* was to return to England immediately, whilst Frobisher would take the *Gabriel* and *Michael*, having loaded extra victuals from the *Ayde*, to press on westwards, force the passage and sail on to Cathay.[3]

Admirably flexible though these instructions seem, in reality the expedition was equipped only to service the mining operation, as the commissioners did not provide for any more possibility of profit arising from the fall-back 'Cathay' option than in the previous year. No further merchandise was purchased to take in the barks, though the trifles acquired in 1576 were loaded once more.[4] Unless that particular goal had assumed the nature of a purely scientific endeavour, therefore, we may assume that the passage project had been as effectively abandoned in the minds of the Privy Counsellors as among their fellow adventurers.

The ships departed from Harwich, their assembly port, on 26 May 1577.[5] As in the previous year, their course was laid due north until they came almost to 60°N, and thereafter westwards; utilizing the simple 'westering' technique employed by generations of Bristol fishermen. A brief and uneventful passage in fair weather brought them once more to sight land in the vicinity of Kap Farvel in southern Greenland. Having tried and failed to land there in 1576, Frobisher had been instructed to make a further attempt, to assess its potential for supporting English colonists (he had been

---

[1] PRO EKR E164/25, pp. 85–7; the total subscribed stock was £5,150 (of which £875 was allocated to cover the debts of the previous year). Possibly the prospect of the Queen's heavy hand upon the enterprise was a further disincentive.

[2] PRO SP12/111, 49. Lok (document 5, p. 74) later claimed that Frobisher had initially urged an even greater expedition, of three ships and the two barks: another manifestation, it was suggested, of his self-aggrandizement. There is no evidence to corroborate this accusation.

[3] There are three extant versions of instructions for Frobisher's 1577 voyage. All differ in minor respects, and it is not known which constituted the final draft. These are held in BL Add. MS 3583I, ff. 23v–24r, BL Sloane MS 2442 and PRO SP/12/113, 12.

[4] A preliminary plan for the voyage, drawn up before the ore became an issue (possibly in January 1577), had provided for further merchandise to the value of £1,200 (PRO SP/12/111, 49). In a subsequent, cost-cutting refinement (PRO SP/12/119, 33), this was scaled down to £300; but following the virtual abandonment of the Cathay plan in favour of the ore-mining project, all provision for further expenditure upon tradeable goods was dropped.

[5] There are only two contemporary sources for the 1577 voyage – both from eyewitnesses. George Best sailed in the *Ayde* as a gentleman-volunteer and recorded his experiences in his *True Discourse*; another 'gentleman' in the *Ayde*, Dionyse Settle, produced his *A true Reporte of the last voyage into the west and north-west regions &c., 1577. worthily atchieved by Capteine Frobisher of the sayde voyage the first finder and generall* (London, Henry Middleton, 1577), the first account of any of Frobisher's voyages to be published.

provided with ten convicted felons to conduct this experiment, but being overmanned had set them down at Harwich, contrary to his instructions). Again, he failed; the dangers presented by icebergs and mists on that coastline outweighed the subsidiary priority of exploring what lay beyond it. The fleet therefore pressed on, and despite encountering the expected storms in the Davis Strait, Hall's Island was sighted on 17 July.

Curiously, no further samples of the black ore were found upon Hall's Island, but following a brief reconnaissance of the southern shore of Frobisher Bay (during which several of the 'gentlemen' carried in the *Ayde* managed to ignite a brief war against the Inuit, killing five of their number and taking hostage a Inuk woman and child), deposits of an ostensibly similar mineral ore were discovered on an island in a sound on the northern shore, named Sussex Island and Beare Sound respectively. Some mining of this was undertaken in the following twenty-four hours; however, the site was dangerously exposed to the elements, and the shallow waters treacherous for deeper-draughted vessels. Leaving the extracted ore stockpiled there, the barks moved north-westwards along the northern shoreline, until ample sheltered mooring was discovered in a large bay, and further samples of mineral ore on a small island therein. Frobisher named these the Countess of Warwick Sound and Island in honour of the wife of his most enthusiastic noble patron. Upon the island – which also had the advantage of providing natural security against any future aggression from the Inuit – a base camp was established, and mining began immediately. Little more than a week later, approximately 160 tons of ore had been extracted and loaded into the ships. On 22 August, with signs that the brief 'summer' had run its course, the mariners' tents were taken down and the expedition hurriedly re-embarked.

No attempt had been made to explore further the 'strait', nor to search for the five men taken by the Inuit in the previous year (though Frobisher had parleyed with the Inuit and been told that they lived still; and had even drafted a letter to them at the Inuit's suggestion, 'for they knewe well the use wee have of writing').[1] The supposed passage to Cathay had been penetrated to a depth, according to Best, of no more than thirty leagues. Burdened by the prospect of heavy storms descending upon ships that now lay too low in the water, Frobisher ignored his instructions to revisit 'Friesland' and turned his vessels southwards instead, seeking a gentler latitude in which to make the eastward passage to England. In storms that chased them into the Atlantic the *Michael* went missing once more; though her captain, Gilbert Yorke, brought her safely into Yarmouth having made the more familiar, if more dangerous northern crossing. Meanwhile, The *Ayde* and *Gabriel* came into Milford Haven on 23 September, having lost only two mariners from a total complement of one hundred and forty three men.[2]

By contemporary standards, and other than upon the minor matter of providing a profit for its backers, the expedition appeared to constitute an admirable achievement. Despite minor – and, usually, pragmatic – diversions from his official instructions,

---

This was to be the most successful literary legacy of the voyages, and editions in French, German, Latin and Italian were produced between 1579 and 1582.

[1] The phrase is that of Best.

[2] One of whom was the unfortunate William Smith, master of the *Gabriel*, who fell overboard immediately after revealing a premonition of drowning (Best, 1577; Hakluyt, *PN*, 1598–1600, vii, p. 315–16).

Frobisher had proved an adept sea-commander. In addition to the singular dangers of an oceanic passage at high latitude, he and his men had been subjected to the rigours of a climate almost beyond the experience of Englishmen, whilst performing heavy manual labour with tools that almost certainly had been inadequate for their task. To excite the necessary popular attention in England, a further three Inuit captives had been secured, and though they would prove to be no more robust than their unfortunate compatriot taken in the previous year, they were at least palpable tokens of an exotic and alien land: one to which the Queen, by right of exploitation, might now lay a firm claim. In contrast to the human disasters that had scarred the early Muscovy and Guinea ventures, this had been a happy and, for the moment, an auspicious voyage.

However, its bare achievement (which, in scale, was to be far surpassed in the subsequent, 1578, voyage) was meaningless without the further success that had been promised upon the back of numerous assays upon a single, small piece of rock. Whilst the expedition – and its chief assayer, Jonas Schutz – had been at sea, no further progress towards definitively valuing the ore had been made. To date, a little less than £6,000 had been raised from the purses of the adventurers, and still there was no firm indication of when some of this might be recouped. Indeed, the post-costs of discharging the men who sailed with Frobisher in 1577 required yet more money. Even whilst the expedition was out of England, growing financial pressures had caused the Privy Council to write to the Lord Mayor of London, asking him to invite the 'substancial merchauntes of the Citie' to come forward and participate in the venture.[1] Not one of their number had done so. Disappointed in this optimistic strategy, the Council ordered Michael Lok to take up loans in the City to meet the increasingly urgent bill for wages. His failure to secure monies on the security he was able to offer, 'even upon interest', was predictable but chastening nonetheless. Bowing to the inevitable, the Council on 16 October 1577 ordered an extraordinary assessment of 20 per cent upon the adventurers' existing stock; the first of several such unanticipated recourses to their pockets.[2] Though several other occasions recommend themselves, it was probably at this moment that the former mood of optimism for the future of the enterprise first became tinged with real anxiety.

During the next few months, the scant progress of assays and reports upon the ore returned in the 1577 voyage did little to reassure the adventurers. Schutz performed three 'great proofes' upon large quantities of the ore between 1 November 1577 and 6 March 1578; none provided hard evidence of that value he had formerly proclaimed. In the meantime, another German metallurgist, Burchard Kranich, had been introduced to the enterprise by Francis Walsingham in an attempt to bring some clarity to the process of establishing the ore's true value. His strategy had precisely the opposite effect. Schutz and Kranich contracted an immediate and profound mutual loathing: each man's claims for his own expertise and the other's incompetence, and their strident efforts to secure the sole right to work the ore, brought inflated claims of what might be achieved and gave an unfortunate impetus to the enterprise at a time when all

[1] *APC*, 4 August 1577.
[2] PRO SP/12/116, 24.

common sense should have killed it off.[1] Kranich soon fell from grace, having been discovered to be salting his assays with silver-bearing 'additaments'; by then, however, the adventurers' first faint misgivings had been assuaged by the very intensity of the assayers' rivalry. Preparations for a new voyage commenced, though the logic of its scale, and the level of new commitment demanded of the adventurers, had been determined upon profoundly flawed assumptions.

At the conclusion of his second 'great proofe' on 4 December 1577, Schutz had indicated that gold and silver to a value of some £40 per ton lay within the ore.[2] This was far short of his original estimate, and indicated that much more ore would be required to realise a profit than had been anticipated previously. Accordingly, a new plan was drafted sometime before March, which proposed the mining and transportation of more than 2,000 tons of ore.[3] Schutz's third 'greate proofe', of 6 March, produced even less optimistic results and a correspondingly greater need for the raw material that would secure the adventurers' profit.[4] Furthermore, all of his assay reports had concluded with the statement that much gold and silver had remained in the melted slag; to obviate this, he claimed that new and bigger – much bigger – furnaces were required to successfully refine the ore.

These two seemingly logical extensions to current financial commitments did much to determine the nature and scale of the coming voyage. However, Michael Lok also gave credit to Frobisher for a further, major expense; claiming that he had testified to the commissioners charged with preparations for the 1578 voyage of a planned French expedition to take possession of the straits and forestall any future English claims to the land and resources of Meta Incognita.[5] This supposed threat, and the perceived need to secure more ore than the coming expedition, even in its enlarged form, would be capable of providing, had made a further refinement to existing intentions a matter of necessity. As part of the draft plan which had anticipated a hugely increased volume of raw ore, the means by which its sources might be protected were also mooted for the first time in a proposal for the establishment of a semi-permanent foothold in Meta Incognita – a presence, if realised, that would have constituted the first English colony in the New World.

Thus, the north-west adventurers were faced in the early months of 1578 with a massive incremental financial commitment over that of the previous year: not a corollary of any excessive optimism for the future, but of the flawed logic that demanded an adequate level of return upon existing and anticipated expenditure – and, as in so many other late-sixteenth-century maritime ventures, of the necessity of allowing the Queen to finance a strand of her foreign policy from the pockets of others.

[1] PRO SP/12/118, 36: (Michael Lok, 23 November 1577): '... eche is jelous of other to be put out of the work and therby lothe to shew their conynge or to use effectuall conferens'. The most detailed account of this vicious and diverting contest, also written by Michael Lok, is 'A little bundle of the tryeing of the North-west Ewre. By D. Burcot, Jonas Schutz, Baptista Agnillo, etc.' (PRO SP/12/122, 62).
[2] PRO SP/12/122, 62.
[3] PRO SP/12/124, 1.
[4] PRO SP/12/123, 5. The refined value of a ton of ore had now fallen to an alleged £23. 15s.
[5] Document 5, p. 84.

2. PREPARATIONS FOR THE 1578 VOYAGE

The Adventurers

Soon after the return of the 1577 voyage, a list of twenty-five potential new investors had set down their names in a provisional list to finance a third voyage to Meta Incognita.[1] The intervening months, in which successive assays upon the ore had failed to provide hard evidence of precious metals therein, had not added to this list; in fact, it had inclined twenty-one named therein to withdraw. Only sixty-one investors officially subscribed in the coming voyage. Two of the original venturers, the mercers William Burde and Christopher Andrews, now dropped out, as did two 1577 adventurers, Lady Anne Talbot and Sir William Winter – the man who, with Lok, bore the greatest responsibility for the rise of the ore project: a defection that must have provided a powerful disincentive to prospective investors. The grand total of new subscribers in 1578 was therefore seven.[2]

Notwithstanding the adventurers' pronounced lack of success in attracting new subscribers, a cursory examination of the profile of investment confirms the heterogeneous nature of contemporary interest in speculative ventures. Indeed, the north-west enterprise exemplified the phenomenon: the roll of Privy Counsellors, courtiers, poets, soldiers, merchants and, not least, their sovereign, comprised possibly the most diverse company of English adventurers to invest in a single project since the 1553 voyage of Willoughby and Chancellor. It would not be equalled again until the outbreak of war with Spain, and its commensurate promise of plunder, provided a similarly tempting prospect of gold to be had easily.

It is important, however, to distinguish between the breadth of support for the enterprise and its depth. We have noted how few new investors were secured by the promise of gold. Furthermore, the majority of those who had invested for the first time in 1577 and now in 1578 did so by reason of their personal connection with existing stockholders, not by wider advertisement of its attractions. Michael Lok, whose own investment represented a major part of 'company' stock, had additionally subcribed for thirteen members of his family; the earls of Warwick, Sussex and Pembroke had been joined by their wives; and the mercers and Muscovy men who had formed the predominant group of 1576 adventurers secured – by word of mouth – a number of further participants from the same companies. There were few new names, either in 1577 or 1578, who did not have known associations with the original adventurers. Even allowing for the parochial nature of sixteenth-century London society, this was a relatively discreet group.

Nevertheless, there had been some telling shifts in the character of investment since the inception of the enterprise. Superficially, it would seem that the variegated nature of investment in 1578 largely reflected that of 1576, and thus that the shifting goals of

---

[1] PRO SP/12/119, 44.

[2] Document 1, pp. 55–7. The name of the Earl of Oxford is missing from this subscriber's list; he subsequently took up a portion of Michael Lok's existing stock.

the enterprise had a minimal effect. However, looking at the stock of the adventurers proportionately tells a different story. If we use a broad and arbitrary division – of mercantile and non-mercantile investment, rather than a misleading 'City' and 'Court' distinction – the respective groups' percentage of investment in 1576 was approximately 65/35. The ratio in the provisional list for the second voyage (that of 30 March 1577, set down before news of the ore became widespread) was not significantly different: removing the disproportionate (and unrepresentative) subscriptions of the Queen and Michael Lok, the percentages now became 64 per cent and 36 per cent respectively. However, news of the ore changed this situation dramatically. The final subscribers' list for the 1577 voyage shows the non-mercantile proportion of investment to have risen to 53 per cent. Given the very small fluctuation in the profile of investors between the 1577 and 1578 voyages, this latter percentage remained almost constant, though with one significant exception. Absent from the original list of 1578 adventurers is the name of the earl of Oxford; yet even as it was being drawn up, Lok was negotiating to sell to him £1,000 of his own, huge stockholding. By the time the expedition returned, Oxford had become a major investor, just in time to bear several large extraordinary calls upon his stock to meet the debts of the failing enterprise. Alone, the data gives little more than a hint of the speculative tastes of the Elizabethan court; nevertheless, it is clear that as the north-west passage project was downgraded in the adventurers' plans, the interest of London's mercantile community dimmed accordingly.

From a purely propagandist perspective, the enterprise had some august support. In addition to the Queen herself, almost every one of her principal councillors was an investor by 1578. Whilst this undoubtedly had a positive effect in promoting the aims of the adventurers as a whole, a less fortunate corollary was that their individual authority – that is, their influence upon the aims of the enterprise and the pace of expenditure thereon – had been entirely expunged. Stock held in the enterprise continued to carry the promise of commensurate rewards, but it did not bring voting rights. There are no extant 'company' papers which record the deliberations of the adventurers, because no such deliberations took place. The record of the business of the Company of Cathay is to be found entirely in Privy Council and other state correspondence, and in the various responses thereto. The commissioners appointed by the Council – in early 1578, these were Michael Lok, Sir William Winter, Thomas Randolphe, Edward Diar, Richard Young and, occasionally, Martin Frobisher – had the entire responsibility for preparations for the new voyage. The enterprise had become a royal project in all but name; and if the other adventurers were informed of how their money was being spent, it was by word of mouth only – an acutely unsatisfactory basis for investment.

The proposed colony

The adventurers could draw upon no precedents in providing for a semi-permanent presence in Meta Incognita. The first English colony outside the British Isles – one, moreover, that would be established in an extremely harsh climate – presented unique problems; and whilst these were almost certainly underestimated, much attention was devoted to the detail of the colonists' provision. According to the draft instructions, there were to be one hundrd inhabitants of this new Crown possession, comprising 'fortie hable mariners, gonners, shipwrights, and carpentars, 30 soldiers and 30 pyoners'.[1] Rather than oblige these men to endure a life under canvas whilst finding raw materials locally to build something more substantial – which their previous experience of the empty landscape of Baffin Island suggested would be a forlorn undertaking – a large, prefabricated blockhouse was conceived, of some 132 feet in length and 42 feet in breadth, its frame dismantled into sections to be carried in the ships.[2] Bricks and mortar were provided for the external walls, indicating that this structure was intended to endure beyond the stated life of the colony – or, perhaps, the colony's first 'shift' of men.

These men were to work with the mariners, soldiers and miners who would return with the *Ayde* and freight ships, but would thereafter winter in the new land and, when the weather permitted, commence further mining activity prior to the arrival of a 1579 expedition.[3] Their commander was to be Edward Fenton, Frobisher's lieutenant-general in the coming voyage. Fenton, a 'professional' soldier (insofar as that calling could provide steady employment) who had served previously in Ireland under Sir Henry Sydney, was not an uneducated man; like George Best, he had a keen interest in the natural world, and possessed similar pretensions to underpin his enquiring nature. He was the author of *Certaine Secrete wonders of Nature … Gathered out of divers learned authors, as welle Greek as Latine, sacred as prophane* (a 1569 translation, with supplementary material, of Launay's 1567 *Histoires prodigieuses*). Patronized by the earl of Warwick, he had sailed with Frobisher in 1577 as captain of the *Gabriel*. Now, as the leader of the intended colonists, Fenton was to put his intellectual curiosity to practical use. The draft instructions stipulated that he was to observe the state of the air, nature of the countryside thereabouts and identify the season in which the strait was most free of ice; all necessary prerequisites for the future success of English voyages to the region. His ships were also to reconnoitre the coastline of the strait and its environs within a radius of 200 leagues; a task which, if not attempted by Frobisher whilst in Meta Incognita (his instructions directed him to do so only 'yf leasure and tyme wille permitt'), would inevitably have given Fenton the glory of completing the navigation of Frobisher's 'strait' – if that is what it proved to be – into the Pacific Ocean:

---

[1] Document 2, p. 58.

[2] HM 715, f. 12; Pepys MS 2133, f. 12.

[3] It has been suggested that the eventual profile of colonists (HM 715, ff. 15–18) was significantly different than that provided for in the draft instructions (eleven named miners and labourers, as opposed to the 30 'pyoners' allowed for), and thus that the mining activity to be undertaken thereby had been downgraded in the intervening months (Hogarth, Boreham & Mitchell, *Mines* (hereafter cited as *HBM*), p. 43). Lok's summary of the actual colonists refers to '28 men/Artificers, myneres/Laboreres and otheres', which indeed suggests a broader group than miners alone; however, following the return of the voyage, Lok's reconciliation of personnel (PRO EKR E164/36, p. 98) still refers to the 28 'mynars' appointed to remain with Fenton, whilst the earlier number of mariners he had given for the *Judith*, *Gabriel* and *Michael* was reduced correspondingly. It seems therefore that many of the mariners were included under the ambiguous umbrella of 'artifiers', intended to act as miners' labourers during the life of the colony (as in fact had been the case during mining operations in 1577 and 1578), and that the intention to secure c. 2,000 tons of ore before the arrival of a fourth expedition therefore remained a firm one. Writing after the voyage, Best (document 11, p. 206) also states that 30 miners were to be left in the new land 'for gathering the golde Ore togyther for the nexte yeare …'. Even so, the equation was impossibly optimistic; as it transpired, a total of 155 miners in the 1578 expedition, assisted by mariners, were to scrape just 1,200 tons of ore from the ironhard ground in an entire 'summer' month.

one reason, perhaps, why Frobisher himself was to be so antagonistic to the colony project.[1]

To enable these aims, the colonists required feeding. The victualling lists suggest that eighteen months' supplies were provided, though the colony's relief expedition was to return within one year.[2] The lists do not give precise allowances, but a recent analysis of the victualling rates for the 1577 voyage allows broad assumptions to be made.[3] Because of the utter novelty both of the experiment itself and the climate in which it would be conducted, it is clear that the planners could draw upon no directly relevant experience. Accordingly, there is much evidence that the assumptions which provided for the colony were in little manner different than those which informed the only other activity which required the Englishman to be absent from his homeland for long periods - the oceanic voyage. Precisely like the mariners who would accompany them to the New World, the colonists were to enjoy four meat days per week (principally beef or pork, an allowance of 1lb per day, with bacon supplied for when stocks of the more perishable fresh meat were exhausted); dried fish (stock, habardine and rodfish) and cheese (1lb per day) providing protein for the remaining three. Beer, obviously, was to be the principal liquid nourishment, but a quantity of expensive wine-sack was purchased also; possibly to minimize the risk of enteritus.[4] The only green vegetable capable of surviving the long voyage and subsequent occupation of a harsh, infertile land was the pea; 36 quarters were purchased (almost certainly of the dried variety), though the provision of 'sallet oil' suggests that Frobisher had taken heed of the Inuit's habit of eating local varieties of 'grass' (more correctly, lichen) to supplement their diet, and had decided to test its value.[5] The colonists' staple was bread; 150 quarters of wheat meal and 160 bushels of biscuit were supplied, in addition to 64 dozen ready-baked loaves for the outward voyage. Small quantities of oats and rye were also purchased, almost certainly for nourishment of the sick. To flavour this rather monotonous diet, only salt and the ubiquitous mustard seed were supplied (again, small quantities of honey, sugar, cinnamon and ginger – all relatively expensive items – were provided for the enjoyment of convalescents only).

The evidence suggests therefore that the colonists' diet would have been tedious but adequate; its calorific value more than sufficient to meet the needs of the climate. Undoubtedly, an element of spoilage was anticipated, but the implied over-provision indicates that 'living off the land' – fishing and some hunting apart – was not

---

[1] Document 2, p. 60.

[2] The stated period of provision is mentioned only in the preliminary estimates for the colony (document 4, p. 66), in the initial plans for the third voyage (ibid.), and, subsequently, by ambassador Mendoza in his report to Philip II following the return of the voyage (document 13, p. 251). However, the final victualling list for the colonists (HM 715, ff. 13r–14v) reveals little difference in the scale of provisioning. For example, the preliminary estimates provided for, among other foodstuffs, 15,600 lbs of beef, 6,400 lbs of pork/bacon and 133 tons of beer; whilst the actual provision for the colony included 16,750 lbs of beef (unbutchered), 7,028 lbs of pork (unbutchered), 1,480 lbs of bacon, and 137 tons of beer.

[3] For the 1577 voyage, see Watt, 'Medical Record of the Frobisher voyages', in Symons, II, pp. 613–17.

[4] Lok's accounts (HM 715, f. 14) state that the wine sack – some six butts – were provided for 'provision of the voyage', an amount the seems excessive for an expected passage of only three weeks. Furthermore, several tons of wine-sack bought from William Bond for the 1576 voyage had been returned and sold to the 1577 account; some of this may have been loaded once more for the new expedition (the alternative, that it was taken in the *Ayde*, cannot be verified, as Frobisher, who had responsibility for the victualling of his flagship, was an acutely unsatisfactory accountant).

[5] The suggestion is made by Watt, 'The Frobisher Voyages', p. 615.

envisaged. Acknowledging this necessarily unavoidable limitation, the hiring of a broad community of shipwrights, carpenters, coopers, bakers, fishermen, shoemakers, a taylor, two surgeons and a preacher to serve the colony, in addition to the soldiers who would protect it, emphasizes the commissioners' desire to make this first colonial experiment as self-sufficient as any all-male community in a barren land might be. Even the three ships that were to remain with the colonists would be scrupulously preserved during the winter months: large 'crabs' (wooden clamps) were purchased to allow them to be secured and hauled out of the water during months when ice packed the straits.[1]

Thus, the hazards of the new world, as experienced in 1576 and 1577, were reasonably well addressed by men with no previous experience of ensuring the survival of an English community abroad. Whether the potential psychological dislocation of the colonists' condition was similarly anticipated – particularly the effect of their prolonged isolation, and the near-impossibility of escaping that condition when, in the winter months, it would press most severely – is doubtful; though the provisional list for the colony did provide for a small source of spiritual comfort in the three bibles and twenty-four each of psalm books and catechisms it proposed. The ministrations of the 'pious and godly' reverend Wolfall were no doubt expected to be a popular recourse for desperate men.

Ships and men

The preliminary plan for the 1578 voyage (that in which the form of the proposed colony was also considered for the first time) had envisaged a fleet of four ships; that is, the *Ayde*, *Gabriel* and two naval vessels ('procured … of her Majestie'): one of 400 tons, the other of 200.[2] The cost of these latter vessels was estimated at £3,600. In the months that followed, it became clear that this level of expenditure could not be supported; in any case, the total capacity of such an expedition – some 830 tons total burden – would be inadequate to carry the anticipated cargo of 1,200 tons of ore to be mined and brought back to England immediately. The alternative – to charter vessels from non-adventurers – had several intrinsic advantages. It was cheaper, of course, to pay tonnage rates than to buy ships outright. Furthermore, should such hired vessels be lost at sea, there would be neither incremental cost nor capital loss to the enterprise, other than in respect of the ore that would go down in them. Finally, the use of several smaller vessels, rather than the two or three larger ships as originally envisaged, would spread the risk of that loss.

The core of the fleet, as eventually provided, comprised four 'company' ships, *Ayde*, *Gabriel*, *Michael* and a further, large bark, the *Judith* (of some eighty tons burden, purchased from William Borough for £320),[3] all forming part of the common stock in the enterprise. Of these, all but the *Ayde* were to remain in Meta Incognita to service the intended colony. The ore that was to be returned in 1578 was to be loaded in eight

---

[1] HM 715, f. 8: 'paid to thomas bodnam Carpinter … for Crabes for the Landing of the Shippes that shall remayne in the new Land. li. 3. 7. 0.'

[2] For some reason, the *Michael* was omitted from this preliminary schedule, though her inclusion would have represented no incremental charge other than for her re-fitting. It may be that her carrying capacity was thought inadequate in a fleet of such few vessels (she would sail with the 1578 voyage as eventually constituted and, like the *Gabriel*, be employed to carry shifts of ore from outlying mine sites to the principal freight ships awaiting their lading in the Countess of Warwick Sound).

[3] HM 715, f. 8.

ships: the *Ayde* herself and seven hired vessels, *Thomas Allen* (owned by the adventurer of the same name: a leading London skinner, the Queen's Merchant of the Baltic Stores and future treasurer of the enterprise), *Anne Frances*, *Thomas of Ipswich*, *Beare Leicester* (owned by Richard Fairweather the elder and, possibly, by Michael Lok also), *Hopewell*, *Frances of Foye* (Fowey) and *Moon of Foye*.[1] Under the terms of the charter party arrangements, the adventurers agreed to pay the freight ships' owners at the rate of £5. 2. 8 per ton of ore loaded (£5 freightage plus 2s. 8d primage and average), and to provide victualling for their mariners at a flat rate of 16s. per month.[2] The latter was broadly that allowed the 'company's' own mariners, at a daily equivalent rate of 7d; but the freightage rate appears to have been extremely generous, no doubt a reflection of the hazardous nature of the job for which the vessels were hired (almost a century later, private freight ships carrying naval stores on long-distance voyages were contracted at rates of between £2 and £4 per ton, for mixed cargoes that were infinitely more troublesome to load and preserve *en route* than the mineral ore which Frobisher's men would gather).[3]

This was not, however, the full complement of ships that was to comprise the 1578 fleet. In the early months of 1578, whilst in the West Country to arrange for the refitting and victualling of the *Ayde* and *Gabriel* (which had laid at Bristol since the return of the 1577 voyage), Frobisher had spoken with a number of old acquaintances from his privateering days and arranged for a further four vessels to join the expedition. These were the *Salomon* of Weymouth (owned by Hugh Randall, she had been involved previously with Frobisher in the illegal seizure of the *Mari* of Mortaigne in 1569),[4] *Emanuel of Bridgewater* (referred to also as the *Manewall* and *Busse*, owned and commanded by Richard Newton), *Emanuel of Exeter* (known also as *Armonell*, Thomas Courtney), and a large bark, the *Denys* ('captain' Kendall).[5] Frobisher seems to have arranged for these vessels to join him directly at Harwich, where, according to Lok's later testimony, he victualled them with some of the provisions intended for the colony.[6]

The motive of the owners of these unofficial vessels in joining the enterprise is not difficult to discern. England's improving relationship with Spain following the crises of 1569–71, manifested in the resumption of trade with the Low Countries and the

---

[1] The commissioners had allowed for six freight ships; however, Lok – perhaps seeking to recoup from freightage income some of his heavy losses to date – jointly financed (or perhaps owned, with Richard Fairbrother) a further vessel, the *Beare Leicester*, and persuaded the other commissioners to admit her charges prior to the departure of the 1578 voyage (perhaps the *quid pro quo* to divert or forestall Lok's claims for interest and other expenses incurred during his tenure as treasurer of the 'company'). Her captain, Richard Philpot, was obviously well regarded, as he was immediately appointed to Frobisher's 'land council'. Nevertheless, the *Beare Leicester*'s participation was not unequivocally sanctioned; the Queen's auditors later disallowed payments made in respect of victuals for her crew, whilst allowing her freight charges (HM 715, ff. 24–5).

[2] PRO EKR E164/36, pp. 63–93, *passim*; HM 715, ff. 23–4.

[3] Oppenheim, *Administration of the Royal Navy*, p. 343. The lower rate was paid on stores shipped to Gibraltar; the higher to Jamaica.

[4] PRO HCA 13/17; 15 June 1569.

[5] Short biographies of Courtney, Newton and Randall are found in *HBM*, pp. 147–8. Kendall has been tentatively identified by Quinn (*Roanoke Voyages*, I, p. 291, n. 1) as the Abraham Kendall who subsequently served as master of the bark *Francis*, a vessel in Drake's 1585 West Indies fleet that was to have remained with the first Roanoke colony.

[6] Document 5, p. 86.

Anglo-Spanish Treaty of Bristol of 1574, had brought renewed, if often ineffective, protection for Netherlandish and Spanish ships vulnerable to English privateers. With proclamations against acts of piracy (1572) and – another loophole closed – against English mariners taking up foreign commissions (1575), the privateering trade was experienced a mild, if short-lived slump during the mid 1570s.[1] The transportation of mineral ore from the New World may have seemed a relatively mundane undertaking to men who, habitually, took their profits by more direct means; yet the insecurity of their principal trade made extemporization a necessity. In relatively lean times, anything which offered a profitable return on under-employed resources was to be welcomed. Furthermore, it is likely that the owners and crews of these vessels anticipated the 'diversion' of a proportion of the ore they carried; though in the event, security measures conceived by the Privy Council and commissioners made such pilferage impractical.

Frobisher's own intentions in bringing in these surplus ships are more obscure. Clearly, he could not have hoped to deceive the other adventurers beyond the moment at which the fleet concentrated at its port of departure, and any incremental quantities of ore secured by the non-chartered vessels would have fallen to the enterprise as a whole. It may simply be the case that he had been quizzed about the prospects for his venture by old comrades, over-stated his case, and found himself with unwanted but persistent volunteers. Only Lok gave a specific reason for it, and that was almost certainly a spurious one: that Frobisher's vanity required as large an expedition as might be arranged, to reflect the better upon his growing reputation.[2]

The scale of the expedition was indeed an impressive one. To man the fleet (that is, the official ships of the fleet), 270 men were appointed by the commissioners.[3] These were the mariners for the adventurers' four ships, plus miners, soldiers, surgeons and the numerous 'artificers' who would support the principal activities. In fact, some 360 men actually sailed with the expedition (excluding the crews of the freight ships), a surplus for which, it seems, Frobisher must take much responsibility.[4] Lok later

---

[1] Hughes & Larkin, *Tudor Royal Proclamations*, II, 585, 609.

[2] Document 5, p. 86.

[3] The most complete reconciliation of those appointed, and those who actually sailed in the voyage, is contained in Lok's accounts, PRO EKR E164/36, p. 98.

[4] *HBM* (pp. 28–9) calculates the identifiable expedition complement (that is, excluding the mariners of the freight ships) to have been 391. An earlier attempt by Hogarth to identify every named man on the voyage, drawn from the wage lists in Lok's account books ('The ships' company in the Frobisher voyages', in W. W. Fitzhugh & J. S. Olin, *Archeology of the Frobisher Voyages* (Smithsonian Institution Press, 1993), appendix 1) provided a total of 397. It is the present editor's opinion that both estimates may be a little too high, possibly because of a degree of double-counting or mis-identification of certain names (see, for example, the case of Thomas Batters, also Batterby, Batterick – p. 124 n.1). Lok, very keen to advertise any and all of Frobisher's 'doinges' by the latter months of 1578, had every reason to present the full extent of over-manning in his accounts; but his detailed lists of payments and amounts outstanding to individual, named soldiers, mariners and miners (PRO EKR E164/36, pp. 55–62, 95, 98) indicate that some 360 men sailed with the voyage (again, excluding the freight ships' mariners). Taking, for example, the complement of a single vessel, the *Ayde*, Lok gives the names of sixty-eight mariners, a figure which is precisely verified by that in Frobisher's 'boowk' (PRO EKR E164/35, pp. 284–7). Using Hogarth's earlier work, *HBM* (p. 28) state her total complement (including 27 miners) as 134; yet even had the *Ayde* alone carried all of the thirty-two (non-colonist) gentlemen and soldiers – which she did not – this latter figure would appear to be excessive, though it is claimed to be the *minimum* number who sailed. Absent the crew lists for the unofficial vessels, we must accept that the total number of men who sailed with the expedition will remain, at best, a matter for informed speculation.

accused him of hiring many 'miners' in the West Country from a pool of artisans who had little or no experience of mining (the inference being that Frobisher had then pock-eted the balance of monies provided for their wages).[1] Furthermore, it seems that sev-eral mariners and miners examined and found unfit for service by the commissioners were subsequently taken on by his acquaintances in the unofficial freight ships;[2] whilst almost double the planned number of gentlemen and soldiers – men moved by Fro-bisher's own enthusiasm or the perennial lure of new and untested possibilities – had joined the expedition unbeknown to the Privy Council or commissioners. Though they received no money prior to departure, they would require feeding at sea and, eventually, prove to be a further drain upon the adventurers' dwindling resources.

Even before the financial implications of this overmanning had worked through, the total cost of setting out the new expedition came to almost £9,000, yet the adventur-ers' total subscriptions supplied only £8,370.[3] This was obviously a matter for concern. The earl of Oxford, though now a major investor, had taken up existing stock and therefore brought no new money to the enterprise. Three of the other new adventur-ers had come in for the minimum subscription of £33. 15s., three for £67. 10s., and the remaining one for £101. 5s.; thus ensuring that the financial burden of the huge expan-sion of the enterprise fell squarely upon those whose pockets had been heavily depleted in the previous year. Their response was less than enthusiastic. Earlier in the year, on the 19 January, an extraordinary assessment of 20 per cent of existing stock had been raised to finance the building of a new refining complex at Dartford.[4] This realised £1,030, though by 3 May, £265 remained outstanding. Of more immediate sig-nificance, almost £1,900 of subscriptions to set out the 1578 voyage had not been secured by the same date, and this was almost certainly the principal reason why the expedition was not despatched at the beginning of that month, as the draft instruc-tions had stipulated.[5]

Those who had yet to pay their full subscriptions (or in many cases, *any* of the due amount) included every participating member of the Privy Council other than Dr Thomas Wilson, many of the principal merchants such as Gresham, Brocket and Ducket (though Lok, the most heavily assessed of their number, appears to have paid in full) and, not least, Martin Frobisher himself. Except for the latter, perhaps, this was clearly not a matter of temporary fiscal embarrassment, but of a lack of will to go fur-ther without receiving some firmer expectation of when – or if – the ore secured to date might provide a palpable return upon their existing investments. The attitude of

[1] Document 5, p. 85.

[2] For example, the name of Thomas Wiars, boatswain of the *Emanuel of Bridgewater* and author of the report on the supposed discovery of 'Busse Island' by her crew (reproduced by Hakluyt, *PN* 1589, p. 635), is listed in Lok's accounts for the outfitting of the voyage under the heading: 'These maryners & others were discharged, and went not on the third voyage being found unfytt for service' (HM 715, f. 18r). Wiars had previously sailed as boatswain of the *Michael* in the 1577 voyage (PRO EKR E164/35, 145). The dis-qualification may have been the cause of Wiars's prudent description of himself as a 'passenger' in the *Emanuel of Bridgewater*.

[3] HM 715, ff. 3, 26.

[4] PRO SP/12/122, 9.

[5] PRO SP/12/130, 35; SP/12/124, 2. EKR E164/36, pp. 171–3. Lok's accounts differ slightly from the estimate presented in the state papers; the latter gives the total assessment for Dartford as £1,030, the former as £1,080.

the Privy Counsellors was particularly disingenuous; it was they who had assumed the entire direction of the enterprise, determined its aims, form, and scale, and put their names to the documents that had authorized the very sums that they were now refusing – or forgetting – to pay promptly.

Nevertheless, the momentum that had seized the project carried the preparations through the minor impeachments of unpaid suppliers. No doubt Lok, their principal point of contact, was sufficiently enthused still to persuade them that the credit of the 'company' remained excellent (the secrecy imposed upon the results of Schutz's assays was entirely helpful in this respect, if in no other). From 22 May, the ships of the fleet commenced their concentration at Harwich (Fenton's *Judith* was the last to arrive at the Naze, on 27 May);[1] at anchor in Orwell Pool, the vessels took in their final supplies during 29–30 May. On the following day, they departed from Harwich, bound upon their great business. In London, almost simultaneously, Lok was drawing up a schedule to the accounts for the eyes of his masters in the Privy Council: his first bid for wages, calculated at 3 per cent of the adventurers' total stock in the voyage.[2] It is difficult to know who was embarking upon the more optimistic endeavour.

---

[1] Document 8, p. 137. According to Selman (document 9, p. 177), the ships *Ayde*, *Gabriel*, *Frances*, *Moon*, *Emanuel of Exeter* and *Denys* came into Harwich on 22 May, the remaining vessels five days later.
[2] HM 715, f. 27.

3. THE 1578 VOYAGE

Outward passage

The fleet departed almost exactly one month later than the date stipulated in Frobisher's instructions. The delay, caused principally by the difficulty in securing the due subscriptions, appears to have been anticipated; the same instructions had also indicated that its precise sea-route to Meta Incognita was a matter for Frobisher's discretion, requiring only that he set a course 'as the winde will best serve you'. Given his foreshortened schedule and the brevity of the summer season in the new lands, Frobisher decided upon the shortest possible passage. Accordingly, his fleet did not retrace the route of the 1576 and 1577 expeditions, both of which had sailed due north to approximately 60°N and set their course directly to the west thereafter. The ships made instead for the English Channel; on 1 June they were off Folkstone, where, briefly, they chased a French man-of-war (possibly because it was believed that she was shadowing the expedition); on 3 June, the fleet came into Plymouth Sound to take on more water – having identified their faulty casking (an inevitable hazard) in the intervening days – but by the evening of the following day, the fleet had passed Land's End. Off Cape Clear on 6 June, a lookout in the *Ayde* sighted the Bristol bark *Grechwinde*, taken and despoiled a number of days earlier by French privateers.[1] Briefly, Frobisher had his ships heave to; barrels of biscuit, butter, peas and cheese were lowered into the stricken ship to relieve her half-starved crewmen, and Edward Selman gave them a letter to send on to Michael Lok. Thereafter, the fleet made its point of departure WNW from Cape Clear, and passed out into the Atlantic Ocean.

The outward passage was prosperous and uneventful. For several days, Christopher Hall (appointed chief pilot of the expedition, he sailed in the vice-admiral *Thomas Allen* on the outward passage) reported a 'fayre gale' of wind, usually from the southeast. A brief calm interrupted their progress on 11/12 June, but otherwise, only the contrary pull of the Gulf Stream off western Ireland (noted by George Best, the earliest known witness to its effect)[2] offered a slight impediment to their progress. At two o'clock on the morning of 20 June, Hall sighted Kap Farvel.[3] The first and longest leg of their Atlantic passage had been accomplished in just thirteen days; in 1576 and 1577, the navigation via the alternative, northern route to the same point had required twenty-eight days and thirty-four days respectively.

In the previous two years, attempts to land upon the coast of 'Friesland' in the face of fog and ice had proved too dangerous. The persistence of the Privy Council's desire to have this potential way-station to the east examined required a third attempt to be

---

[1] The *Grechwinde* is identified by name in Fenton's log only (document 8, p. 138), though Best, Selman and Ellis also note the episode.

[2] Document 11, pp. 209–10.

[3] The fleet's formation clearly remained close; Best (document 11, p. 210) reported that Frobisher made the same sighting from the *Ayde* at precisely the same time. Fenton (document 8, p. 140) erroneously dated this sighting – and his subsequent landing there with Frobisher – as having occurred on 19 June.

made. Frobisher's instructions left the timing to his discretion, indicating that a landing during the outward or return passage would be acceptable. Prudently, Frobisher dismissed the option of returning later to this treacherous coast with tired crews and ships fully laden (and thus low in the water), and decided to make the attempt immediately. At five o'clock in the morning, some three hours after sighting land, he had the *Ayde*'s pinnace hoisted out, took in Christopher Hall from the *Thomas Allen*, and together they boarded the *Gabriel*, whose handling amidst ice was by now intimately familiar to them. West of 'Frobisher's Cape' (Kap Farvel), they found clear water to the land and, upon the shore, Inuit tents. Their owners fled as the Englishmen approached the shore; a brief examination of aboriginal artefacts (whose similarity to those of the people of Meta Incognita led both Best and Ellis to surmise that they conducted regular traffic across what would become Davis Strait), and the abstraction of a single whelp from a litter in one of the tents – for which, according to Ellis, Frobisher left pins, knives and other 'trifling thinges' – constituted the only intercourse with the aboriginals during the 1578 expedition.[1] Within two to three hours of landing upon Friesland, the Englishmen had exhausted its delights, and returned to their ships. The most important task had been discharged, however; in the act of setting foot upon that desolate place – 'being the fyrste knowen Christians that we have true notice of', as Best claimed with some justice – Frobisher and his men had asserted the Queen's right of possession and future exploitation.

Significantly, several of the accounts refer to the potential for settlement upon this coastline; Fenton noticed its 'grasse & herbes', whilst Best regarded the land as having 'good hope of great commoditie and riches, if it maye be well discovered'.[2] The cape they had briefly explored lay almost exactly in 60°N. Englishmen's experience of other lands at this latitude – particularly the Shetland and Orkney Islands – suggested that their compatriots might well survive the seasons here, notwithstanding the harsh lessons derived from Meta Incognita, lying only some two and a half degrees to the north. Without knowledge of the Gulf Stream's fundamental influence upon the western European climate, such a misconception was natural, though it was one that experience would cause to be corrected very quickly.

This brief reconnaissance over, the fleet rounded 'Cape Frobisher' and moved north-westwards, with the intention of observing the coastline of this new English possession. However, a heavy fog prevented this; for much of 21 June, each ship's crew used their drums and trumpets to remain in touch with the other vessels of the fleet, though by the time that the fog cleared, the ever-unlucky *Michael* – commanded this year by one of the original 1576 adventurers, the mercer and shipowner Matthew Kindersley – had gone missing. A few distant sightings apart, she was to be alone for almost four weeks thereafter. The other ships, faithful to their instructions, did not attempt to find her; the rendezvous point was known, and any ship leaving the fleet was obliged to find her own way there.

For four days, the fleet moved north-westwards across the Davis Strait. Ice was observed in ever greater quantities as the ships neared its western shores (then, as now,

---

[1] A further, clandestine act of brigandage was committed when, unbeknown to Frobisher, the *Ayde*'s trumpeter, Christopher Jackson, stole a second pup (document 6, p. 112).

[2] Document 8, p. 140; document 11; p. 210.

carried swiftly before the coastline by the strong Labrador current). By 26 June, the *Judith* had also become separated from the fleet.[1] The following day, members of the *Thomas Allen*'s crew had sight of land to the west, but the fleet lay becalmed in much ice; Fenton also had made out what he took to be Hall's Island, but the *Judith*, seeking to rejoin the other ships by performing a series of 'bordes' or tacks, only succeeded in burying herself further into ice-floes. Eventually, Fenton was obliged to order her about to the southeast, and by 29 July had lost all hope of regaining the fleet (having moved as far south as 61°34′). Meanwhile, the thirteen ships still in contact edged through and around the ice until the land to the west was clearly resolved. A little to the west of the other ships, the *Thomas Allen* made the first positive sightings: in his log, Hall recorded: 'The first of July *Meta Incognita* sene *Latitude* 62de.–14m.', with marginalia: 'Lockes Land. Hawles Iland. Quenes foreland'.[2]

At this point, thirty-one days out of Harwich, the fleet lay at most some one hundred and twenty miles from the Countess of Warwick Sound, its destination. It would require a further four weeks for Frobisher and his mariners to make that short, fraught passage.

2/3 July: the Great Storm

The *Thomas Allen* was the first ship to attempt to reconnoitre the supposed strait on 1 July, the day of the fleet's arrival at its mouth. As she did so, a great flock of wilmots and 'sea pyes' descended upon her mainmast; one mariner climbed it and was able to pluck three of the seabirds out of the air with his hand. As ill-favoured testings of fortune go, it was to have particularly swift consequences. To the west, 'a whole land of yse' confronted the *Thomas Allen*; prudently, Hall and her captain Gilbert Yorke brought her out again during the early morning of 2 July to warn the other ships. Unfortunately, the day was clear and promising; the rest of the fleet, buoyed by this happy prospect after days of poor weather, fairly flew past under full sail as Hall vainly hailed them to warn of what lay ahead. The bark *Denys* was the fleet's vanguard that morning; her master, one Dabney, half-heeded Hall's cries but was carried on ahead in a moment. Then the *Hopewell*, whose own master, Andrew Diar, seems to have been fully persuaded by Hall's warning, but was likewise swept on by the momentum of the fleet. The eleventh ship in this suicidal procession was the flagship *Ayde*; Frobisher himself seems not even to have noticed the *Thomas Allen*, which, forlornly but faithfully, turned and followed on after the fleet.

Much ice was clearly visible to the west; but caught in the bright sunlight of that morning it seemed to hold little of its habitual threat. Now well to the north of the fleet once more, Fenton in the *Judith* made out the other ships' passage into the mouth of the strait and set a parallel course to follow. The wind, as yet favourable, encouraged their intention; but it also encouraged further ice floes to follow the vessels and congest the sea behind them.

---

[1] On that day, Fenton observed his latitude at 63°3′, yet less than twenty-four hours earlier, Hall had observed his own – and the fleet's – to be 61°24′, and since that time the *Thomas Allen* had made only twenty-one leagues NNW (document 8, p. 142; document 6, p. 113).

[2] Document 6, p. 114.

Later, both Best and Selman would speculate upon the great quantity of ice they encountered in the voyage, which far exceeded that of the previous two years. Both men blamed the prevailing winds, 'whiche blowing from the Sea directlye upon the place of our straites, hath kept in the Ise, and not suffered them to be caryed out by the ebbe to the maine Sea ...'[1] In the immediate sense, this was certainly a contributory factor to the peculiar conditions they were to experience in the following twenty-four hours; but the principal underlying cause of their affliction seems rather to have been the mildness of the Arctic spring that year, which had resulted in the calving of an unusually large number of icebergs from the northern coast of west Greenland.[2]

All the extant accounts dwell at some length upon the ordeal of the night of 2/3 July; an indication of its painful novelty to the English commentators who endured it.[3] Moving westwards into the strait, the ships were initially almost enclosed by ice. However, they eventually came to a polynya, some three leagues in diameter according to Selman (Ellis put it at one league, the fleet being as if enclosed by 'the pales of a Parke'). For a time, the continuing fair weather made this partial confinement no more than a distraction; Hall called it a 'pretty plasser' to ply up and down, waiting for the ice to clear sufficiently for the fleet to make for the Countess of Warwick Sound. As a precaution, most of the ships' sails were furled, but the bark *Denys* continued to bear canvas, and in coming about under sail struck an iceberg. A large hole was rent in her side, and within thirty minutes she had sunk.[4] Fortunately, Captain Kendall managed to fire off one of his guns to alert the other ships to his plight, and the *Beare Leicester* and *Ayde* were able to put out their boats in time to rescue his crew; however, much of the frame of the great prefabricated house went down in the *Denys*, thus ensuring that any subsequent attempt to establish the intended colony would be a much more hazardous undertaking.[5]

The loss of the *Denys* in calm weather was an unnecessary misfortune; but that which followed was entirely beyond human government. The wind, rising, began to impact the boundaries of the polynya; four ships that lay easternmost – the *Anne Frances*, *Moon of Foye*, *Francis of Foye* and *Gabriel* – were able to force their way a little towards the mouth of the 'strait', where the incoming ice was less dense; but as the evening drew on, the remaining nine vessels were entrapped within a rapidly closing curtain of clashing icebergs. The first-hand accounts of this ordeal (and that of Best, not personally observed but taken from the testimony of witnesses) provide some of the earliest known data upon how wooden ships were preserved, if at all, in such supremely adverse conditions.

---

[1] Document 11, p. 212.

[2] C.f. Fenton's journal entry for 17 July (document 8, p. 150): '... we drove northwardes into much ize, so that we saw no waie to cleare theim being verie strau*n*ge, for that the last yere on the same daie and monthe, there was litle or no ize to be seen within 8 or 10L.'

[3] Best's (document 11, pp. 212–14) is the most detailed description of these events (and the most florid); but Selman (document 9, pp. 179–80), Ellis (document 10, p. 197) and Hall (document 6, p. 115) contribute their own, useful perspectives. In the *Judith*, Fenton (document 8, pp. 143–4) and Jackman (document 7, p 134) recorded their lonely ordeal. See also McDermott, 'Frobisher's 1578 Voyage: Early Eyewitness Accounts of English Ships in Arctic Seas', *Polar Record*, vol. 32, no. 183 (1996)' pp. 325–34.

[4] Ellis (document 10, p. 197) called her 'but a weake shippe', which seems unlikely, if she were indeed a sometime privateer.

[5] Selman (document 9, p. 179) differs from the other accounts, in describing the sinking of the *Denys* in high seas and the rescue of her crew by boats sent out to clear a passage through ice.

As the polynya closed, the crews of individual ships responded in different ways. Some of the smaller vessels managed to ply a narrow channel with sails raised still (though this had proved to be a dangerous tactic). Others anchored upon the lee of large icebergs, attempting both to reduce their own rate of tossing and shield themselves from the faster-moving, smaller bergs. Most of the crews armoured their ships' hulls with cables, bedding and planks, and used spars and oars to fend off the clashing floes. The greatest ordeal seems to have been borne by several of the larger vessels, particularly the *Ayde* and *Thomas Allen*, which were so entirely enclosed that they could not make any way in the sea, nor even to come about. Their crews disembarked at the most dangerous moments; going out on to individual icebergs to prise them apart and relieve the pressure upon their vessels' hulls (the *Ayde*'s topmasts were taken down and expended as fenders in this manner).

It should be recalled that all of these measures were hampered by an increasingly violent storm. Some of the men, overwhelmed by the hopelessness of their predicament, simply fell to their knees and prayed. Significantly, Best did not condemn nor play down the role of these 'of more mylder spirit'; indeed, he regarded their efforts as important as those of their more practically-minded comrades, crediting their belief that it was 'by no other meanes possible, than by a diuine miracle, to haue their deliuerance'.[1]

According to Hall, his own vessel, the *Thomas Allen* (probably the largest ship in the fleet after the *Ayde*), bore this torment for fully thirteen hours. To the north, the *Judith* and *Michael* were separately bearing similar hardships, though having neither company nor polynya to ease their plight. There are no first-hand accounts of the *Michael*'s ordeal, but both the *Judith*'s captain and master provided narratives which suggest that their own experience was potentially more dangerous even than that of their colleagues. For most of the evening of 2 July, the *Judith* turned in the ice, keeping a small pool of clear water; however, she became entirely enclosed in the early hours of the following morning, and the pressure of the impacted ice threatened to cave in her hull. The high winds which tossed both the ship and ice were, remarkably, complemented by a thick fog which served to make their isolation seem even more complete. Under such conditions, morale appears to have collapsed as the mariners' strength failed – 'we supposed ourself lost forlorn hope', as even the phlegmatic Jackman later recalled. Only the timely professional intervention of the intended colony's chaplain, Reverend Wolfall, raised the spirits of the *Judith*'s seemingly doomed crew sufficiently to have them renew their struggle.[2] At about eight or nine o'clock in the morning the wind slackened, and at the same time veered from south-easterly to due west. Gradually, the impacted ice parted once more, providing channels through which the *Judith* and, to the south, the other battered vessels of the fleet moved back towards the mouth of the strait. Remarkably, throughout the hours of desperate danger they had endured, not a single life had been lost.

---

[1] Document 11, p. 213. Best's, it should be noted, was not strictly an eye-witness account, evocative though his prose is. His own ship, the *Anne Frances*, was one of the fortunate four vessels that forced their way back out into open water before the tempest impacted the ice, they 'beeing fast ships'.
[2] Document 7, p. 134 See also document 3, pp. 64–5 for a taste of Wolfall's effective if grammatically challenging style.

It is tempting to believe that the recipients of this seemingly miraculous deliverance had exaggerated their plight; but the various accounts of the storm and its dangers tally too precisely to represent mere hyperbole. These are earliest known accounts of English ships entrapped in ice, excepting the necessarily incomplete journal that recorded the travails of Sir Hugh Willoughby's doomed expedition some twenty five years earlier.[1] It is clear that the movement of pack-ice and icebergs in confined, stormy waters was something that not even the Muscovy mariners who accompanied the expedition had faced previously; certainly, neither Christopher Hall nor Charles Jackman make what would otherwise be obvious comparisons to their former experiences. Nor do the other authors attempt to play up their own hardships by making similar, if uninformed comparisons; the inference is that all believed themselves to be undergoing an ordeal which, though partially anticipated by Richard Grenville as early as 1574, was something new in English oceanic voyaging.[2]

Error and discovery

With the exception of the *Judith* and *Michael*, the surviving ships continued to move slowly sea-ward throughout 3 July. The following day, most lay adrift in open water, their crews performing urgent repairs to their bruised hulls. The *Michael*'s movements at this time are unknown; for nine days thereafter she was to make her own, solitary way through ice-packed seas without a chronicler to record it. Meanwhile, the *Judith* had emerged from the strait on 4 July, too distant from the other ships to track their course. On that day, she passed south-westwards behind the Queen's Foreland, thus confirming it to be an island, rather than the archipelago previously assumed; unfortunately, Fenton soon abandoned this worthwhile reconnaissance and turned the *Judith* about once more into the strait, thus carrying her even further from the fleet; which, now out of sight of land, had begun to drift south, carried by the prevailing south-westerly continental current. For several days thereafter, Frobisher seems to have attempted to correct this, setting his course northwards once more whenever his ships raised sail. However, he and almost all of the ships' masters underestimated the strength of the current; when, on 9 July, land was once more clearly sighted to starboard, they, led by Frobisher, declared it to be the northern shore of his 'strait'. Christopher Hall (who appears, upon this and other evidence, to have been by far the most adept master in the fleet), disagreed. Though cloud cover prevented them from observing their correct latitude from the sun, Hall recalled his experience of two years earlier, when he had remarked upon the strength of that current: 'I iudge a ship may drive a league and a halfe, in one howre, with that tide'.[3] He suggested now that they had probably passed far to the south of their intended position, and were looking upon

---

[1] Willoughby had not recorded the final tribulations of his men. In the final entry of his journal, he merely referred to the onset of their ordeal: 'very evill wether, as frost, snow, and haile, as though it had beene the deepe of winter ...' (Hakluyt, *PN*, 1598–1600, ii, p. 223).

[2] In 1573, arguing against the feasibility of a viable northern sea-route to the east (principally to promote his own intended attempt via the south), Grenville had percipiently foreseen the freezing of any such passage, though not the danger from moving ice (BL Lansdowne MS 100/4).

[3] Hakluyt, *PN*, 1589, p. 620.

an entirely strange shore. Frobisher's fury at this imagined insubordination, graphically and wittily recorded in Hall's log, was excessive, but the error was hardly his alone.[1] As he and his masters prepared to re-enter his eponymous strait, the fleet in reality lay off the entrance to what would become known as Hudson Strait, almost a full degree of latitude south of its imagined position.

Hall maintained his contradictory assessment. Robert Davis, master of the *Ayde*, was the only other member of his profession to concur openly, but, being too proximate to his admiral's wrath, wisely did not push his opinion too strenuously. However, Hall had clearly convinced more of those present during his argument with Frobisher than Davis alone. He returned to the *Thomas Allen* and successfully persuaded Gilbert Yorke of the common error; when, at four o'clock the following morning, a thick mist descended once more, three other vessels – *the Anne Frances* (whose own master, James Beare, had been one of the strongest against Hall's opinion but who was now, apparently, over-ruled by his captain, George Best), *Emanuel of Bridgewater* and *Francis of Foye* – failed to follow when the other ships in the fleet raised their sails and set a course westwards. Instead, they turned directly eastwards, towards open water once more. It was the first, and certainly the most striking disregard of Frobisher's authority.[2]

Meanwhile, the remaining eight ships of the fleet pressed on to the west, though in Ellis's pungent phrase, 'we scarse knewe where we were'. Best later claimed that Frobisher himself soon realised his mistake, but continued to test this new body of water for a number of days thereafter. The claim is hardly supportable. Until 17/18 July,[3] when prevailing cloud cover parted briefly to allow the fleet's latitude to be observed, there is no indication that any member of the expedition was aware of the magnitude of their error; indeed, on 16 July, when Frobisher sent the *Gabriel* towards the shore to their starboard, it was because they had sighted an inlet which they took to be the Countess of Warwick Sound: 'all men that had sene it the yere before (except two, called Stobern & But) allowed yt to be the same ...'[4] By this time, the fleet had passed some 120 miles to the west, almost as far as Big Island; for an expedition whose schedule had been compromised already, it had been a costly error.

It did not appear to be an entirely unproductive one, even so. The *Gabriel*'s in-shore reconnaissance had allowed a new contact with the Inuit, some of whom, seeing the landing party, readily brought fish, bear-skins and fowl to the shore-line to trade for the Englishmen's knives, bells and other trinkets. These local commodities were hardly necessities for an expedition that was as yet well-provisioned; nevertheless, they held out at least a promise of sustenance to be had from a land which, to date, had

---

[1] Document 6, p. 116. One must assume that Frobisher's threat, to take his own life if Hall did not concur with his judgement, was neither entirely sincere nor particularly effective.

[2] Not surprisingly, Best and Hall chose to portray this as an honest mistake rather than desertion; both wrote of having 'lost' the other ships of the fleet whilst their own vessels lay at hull still, after which they attempted to move clear of the ice and await sight of the sun to observe their correct latitude. Cf., however, Edward Selman's interpretation of Best's later defection (document 9, p. 183, n.3).

[3] There is disagreement between the texts here; Selman stating it to have been 17 July, Ellis – somewhat vaguely – the day following (see document 9, p. 181; document 10, p. 199). Further east, Hall was able to observe his latitude from the deck of the *Thomas Allen* on 16 July, which he made to be 61°17'; two days later, he pointed out the detail of the southern shore of the Queen's Foreland with considerable (and, one suspects, didactic) care to his captain and master.

[4] The claim is Selman's: document 9, p. 181 (*recte* Stobern and Lunt).

offered little in the way of natural resources. A more profound discovery, supported by careful observation of the body of water through which the ships had passed, was that the Mistaken Strait (as such it was now named by Frobisher) appeared to offer a more feasible passage to the 'Mare del Sur' than that which he had first entered two years earlier. Reasons for this assumption, recalled by Best, included the great indraft of water noted at the entrance to the strait, with no apparent corresponding outflow; the absence of large amounts of ice in the strait, which seemed to indicate a free-flowing passage; and the discovery of pieces of driftwood from the lost *Denys* therein, which, together with the testimony of several mariners in the *Gabriel*, suggested that Frobisher's own 'strait' was but a tributary of the new body of water.[1] None of this evidence was adduced in the other accounts of the voyage; nevertheless, it was to provide much sustenance for further speculation regarding the viability of a strait or passage in this area until John Davis's observations during the 1580s – married to the apparent confirmation of the existence of Friesland – undermined any vestigial confidence in Frobisher's 'achievement'.

The return of the fleet eastwards following the discovery of their error brought further dangers. Having had little sight of the shoreline during the westward passage, its features now offered few clues to allow an accurate assessment of precisely how far the ships has passed into the new strait. On the evening of 18 July (Best, who was not present, stated it to be 21 July), Frobisher and several of the ships' masters sighted what they took to be the Queen's Foreland, and the fleet's course was set due north. The manoeuvre was premature. Rather than clear the foreland, they entered what is now Annapolis Strait, between the Meta Incognita peninsula and the Lower Savage Islands. In fog, and with large quantities of ice bearing into the same, confined waters, the fleet dispersed entirely. The depth of water in the passage prevented the ships from anchoring clear of lee-shores that featured extremely jagged rock formations, some of them just below the water's surface. Ships' boats were set out before their mother vessels to sound for safe passage, but in several cases the ships' crews were thereafter obliged to kedge with their anchors to drag themselves away from rocks on to which the prevailing currents strongly urged them. Only a fortuitous variation in wind direction, which briefly lifted the fog and dispersed low clouds, allowed the mariners to react to their predicament before disaster overwhelmed them. As it strengthened, it also allowed them to set their sails and move slowly southeastwards against the current's pull. Even so, the persistence of fog made their escape hazardous; Selman in particular records the painful search for clear water beneath the ships' hulls, and the lashing together of the *Ayde*'s cables to allow her to anchor in eighty fathoms and prevent her being swept back in-shore again on the flood tide.[2] According to Ellis, it was the prudent action of

---

[1] Document 11, pp. 216–17. Best recalled the insistence of some of the *Ayde*'s mariners that the flood tide ran for some nine hours in the strait, and the ebb tide but three hours. On 31 July 1587, John Davis would pass across the mouth of Hudson Strait and noted there 'the water whirling and roring, as it were a meeting of tides'; subsequently provided to Emeric Molyneaux, this data was to be responsible for the nomenclature 'Furious Outfall' at this location on the latter's 1592 globe (Hakluyt, *PN*, 1589, p. 792; Markham, *John Davis*, p. xxxvi).

[2] Document 9, p. 182. This passage is one of the most technically adept in Selman's account of the voyage; its detailed record of soundings taken by men in the ship's boats leads one to suspect that it was drafted with the assistance of the *Ayde*'s master, Robert Davis.

the rear-admiral, Henry Carew in the *Hopewell*, who fired off his ordnance continually once his own vessel had reached safety, that brought the other ships clear of the ice and rocks without mishap on 19 July.[1]

The following day, with the ships assembled once more, the Queen's Foreland was sighted to the north. To the west of that landmass, a body of water hinted at a clear passage through into Frobisher's strait. This time, however, only a single ship was risked in testing the possibility. The *Gabriel*, with great difficulty, forced the ice-bound passage as the remainder of the vessels, led by Frobisher's *Ayde*, circumvented the Queen's Foreland to seaward. In honour of her achievement (one that the *Judith* had accomplished over two weeks earlier), the navigation was named – and remains – Gabriel Strait.

On 23 July, the fleet made contact once more with Best's *Anne Frances*, which, since her desertion thirteen days earlier, had laid off the mouth of Frobisher's 'strait'. Best's account of these days emphasizes the dangers of ice and his repeated attempts to reach Countess of Warwick Sound; yet the circumstance of their early rendezvous with Frobisher suggests that he had been content merely to await the return of the fleet whilst avoiding unnecessary risks. Similarly, Hall's log of the *Thomas Allen* indicates that she had done little more than lay off and on for almost two weeks, attempting to make contact with the fleet only when Frobisher had realised his error (on 21 July, she briefly put into Frobisher Bay but emerged swiftly when ice threatened to close about her).[2] On 22 July, she, the *Francis of Foye* and *Emanuel of Bridgewater*, which had likewise failed to follow the fleet into the 'Mistaken Strait', met with the *Gabriel* as she emerged from behind the Queen's Foreland. A further attempt by these four vessels to enter the ice on the following day was unsuccessful, though they managed to pass almost as far as Jackman Sound on the southern shore before being repulsed.

Meanwhile, Frobisher's fleet of eight ships, somewhat to the south and west, prepared also to enter his 'strait' once more. The wind, previously unfavourable, now promised to carry them in as it had done on the near-disastrous evening of 2 July; fortunately, the *Frances of Foye*, fleeing from her own forlorn attempt to make Countess of Warwick Sound, met with the advancing fleet on 23 July and reported the conditions ahead. Even the headstrong Frobisher heeded this latest warning; he had the ships anchor in a small sound on the northern shore of the Queen's Foreland near the latter-day Cape Warwick while he went ashore briefly to reconnoitre for potential ore deposits. By the following morning, however, he was once more in the *Ayde*, and ready to defy both the weather and sage counsel. Best, a generally sympathetic interpreter of Frobisher's motives, reveals something of the frustration that weeks of profitless labour had brought:

> 'The Generall … determined with this resolution, to passe and recover hys Porte, or else there to bury himselfe with hys attempte, and if suche extremitie so befell him, that he muste needes perish amongst the Ise … esteeming it more happye so to ende hys lyfe, rather than himselfe, or anye of hys companye or anye one of hir Majesties Shyppes shoulde become a praye or spectacle to those base bloudye and man eating people.'[3]

---

[1] Document 10, p. 199.
[2] Document 6, p. 117.
[3] Document 11, p. 220.

Best does not recall the reaction of the mariners to their implicit role in this somewhat extreme strategy; but it seems that he, no less than they, regarded it as being far in excess of their duty. The following day, *Ayde* set a course into the ice-bound strait. She had the company of only four other vessels – the two *Emanuels*, the *Hopewell* and *Bear Leicester*; the five remaining ships, including Best's *Anne Frances*, slipped away once more under cover of a snow storm, to make their own way to the agreed rendezvous.

Ellis, one of only two commentators now remaining with the fleet, has nothing to say of its passage into the ice. Selman, whose narrative is coloured by his employer Michael Lok's growing distaste for Frobisher, criticizes his decision to proceed, refers to the fleet's repulse on 27 July, and, upon its second attempt, comments in some detail upon his admiral's poor skills as a navigator. As the fleet moved slowly north-westwards in now-calmer weather, successfully avoiding the greatest concentrations of ice, Frobisher appears to have misidentified in turn Jackman Sound, Yorke Sound and Gabriel Island (the trumpeter, Christopher Jackson, convinced him of the latter error). This was his final mistake, however; by 30 July, the ships were sufficiently close to their destination for Frobisher to take a pinnace and go on ahead into Countess of Warwick Sound, ordering the fleet to follow when they had sufficient wind. Once into the sound that afternoon, he found the *Judith* and *Michael*, long feared lost, awaiting the remainder of the fleet.

Fenton and the *Judith*

The *Judith* and *Michael* had been last sighted on the evening of 2 July, bearing into Frobisher Bay to the north of the fleet. Their ordeal since had been prolonged and extreme; perhaps more desperate even than that of the remainder of the fleet. The log of the *Judith* recounts in great detail her own near-constant dangers, and, after 13 July, of the *Michael* also.

Edward Fenton, captain of the *Judith*, lieutenant-general of the expedition and prospective commander of England's first colony in the New World, remains an enigmatic character. Later, his appalling performance as commander of an intended Moluccas voyage (1582) was to reveal deep flaws in his character that had been anticipated even before its departure. The merchant Henry Oughtred, responsible for much of the preparations for that expedition, was to express an extremely blunt opinion of him: 'his experience is verye small his mynd highe, his (temper) of the manne(r) colerick, thrall to the collycke and st(ubborn) ...'.[1] Yet his record during the 1578 voyage was to be exemplary; indeed, the obvious jealousy that Frobisher exhibited towards him both in 1577 and 1578 strongly hints at a grudging appreciation of his talents. At no time were these more in evidence than in the days following the *Judith*'s emergence from Frobisher Bay following the storm of 2/3 July. After examining the passage of water to the north and west of the Queen's Foreland – 'so that I judge certeinlie the Quenes forelande but an ilande' – and briefly landing upon its shores to take on water and ballast, Fenton ordered the *Judith* back into the strait from which they had fled only

---

[1] BL Cotton MSS Otho E VIII, f. 127; Oughtred to Leicester, 12 March 1582; Taylor, *Fenton*, p. 34.

twenty-four hours earlier. Though some two weeks were to elapse before she was able to make her destination, she would emerge from the straits only briefly during this time, to flee the most immediate dangers from ice before renewing the struggle. In repeatedly attempting this seemingly suicidal navigation, the *Judith* came close to disaster on several occasions. Twice on the same day – 6 July – she was almost driven on to a lee shore (she escaped by means of her crew kedging with their anchor on icebergs to seaward). Two days later, when ice formed entirely around her hull, Fenton was obliged to send his men out with pikes and other implements to break a passage back to open water. On several other occasions, she was lashed to larger icebergs to shelter from the hazard of smaller, fast-moving pieces whilst her exhausted crew rested. Most dangerously, she was almost crushed by clashing icebergs on 11 July, when her hull was breached upon each flank simultaneously; fortunately, her crew managed to heave off and force their way out into clear water once more, and effect urgent repairs.[1]

The *Judith*'s lonely odyssey was partly ameliorated on 13 July, when the *Michael* was sighted to the southeast. It seems that she also had re-entered the 'strait' – if, indeed, she had left it – soon after the storm of 3 July, and had remained there since, seeking the prearranged landfall with no less assiduity than Fenton's crew. *Michael*'s captain, Matthew Kindersley, had perhaps the added preoccupation – or incentive – of his personal investment in the enterprise (some £83. 15s. to date) to focus his attention upon their goal.[2] Their meeting on 13 July was doubly fortuitous; a brief dispersal of ice in the northern passage of the bay had allowed both vessels to make separate attempts to reach Countess of Warwick Sound, but almost immediately following their contact, a fog descended that was to endure for more than three days thereafter. In calm, ice was not the persistent problem that it had been in previous days; but lacking both wind and visible points of reference, the *Judith* and *Michael* were unable to make further progress towards their goal – though again, the physical exhaustion of their mariners appears to have been a factor also. Significantly, on 15/16 July, even with brief sightings of Countess of Warwick Sound and reasonably clear water between, boats were not put out to tow the becalmed ships – they remained anchored instead to a large iceberg, until the return of a great number of its fellows drove the tired crews to try for their landfall once more.

Their ordeal continued for a further four days. Unable to bear sail safely in the congested waters, the *Judith* and *Michael* drifted away from the northern shore of the bay, carried by the same currents as the ice that entrapped them. Again, on 20 July, the ships anchored against a great iceberg, the mariners 'utterlie wearied with towing'; however, later that day, a partial break-up of ice to the east encouraged the exhausted men back into their boats. With only a brief pause during the night, they continued to tow for more than twelve hours, and by the morning of 21 July were within three miles of their harbour. From there, careful sounding and slow towing brought them into the sound's northern reaches by noon, at which Fenton immediately gave his men their

---

[1] His description of one of these encounters (document 8, p. 151) was typically laconic: 'we abode some knockes (which were not daintie to us).

[2] PRO EKR E164/35, p. 86; HM 715, f. 3.

well-earned dinner. The *Judith* and *Michael*, truants from the fleet for more than three weeks, were the first English ships to attain the appointed rendezvous that year.

In the days between his arrival and that of the main body of the fleet on 30 July, Fenton and a party of soldiers explored the immediate environs of Countess of Warwick Sound. According to his instructions to observe the nature of the land and its potential, he noted the quality of the terrain ('marshe lik but of no depthe of earthe' in general, though he also noted one small area of adequate pasture),[1] the incidence of wildlife – principally reindeer and partridge-like fowl – and, particularly, all signs of recent Inuit activity. He also discovered an apparent abundance of a similar sort of ore to that of Countess of Warwick Island; a discovery that was responsible for the establishment of at least one mine-working there – 'Fenton's Fortune' – following the arrival of the remainder of the fleet.[2] That Fenton's miners were unable to open this working themselves was yet another repercussion of 'thindesreccon' of the pursar (either Nicholas Chancellor, pursar to the colony, or Thomas Thornton, responsible for the provisioning of the non-company ships), who had arranged for the intended colony's mining tools to be loaded into the *Thomas Allen*.

Mines and colonies

With the arrival of most of the other vessels of the fleet on 31 July (the *Anne Frances*, *Moon of Foye* and *Thomas of Ipswich* remained at sea), the main business of the expedition could begin. Sensitive to the time he had lost, Frobisher took in hand the search for new deposits of ore with exemplary industry. On that first day, he was unavoidably occupied with emergency repairs to the *Ayde*, breached by her own anchor (the hole had been stopped up hurriedly with a side of beef, a necessarily temporary measure); but on the following morning, he organized the reopening of the mining trench on Countess of Warwick Island, and, on 2 August, set out with two pinnaces south to Beare's Sound, to recover samples of ore mined and stockpiled there in 1577.[3] He returned by evening; the next day being Sunday, he went only so far as Winter's Furnace, some four kilometres west of his base camp, and after briefly surveying the site, decided against re-opening the old mine-working on the island (the ore deposits there lying, according to Fenton, 'uncerteinlie and crabbedlie to gett'). On 4 August, it was the turn of Jonas's Mount, approximately ten miles to the north and east of Countess of Warwick Sound, upon which Frobisher descended with a party of eighty soldiers and pioneers. Despite the supposed discovery there of a rich, red ore by Schutz in the

---

[1] Document 8, pp. 153–4: 23–24 July.

[2] The location of 'Fenton's Fortune' has not been established, but Fenton's own references thereto appear to place it somewhat to the north and west of 'Denham's Mount' on the eastern side of Countess of Warwick Sound.

[3] The 1577 working on Countess of Warwick Island (the 'ship's trench') was not in fact mined significantly in 1578; recent archeological excavations there have shown that the focus of new activity created what is now known as the 'reservoir trench', close to the centre of the island (McGee and Tuck, in Alsford, *Field Studies*, p. 10; *HBM*, p. 108). This appears to have been worked only upon days when the weather did not permit the passage to more outlying sites (cf. document 8, p. 158: 7 August), and it, too, was swiftly abandoned. The ore of the island was said to be 'hardly had'. The precise location of the mine working in Beare Sound has yet to be rediscovered, though excavations during 1991 identified possibly old mining

previous year, only samples of black ore were found and brought back to Countess of Warwick Island for assaying.[1] The following day, Fenton led his general to 'Fenton's Fortune', which was to provide anything but (according to Selman, Robert Denham examined the site on 9 August and thought it unlikely to produce forty tons of ore, '& that with great travayle'). Poor weather, and the vulnerable anchorage at which several of the fleet's vessels had remained, interrupted the search for ore for the next two days. It was a measure of Frobisher's impatience that on 7 August, notwithstanding high winds and seas, he attempted to take several pinnaces back to Fenton's Fortune, though by the time they had made a mile in the sea, Fenton's boat had lost her mast and sails, and Captain Courtney was reduced to near-panic by his own boat's parlous plight.[2] Forced to return to Countess of Warwick Island, the miners passed the day attempting to dig ore from the hard ground of the reservoir trench.

Despite these minor frustrations, Frobisher's efforts appeared to find their reward on 11 August, when Robert Davis and Thomas Morris, respectively masters of the *Ayde* and *Francis of Foye*, reconnoitering the coast some eight miles to the north and west of Countess of Warwick Sound, discovered apparently rich veins of ore, including one carrying the elusive red variety. Robert Denham swiftly confirmed their promise during assays conducted on samples from the site, and the *Francis of Foye*'s miners opened a major mine-working there, which was named Countess of Sussex mine. With the mine on Sussex Island in Beare Sound, this would prove to be the most productive site, and its apparent fertility swiftly encouraged the assayers and miners to abandon Fenton's Fortune - where, beyond expectation, some seventy tons of ore had been secured by 15 August, though with great difficulty.[3]

With all of the expedition's available miners now set to their appointed tasks (some of their colleagues remained at sea still, in the *Anne Frances* and *Moon of Foye*), there was time to consider its other goals. As early as 9 August, the question of the colony had been raised (no doubt the matter was pushed somewhat by Fenton, eager to have it furthered in the face of Frobisher's obvious reluctance). Best and Fenton report the discussion of the land council that day in some detail, with Lok later providing his

---

activity on the north shore of Lefferts Island (Fitzhugh, *Archaeology of the Frobisher Voyages*, p. 114); a site which, unfortunately, is submerged at high tide in the modern era.

[1] The failure to rediscover traces of the red ore was considered one of the principal failures of the voyage. Assays carried our by Kranich in November 1577 had shown this to carry the greatest potential value, of some forty ounces of gold per ton, or four times that in the black variety (PRO SP12/118, 41). Lok (document 5, p. 82) put the blame squarely upon Frobisher for this, though presumably the other eighty men who assiduously scoured the site on 4 August should share that responsibility. Neither Best nor Settle mention Schutz's discovery of red ore or the naming of Jonas Mount, and as no mining activity was conducted at this site, modern attempts to locate it have been unsuccessful. Re-examining the site on 30 July 1578, Fenton (document 8, p. 156) implied that it lay north-east and by north from Countess of Warwick Sound, which seems to place it somewhere in Napoleon Bay. Given the aggressive posture of the Inuit parties around Countess of Warwick Sound during Frobisher's time there in 1577, it is almost certain that it lay on, or within sight of, one of the shores there.

[2] Document 8, p. 158: 'Capten Courtney with his companie in great daunger of drowninge, who in the night dreamed he was sinking in the sea, and so troubled therwith in his sleepe, that he cried with such lowdnes, Iesus have mercie upon me, that we in the other tentes were awaked therwith, mistrusting a larom ....'

[3] Document 9, p. 186. For the fertility of the southernmost mine-site, we have only Lok's testimony (document 5, p. 90): '... beare Sownd, wheare most of their ladinge was had ...'.

own, partial interpretation of events. Clearly, the loss of the *Denys* on 2 July with part of the frame of the 'great house' compromised the original plan. A further section of the frame was at sea still, loaded in the *Anne Frances*, and it was not known whether she survived at that date. The pieces available to the intended colonists comprised only the east and south sides of the original structure, and their modification to serve a more modest plan would have been a difficult and time-consuming process.[1] Also – and this appears to have constituted the principal setback to Fenton himself – eighty-four tons of beer intended for the colonists' consumption had been loaded in the *Thomas of Ipswich*, which the previous night had deserted the expedition to return to England (though the land-council would have had no knowledge of her loss to the expedition until mariners of the *Anne Frances* reached Countess of Warwick's Sound on 22 August).[2] In light of these difficulties, Fenton offered to remain in Meta Incognita with just sixty colonists. Fortunately for him and the prospective colonists, the carpenters and bricklayers who were to erect their home in the new land, called before the land council, calculated that their work could not be done within eight or nine weeks (the expedition's schedule gave a maximum of twenty-six days remaining). Therefore, the apparently unanimous decision to entirely abandon the colony project for that year was a sensible one. Michael Lok, seeking once more to portray Frobisher in the worst possible light, claimed that Fenton had made his offer *before* the land council convened, and that it had done so subsequently only upon Frobisher's order, so that he could have the expected objections aired in the most forceful manner possible. There may be some justice to this; yet in calling the council to discuss the matter, Frobisher had acted entirely properly. Indeed, in view of the attrition upon the colony's allocated supplies, it might be argued that he would have been acting within his authority to dismiss the attempt outright, rather than have it discussed in council and put to the vote thereafter. Fenton, who in terms of reputation stood to lose most by the colony's abandonment, offered no criticism of the decision, even implicitly – indeed, it was his account alone which revealed that the loss of wooden boards (probably expended as fenders during the storm of 2/3 July) meant that the construction of a habitation to house even forty men was probably unfeasible. Selman – Lok's partisan – made no mention of the incident in his account, though clearly, it was his personally-expressed version of events that Lok later used (a presumably disingenuous version, given that it had been Selman, as the 'registrar' of the voyage, who had set down the council's decision not to proceed with the colony); but Best supports Fenton's version in all respects.

Despite the admirable level of foresight that had informed the commissioners in preparing for this, the first English settlement in the New World, the future history of early English plantations suggests that the colony, even had sufficient supplies been available to allow its establishment, must have perished during its first winter in Meta

---

[1] Document 11, p. 226.

[2] In fact, that the *Thomas of Ipswich* had defected rather than merely gone missing was not fully understood until the fleet returned to England. Best comments upon it in his retrospective account, but it seems that he was able only to report her absence when he met with Frobisher. As late as 30 August, when the expedition was preparing to depart from Meta Incognita, Frobisher risked a pinnace – and the safety of one John Gray, master's mate of the *Anne Frances* – to return to the Queen's Foreland to search for the truant vessel (document 8, p. 167: margin note).

Incognita. Though no suitable site was identified in advance, it is almost certain that the 'great house' would have been built in the vicinity of Countess of Warwick Sound; not primarily for the proximity of the 1577/8 base camp, but because the sound offered the best (that is, most sheltered and ice-free) harbour yet found in the region. Yet the area is hardly suitable for European settlement, even today. A small well had been discovered on Countess of Warwick Island in 1577, but the locality offered little else in the way of resources. Fenton had noticed the presence of wild fowl and deer on the mainland to the north, but not in such quantities that their use as supplements to the colonists' diet could easily be organized. Most importantly, even setting aside the threat to English hunting parties from the Inuit (which against an organized and well-armed defence could not have been significant), the necessary attitudes required to exist for prolonged periods in such sparse and adverse conditions had yet to be acquired by Englishmen (witness the abject disillusionment of the first Roanoke colonists, rescued by Drake from the relatively fertile Carolina Banks in 1586), and a more challenging environment than that of Baffin Island had yet to be experienced by western Europeans. Furthermore, the collapse in confidence in the enterprise in the latter months of 1578 would have made the prospect of a further, relieving expedition a poor one indeed. Fortunately, the loss of the *Denys*, and the fleet pursars' disregard (or, perhaps, over-zealous interpetation) of their instructions: that 'the victalls, munitions and other thynges to be carryed equally distributed into *the* shippes'[1] ensured the colony could not be attempted; perhaps the only felicitous outcome of a voyage that was otherwise to have almost entirely unhappy results.

The council's deliberations on 9 August had proceeded precisely as the adventurers – or, rather, the Privy Counsellors among their number – had intended. Despite Frobisher's reputation as an autocrat, he was scrupulously to observe the mechanics, if not the spirit, of taking 'good counsel' during his time in Meta Incognita. Nevertheless, it is clear that he did so much in the manner that Francis Drake was to make familiar to future generations; and occasions upon which his commitment to an oligarchical mode of government was tested may be easily discerned in the explosions that followed any display of dissent, no matter how minor. Even so, most of these appear to have turned upon the point of authority *per se*, rather than upon the consequences of its exercise. Prior to the expedition's departure from England, the adventurers seem to have had the greatest difficulty in persuading him to acknowledge Fenton's authority as lieutenant-general of the expedition, notwithstanding the latter's appointment as governor of the proposed colony. Whether this resistance grew from personal antipathy towards his subordinate, the implicit diminution of his own authority it appeared to represent, or, indeed, as a reflection of his unwillingness to see the project furthered cannot be determined; but it was apparently necessary to require his signature upon a document that confirmed Fenton's role in the coming voyage.[2] The consequences of this device were not entirely fortuitous.

[1] Document 2, p. 62.
[2] The only account of this struggle is Lok's (document 5, p. 87), and his claims should not be assessed uncritically. Nevertheless, the subsequent antagonism between Frobisher and Fenton, corroborated in detail by Selman and, apparently, overwhelmingly at Frobisher's instigation, supports much of the tenor of Lok's complaints.

By 19 August, the pace of mining appears to have remained unsatisfactory. On the previous day, Fenton's log had noted that the expedition had secured less than a third of more than 1,000 tons of ore provided for in the fleet's instructions. The burden of this shortfall may have weighed upon Frobisher, and frayed his unsteady temper accordingly. Perhaps unwisely, Fenton complained to him that day of the attitude of some of the *Ayde*'s mariners – particularly the boatswain, Frobisher's kinsman, Alexander Creake – who refuse to accept orders from Fenton.[1] The conversation degenerated into a hot dispute upon the nature of Fenton's authority, and whether it derived from the Queen or Frobisher himself (who adduced his hand upon the commissioner's warrant as proof of the latter, though claiming, pettishly, that he would prefer Fenton to be the Queen's servant rather than his own). The incident was relatively inconsequential, possessing little of the magnitude or implication of more famous encounters; but the similarity between the matter of contention here and Drake's quarrels with Thomas Doughty (1578), Francis Knollis (1585) and William Borough (1587), suggests that the precise span of a commander's authority at sea was not an uncommon source of strife in contemporary voyages, particularly where officers owed their rank and responsibilities to other than the patronage of their immediate superior. It is therefore somewhat ironic that Frobisher's own later antipathy towards Drake, expressed most memorably following the Armada campaign, almost certainly derived from his experience as Drake's lieutenant during the West Indies Raid of 1585.[2]

The matter was laid to rest four days later, when the land council convened once more. Even Frobisher must have realised that he was defending an untenable position; one that flew not only in the face of instructions he had received from the Privy Council, but also of those he himself had issued following his arrival at Countess of Warwick Sound some days earlier.[3] He probably urged, or commanded, Creake and his cronies to make their peace, and in return they were merely admonished – a notably light punishment for an offence that in extreme cases merited the death penalty.

The air of reconciliation was no doubt encouraged by the urgency which permeated the efforts of the expedition. Since his arrival, Frobisher had hardly paused. Accompanied most days by his supposed lieutenant Fenton, he had reconnoitred the shores immediately adjacent to the sound, directing and re-directing his weary miners to where the latest or most promising discovery lay. Weariest of all, one suspects, were the assayers; Denham in particular appears to have taken on the role of site-inspector, performing assays 'at the vein' as new deposits or varieties of ore were uncovered, a task that would have required the near-constant dismantling and reassembly of his brick furnace.[4] On 16 August, a new mine-working was opened at Diar's Sound (named after Andrew Diar, master of the *Hopewell*),[5] an inlet some miles to the south

---

[1] Their precise relationship is not known.
[2] See McDermott, *Frobisher*, pp. 352, 354 on the likely genesis of this near bloody antipathy.
[3] Document 11, p. 225.
[4] Cf. Fenton's journal for 14 August (document 8, p. 160).
[5] Diar, according to Lok (document 5, p. 88), was Frobisher's long-time associate, a man 'so unskillfull as he can neyther wright nor redde so inexpert of the sea, as he was never further from England then Fraunce, and Ireland, and so honest and so trewe that syns his retorne home he is gonne owt with his Fellowes to Sea in evill ventures … '. If his relationship with Frobisher was indeed a venerable one, it is not difficult to imagine the nature of these 'evill ventures'. Diar came to a violent end; master of the ship *Jesus* in

east of Countess of Warwick Island. The mine, named Denham's Mount, yielded some four types of black ore and proved productive, being surpassed only by the Countess of Sussex and Beare Sound sites. With this discovery, no further exploration was made, and all efforts were devoted to extracting ore from existing mines.

This was not done without cost. There can be little doubt that the rigours of the expedition to date – particularly those suffered during the protracted struggle to reach the pre-arranged landfall – had weakened the men who were now required to expend the labour of weeks in a matter of days. Mortalities, though not large in absolute numbers, were noted almost as soon as large-scale mining commenced (Best was to calculate that 'no more than fortie' men died during the entire expedition, though he had no information on post-voyage fatalities). Significantly, the dead were not all, nor even predominantly, miners. On 16 August, three men died: democratically, one was a mariner, another a miner's labourer and a third, Philip Ellarde, described as a 'gent' in Fenton's journal, had charge of the expedition's winter clothing. On the 19 August, mariners of the *Denys*, *Emanuel of Exeter* and *Frances of Foye* were buried; on 28 August, Roger Littlestone, described by Selman as the 'General's servant', died, 'who by the judgment of the surgian had the horrible disease of the pox', and, three days later, the quartermaster of the *Ayde*, Anthony Sparrow, was buried – apparently the last Englishman to die upon the soil of Baffin Island for several centuries to come (though by no means the final fatality of the expedition).[1] This 'spread' of mortality is hardly conclusive – we cannot say whether the various accounts of the voyage reported all the fatalities or just the more notable examples – but it suggests that Best's claim that 'the Gentlemen for example sake laboured hartily, and honestlye encouraged the inferiour sorte to worke', if overstated, nevertheless represented more than literary hyperbole.

The significant depletion (or non-arrival) of the men's provisions must have been a contributory factor to these fatalities, as it was to the general rate of morbidity and weakening of the men's constitutions – though again, precise statistics are not extant. Fenton's journal is the best source for the shortage of victuals, particularly those of the *Ayde*, which he appears to have taken as the measure for the entire expedition. On 17 August, he reported that she had only seven tons of beer remaining; two days later, her supplies of butter were depleted to just three firkins and half a 'kilderkin' (a small barrel); on 22 August, her store of dried fish comprised 250 stockfish and 240 'poor john' (haberdine).[2] With the fleet arriving at least four weeks overdue its original schedule, such shortages were to be expected, and if the flagship's provisions were so acutely stretched, the situation could hardly have been easier elsewhere. Yet the intended colony – whose foundation had now been abandoned – had been provisioned for a minimum of one year (of butter alone, Fenton's particular concern, over twenty one large barrels had been provided).[3] It is hardly likely their stores had been so spoiled that there was now no more than what was necessary for the hundred failed colonists during their brief time in Meta Incognita. In fact, it appears that a form of

---

a Levant Company voyage of 1583/4, he was seized and hanged from the walls at Tripoli upon the orders of the local 'king', following unsatisfactory trade negotiations there (Hakluyt, *PN*, 1598–1600, v, pp. 297–8).

[1] Document 8, p. 166; document 9, p. 187, 189.
[2] Document 8, pp. 161–3.
[3] HM 715, f. 13.

rationing had been imposed, and that these supplies were held back deliberately – perhaps a reflection of fears that the return passage would be as protracted as that which had brought them to Countess of Warwick Sound. In this respect, it seems significant that on 29 August, as the expedition prepared to depart upon the return voyage, Fenton distributed supplies ear-marked for the colony to several ships, 'victuallinge every one of all thinges necessarie for ix weekes following'.[1] For a passage that was capable of being accomplished in less than three weeks under favourable conditions, this seems less like caution than acute pessimism.

These shortages, however artificial, may have been alleviated by the arrival of the final elements of the fleet. On 22 August, Fenton, laboriously making his way by sea to Countess of Sussex Mine against contrary winds, sighted a pinnace to seaward of his own boat. Correctly, he assumed it to belong to the ship *Anne Frances*, George Best's command. Since separating from the fleet on 26 July, the *Anne Frances* had kept the company of the *Moon of Foye*; their persistent attempts to re-enter the 'strait' from its southernmost approach near the Queen's Foreland had largely proved near-disastrous. Usually, the winds were unfavourable, coming from the north and west. This, of course, meant that the vessels were most effectively prevented from achieving their goal at precisely the time when the body of water before them was least pestered by ice. When the winds changed to the good, it was usually to bring thick fog and ice once more, making each new attempt as fraught as previously. Briefly, they kept company with the *Thomas of Ipswich*, which had laid on and off for several days in the vicinity of the northern shore of the Queen's Foreland, but they lost contact with her during a storm on the evening of 3 August. Three days later, they had beaten westwards no further than 'Leicester Point' (probably the northern extremity of Edgell Island); there, in yet another squall, the two ships parted company. However, they, and the *Thomas of Ipswich*, met once more on 8 August, and the three captains – Best, Upcot and Tanfield – met in the *Anne Frances* to discuss their impasse.

Best's portrayal of this conversation is so protracted (and in many ways self-serving) that it is tempting to see it as a personal apologia. Having left the fleet – possibly deliberately – on three occasions, and being as far from making his landfall as when the fleet had first arrived in these waters some six weeks earlier, his record to date was hardly an impressive one: particularly for a man who still expected to be Fenton's lieutenant during the life of the proposed colony. Accordingly, it was claimed to be his forceful reminder of their common duty that persuaded the other captains to press on, rather than to abandon their search for the rest of the fleet – of whose survival they had as yet no information – and return to England. With their men now near exhaustion, however, it was proposed that the three vessels' miners explore the nearby southern shore for a few days, to allow time for the *Anne Frances*'s pinnace to be assembled. Ice in the strait remained too thick for the ships themselves to make any further progress towards their elusive goal – a fact reinforced by circumstance when, on 10 August, the *Anne Frances*'s hull was badly damaged as her mariners attempted to bring her into safer harbour. Upcot, commander of

---

[1] Document 8, p. 167.

the *Moon of Foye*, agreed to this strategy readily enough; but the crew of the *Thomas of Ipswich*, whose captain had also assented, quietly took their ship out to sea that night under cover of partial darkness, and ran for home with Fenton's beer in their holds.

On 9 August, Best and Upcot began to examine their immediate locality in the ships' boats. Upon very little evidence (neither the *Anne Frances* nor *Moon of Foye* carried an assayer), they swiftly concluded that ore deposits identified on 'a great blacke Iland' off the Queen's Foreland were potentially rich, and significant mining began at what was named Best's Blessing immediately following its discovery that day.[1] As this activity continued over several days, the carpenter-smith of the *Anne Frances* slowly jerry-built his ship's dismantled pinnace without nails or wooden knees, using pieces of metal fashioned from tongs, gridiron and a fire-shovel. His opinion of its seaworthiness – on 19 August he presented the vessel to his captain and told him 'he would not adventure himselfe therein, for five hundreth poundes' – was probably an astute one;[2] nevertheless, Best and Upcot, with eighteen others, put out into the 'strait' that day to discover the fate of their fellow voyagers, leaving their mariners and miners to continue to mine and load the ore of Best's Blessing.

This happy voyage lasted three days, during which the pinnace appears to have more than repaid her architect's pale faith. Despite having no wind and therefore obliged to row for hours at a time, her crew's luck held as the 'strait' remained calm and relatively ice-free. On 22 August, they lay off Countess of Sussex mine (which was as yet unknown to them), where they sighted one of the other ships' ensigns and immediately assumed the expedition to have fallen prey to the Inuit. Fortunately, Fenton sighted them from his own pinnace and was able to assuage their fears before Best and his companions 'resolved to recover the same Auntient, if it were so, from those base, cruell, and man eating people, or els to lose their lives, & all togither'.[3] Their rendezvous marked the moment at which all elements of the fleet that had first sundered on 2/3 July, some seven weeks earlier, were finally in contact once more.

That fear of Inuit aggression, so prevalent in the published accounts of the voyage, was undoubtedly overplayed for popular consumption. Compared to the experiences of the previous two expeditions, there were few sightings of, much less contact with, the local population. Anticipating trouble at some of the outer-lying mine-workings, Frobisher had organized shifts of armed parties to protect the miners as they laboured, and this measure appears to have been entirely effective. The prospect of a huge fleet of strange vessels, with over five hundred well-armed white men swarming over the vicinity of Countess of Warwick Sound, inclined the Inuit to great circumspection – the more so, one suspects, because the efforts of these intruders did not impinge in the slightest degree upon resources in which they themselves had any interest. On 15 August, organizing the transportation of the last of the miners from Fenton's Fortune

---

[1] The island cannot be identified with certainty. According to Best, it lay 'under' Hatton's Headland, the south-easternmost tip of Resolution island. There are many small islands in that fractured archipelago, any of which might have yielded the c. 130 tons of low-grade ore collected by the miners and mariners of the *Anne Frances* and *Moon of Foye* (see p. 39 n. 3 below). Modern archaeological examination of the area has not established the site to date.

[2] Document 11, p. 231.

[3] Ibid, p. 232.

to Countess of Sussex mine, Fenton had sighted two Inuit in their boats; wisely, he had ordered his men not to show themselves or otherwise encourage any new confrontation. With only Gilbert Yorke to accompany him, Fenton had then attempted to parley, but the Inuit, perhaps recalling the previous year's 'parley' at Bloody Point (in which Yorke himself, coincidentally, had played a prominent and sanguinary part), hurriedly made off. This was to be the only close sighting of the 'newe prey' in 1578. Coming from Beare Sound, mariners of the *Salomon* later claimed to have seen several larger Inuit boats there, at which Frobisher berated his old privateering crony, Hugh Randall, for leaving the miners at Sussex Island alone and unprotected before his relief arrived (a rare, overt declaration of concern for his charges); and Frobisher himself saw two Inuit far from him in Beare Sound on 28 August, when according to Ellis, he sought to capture one or more of them.[1] These incidents apart, the Englishmen appear to have found little evidence of recent settlement in the area. Best's detailed description of Inuit artefacts, habits and mores, appended to his account of the 1578 voyage, has been included in the present volume; but it is almost certain that his material was drawn from the experiences of the previous year. Ellis, present only on the final voyage, had nothing to say of the Inuit – a remarkable omission from a work intended for public consumption, had there been the opportunity to observe them at first-hand.

With the *Anne Frances* and *Moon of Foye* now with the fleet once more (Best returned to Resolution Island on 24 August to load the ore his men had mined at Best's Blesing and bring the ships to Countess of Warwick Sound thereafter), the expedition finally had its full complement of miners – other than the fifteen of their fellows obliged to return prematurely to England with the *Thomas of Ipswich*.[2] Yet the fleet was due to depart in little more than a week hence, and the pace of activity remained frenetic. Frobisher continued his near-constant perambulations between the mining sites, exhorting and cajoling his increasingly exhausted men, and rattled his captains into making a similar effort. From 24 August, however, preparations to evacuate the site commenced. On that day, Fenton began to allocate a proportion of the remaining victuals (principally peas and meal, items that even growing hunger had not tempted the mariners and miners to deplete significantly) that would otherwise take up valuable storage space in the ships' holds to be buried on Countess of Warwick Island, together with those timbers of the 'great house' that had survived. He also began the remarkable task of constructing the first stone dwelling in America north of the Spanish occupation: 'to prove what the vehemencie of winde and weather would do therwith this winter, to thende, that if the nexte yeare habitacion shoulde be performed there, that then by this litle begynninge, a juste occasion and experiment should be given how we shoulde deale in building greater howses.'[3] However modest, the creation of his house (or 'Fenton's watch-tower', as its architect named it) was moved by an

---

[1] Document 10, p. 201. Hall, who was with Frobisher during this episode, claims that it took place on 26 August, but that no Inuit were sighted (document 6, p. 121).

[2] PRO EKR E164/36, p. 162: Edward Selman's accounts recording their discharge. They received five months' wages, as opposed to seven months for those miners who remained in Meta Incognita until 1 September.

[3] Document 8, p. 165.

admirably untainted spirit of scientific inquiry. Its walls – some fourteen feet in length and eight in breadth – were faced with lime-wash, and a roof of ships' boards placed above them. Fenton also planted seeds around the house, and freshly-baked bread was placed within to entice the Inuit following the evacuation of the island by the English-men: a somewhat thin propitiation in light of the indignities endured by the local pop-ulation in the previous year, and rather shabbily explained by Best as the means to ' … the better allure those brutish & ucivill people to courtesie …'.[1]

Meanwhile, the lading of ships had commenced. Since Christopher Hall's own arrival at Countess of Warwick Sound in the *Gabriel* on 2 August (he had left the larger *Thomas Allen* in Gibbes Sound[2] on the southern shore of Frobisher Bay, returning for her five days), he appears to have taken charge of the complicated process of allocating ore to each vessel and supervising its transportation from the various sites. As late as 11 August, the only significant quantity of ore ready for lading was that stockpiled at Beare Sound; on the same day, the old ballast of the *Gabriel* and *Michael* was discharged into the water there, and the two barks brought their first cargoes of ore back to Countess of Warwick Sound, where they were transferred into the *Ayde*. In the following days, several of the freight ships also vis-ited Beare Sound, but the largest vessels were not sufficiently shallow-draughted to risk the relatively treacherous waters of Beare Sound.[3] To the north, Countess of Sussex mine had produced sufficient quantities of 'good' ore for lading by the ships *Thomas Allen*, *Frances of Foye*, *Judith* and the two *Emanuels*; its location immedi-ately beside relatively deep water allowed them to load their cargoes directly. Simi-larly, ore secured from Denham's Mount in Diar's Sound – a narrow but deep inlet – was loaded directly into the *Hopewell*, with other vessels taking small amounts from this mine.[4]

By 30 August, the ships were loaded almost to their full capacity; Selman noted that the *Ayde* lacked ten or twelve tons at most on that day, which was subsequently met by further loads from Countess of Sussex mine. Other vessels with capacity remaining received small parcels of ore from the minor sites – Countess of Warwick Island, Winter's furnace or Fenton's Fortune. Selman's summary of the lading of ore through the fleet, though not entirely accurate, provides the only extant evidence of the relative productivity (tons of ore) of the various mineworkings:

[1] Document 11, p. 233.
[2] The precise location of this feature has not been established, but Hall's log appears to put it somewhere on the northern shore of Resolution Island; perhaps to be identified with the present-day Sorry Harbour. Other locations named in his log but not elsewhere – Pamors (?Palmer's) Point and Harves (?Harvey's) Gulf – seem to be features of the same shoreline.
[3] The *Thomas Allen*, one of the three largest vessels in the fleet, went to Beare Sound on 24 August to take in 60 tons of ore; but it is likely that she stood off from the shore and was loaded in shifts by the pin-naces that served the miners there. Selman reported that on the same day, the *Anne Frances* – again, one of the larger vessels – had taken in the shallower-draughted *Moon of Foye*'s lading of (Queen's Foreland) ore so that the *Moon* could take on a further 100 tons of ore from Beare Sound; a transfer that suggests some difficulty was anticipated (document 9, p. 188). Selman's later statement that the *Moon of Foye* remained loaded with 100 tons of ore from the Queen's Foreland – and, by inference, that mining at the site had yielded a total of some 230 tons of ore – therefore appears to be mistaken).
[4] Fenton's journal for 5 August first identified Diar's Sound: 'In our reatorne home we serched (dyers) sownde for harbour for our shipping which we founde verie good …' (document 8, p. 157).

Beare Sound	450	Countess of Warwick Island	65
Countess of Sussex Mine	455	Denham's Mount	260
Queen's Foreland	130 [1]	Fenton's Fortune	5 [2]
Winter's Furnace	5		

In total, 1,370 tons. If Schutz's final pre-voyage estimate of £23. 15s. per ton refined could be sustained, the freight ships' cargoes held a nominal value of some £32,500: a reasonable, if not spectacular, return upon the c. £16–17,000 spent to date (and certainly more impressive than the £19,000 anticipated upon the 800 tons specified in the official instructions). Problems were already anticipated in this respect, however. Even before the departure of the fleet, Selman claimed that the latter stages of the ships' lading had been haphazard, and that much ore not specifically certified in the register book had been loaded by 'many symple men'. No doubt the looming prospect of departure from that savage place had been a powerful incentive to fill the ships indiscriminately. Michael Lok was to make much of this failure to maintain control of the lading; yet the evidence of all future assays makes it clear that all types of the ore, wherever mined, however certified, and by whatever process refined, were almost uniformly worthless.[3]

On 31 August, most of the miners and mariners (other than those still working on Sussex Island) were gathered from the outworks and assembled on Winter's Furnace to hear a 'godly' sermon preached by the reverend Wolfall and take communion thereafter. Immediately following the service, Frobisher convened his land council for the final time – the first occasion, in fact, upon which all of its designated members were present – to discuss one of the intended, if now minor, goals of the expedition that had yet to attempted. His instructions had relegated the search for a passage into the South Sea – the principal goal of the 1576 adventurers – to a composite, sweep-up clause:

> We will then yf Leasure and tyme wille permitt the same that you with the ii barkes shall repaire towardes the place where the first yeare you loste your men, aswell to searche for mynes theire, as to discover .50. or .100. leages (further) westwardes frome that place (as the oppening of the streight by water will lowe), as you may be certayne that you are entride into the Southe Sea (commonly called Mare di Sur), and in your passage to learne all that you cane in all thinges, & take parfect notes therof, not tarringe longe frome your shippes and workemen, but that you maye be hable to retorne homewardes with them in due tyme.[4]

The western exit to the north-west passage was therefore not to be attempted unless the time consumed in that search could be put to other, more productive use. Nevertheless, as late as 24 August, Selman expected Frobisher to make the attempt when

---

[1] This was the lading of the *Anne Frances*, mined at 'Best's Blessing' between 11–18 August, before the vessels re-joined the fleet. The respective figures for ore mined from Beare Sound and the Queen's Foreland have been altered from those given in the text to allow for Selman's apparent error, discussed in note above.

[2] This is the figure for ore loaded, not the total mined (Selman had estimated the latter to be approximately 60–70 tons before the mine was abandoned on 16 August (Document 9, p. 186).

[3] *HBM* (pp. 122–38) provide a comprehensive analysis of the types and properties of the various black ores.

[4] Document 2, p. 60.

time permitted, which indicates that the intention continued to be expressed, if only for duty's sake.[1] At the meeting of 31 August, however, the impracticality of making a further reconnaissance to the west was too evident, despite Best's claim (no doubt intended to assuage the disappointment of his readership), that it was abandoned only after 'long debating'. The obstacles, unanimously recognized by the members of the council, were insurmountable. The weather, never very favourable, had now deteriorated to the point where the evacuation of the 'strait' was becoming an urgent priority (the day before, Fenton reported 'verie tempestious weather with greate snowe and the winde at northest'); supplies of water and beer had fallen to the point at which further rationing might be necessary simply to get the ships back to England – due in no small part to the master of the *Anne Frances*, whom Fenton accused of negligence in 'losing' some eighteen tons of beer allocated to the *Judith* – and, not least, the fabric of all the ships was now seriously compromised by the attrition inherent in their employment as ore-transports (particularly the little *Gabriel* and *Michael*, which had been loaded and unloaded upon more occasions than any other vessels in the fleet, but which were now to be the instruments of the proposed reconnaissance). In view of these difficulties, any discovery of the western exit to the 'strait' in 1578 was declared to be 'a thing verye impossible' to achieve. Predictably, Michael Lok later placed the worst possible construction upon the same discussions. In his version, Frobisher had been urged by Christopher Hall and Charles Jackman throughout the month in which they remained in Meta Incognita to make some attempt upon the passage or allow them to do the same.[2] He had apparently put them off, claiming, firstly, that there would be time enough to explore, and subsequently that no time remained to do so; in Lok's opinion, these obfuscations had a single cause: ' … his mind beinge so vayne glorious, that he will not suffer anye discoverye to bee made without his owne presens …'. There may have been some justice to the latter claim; but Hall's journal makes no mention of his alleged pleas to discover the passage (a journal that is otherwise somewhat critical of Frobisher), and none of the other accounts corroborate Lok. During the period in which ore was being actively mined, the *Gabriel* and *Michael* were needed to assist in the principal task of the expedition – to secure the largest possible volume of ore. Their employment was, therefore, unavoidable; once it was no longer so, further exploration of the 'strait' by one or both of the same vessels had become impractical. Of any of Lok's blasts against Frobisher's motives and performance, this is perhaps the least sustainable. Conversely, Best's further claim – that notwithstanding this rare display of unanimity, Frobisher subsequently took his pinnace and desperately sought to make at least a limited reconnaissance to the 'northwards' during the next twenty-four hours – was also incorrect. From all the accounts (including Best's) we know that Frobisher went directly southwards from Countess of Warwick Sound on 31 August: to Beare Sound, to arrange the final lading of ore and evacuation of miners from Sussex Island. Having dismissed the possibility of making an attempt upon the passage in 1578, he likewise appears to have cleared his mind of any thought of further exploration.

---

[1] Document 9, p. 188: 'The General departed this present towards *Bears Sound* in a pynnas & will return hither agayn before he go up into the Streicts'.
[2] Document 5, pp. 89–90.

There was, however, a further reconnaissance made of the land to the east of Countess of Warwick Sound. This was conducted by Fenton and Thomas Morris, master of the *Frances of Foye*, on 27 August, though their precise purpose is not stated in any of the extant commentaries. Moving to the south of Jonas's Mount (the site of the red ore discovered in 1577), they passed some five miles south-eastwards until encountering 'the northe sea'. Though their precise route is unknown (as, indeed, is the location of Jonas's Mount), it appears that they had crossed the Blunt Peninsula and sighted Cyrus Field Bay from high ground. The island that Fenton described (document 8, pp. 165–6) similarly cannot be identified, being one of many in the headwaters of the bay; but his observation that the land seemed to tend to the north-eastwards indicates that the weather was sufficiently clear that day to make out Cape Farrington and, beyond it, Cape Haven. Their reconnaissance was notable only for being the sole specific observation made upon the Atlantic coast of Baffin Island north of c. 62°30′ during three years' exploration of the region: it was made, and completed, by mid-day.

The return passage

The orders issued by Frobisher immediately following the last meeting of his land council on 31 August 1578 (document 11, pp. 235–6) were drafted with a predominant concern: to protect the cargo carried by the fleet and to prevent intelligence of its source from being disseminated. The fleet was to keep strict formation homewards (or, if separated, each 'truant' ship to be quarantined in its port of arrival pending instructions from Michael Lok); none of the mariners or miners were to have access to the ore, or to abstract any part thereof until the ships had arrived at Dartford; most dramatically, if any ship were to be taken by an 'enemy' – presumably a hostile vessel of any nationality, including a compatriot – its plots and charts to be cast overboard to preserve the secret of the ore's source. All of these admonishments underlined the expectation that others shared the optimism of Frobisher's adventurers for the value of their asset. For a number of reasons – not least, the ferocity of Atlantic storms that marked the homeward passage – they were to prove superfluous; nevertheless, having devoted such tireless energy to securing the fruits of his commission, Frobisher was assiduous in protecting them.

Before the expedition could depart, the mine at Beare Sound had to be evacuated. Frobisher took the *Ayde* and six other ships which were still found to have some small capacity remaining in their holds on the evening of 31 August; leaving behind the *Anne Frances*, half-beached to allow repairs upon her battered hull – the damage she had sustained on 10 August had yet to be made good – and the *Judith*, whose mariners were to assist in the refloating of the other vessel.[1] Several other fully laden vessels – *Emanuel of Bridgewater*, *Beare Leicester*, *Hopewell* and *Moon of Foye* – rode the night at 'Corbett's Point'[2] and joined Frobisher at Beare Sound the following day.

The waters of the sound were calm on the afternoon of 1 September; several ships took in ore from pinnaces plying between their anchorages and Sussex Island, and by

---

[1] According to Best (document 11, p. 233) the *Anne Frances* had eight 'great leakes' in her hull on that day.
[2] Probably to be identified with the latter-day Cape Cracroft; the deep inlet there, almost exactly halfway between Countess of Warwick and Beare Sounds, provides safe harbour for a number of ships.

evening the work was completed. The miners remained on the island, however; by eight o'clock that evening, the wind had risen dramatically, making their evacuation impossible. Frobisher himself was with them, having taken charge of the final lading of the *Gabriel* and *Michael*. Sussex Island was one of the more heavily worked mines in the latter stages of the expedition's tenure in Meta Incognita, and it appears that several ships' allocations of miners had been taken there from other sites. These were made as comfortable as possible for the night, having few supplies and little cover to shelter them, with the mariners of the *Gabriel*, *Michael* and several pinnaces adding to the general congestion.

Out in the sound, the ships of the fleet rode dangerously, the ebb having made their anchorages dangerously shallow, whilst high winds threatened to drive them on to the lee shore (the *Hopewell* was particularly troubled, having icebergs close by on her seaward side). Christopher Hall had been with Frobisher on Sussex Island earlier in the evening, but had returned to the *Ayde* before the weather turned, having been assured that his admiral would be following on.[1] Optimistically, he hung out a light to guide in the *Ayde*'s pinnace, but at midnight the wind had grown so strong that the ship's anchor cable sheered through, and he was obliged to stand off under sail.

By first light, almost all the ships in the fleet were busily staving off disaster. A number of their pinnaces had already sunk; fortunately, most of these had been empty, and riding at their mother ships' sides. Having lost her own pinnace, the *Judith* had put over to the relative safety of the Queen's Foreland, where Fenton awaited the rest of the fleet. It was not as a fleet, however, that its component parts departed from the new land that day. One by one, their masters giving up the struggle to keep distance from the lee shores of Sussex Island, the ships raised sail and moved precipitately towards the mouth of Frobisher Bay. Hall, waiting in the *Ayde*, managed to hail the *Beare Leicester* and *Emanuel of Exeter* as they fled, but could get no news of the other vessels, or of those that remained upon Sussex Island. Finally, on the evening of 2 September, Frobisher's pinnace – without Frobisher in it – returned to the *Ayde*, her mariners claiming that their admiral came on after in the *Gabriel* in the company of the *Anne Frances* and *Judith*. This was enough for the preoccupied Hall. He took the *Ayde* across the 'strait' to the Queen's Foreland and lay at hull that night in the company of the *Thomas Allen* and *Moon of Foye*. The following morning, at 7 o'clock, the three ships raised their sails and put out into the ocean.

The mariners who had brought news of their admiral had omitted several important details. Frobisher was indeed in the *Gabriel* by now, and had departed from Sussex Island in the company of the *Michael*; but initially their situation had been parlous. Each of them carried more than double their usual complement, and towed pinnaces precariously packed with more miners and men, including George Best. They also carried victuals for six days at most. Fortunately, the master of the *Anne Frances* (upon whom Best subsequently, and understandably, lavished great praise for his 'good regard of dutie'), had waited for his captain in safer waters in the middle passage of the bay, and was able to take on the men in the *Michael*'s pinnace, moments before it, too, capsized and sank. Off the Queen's Foreland, a rendezvous with the *Judith* relieved

---

[1] Hall had transferred from the *Thomas Allen* for the return passage.

the *Gabriel*'s similar predicament; but both vessels continued to carry far more men than their supplies could furnish (*Judith*'s complement on the outward passage had been forty mariners and miners; she returned to England carrying sixty-seven men).[1] To Frobisher, the disappearance of his flagship looked like abandonment, and it was one of his more justifiable rages that George Best, hailing the *Ayde* from the deck of the *Anne Frances* in mid-Atlantic on 21 September, reported to a nervous Christopher Hall.[2]

The voyage homewards was therefore a dispersed affair. Hall's *Ayde* had intermittent company; from 2 to 5 September, she kept formation with the *Thomas Allen* and *Moon of Foye*, but lost the latter on that day. On 11 September, when the *Ayde* lost her main yard in a squall, the *Thomas Allen* continued alone. Several days later, the *Ayde* met with the *Hopewell* (which had kept company with the *Beare Leicester*, *Salomon*, *Emanuel of Exeter* and *Frances of Foye* before losing sight of them during a storm) and then the *Anne Frances*, from which Hall transferred some of her excess complement into the *Ayde*; but lost them once more on 23 September. Meanwhile, the *Judith*, having kept the company of the *Gabriel*, *Michael* and *Anne Frances* until their separation on 8 September, had a lonely passage thereafter until 27 September, when she met with the *Anne Frances* and *Salomon* west of the Scillies. By the end of the month, the ships began to arrive, singly and in pairs, at Portsmouth, their designated assembly port.

Despite the severity of the Atlantic weather, only one ship failed to make that rendezvous. The *Emanuel of Bridgewater*, or *Busse*, had last been sighted off Sussex Island, perilously close to a lee-shore and, in the minds of all who witnessed her struggle, already lost. Her crew managed to kedge her away from the rocks, however, after which she sailed eastwards in a higher latitude than the other vessels (as during the return passage of 1577, they had made for warmer latitudes before setting a due east course). She was off 'Friesland' on 8 September; four days later, some fifty leagues southeast and by south from that mythical place, she encountered another mysterious land. Twenty-five leagues long, with two great harbours ('the land seeming to be fruiteful, full of woods, and a champion countrie', as Best later embellished), this strange, uncharted land – Busse Island, as it was named – was to employ successive generations of cartographers, none of whom were able to consult anyone who could claim to have seen it. The *Emanuel of Bridgewater* made the Galway coast on 25 September, at which the *relation* of her boatswain, Thomas Wiars, prudently ends.[3] Some days later, apparently attempting to beach her at Smerwick herbour, her crew ran her aground and wrecked her, though they survived. Her ore, seized and retained by the Earl of Desmond despite the remonstrations of the Privy Council,[4] was eventually used to repair the damage that the walls of Smerwick fort endured during the brief, savage siege of 1580. The complement of the *Emanuel of Bridgewater* had returned to England by the early months of 1579; on 10 March, her seven miners received their

---

[1] PRO EKR E164/36, p. 96; Document 8, p. 174. It should be recalled that the *Gabriel* – a bark of 25–30 tons burden – also carried some twenty tons of ore.

[2] Document 6, p. 129: '… the Capteyn of the An fraunces told me that my Generall was in great coller against me …'.

[3] Document 11, pp. 247–8.

[4] *APC*, xi: 26 February, 25 March 1579.

seven months' wages from the hands of Thomas Allen, Michael Lok's successor as treasurer. Her captain and owner, Richard Newton, and his mariners were not so lucky. Having failed to bring their allocation of ore to Dartford, no freight charges were paid by the beleaguered adventurers.[1]

---

[1] PRO EKR E164/36, p. 133; E164/35, p. 290: the auditors of Frobisher's 'boowk', in a list of entries headed 'These parcelles Foloweng bedies other*es* nott allowable in these Accounttes ...', disallowed advances of £3. 10. 0. he had made to three mariners of the *Emanuel of Bridgewater* on the basis that 'it is no frayghted ship in Irland'.

4. AFTERMATH OF THE VOYAGE

From Portsmouth, the ships passed on, singly or in pairs, to Dartford Creek, and between 22 and 28 November discharged their cargoes there, to be carried to their store at the Queen's House (formerly Dartford Priory, where most of the ore from the second voyage lay) and laid up precisely, according to each batch's mine of source and ship of lading. From there, quantities were carried on to the new refining site at Bignoures mill, about a mile distant on a tributary of the river Darent, to be assayed.[1] Jonas Schutz took possession of his expensive new furnaces, and the first 'proofe' of the ore was conducted there on 8 November. Despite the putative advantages of the new equipment, built at his urging and to his specification, Schutz could do no more than produce results that according to Michael Lok, were 'verye eville'. A subsequent assay, conducted a week later, 'had suche evill success as cowld not be worse'.[2] Three further large assays between that time and February 1579 promised slightly more, but failed to prove anything tangible; we may assume that it was only the presence of Frobisher himself, at an assay conducted on 10 January, that inclined Schutz to 'discover' gold and silver to a value of £10 per ton, though subsequently he was not able to produce the fruits of this success. The assay of 17 February, of half a ton of ore of the *Judith*'s lading (ore from Countess of Sussex mine) was the final attempt at Dartford to wrest some value from the ore. Its results apparently indicated that gold and silver remained in the slag, to a value of just £5. 2. 0. Schutz was to conduct only one further, reported assay – at Tower Hill, on 22 March 1579 (its results were reported two days later). This was ordered to be conducted in the presence of new commissioners (the old ones were considered compromised by their previous exposure to Schutz's methods), who had become suspicious of his 'evill worke' at Dartford. Once more, Schutz utilized his obfuscating skills, and convinced his supposedly sceptical audience that its results were optimistic, promising to yield a net £15 per ton of ore refined.[3]

Yet whatever they thought they had seen, there was no longer any possibility of resurrecting any palpable enthusiasm for the enterprise among its most important constituency – the adventurers of the 'Company of Cathay'. The bulk of them were not merely disillusioned by the end of 1578: they had ceased to regard themselves as an entity. Their pockets assaulted by a further, massive assessment of 85 per cent upon existing stock following the return of the voyage – to pay off the crews and to meet freight charges that were some fifty per cent higher than anticipated – they had progressively lost hope of recouping any part of what had been expended to date.[4] Most of

[1] PRO EKR E164/35, pp. 210–11: accounts for the payment of carters.
[2] Document 5, pp. 92, 97.
[3] PRO SP/12/129, 2; 12/130/15; document 5, pp. 98–9. The most modest assumptions made by Schutz of the ore he assayed indicated concentrations of gold and silver therein some two to three hundred times greater than the most promising modern analyses of samples of the same ore have yielded (*HBM*, p. 137).
[4] PRO SP/12/126, 20. Though he had ceased to be treasurer by this time, Michael Lok drew up his 'State

the mercantile investors, bound by the imperatives of their personal credit in the marketplace, paid their full dues and wrote off the experience. The Queen also honoured her commitments, but other than her secretary Thomas Wilson, every member of the Privy Council who had invested in the enterprise remained debtors, for which Michael Lok, ultimately, paid the price.[1] Utterly ruined by his own vast investment and outstanding loans, he had petitioned once more for wages and interest of some £1,200, though with no apparent success.[2] Frobisher and he had become gradually alienated; though this was ostensibly upon a point of money (Frobisher had received no wages for almost fifteen months, and blamed Lok), it was rather the inescapable consequence of the natural antipathy between their respective characters. With Frobisher leading accusations of mismanagement and even misappropriation against him, Lok had been removed as treasurer some time before 8 December 1578.[3] Subsequently, though cleared of the specific charges that had led to his dismissal, he was the victim of a number of lawsuits brought by creditors of the enterprise – including his fellow adventurer, William Borough, who was still owed £96 on the purchase price of the ship *Judith*.[4] At the commissioners' direction, Lok had entered into charter parties with the freight ship owners in his own name before the despatch of the 1578 voyage; now, relieved of the burden of their own culpability, they allowed the fact of his signature upon the documents to speak for itself.[5] Effectively bankrupted, Lok went to debtor's prison upon at least eight occasions in the subsequent three years. From one or more of these institutions, he penned the pedantically detailed and damning 'Doinges of Captayne Furbusher' – a small revenge for his persecution. This minor satisfaction apart, the repercussions of his involvement with Frobisher were to hound him for the remainder of his extremely long life.

Frobisher himself escaped any formal censure; nevertheless, any ambitions he may have had of becoming the English Columbus and/or Cortes were over.[6] For the next six years, his employments were few and modest, and his disappointments substantial. He was appointed to lead the 1582 Moluccas project sponsored by Leicester and Drake, but stepped down or, more likely, was removed upon rumours of improbity before that disastrous voyage commenced. The following year, he was one of three

---

of the Company' on the final day of December 1578 (PRO EKR E164/35, pp. 200–208). It showed unpaid subscriptions £2,618.6.8. due from the adventurers (the final auditors report, issued approximately eighteen months later, showed this figure to have been marginally optimistic: it had actually risen by some £29 in the intervening period). Even at this late stage, Lok continued to record the ore as an asset, at a nominal net value of £16 per ton, giving a paper worth of £20,800.

[1] PRO EKR E164/36, pp. 321, 323: auditors' report (undated but post-6 May 1581): outstanding subscriptions owed by members of the Council, their wives and the earl of Oxford totalled £1,340; Michael Lok, whose entire stock in the voyage came to £2,180, owed only £27.10.0. by this date.

[2] Neale and Baynham, the auditors appointed by the commissioners to examine the accounts of Lok and others, assessed Lok's claims and agreed – reluctantly – that a reimbursement of some £836 might be appropriate (PRO SP/12/126, 35). However, with no funds remaining, and many of the mariners and other creditors yet to be paid off, Lok had no more than a moral victory.

[3] Thomas Allen was acting treasurer by that date (PRO SP/12/127, 12; 8 December 1578: letter from Allen to Walsingham, requesting his assistance in securing the adventurers' outstanding dues).

[4] PRO EKR E164/36, 29.

[5] PRO SP/12/149, 42 (xi).

[6] Cf. document 5, p. 84: '… as alredy by discoverye of a new worlde, he was become another Columbus so allso nowe by conquest of a new world he woold become another Cortes …'.

captains named to undertake a voyage to North America to secure lands to be colonized under George Peckham's licence from Humphrey Gilbert, but the project collapsed with Gilbert's death and Peckham's imprisonment. These non-engagements apart, a number of very modest naval duties and a probable return to privateering were Frobisher's only sources of sustenance. It was not until 1585, with the growth of Anglo-Spanish enmity and the recognition of his true talents – as a fighter – that he was restored to favour, to be Drake's vice-admiral in the West Indies raid.[1] Thereafter, his career was distinguished, if coloured by his abiding inability to distinguish friendly vessels from legitimate prizes. He was never again to be involved – passively or actively – in any commercial arrangement that did not seek to take its profits directly from other men's pockets.[2]

---

[1] Anecdotal evidence suggests that Frobisher was part, or the bearer, of an embassy to the Danish Court in 1584 (Gad, *History of Greenland*, pp. 196–7), but the source – Frederik II's later letter to Elizabeth, in which he claimed to have 'approached' Frobisher – is ambiguous, and cannot be verified.

[2] For Frobisher's later career, see McDermott, *Frobisher*, pp. 257–423, *ad finem*.

5. LEGACY OF THE 1578 VOYAGE

In contemporary minds, the most immediate lessons of Frobisher's enterprise were negative, and with justice. Subscriptions from the adventurers, together with extraordinary assessments upon stock, had eventually reached some £20,345 (though almost £3,000 of this remained unpaid). The actual cost of the enterprise, including creditors' unsatisfied demands, was close to £25,000. On the debit side of the balance sheet, some 1,530 tons of an exotic black ore had been made available to effect repairs upon walls, roads and privies in Dartford and its environs. A major new refining facility – the largest of its kind in southern England – had been built just outside the town, though it was to be entirely abandoned within a year of its construction. The final assessment of the furnaces' technical attributes was that of Daniel Hochstetter and George Needham, following trials in 1580 to determine whether lead and copper ore might be smelted there. Ironically, Needham had been one of two men to whom Michael Lok had first passed samples of his ore in the final months of 1576. Then, he had determined it to be worthless – an assessment which Lok had chosen to ignore. Four years later, Needham's opinion of the mechanism that was to have prised the riches of the New World from the same ore was equally damning:

> ' … the furnace there was not so orderlye made nether the bellowes gave suche apte blaste as they oughte to have donne. We were forced as aforesayd to spende iii dayes and more, *whi*che if we had bene at Keswicke at the worste of *our* owne furnaces we woulde have smolten a greater quantetye of rostyd ure in the space of xvi howers … in the smelting of the sayde rosted yewres we founde suche wante in the buildinge of the furnace and the disorderlye placinge of the bellowes that we coulde not by anymeanes possible perfectlye smelte downe all the sayde yewres … we did finde the furnace … to be so far out of order that yt woulde not serve us …'[1]

Ore that could not be refined profitably, and furnaces that could not refine *any* ore successfully: for the sake of this pale bounty, the original aims of the 1576 adventurers – to find, navigate and exploit an 'English' route to the markets of the Far East – had been overthrown. Frobisher had not even gone so far as to definitively disprove the existence of the passage in the body of water he had incompletely explored: the purpose for which he had first approached the Privy Council in 1574. Can this then be counted as yet another of his failures? Insofar as George Best and others claimed the goal to have been his obsession of some fifteen years' standing, we must conclude that it was – a particularly abject one. However, in practical terms, it is difficult to regard it as a lost opportunity. All Frobisher might have done was to prove that the passage, if it existed, lay in another place. Yet there is no indication that any vestigial enthusiasm to achieve the goal would have brought about a further attempt to seek it

---

[1] PRO EKR E164/36, pp. 307, 309.

in another location before John Davis returned to the region in the mid-1580s, and no further exploration of Frobisher Bay was conducted in the sixteenth century. Even setting aside the tainting proximity of the goal to the commercial disaster of Frobisher's enterprise, it is clear that exploration *per se* enjoyed a very limited natural constituency in London, despite the emphasis that has since been placed upon the longevity of interest in the existence of a north-west passage and English ambitions for its exploitation. That reserve was entirely judicious. Almost all other, ostensibly comparable contemporary projects were to enjoy incremental advantages or incentives beyond those that had engaged the interest of the 1576 adventurers. The Russia trade – perhaps the closest exemplar for Frobisher and Lok – had not been a goal in itself, but had developed to compensate for a similar failure to discover a north-eastern route to Cathay. The Inuit of Baffin Island were hardly able to provide a similar resource to the north-west adventurers. Other ventures of the period – the Guinea, Barbary and, subsequently, the Levant trades – were either English graftings upon existing trade-routes (whose characteristics and potential returns were known or suspected already), or, in the latter case, a commercial arrangement concluded with a political entity already in contact, however tenuously, with those of the West. Superficially, Drake's 1577 project appears to have shared a similar degree of speculative risk, but the comparison is misleading. It is likely that at least some of its backers – perhaps the Queen herself – had prior knowledge of his intention to supplement legitimate returns with Spanish assets he might seize *en route*.[1] For sound commercial reasons, the search for the north-west passage (other than as a purely subordinate goal) was to be a very discreet and economically-funded phenomenon, with the exception, and in large part because, of Frobisher's own experiences.

The geographical legacy of these voyages was much more persistent, and pernicious. Charts prepared by Michael Lok and an unknown cartographer (plates III and V) were rudimentary, and soon forgotten (Halkuyt commissioned Lok's chart for the 1582 *Divers Voyages*, but had discarded it for the first edition of *Principall Navigations*). However, the existence and location of 'Friesland' had been confirmed to contemporary cartographers, and they, in turn, propogated the myth; though at least that particular land had a palpable form, even if its identity was misunderstood. Busse Island also became a feature upon contemporary charts, though having been seen by no one other than the over-imaginative crew of the *Emanuel of Bridgewater*, its location was more of a moving feast. Henry Hudson was the first known navigator to seek it out on the outward passage of his own, 1609, voyage to find the north-west passage; his inevitable failure did not discourage others. By 1673, this persistent little wraith had even acquired detailed topographical features, named after a later generation of notables: Albemarle's, Viner's and Craven Points, Cape Hayes and Arlington and Shaftesbury

---

[1] John Cooke's narrative of the voyage (ed. Temple, *The World Encompassed by Francis Drake*, p. 156) claims that Drake himself implied that his primary intentions were known to the Queen prior to his departure: 'her Maiestie gave me speciall co(m)maundement that of all men my Lord Tresorar shuld not knowe it.' K. R. Andrews (*Drake's Voyages: a reassessment etc.*, p. 57) suggests that the Queen suspected, if she was not explicitly told, of Drake's motives. Given the known anti-Spanish attitudes of Walsingham and Leicester in particular, it is unlikely that they would have been discouraged by the revelation of Drake's true intentions, or, by the same token, that Drake should have hesitated to enlighten them.

Harbours.[1] Seventy years later, however, its continuing non-appearance had brought about its metamorphosis into 'the submerged island of Busse': an ingenious, if somewhat circular, solution.[2] During Frobisher's lifetime, even wilder assumptions were made about his achievements. By 1592, continuing faith in the Zeno data (particularly with respect to 'Friesland'), married with the uncomfortable confirmation, by John Davis, that the southern extremity of Greenland – in a much lower latitude and further to the west than had previously been suspected – was just that, required a sleight of cartography to reconcile the data of the Frobisher voyages with a perceived reality. This was the 'Greenland Transfer': the wholesale relocation of geographical features identified during the 1576–8 voyages from Baffin Island to the coast of Greenland.[3] One of the most enduring falsehoods in the developing science of cartography, the transfer was to enjoy a currency well into the eighteenth century.

With such a catalogue of outright failure and absurd misconception to draw upon, history has not been kind to Frobisher the explorer. The only indisputably positive legacy of his 1578 voyage – of the north-west enterprise as a whole - was an ephemeral one, in providing a further body of empirical knowledge to add to the rapidly expanding corpus of English maritime expertise. In the process of doing so, it suffered possibly the lowest rate of mortality of any contemporary trans-oceanic project. Such a laudable achievement would not have been sufficient in itself to ease the pain of monies lost in the bursting of England's first investment 'bubble'; nevertheless, the episode was quickly forgotten amidst the accelerating pace of new ambitions that marked the slide towards outright conflict with Spain, not least because its failures were part of the natural process of pushing out into new regions. Michael Lok, who remained faithful to the goal, believed those failures to derive entirely from Frobisher's manifold faults. Thomas Fuller had the advantage of several decades' further perspective upon which to base his opinions, and used it perceptively: '… no wise man will laugh at his mistake, because in such experiments they shall never hit the mark who are not content to miss it.'[4]

---

[1] Babcock, *Legendary Islands of the Atlantic*, p. 176.

[2] Perhaps the best explanation for the non-appearance of Busse Island may be found in the often-seductive synthesis of vainglory and acumen. The kudos of first discovery is a powerful incentive to dishonesty, and having staked their claim, the crew of the *Emanuel of Bridgewater* had positioned themselves for further employment, should curiosity have financed an early attempt to explore the island.

[3] The first manifestation of this treatment appears to have been upon Emeric Molyneux's globe of that year, upon which Busse Island also made its first appearance.

[4] Fuller, *Worthies*, III, p. 419.

DOCUMENTS

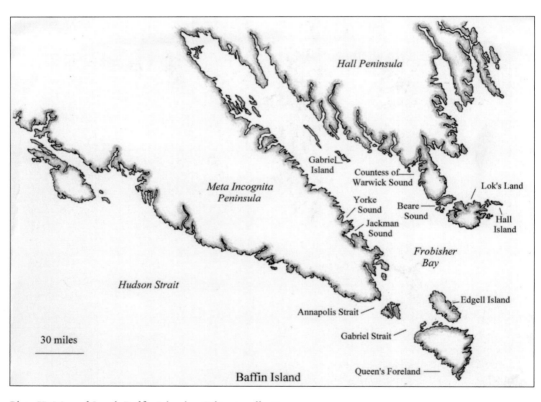

Plate II: Map of South Baffin Island.   *Editor's collection*

DOCUMENT 1

List of Adventurers, 1578[1]

Yere 1578 /

The Receytt of Money by me Michael Lok mercer /
Tresorer of the Companye for discovrye of
Cathai etc / by the Northwest partes.

Receaved of the venturars for their Stok & venture outwardes in the third voiage for the dyscovrye of Cathai, etc / by the Northewest partes – made Anno 1578 / by Conduct of Martin furbusher esquier / begon in the monthe of May 1578 /

Receaved of them, aswell for the furnyture of the ship Ayde, & other ships fraighted to retorne home this yere / as also for furnyture of the iii ships to saye the Judythe / the Michael, and the Gabriel, with C men, appoynted to remayne & dwell there in that Countrye this yere / under charge of Edward fenton their Captaine / I saye Received of them as followithe /[2]

Receavyd of the Queenes Maiestie	li	1350.
Receavid of the Lorde Highe Treasorer	li	135.
of the Lorde highe Admirall[3]	li	135.
of the Lorde Chamberlayne Earle of Sussex	li	135.
of the Earle of Warwicke	li	135.
of the Earle of Leycester	li	202. 10.
of the Lorde of Hundesdon	li	67. 10.
of Sir Frauncys knowles tresorer, etc	li	67. 10.
of Sir Frauncys walsingham secrytarye[4]	li	270.
of Master doctor Willson secrytarye	li	67. 10.
	£2555 –	

---

[1] Henry E. Huntington Library HM 715, ff. 1–3.

[2] The new subscription constituted a 135 per cent levy upon existing stock.

[3] Edward Fiennes, Baron Clinton and Saye, Earl of Lincoln. Lincoln had been a patron – and, possibly, a customer – of Frobisher from his privateering days (McDermott, *Frobisher*, pp. 71–2, 74).

[4] Walsingham's stock in the enterprise, double that of any other Privy Councillor, gave the lie to his apparent scepticism regarding the results of early assays upon the ore, which he had referred to previously as 'but devyses of alchamists' (PRO SP/12/112, 25).

of the Earle of pembrooke	li	202. 10.
of the Countesse of pembrooke	li	33. 15.
of the Countesse of warwicke	li	67. 10.
of the Countesse of Sussex	li	67. 10.
of Master philipe sydney[1]	li	67. 10.
of Sir henry Wallope knight	li	67. 10.
of Sir thomas greshame knight	li	270.
of Sir Leonel duckett knighte	li	67. 10.
of Sir John brockett knight	li	67. 10.
of Master william pelhame	li	67. 10.
of Master thomas Randoll	li	67. 10.
of Master Edwarde Dier	li	33. 15.
of John Somers	li	67. 10.
of Symon boyer	li	33. 15.
of John dee	li	33. 15.
of Anthonye Jenkinesone	li	67. 10.
of Martine Furbusher Captaine[2]	li	135.
of Edmund hogaine mercer	li	135.
of Richard younge Customer	li	67. 10.
of thomas allyn skynner	li	67. 10.
of Mathew Filde mercer	li	67. 10.
of Christofer hoddesdon mercer	li	67. 10.
Summ this syde	li	4455.

of William painter	li	67. 10.
of Jefferye turville	li	67. 10.
of William burrowe	li	67. 10.
of Thomas Owine gent.	li	33. 15.
of Richard Bowlande	li	67. 10.
of william Bonde haberdasher	li	135.
of Robert Kindersley	li	67. 10.
of Anne Frauncys wydowe[3]	li	101. 5.
of Mathewe kindersleye[4]	li	33. 15.
of william harington	li	33. 15.
of william dowgle	li	33. 15.
of Anthony marler mercer	li	33. 15.
of william Ormeshaw	li	33. 15.

[1] Sydney's interest in the enterprise (he was one of the original 1576 adventurers) may be traced to his extended stay at Kenilworth, the house of his uncle, the earl of Leicester, during the summer of 1575, when subscriptions for a north-west voyage were first discussed (Boas, *Sir Philip Sydney*, p. 28).

[2] Frobisher was not a willing adventurer. His 'stock' consisted of unpaid wages that had metamorphosized for want of monies to meet them (PRO EKR E164/35, p. 288: his answer to the auditors regarding his wages: 'I was fane to lett it rone for my aventure which doth remane ther ...').

[3] Not the owner, nor connected with, the vessel of the same name which sailed in the voyage.

[4] Kindersley, one of the original adventurers of 1576, commanded the ship *Michael* in the coming voyage.

of zacharie Lok	li	33. 15.
of Eleazer Lok	li	33. 15.
of Gerson Lok	li	33. 15.
of Benjamin Lok	li	33. 15.
of Mathewe Lok	li	33. 15.
of henry Lok	li	33. 15.
of Michael Lok Junior	li	33. 15.
of Julio Cesar Adelmare[1]	li	33. 15.
of Thomas Cesar Adelmare	li	33. 15.
of Charles Cesar Adelmare	li	33. 15.
of henrye Cesar Adelmare	li	33. 15.
of william Cesar Adelmare	li	33. 15.
of Elizabethe Cesar Adelmare	li	33. 15.
of Dame Elizabeth Martine[2]	li	33. 15.
of Michael Lok mercer and the remayner of the second voyage being li 1750	li	2232. 10.
	li	3915.
	li	4455.
Sum*m* of all the Stok of the venturars	li.	8370.

[1] The Adelmares were Lok's step-children by his second marriage, to Margery Adelmare. Julius Caesar Adelmare (more commonly known thereafter as Julius Caesar), was subsequently knighted and appointed Judge of the Admiralty upon the death of his predecessor, Thomas Lewes, on 27 April 1584.

[2] Probably the widow of Robert Martin, an adventurer in 1576 and 1577, who, jointly with Christopher Andrews, had been the former owner of the ship *Michael*.

DOCUMENT 2

Instructions for the 1578 voyage[1]

Indorsed .1578. Commyssion instructions to Master Furbusher to goo to sea, Anno 1578.

Instructiones geven to our lovinge frind Martine Frobisher esquier, for the order to be observed in the voyage nowe recommendid to him for the Lande now called by hir majestie *Meta incognita* to the Northwest partes & cathaye.

Fyrst, you shall enter as capten Generall into the Charge and government of theis shippes and vessells, viz., the Ayde, the Gabriell, Michaell, Judethe, the Thomas Alline, Anne Fraunces, the hoppewell, the mone, the Fraunces of Foy, the thomas, & the[2]

Item, you shall appoynte for the furnishinge of the Ayde, gabriell, Michaell and Judith, Fourskore and ten hable and sufficient Marinores and .130. Pyoners and .50. soldiares, for the sarvyce and ladinge of all suche shippes and vessells as shall go under your charge and be appoynted to retorne againe with you for that purpose, and of the sayd shippes or vessells and maryners, pyoners and soldiors you shall leave to remayne and to inhabite in the lande nowe called *Meta incognita*, under the charg and government of Edward Fenton gent your Lieutenaunte generall, the Gabriell, the Michaell, and the Judethe, with fortie hable marioners, gonners, shipwrightes and carpentares, 30. soldiors and .30. Pyoners, with sufficient vittalle for xviii monthes for their provisione, releife and mayntenance, and also munition and armoure for their defence, which number of persones befor specified, you shall not exced to carrie nor leve their.

Item, that the vittalles for vii months which you deliver into the ayde for provisone of .90. persones goinge and to retorne in the said shippe you shall carefulye see the same preserved and used in sarvyce without spoyle or hurte takinge by necligence, And the like care you and your Lieutenaunte Generall shall have of the victualls that shalbe by you delivered into any shippes or vessells whatsoever, for the provision of the .100. men appoynted to inhabite their.

Item, you shall make a juste inventorie of every shippe to the companie belonginge of all the takell, munitione, and furnitur to them belonginge at their settinge fourth from hens and the coppie therof under your hand to be delivered to the tresorer. And the like to be done at your retourne home, of all thinges then remaynyng in the said ships.

---

[1] PRO CO1/93 (copy in PRO SP/15/25, 81). This is a rough draft of the instructions; no more definitive version is known to survive. It was set down by Michael Lok, with further insertions and corrections by Lord Burghley. Collinson's original transcription of this document was somewhat flawed, and was later reproduced verbatim by Stefansson & McCaskill. A new transcription is presented here.

[2] *Sic.* Supply *Beare Leicester.*

Item, you shall not receve under your charge & government any disordred or mutinous persone which shall be appointed to goo or remayne theire, but upon knowledge had to remove him before you departe hence, or ells by the way as sone as you can avoyd hym.

Item, you shall use all dilligence possible to departe with your said ships and vesselles frome the portes where they now remayne, before the firste of may next cominge, and to make your course eather by the Northe or the west as the winde will best serve you.

Item, when you shall passe the landes of England Scotlande or Irlande you shall direct your course with all your shippes and vessells to the lande now called *Meta incognita*, and to an Iland and sounde there called the countess of warwickes Iland and sounde, being within the supposed straight which we name Frobisers straight discovered by your selfe 2 yeres past, and in your voyage thither wardes you shall have speciall regarde so to order your course as your shippes and vesselles do not losse the Companye one of an other, but may kepe Company together. And the lyke also at your retorne homewardes. And yf any wilfulnes or negligence in this behalfe shall appeare in any persone or persons that shall have charge of any of the shippes aforesaide, or yf they or any other shall doo otherwyse then to them apperteyneth, you shall punishe suche offendor sharplye to the example of otheres.

Item, that at your arryvall at the countesse of warwikes Iland and sounde you shall their in saffitee harbour your shipps & vesselles, and frome thence you shall repayre to the Mynes and Myneralles of the same Iland wher you wrought this laste yeare with myners & other men & furnyture necessarie, and their shall place the myners and other men to worke and gather the oare, foreseinge they may be placed aswell from Dainger and malyce of the people, as frome anye other extremitye that maye happen.

Item, whyle these mynars are workyng in warwyke sound, you shall cause serche to be made for other mynes in other places, and yf uppon good proofe made, you shall happen to fynde other mynes to be richer then theis frome whence you had your laste yeares ladinge, then you shall presentlie remove the shippes & mynars to the same place of mynerall, and to lade of the same yf that may be done convenientlye.

Item, to searche and consider of an apte place wher you maie best plante and fortefye theise .C. men which you shall leave to inhabite theire, aswell against the dainger and force of the natyve people (of the countrey, and any other that shall seke to arryve ther from any other part of Christendom),[1] as also to prevent and fore see as neare (as you cane) all other extremities & perills that maye happen, and necessarie to be considered of for them.

Item, you shall leave with Captan Fenton your Lieutenaunte generall the government of those .100. persones to remayne in that countrie with instructions howe he maye best observe the nature of the ayre, and as moche as may be discover and knowe the state of the countrie, and what tyme of the yeare the Straight is most free frome eysse (kepyng to thend from tyme to tyme a journall wekly of all accountes),[2] with whome you shalle leve the vessels named the Gabriell, the Michaell and the Judith with suche proportion of victualles and other necessarie thinges as are alredye appoynted to him and his companye for that purpose suppliing his want with able and skyllfull men for that purpose, & with any other thinges necessarie, which you or any other of the shippes maye convenientlie spare at your reatorne.

[1] Editor's parenthesis: insertion in Burghley's hand.
[2] Editor's parenthesis: insertion in Burghley's hand.

Item, we require that you shall instructe all your people rather to muche then any thinge to littell, aswell for your owne saffetye there, as of suche as you shall leave behinde you, that when you or they shall happen to come to have conferrence with the people of those partes wher you shall arive, that in all your doynges & theirs you so behave yourselves towardes the said people, as maye rather procure their frindships and good lykinges towardes you (by courtesyes)[1] then move them to any offence or myslikinge.

Item, uppon your arrivall at the place before specified, and after you have bothe harbored safflie your ships, sett your mynars one worke, and also have taken sufficient order for plantinge of those men which shall inhabite their, and appoyntinge in your absence governers for all theis causes: We will then yf Leasure and tyme wille permitt the same that you with the ii barkes shall repaire towardes the place where the first yeare you loste your men, aswell to searche for mynes theire, as to discover .50. or .100. leages (further) westwardes frome that place (as the oppening of the streight by water will lowe), as you may be certayne that you are entride into the Southe Sea (commonly called Mare di Sur), and in your passage to learne all that you cane in all thinges, & take parfect notes therof, not tarringe longe frome your shippes and workemen, but that you maye be hable to retorne homewardes with them in due tyme.[2]

Item, you shall well consider what place may be most aptest further to fortifye upon hereafter (yf nede requier) bothe for defence of the mynes and also for possessinge of the countrie, and bring home with you a parfecte platt and parfecte notes therof, to be kept in secreat, and so delyvred unto us.

Item, you shall not suffer any shippe or shippes beinge laden with oare to sett sayle or departe frome the place of their ladinge till the daye fixed in their charter partye except you see good cause otherwyse. And beinge so laden & redy to retorne homeward you shall reatayne them in flete & in companie all togethers as muche as in you liethe, & as the wether wyll suffer, untill your retorne into this realme of England and arrivall at the place appoynted in the River of thammes for unladinge of the same.

Item, for the succession of the Generall governour of this whole voiage (yf he should fortune to die) for avoydinge of stryffe & kepinge of peace & fryndship, there be the names of iiii gentlemen privatlie sett downe to succeade him in his place (one after the other, which ar severally wrytten in paper included in balls of wax, sealed with hyr Majesties sygnett and put into boxes, locked with severall keys, wherof on in your custody).[3]

Item, for the better and more circumspecte execution and determinacon in any waightie causes incident on land, we will that you shall call unto you, for assistantes your Lieutenant generall, Captayne Yorke, Richard Philpott, george Beast and henry Carewe gent., with whome you shall consult and confere what is beste to be done in the said causes, matteres and accions of ymportaunce towchinge this service under taken: And in all suche matteres so handeled, argued & debated upon, the same to rest to be allowed or disallowed at your owne ellectione, and that alwaies to be executed which you shall thincke meeteste with assent of any ii of them in general consent. And like wyse in matteres of weight concerninge

---

[1] Editor's parenthesis: insertion in Burghley's hand.
[2] All parentheses in the preceding paragraph denote insertions in Burghley's hand.
[3] Editor's parenthesis: insertion in Burghley's hand. A margin note here, also by Burghley: '3 keys: Frobisher. Fenton. A master of a ship'.

all your shippes good government aswell at the sea as in harboure, our wille is that the fore-named gentlemen and Christofor Hawle, Charles Jackeman, James Beare, and Andrew Dier, masters in certayne of your shippes, presentlie ymployed in this north-west service shalbe assistaunte unto you and consentinge to all Determynacones concernynge the same. And in casse that of suche conference and discoursinge the opiniones of the aforesaid assistaunce be founde in effecte any waye to differ, then our will is, that thexecution of all suche mat-teres so argued upon shall rest to be put in execution in suche sorte as you shall thinke most metest, having the assent of any ii of them.[1]

Item, because the temprature of those Northewest partes and boundes of seas and landes are not yet sufficientlie knowne (which thinges we principallye desyere), and for as much as verye good opertunitie in sundrie respectes maye falle out in tyme of your absence to purc-haze or attayne to the same, we thinke yt verye necessarie and to your better desert worthe-lie apperteninge, that you shall enforme advise and aucthoryse by your owne hande writtinge in the beste manner you cane devise, howe any further discoverye understandinge or knowlege of the foresaid landes or seas (confynynge borderinge or lyinge within .200. leages of the place wher at this voyage the habitacone or fortification of our people shalbe setled or Cituated) maye be executed and acheved by your aforesaid Lieutenaunte generall, or by suche other parson as he or the most parte of suche as hereafter shalbe named to be his assystance shall deme and judge most apte and sufficient for the accomplishinge of the sar-vice their unto apperteyninge.

Item, that you shall have speciall care and geve generall warninge that no persone of what cawlinge soever he be, shall make an assaye, of any manner of mettalle matter or oare on the foresaid partes of *Meta incognita*, but onlie he or they to whome the offyce or seate of assayes makinge is asigned or comitted (onlie your selfe your Leutenaunte generall and your substitutes before named from this article to be excepted). Nor any persone under your governement shall take uppe or keape to him selfe and his private use anye parte or parcell of oare, presious stone or other matter of comoditie to be hade or founde in that lande but he the said person so seazed of such oare, stone or other matter of comoditie shall withall speade or so sone as he cane, detecte the same and make deliverey therof to your selfe or your Lieutenaunte generall, upon payne to forfite for every ounce therof the valewe trible of any wages he is to receave after the daye of suche offence committed, and further to receave suche punishement as to hir Majestie shall seme good.

Item, our will is that you shall cause a recorde dilligentlye to be kept in wryttyng of all suche oare, myneralls, stones and other matters of vallew gotten or founde in that countrie, aswell of the time and places when or whear all and everye suche oare Minerall and other matter of suche vallewe is or shalbe founde or gotten, as also some parte, porcion or exam-ple of all and everye the said oares Mynneralles and other matter of vallewe, in apte and pecu-liar boxes cause to be reserved with theire due titles and notificacones. And further cause dulye to be layed uppe in the said boxes the severall rates & tryed valuacions of all assayes their made of any the foresaid oares and mynneralles, and allso those foresaid boxes so fur-nished and distinctlie noted, at your reatorne to the citie of London you shall deliver or cause to be delivered to the Tresorer of the companye of adventurers for those Northewest affayres, aswell for the better directione and dealinge heareafter with any the foresaid oares

---

[1] Margin note (Burghley): 'having the assent of any ii'.

or myneralles ther, as for the better and speedie account and reckoninge makinge in grosse heare at home of the valewe of suche quantitie or masse as any of them shall hether be brought. And of these doinges make two bookes, to be kept in ii severall shyps.[1]

Item, that the Marioners of all the hired shippes imployed in this service, shall geve jointlye withall the other companies of our owne ships iii or iiii dayes travall and labor towardes thintrenchinge and fortifiinge of the place wher the Leutenaunte generall with his charge shall remayne to inhabite there.

Item, that you shall make your directe course from hence as neare as you cane, with all suche shippes as passe under your government to the land now called *Meta incognita*, and their lade .800. toones or so muche more as the shippes of retorne cane safflie carrie of suche oare as you alredie have founde their this last yeare, or rather richer yf you cane fynd the same. And so havinge laden your shippes with the said number of .800. tonnes or more as is aforesaid, shall make your direct course frome thence into this realme of England into the River of Thames, where the shippes be appoynted to be unladen of the same.[2]

Item, that everye Capten and Master of every shippe appoynted in this voyage shall joyntlie under their handes writing by Indenture deliver unto you a note and estimacone of suche nomber of toones of oare or other matter of vallew as they shall receve into their shippes theire. And all the same indentures, to be registred in one booke, wherof iii copies to be made, and to be put in iii severall shypes to be delyvred to the Tresorer of the companie at retorne home of the shypps.[3]

(That a minister or twoo do go in this Jorney, to use ministration of devyne service & sacramentes, accordyng to the order of England. nota, that the victalls, munitions and other thynges to be carryed to be equally distributed into the shippes, for dout of miscarrying of some of theme).[4]

Item, in your waye outward bound, yf it wylbe no hynderans to the rest of your voyage, you shall doo your endevour to dyskover the new land, supposed to be Fryzeland, and to gett the best knowledge that you can of the state & nature therof. And yf you cannot conveniently doo it in your waye outward bound, then doo your attempt hence in your waye homeward bound at retorne, yf the same may be done convenientlye.

Item, that yf there should happen any person or persons ymployed in this service of what calling or condicion he or they shall be, should conspire or attempte privatlie or publiklie any treason, mutinie or other disorder, either towchinge the takinge awaie of your owne life or any other of aucthoritie under you, whereby her Majesties service in this voyage might therby be overthrowen and ympugned, we will therfore that upon juste prooffe made of any such treasons, mutanie or other disorders attempted as aforesaid, the same shalbe punished by you or your lieutenaunt generall, etc.

Item, for the succession of the lieutenaunt generall of those c. men which shall remayne & inhabite there, there be named iij parsons, to succede, in order and maner as is sette downe before in the Article for the succession of the generall (which are severally wrytten

---

[1] Margin note (Burghley): 'A Dooble of this book to be made, and brought home in an other shipp'.
[2] Margin note (Burghley): 'A book conteyninge the quantitie laden in every shipp'.
[3] Margin note (Burghley): 'The book to be indented'.
[4] Entire clause inserted in Burghley's hand.

in paper included in bawles of wax, sealed *with* her M*aj*esties signet, and put into two severall boxes, locked *with* iii severall keys, wherof one key in yo*u*r custodie, and one in custodie
of Edward Fenton, and another in custodie of Christofer Hawlle. And the same two boxes
to be put in ii severall shyps, to saye, one boxe in the *Ayde*, and the other in the ship where
yo*u*r lieutenaunt generall shall passe).[1]

Item, that there be made a doble of this Comm*y*ssion, to remayne *with* the Lieutena*u*nt
generall.

---

[1] Words in parenthesis inserted before the first part of this paragraph.

DOCUMENT 3

Prayer for voyagers[1]

O my good god I doe acknowledge & confesse & my conscience doth certifie me *tha*t thou art my mercifull fat*h*er my portion, my comforte, & lyffe for evermore, thou of thy greate goodnes hast fashioned me even of *th*e duste to be a livinge creature according to thyne Image, where if it had pleased the thou mightest have made me one of *th*e monsters of *th*e worlde & of uglie shape but yet thy fatherlie p*r*ovydence in greate mercie towardes me hath breathed into me the spiritt of lyffe & not onlie that, but of thy tender love haste given unto me *th*e knowledge of *th*e misterie of my salvation in *th*e p*r*etious redemption of christe, yea & hast sealed it in my conscience by the holy spiritt, wherby I feele my selfe assuredly begotten to a new lyffe & everlastinglie rooted in a new election whence nothinge shalbe able to remove me, o deare father & heavenly god thou hast done all these thinges for my soule, & more then I am able for my dulnes to repeate unto the, looke downe therfore I beseech the o lorde upon *th*e worcke of thyne owne hand*es*, wh*i*ch havinge often on *th*e lande besoughte thy ayde & founde releife doe now with tricklinge teares from a bleedinge harte beseech the on these horrible seas & fearfull waves to visitt me in *th*e greatnes of thy fatherly kyndnes and doble encrease *th*e comforte of thy spiritt in me, fortifie my fayth *tha*t I waver not & replenish me with thy graces more & more, *tha*t neyther *th*e frailtie of my fleshe dryve me into doubte of thy lovinge kyndnes & fatherly p*r*ovydence towardes me in this most perillous place & daungerous tyme, nor any rashnes of my frailtie for wante of discretion thruste me upon *th*e enterpryse of any such course as is not foreseene in thy heav- enlie counsell to be most for thy glorie, and thou o most deare father who hast alone *th*e end*es* of all thing*es* in thy hand*es*, watche over thy servante with thy holie power in this watry pilgrimage, to blesse my goinge forth & cominge in, soe *tha*t if it be thy good will & pleasure I may returne to *th*e comforte of my native cuntry & christian brethren, & pur- chasinge of *th*e great libertie to serve the (in *th*e congregacion of thy electe)[2] & *th*e stoppinge

---

[1] Magdelene College Library, Pepys MS 2133, p. 8. The prayer is bundled with the manuscripts presented as documents 4 and 8, though written in a different hand. Given this proximity, its author is tentatively identified as Reverend Robert Wolfall, who accompanied the expedition. The strongly Protestant – even Calvinist – tenor of the piece indicates that it may indeed be the work of Charles Jackman's 'good and godly' preacher, and certainly, the script indicates that it was broadly contemporaneous with the enterprise; however, it is equally likely that the prayer was placed with the other material which now constitutes Pepys MS 2133 long after the voyage – perhaps even by Pepys himself, whose orderly archivist's mind may have determined this to be a suitable 'home' for the piece (the pagination mark is ambiguous in this respect). To the editor's knowledge, the first transcription of the prayer is that by Dr William Sherman, whose encour- agement to the editor to reproduce it in the present volume is appreciated.

[2] Words in parenthesis crowded into the text.

of *the* mouthes of thy adversaries, or otherwyse o dear father if thou hast this same determined to gather me unto thy people soe *p*repare I beseech the me therunto, as *tha*t both my
lyffe & death may be to thy glorie & *th*e salvation of my soule in christe Jhesu, also my good
god for my brethren even those fewe soules here with me over whom thou hast appointed
me a governor, may it please the sweete lorde to *p*ermitt me *tha*t am but earth & ashes to
speake unto the to sende amongst them *th*e heavenly blessinge of thy spiritt, to possesse
them with an holie unitie, in *th*e feare & love of thy ma*j*estie *tha*t we all becom*m*inge a con-
secrate nomber in pure affection may seeke *th*e glory of thy name & *th*e atchievemente of
those thing*e*s *tha*t may best make for it whersoever we shall become watche over us o god &
keepe us from all unrighteous behaviour, sinfull intentions & injurious dayling*e*s one
towardes another & finally o deare father graunte *tha*t in thy feare we may possesse heavenly
wysdome, courage & prosperous success freeinge us from all *ou*r enemies & unles thou
haste otherwyse determined, graunte us to returne, to thy hono*u*r & glory creditt of thy
church & *ou*r everlastinge comforte through Jhesus christe *ou*r lorde. Amen.

DOCUMENT 4

Edward Fenton's provisional list for the 1578 Colony[1]

[9] A Portion of victualls, munition and other thinges sett downe
for 100 men for xviii monthes appointed to inhabitt in the Lande
now called Meta incognita, under the charge of Edwarde fenton, gent.
Lieutenant generall unto Martin Furbusher Esquier Captain generall
to her Majestie for the discoverie of Cathaia by the northwest partes/
Anno mdlxxvii. 1577. viz.

In Biskett for vi monthes, 1600 at xi.ˢ vi.ᵈ le 100 –
Meale for xii monthes at one quarter for a man
  by the yere, cometh to 150 quarters at ( ) le quarter –
In Smale Beare 43 toones at ( ) le toone –
Beefe for iii quarter of a yere 15600 pownde weighte
  at i.d demi le pownde –
Porke for iii monthes 1200 powndes weight at i.d demi le pownde –
Bacen for vi monthes at half a pownde le daie for a man
  amounteth to 5200 powndes weight cometh at ii.d le pownde –
Habardine[2] for vi monthes cometh to 1300 at ( ) le 100 amounteth to –
Stockfishe[3] for one yere 5200 fishes at ( ) le 100 amounteth to –
Butter for xviii monthes at iii powndes le man for a month
  amounteth to 100 firkins at xiii.sh iii.d le firkin –   lxvi.li xiii.sh x.d.
Chese for xviii monthes at one pownde for a man for iii daies
  cometh in xviii monthes to 68 powndes[4] weight is ( ) le pownde –
Peaz for xviii monthes at iiii busshells for every man at ( )

---

[1] Magdelene College, Pepys Library MS 2133, pp. 9–12. Drawn up at some time in the first few months of 1578 (but before 25 March), which assists in broadly dating Fenton's appointment as commander of the intended colony. All blanks in parenthesis, indicating missing rates, are Fenton's own; which suggests that he was writing prior to the commencement of purchases for the expedition.

[2] Air-dried (as opposed to salted) codfish.

[3] Salted haddock, hake or cod.

[4] The cheese was predominantly of the harder Suffolk variety, which kept well at sea; but quantities of Cheshire, Essex and Dutch varieties were purchased for the voyage also. Fenton's calculation here is ambiguous. If he meant one third of a pound of cheese per man every day for eighteen months, his total should have been 182 pounds per man; if he meant one pound per man per day for three non-meat days per week, it should have been 234 pounds per man; if – as seems most likely – he referred to an allowance of one third of a pound per man for three days in each week, the total should have been 78 pounds.

le busshell amounteth to 50 quarters –

Summ page

[10]

Otmeale for xviii monthes xii quarters at ( ) le quarter
    amounteth to –
Salte iii toones –
Vinegar i toone –
Sweet Oyle ii hogesheades –
Sack iiii toones –
Aquavita ii hoggesheades –
Muster seede I quarter pd. –
Rize 1000 weight –
Trayne oyle I toone –
Candells 500 weight –
Honie I hoggesheade –
For spicerie and potticarie ware[1] –
The furnishing of ii surgions chestes –
Iron lampes xii –
Waxe 100 weight –
Brimstone 200 weight –
Rosin[2] 500 weight –
Tallow 200 weight –
Okeham[3] 50 stone –
Tarre iiii Barrells –
pitche iiii Barrells –
Corne powder one laste –
matche 1000 weight –
Tanned hides vi –
Bonge barrells vi –
Staves for ladells xii –
heades and Rammers xxiiii –
Leather bagges vi –
Calivers 60 –
Bowes 60 –
Arrowes 180 sheffes –
Bowstringes 60 dussen –
Black billes 50 –

---

[1] For a detailed analysis of the drugs and herbal preparations taken on the 1576 voyage (and which, presumably, were identical to those intended for the coming voyage) see Watt, 'The Frobisher Voyages', pp. 610–12.

[2] Resin.

[3] Oakum: the coarse part of the flax or unpicked old rope; used for caulking ships' seams.

Pikes long 50 –
Targettes 50 –
Jackes 80 –
Leade 1000 weight –
Crosbowes vi –
Baskettes 400 –

Summ page

[11]

Shovells 10 dussen –
Spades 3 dussen –
Whele barowes 20 –
hand barowes 20 –
Crowes of Iron 30 –
Mattockes[1] 100 –
Pickaxes 30 –
helves for pickaxes 300 –
Sledges of 24 weight 12 –
Smaller sledges of 8 weight 12 –
wedges 100 –
Wooden trayes 12 –
Wooden platters 12 dussen –
Wooden Cannes 12 dussen –
Leather Jackes of a gallon le peic iii dussen –
Trenchers xii dussen –
Lantarnes xii –
Gride Irons vi –
Frying pannes vi –
Kettells of vi gallon le piece iiii – and one of xii gallons –
pottes of iron of vi gallons le peice –
A great Caldron of Copper of xii gallons –
Axes xii –
hatchettes xii –
Billettes[2] 20,000 –
Seacooles 80 Chalders –
Iron Stoves 4 –

---

[1] A tool for loosening and breaking up hard ground: a wooden pole surmounted by a socketed, iron head with an adze-shaped blade. The number of these and other implements provided for do not indicate that they were meant only for the use of the eleven men identified as colonist-miners in the account books (cf. p. 12, n. 3).

[2] Probably billets of firewood.

Soope 400 weight[1] -
Skalles and weightes ii paire –
Larem Belles ii of 20 weighte le pece –
Clockes with whych to show and strike
   with a good bell ii –
Brike 2000 –
Tile 2000 –

                                    Summ page

[12]

Unslect Lyme 2000[2] -
Bibles 3 –
Bookes of comon prayer iii –
psalm bookes 24 –
Catechismes 24 –
paper writing i reame –
partchement i Roole -

A howse of timber heavie framed for our Lodging & storhowses conteyning 132 foote in Lengthe and 42 foote in breadthe with ii ( )[3] at either ende therof conteyning in Lengthe ( ) foote and in bredthe ( ) foote with iii other bulwarkes of defence thereat adjoyninge, amounteth to the some of –

---

[1] At less than four and a half pounds per man for eighteen months (both for personal use and laundry), this hardly seems an adequate allowance. Contrasting with the excellent provision of works of devotion, it seems that cleanliness was not considered remotely adjacent to godliness.

[2] I.e., unslaked. Presumably, Fenton meant 2,000 weight here.

[3] Supply 'blockhouses'. Despite its omissions, this is the most detailed description of the nature and dimensions of the intended 'great house'.

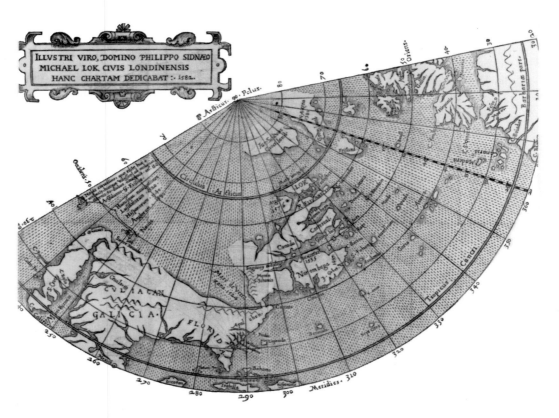

Plate III: Chart of the North Atlantic, by Michael Lok. Commissioned by Richard Hakluyt for his 1582 *Divers Voyages*, this extremely rudimentary recollection of Frobisher's discoveries emphasises the elusive understanding of the region in the minds of contemporary Englishmen. Lok's incorporation of data regarding the Pacific coastline of America from Drake's circumnavigation is similarly flawed.

By permission of the James Ford Bell Library, University of Minnesota.

DOCUMENT 5

Michael Lok's testimony[1]

1576. 1577. 1578.

The doynges of Captayne Furbusher;
Amongest the Companyes busynes /

[f.1r] The doinges of Captaine Furbisher / amongest the Companyes busynes /

Captaine Furbisher was sett owt his first voyadge made departinge from London the 20 May 1576 with twoo smale Shipps, and a pynnas at the Charge of divers honnorable, and worshipp*fu*ll persons, moved of good zeale towards their naturall Countrye, to discover a passadge by Sea to Cathaye. In w*h*ich voyadge he wente towards the Northewest p*a*rts, soo farre as he coold, w*i*th that smale Shippinge and furniture that he had, untill he arryved one the Northe coste of the land of Labrador, amongest betwene the mayne landes of America and Asia, to passe to Cathay. In w*h*ich place, either by great disorder and evill government of him selfe, or ells by greate disobedience of his men, he loste his Boate and v. of his men, w*h*ich the people of that Countrye toke from him / And afterwards by great pollycye, and greater good happe, he toke one man of that strange Countrye, w*h*ich he brought awaye / and so retorned home againe the 2. October 1576 to harwiche, and the 9. daye to London /[2]

And nowe he beinge thus retorned home againe of that first voyadge he was examyned of

[1] BL Lansdowne MS 100/1. Drawn up by Lok as part of his defence against the charges that had brought about his dismissal as treasurer of the enterprise and subsequent prosecution at the suit of several creditors thereof. It is difficult to precisely date the document. It refers to events which occurred as late as May 1579, and may have been composed soon after. A copy, held in the Public Record Office (SP/12/131, 20) is marked '1581', but this may refer only to the date at which the copy was made. The tenor of the piece – particularly its detail – suggests that the events he described were fresh in his memory, rather than the recollections of some years previously. Also, if this were indeed Lok's defence against charges of impropriety, there appears to be little reason why he would have written the piece at the later date, when his numerous imprisonments had ended and his reputation was rising once more (cf. the Privy Council's order to auditors Baynham and Neale, dated 6 May 1581 (PRO EKR E164/36, post p. 341), urging them to complete their examination of Lok's accounts, 'to thende this poore man may therby be furthered'). The folio references given are Lok's original markings, rather than the italic marks added at a later date, which have the document commencing at folio 2r.
[2] Margin note: 'In his first voyag he tooke a strange man and retorned home'.

his doinges therein; by Sir William Winter, Master Thomas Randolphe, Anthonye Jenkenson, Mychael Lok and others, thereunto appointed by Commyssion of her Majesties honorable pryvye Councell concerninge the passage to Cathay, at which tyme he vowched to them absolutlye with vehement wordes, speches and Oathes; that he had founde and discoverid the Straights, and open passadge by Sea into the South Sea called Mare de Sur which goethe to Cathay / and by the waye had founde divers good ports and harbors for passadge of all the navye of her Majesties Shipps, and affirmed the same by divers arguments of the depthe and culler of the water, the sight of the heade landes one boathe the sides of the Straightes at the west end thereof openinge into the broade Sea, called Mar de Sur, and the settinge of the tydes with a fludd frome the west owt of the sayde sowthe Sea / and by divers other arguments by demonstracion in the Cartes and Mappes, which things the Commissioners beleved to be trewe uppon his vehement speches, and oathes of affirmacion / All the which matter by him affirmed, is fownd to be false by his twoo latter voyags, made thether synce that tyme, wherein these affirmyd mayne landes, of America and Asia, are fownde to be but smale Ilands, and the tydes settinge from west, is like to be nothinge but the settinge of the streame from one hedlande to an other of those Ilands, which are there in nomber infynit[1] / And nowe the passage of Cathay is by him left unto us as uncertaine as at the beginning, thoughe thereuppon hathe followed great chargs too the Companye /

In that first voyadge one a little Ilande of Rocke of halfe a mile circuit which they namyd Hawlls Iland, after the name of Christofer Hawlle, Master of the Shippe, who was the first mane that landed thereon, Captaine Furbusher not beinge one land at all, but remayninge still in the Shippes at Sea x. milles from it. One this Rocke was fownde by chaunce by a maryner namyd Robert Garrard, who was one of the v. men which afterwards weare taken with their boate, by the people of that Countrye, a blacke stoune, as great as a halfe pennye loafe, beinge one the grownd losse, which he thought to be a Seacoole which he brought a boorde the Shippe to prove yf it woold burne for fyre, whereof they had lacke /[2] This stone beinge thus brought home, Captaine Furbysher gave a pece thereof to Mychael Lok, sayenge that it was the fyrst thinge that he fownd in the newe land, and therefore gave it unto him according too his promyse. And Mychael Lok caused to be made divers proffes and tryalls of that stone, by divers men of arte, and namely by John Baptista agnello, and by Jonas Shutz, whereby it was fownde

[f.1v] to be a peace of a mynerall Ewre of a gold mynde, whereof hee gave knowledge to her Majestie, accordinge too his dewtye, whereuppon mutch merveile was made, and mutch enquirye and tryall made by divers,[3] and specyally by Sir William winter and others of great creditt, by whome at length it was confirmyd to be trewe, and so was certyfied to their honners of her Majesties honnorable pryvie Councell / whereuppon Commyssion was

---

[1] Cf. the representation of the region possibly to be attributed to James Beare, master of the *Anne Frances* (plate IV). Lok's claims here are somewhat belied by his own c. 1582 chart (plate III), which does not close off the western extremity of Frobisher's 'strait'.

[2] Margin note: 'A stone of Ewre is fownd one hawlls Ilande'. Garrard was one of the five men lost to the Inuit several days later.

[3] *Sic.*

directed from their honnors unto Sir William Wintar, Master Thomas Randolphe, Master Dyar, Anthonye Jenkenson, Edmund Hogan, Mychael Lok, and others to enquire of the state of this matter, and for the settinge owte of a Seconnd voyadge, whereuppon they called before them Captaine Furbysher and Christofer hawlle Master / And amongest other matters enquired of them, what quantitye of this Ewre was to be had in that newe country, whereunto Christofer hawl answered, that he coold not certanly tell what quantity, for that he fownd no more but this stoune, nor sowght for no more, for that he regarded not this stoune, to be anye suche thinge, but he thought that where this was, there was more too be had / And there-withall C. Furbysher vowched to the Commissioners, with great speches & oathes, that there was Inoughe of it to be had in that Countrye, too lade all the Queenes Shipps and sayd that as they sayled alongest in the straights he sawe the lyke thereof afarr of one that Iland, and one Loks lande alongest the shore, by the water lyenge lyke redd sande, glisteringe and one the rocks syddes of the shore, and at Gabriells Iland ynoughe of it, with that Ewre of hawlls Ilande, which the commyssioners did credit and so certyfyed of their honors /[1]

And hereuppon her Majestie was pleased to be a great venturer in that second voyadge, and that secounde voyage was furnished, with mutch greter provycion then was purposed before, havinge nowe one great shippe of her Majestis named the Ayde, and twoo other smale shipps well manned and furnished, which cost v^m ccc. pounds wherewithall he depar-tyd from London the 26 Maye 1577. And he had specyall Commyssion in writinge to lade the Shipps, with that Ewre of hawlls Iland, which he promysed to doo, and for that purpose Jonas, Denham and Gregorye, the goldfyners, and a nomber of myners and men were sent with him in this voyadge, And when they cam to hawlls Iland, he and those workemen, and a nomber of other men, went aland with their toolles, too seke and digge for the mynes promysed, and remayning one that Ilande, almost a holle daye, in which tyme they passed over & over all the Iland, and rownd abowt, & crossinge euery waye; seking and searchinge, and could fynde noe mynes at all / whereuppon Jonas and the goldfyners felle intoo great greyfe, and into desperatt minde, of findinge anye mines to lade the Shipps, and therefore wisshed them selves rather dedd than alyve, and so cam abord the Shipps agayne, and departed thence at adventures, whether god woold send them, too seake harbor for the Shippes, And so never after browght home one Stoune more of that ritche Ewre which he browght in the first voyadg, for there was none of it to be founde. [2]

Thus departinge from Hawlles Ilande, without any comfort of fyndinge good ladinge for the shipps, they wandered with their pynnasse boats to seake harbor for their shipps, to avoyd the great danger of the yse / and at thende of iiii dayes, by gods provydence, they found one one the sowthe land, which they called Jackemans sownde, to the which they caryed the Shippe the Ayde, but because they fownd no mynes their too there content, therefore from thence they wandered over againe to the north lande, to seeke for better mynes, to lade their shipps, and for a better harbor for there shipps, and so within viii dayes by like good fortune, they founde an other harbor one the north land, which they called the Countes sounde, whether they removed their Shipps, because that was a better harbor, and was neare to certaine mynes, which they had

---

[1] Margin note: 'he vowcheth Abundaunce of Ewre of hawlls Ilande and findeth none'.
[2] Margin note: 'In second voyadge he promiseth too lade the Shipps with Ewre of hawlls Iland, but there is none at all fownd'.

[f. 2r] founde by good happe in that tyme of wanderinge and sekinge / And with the Ewre of that mine of the Countes Warwick Sownd, they laded their Shipps in the Secound voyadge, which is such Ewre as that tyme & occasion did serve them, whatsoeuer it be, which is not yet certaine / And thus with this great hassard and uncertaintye, and with so great a chardg, this Second voyadge was attempted by this bold Captaine /[1]

When as the Commyssioners had certyfied her Majestis honorable pryvye Councell of their good lykinge to attempt a seconnd voyadge, uppon this confydent affirmacions vowched by C. Furbysher, and that their honnors by that meanes had allso conceaved good oppynion thereof / And by them her Majestie well perswaded therein, And so the whole matter comitted to the Conduct of C. Furbysher by her Majestis lettres patents / and the Commyssyoners assigned, to see him furnished and dispatched / then begane he to shewe him selfe, somewhat lyke him selfe as followethe /

He woold not have benn dyverted by the Commyssioners what Shippinge and what furniture he should have with him, but for causes of Enemyes, of discoveries, and of the Ritches, he woold nedes have had iii talle shipps and ii smale barks, soo well manned and so well furnished, or ells he woold not goo in the voyadge, for so was her Majestis pleasure he sayd / which great furniture the Commyssioners refused, booth for lake of money to furnish the same, and allso for lake of better knowledge of the stat of the newe Countryes, and of assuraunce of the treasour hoaped for, and therefore did furnishe him as he was, with one Shippe and the twoo Barks, with mutch adoo and great difficultye, whereat he made no smale raginnge and owtragious speakinge amongest the Commyssioners before his departure, as he will wittnes.[2]

When as the Commissioners had devised articles for his Commission, and Instructions for the direction and goverment of the voyadge, which wear confirmyd by her Majestis honorable pryvie Councell, even by his owne advice, and for casualtye of deathe woold have joyned unto him Captaine Fenton and some others of the gentillmen that went with him, he utterly refused the same, and swore no smale oathes, that he woold be alone, or otherwise he woold not goe in the voyadge, for he had alredye a higher Commission under the broad seale then they coold gyve him anye, and badd them make what Commission they woold, for when he weare abroade he woold use it as he lyst, and afterwardes becawse he could not be furnished with all thinges to his will, therewithall he flonge owt of the doores, and swore by gods wounds that he woold hippe my masters the venturers for it, at which words Captayne Fenton plucked him secretly, and willed him to be modest / And so at lengthe had all the aucthoritye of the whole voyage in his owne handes, and used it accordinge to his owne witt and discression, as partly you have hard, and more shall heare.[3]

He desired to have with him in the Seconde voyadge, a certaine nomber of Condempned men, sayeng that he woold leave them in Fryzland and in his newe Straights one

---

[1] Margin note: 'he wandreth at venture to seeke mines to lade and harbor for shipping'.

[2] Margin note: 'he rageth at the Commissioners too have much shipping in second voyage'. Lok is the only source here for the reasons for the constitution of the second voyage in its eventual form. Clearly, there is justice in the claim that financial constraints determined its scale; however, whether Frobisher had actively pressed for a larger expedition is uncertain. Perhaps his efforts to secure more backing than was forthcoming were made in his habitually robust manner.

[3] Margin note: 'he woold haue all authoritie in his owne hands alone'. Cf. Selman (document 9, p. 187). This appears to be one of Lok's more sustainable charges.

land to remayne there, to discover the same and to knowe the state of the Countrye and nature of the people / And for that purpose he had graunt for to take these men whereuppon he redemed divers from the Gallowes & did so had speciall chardge and commission in writinge, to take them with him in the voyadge and to use them to that purpose, and to leave vj of them in Frizland / that he had redemed them from the Gallowe, he carryed not one of them with him in the voyadge, but sett them at libertye for freind shippe and mooney, sayenge that they weare unrewly knaives which would make mutynyes in the Shipps and voyadge, and that he woold fyne so manye honest men in their places, to serve that turne, to learne the state of those Countryes, which thinge he hathe not donne at all, and thus hereby he hathe helpen himselfe, & leaft the Companye as Ignorante of the state of those Counties as they weare at the beginninge /[1]

[f. 2v] He had specyall chardge and Commission in writinge in this Seconde voyadge to take with him no more men, but Cxx^tie in all, and for soo manye he had provicion of victuall, and had allsoo specyall greate chardge by lettres of her Majesties honorable pryvie Councell too accomplishe the same, but contrarye to this he toke with him in the voyadge Cxlv men, which is xxv more then nomber, and allsoo he had taken xxx^tie men more which afterwards weare dischardged at harwiche & gravesend by the severall lettres and Comandement of her Majesties pryvie Councell sent too him thether for that purpose, whiche acte of his did cost the Companye more then iiii^c pounds of mooney extraordinarye, and his Shippe victualls of the ordinarye provicion beinge so spent one them, was one cheife cause that noe further searche nor discoverye of the Countrye coold be made that voyadge.[2]

He had speciall Commission and great chardge geven him in writinge boeth at the first voyadge and allsoo in this Second voyadge, and allsoo in the theird voyadge, to use all manner gentillnes, and good dealinge too gett frendshippe and keape peace with the people of that newe Countrye, wheareby to come to knowledge of the state of their Country but contrarye hereto, at his first landinge in this second voyadge he Commaunded to spred his Ensiegne, and sownded trompets, and marched his men to a place which he named mount Warwicke, whiche comyng to their sight, he sayd lett vs goe to them for I will take some of them / And heareuppon signes of truce and peace beinge made betwene them, he sent owte first John Englishe, and an other mane trompeter, who traffiqued for divers things with them in peace and shoke hands, and therewithall he willed Christofer hawlle to goe forwarde with him selfe from the rest of his Companye, to meete twoo of

---

[1] Margin note: 'He redemeth condempned theves for the voyage and releaseth them before they goo hence / contrary to Commission'. It might equally be argued – given the climate of southern Greenland – that in doing so Frobisher had saved the lives of ten men. Certainly, the description of their condition and offences (PRO SP/12/112, 46) does not indicate that they were in any way unusually qualified to survive in that harsh environment. Most were thieves, predominantly working the highways; one, 'long repreved' by the court, was a beggar previously convicted of perjury.

[2] Margin note: 'He tookethe with him xxv menn more then nomber, contrarie to Commission'. It is difficult to assess precisely whether these were mariners hired upon formal contract, or volunteers enticed by the prospect of the newly discovered riches of the new lands (all were regarded as eligible for wages following the return of the voyage). According to Lok's account books, the number who sailed on with Frobisher after the discharge at Harwich was 143.

these men of that Countrye, which cam towards then in peace; willinge him that when they come neare to shake hands, he shold make fast thone and he woold make sure thother / and so beinge Joyned togethers, he plucked one of them to him by vyolence, meaning to have taken him prysoner, but this man with great force brake from him, and rane towards his fellowes, that weare not fare of beholdinge what successe of this conferrence, who thereuppon fell to dealinge soo with their bowes and arrowes, against our men, that our Captaine and Master fledd to their boate and cried shot, shote, shot, wherewithall Nicholas Cunger drewe his dagger, and rane after one of those strange men, and overthrewe him, and brought him prysoner to the boate, who allsoo was browght intoo England, and soo this battayle ceased / And those people rest still at defyaunce of warres with owers / And allsoo within fewe dayes after this, one other Companye of our men went too an other place of that countrye, one the sowthe syde abowt Jackemans sownde, and at their arryvall made open warres uppon other of those people, wheare they slewe iii or iiii of them, and toke prysoner twoo weomen, whereof they browght one with her Child into England / And nowe, uppon this evill dealings of our men, open warre is growen betwen that people and owers, which will not bee appeased againe easely heareafter, for that euer synce they flye from all manner traffique and Conference with our men, as was evydently proved in all the third voyadge, when none of them woold appere or come neare to our men in anye place, but uppon practise of treson, whereby is nowe lost the knowledge of the state of that Countrye, which most cheifly was sought and desired, and was the cause of the beginnyng of these voyadgs, which by peace and frendeshippe might have been obtayned /[1]

He misused Christofer hawlle Master of the Ayde in the second voyadge at the newe lande callinge him aloud cullerablye to goo search Beare sownde where beinge in a furyous humor of temper, he openly revyled him with owtragious speaches and swore by gods bludd he

[f. 3r] woold hang him, and offered too stryke him one the face with his fyst which Captaine Fenton did defend and hawlle did quietly putt upp and all this without anye cause, but onely uppon vayne suspicion of hawlles dewetyfull service, because he spake to him with his Cappe one his heade as is wittnessed by a writing of hawlls owne hande and by the gentillmen that weare presente thereat, whereby followed afterwardes great murmmuringe and evill service of the maryners in their offices, and mutch unquietnes in the Shipp all the voyadge after.[2]

He had specyall chardge and Commission in writing in this second voyadge to send one or twayne of the smale barks to make some discoverye of the Country C. leags or

---

[1] Margin note: 'He maketh warres under culler of peace with the strang people at firste landinge, contrarie to Commission'. Three draft versions of Frobisher's official instructions are extant (PRO SP/12/113, 12; BL Add. MS 35831 and BL Sloane MS 2442); it is not known which of these is the definitive version, but all required him to achieve a remarkably difficult feat: of ensuring that he gave 'least cause of offence' to the Inuit whilst simultaneously securing three or four of them to return to England. He was not of course present during the skirmish at 'Bloody Point', and it is indisputable that Gilbert Yorke and the other gentlemen who tracked and engaged the Inuit were directly disobeying his orders that they should cross immediately to Countess of Warwick Sound.

[2] Margin note: 'He misusethe C. Hawlle master of the Ayd for a Capp reverence'.

twayne beyonde the place where he loste his v. men the yeare before, untill he might have some better certainty of the sowthe sea, for the which he was well furnished and untill the xxiiiith of August being his departure from thence, and the Master hawlle had tyme ynoughe thereto, from the xviiith daye of July beinge his aryvall in the straights and his mate Jackman required him that somethinge therein might be donne / but because that his vayne glorious minde will not suffer anye discoverie to be made without his owne presence and him selfe coold not be at the dooinge so mutch to doo in the ladinge of the Shipps, he putt of the tyme of dooinge untill it was to late to be donn and so retornyd home without anye thinge at all donne therein.[1]

And now Captaine Furbysher beinge retorned home arryved at Mildford in Wales the 20 september 1577 with his Shipp laden with ritch Ewre of gold worth lx^{li} a ton as he openly vowched and with great oathes affirmed, and sutche plenty of precious stones, dyamonds and Rubies, as he had discoveryd, and brought some with him noe smale joye was had of his arryval, and noe smale increase of his reputacion, So that nowe xii or xx men weare to fewe to followe his horsse uppon this his retorne home. [2]

And Commission was geven by her Majesties honorable pryvie Councell the 20 October 1577. unto Sir William Wintar, Master Thomas Randolphe, Master William Pelhame, George Wintar, Anthonye Jenkenson, Edmund Hogaine and Michael Lok, to have conference with Jonas and Denham the workemen that tryall and proffe might be made of the valewe of the Ewre browght home, whereuppon a smale furnasse was buylded by Jonas order at the dwellinge howsse of Sir William Wintar at Tower Hill, and for the proff of the Ewre Jonas did melt and refyne C. weight there of in the presens of Commissioners, which was fynished in the begining of November, which worke was not perfitt for that the furnace and bellowes fayled, and mutch gold remayned in the sladgs, and therefore he mended his furnace, and made a second tryall of an other C. weight of that Ewre allsoo in the presens of the Commissioners which was fynished the 6. December, by boeth the which tryalls it was founde the Ewre to be worth xl^{li} a ton towards chardgs, and so was certyfied to her Majesties pryvie Councell by the Commissioners, nevertheles for that Jonas worke cold not perfitly be donne, in that smale furnace and evill worke howsses but that still remayned goold in the sladgs, which he promised to gett owte perfectly in the great works / And Allsoo for that John Broad and the goldsmithes of London havinge made manye smale sayes of Ewre colde fynde no gold at all therein, Jonas dooings was suspected / And therefore it was thought good by some to have conference with Dr Burcott and trye his cunninge therein.[3]

And allsoo in the meane tyme it was ordeyned that Jonas should make an other third

---

[1] This is inaccurate, as Lok must have known. Frobisher's instructions directed him to take the barks on to the western extremity of the passage only if his mining activity did not 'yealde the substaunce that is hoped for …' (BL Sloane MS 2442, f. 24v). As Schutz certified the ore they collected as 'good', such a further reconnaissance would have been contrary to instructions.

[2] Margin note: 'He retorneth home with great boste of golde laden in the second voyage'. This is the first reference to Frobisher's retinue of 'sarving men', whose diet was to burden the adventurers so heavily following the return of the 1578 voyage (this document, p. 101). Their identity – whether mariners or impoverished 'gentlemen' seeking a patron – is not known.

[3] Margin note: 'Jonas first proffe of cc. Ewre at Tower hill'.

tryall of ii^c. weight of the Ewre after the order and manner of great works, before the bestowinge of so great chardges to buyld the howse for the great works, which Jonas

[**f. 3v**] did willingly graunt to do, but before that he woold doo that, he desyred to be at a certaintye what lyvinge he shoold have, whereuppon he had graunted of her Majestie by pattent C. pounds yearely during his lyef to be payd owt of those works; with Condicion that he make the Ewre worthe xxx pounds a tonn towards chardges / which chardgs shoold not be abowe x^{li} a tonn, this was his owne Condicion and demaunde, and so he thankefully accepted the pattent, And also because that Robert Denhame was knowen for a good workeman in makinge of smale sayes and the proffs of Ewres and a trewe mane and had donne mutch service and must doo more dalye in theise works, to him was graunted a like patent for l. poundes a yeare, during his liefe, And therewithall Jonas and Denham did goo to woorke the third proffe of this Ewre at the Tower Hill, for the dooings whereof Jonas required to have provyded certaine Markesites for additaments to make the Ewre worke kindlye, for that he sayd the Ewre was of wild nature full of Iron and steele which must be consumed in the meltinge by other additaments putt to it, and gave to the Commissioners instructions and some samples of suche Markesits, as he woold have, but the Commissioners knewe not reddely where to provide nor seeke for those markesits / And therefore in the meane tyme he must do this worke as he can, which he did twoo seuerall tymes, in the presents of the Commissioners, and allsoo of Master dee and Master palmer, and allsoo of John Broad, humfry Cole[1] and others thereto appointed, which was fynished the fyrst CC. weight by the 20 of Februarye and the second CC. weight by the 6. of Marche, by the which twoo seuerall proffs and workes the Ewre was founde to be woorthe at the least valewe xxiiii^{li} a ton towards the chardgs and so was certyfyed to her Majesties honnorable pryvie Councell by the Commissioners owne hands writinge bearinge date the viiith daye of Marche.[2]

And because that during this tyme of Jonas works at Tower hill mutch tyme was spent and yet no certaine agrement nor preperacion made for Captaine Furbysher to be sett owtt againe in a theird voyadge for the which purpose the tyme was almost to late and he not beinge able to contynewe him self at home with that reputacion that he was nowe entered into without contynuance of great entertaymentes, and seinge that all the matter rested uppon Jonas dooings in his works, wherein he thowght mutch tyme was delayed one the xv daye of Februarye he cam to the Commissioners to Master Loks howsse in great radge and exclamyd one them and from them went straight unto Jonas to the Tower hill, wheare fyndinge him naked at his worke and verye sick almost to deathe of infection of the smoke of the myneralls he reviled him with villanus speache for that he had not fynished his worke and drewe his dagger one him and threatened him with oathes, that he woold strike it in him, yf he did not with speade dispatche and fynishe his works, that the Shipps might bee prepared for the thirde voyadge, wherewithall Jonas entered

---

[1] In addition to being England's foremost maker of instruments of navigation, Humphrey Cole had been employed as die-sinker at the Tower Mint for twenty years by 1578 (B. J. Cook, 'Humphrey Cole at the Mint', in Ackerman, *Humphrey Cole*, p. 21). Cole described himself as a 'goldsmith' by trade, and was therefore well qualified to assist Schutz (though obviously not sufficiently expert to identify the weaknesses in the Saxon's skills). John Broad was a goldfiner and later (1582) melter at the Tower Mint (Challis, *Tudor Coinage*, p. 21, n. 67).

[2] *Recte* £23. 15s. This was the perceived value upon which plans for the 1578 expedition were based.

into great perplexitye at the evill nature of the Captaine and utterly renownced with soleme vowe, that he woold never more goe with him to Sea, nor have to do anye more with him in anye busines, and longe tyme afterwards did weare his weapon dowtinge the mallice of the Captaine for enemitie with Dr Burcott, whose doings the Captaine did favor and protect /[1]

Allsoo in this meane tyme of Jonas works, one the 10. daye of december Jonas was brought to have conference with Dr Burcott by meanes made, to have them joyne togethers, in the great works & with in iii or iiii dayes Jonas misliked the delings of Dr Burcott, boeth of his evill manners, and allsoo for his Ignoraunce in divers

[fo. 4r] divers points of the works and handlinge of this Ewre, So as he woold not anye more deale with Dr Burcott in worke / but Captaine Furbisher liked so well boeth of D. Burcott in all that he coold, whereuppon great contencion grewe betwen Burcott and Jonas for Mastershippe of the great works, and for the buildings of the great workehowses, eache condempninge others knowledge therein but Jonas alwaies with modest wordes, and D. Burcott and Captaine Furbysher with owtragious speches / And uppon certaine smale sayes, of the Ewre made by D. Burcott, and his greate promises made to performe in great works, after xv. ounces of gold for the ton of the Ewre, he had a patent allsoo graunted untoo him to be cheife workemaster of the great works, with a pencion of C. poundes yearely during his lyef with alowaunce of xx^s a daye when he wrought, and promesse hope of v^c pounds pencion uppon better successe of the ritche redd Ewre to be brought home in the theird voyadge by his Instructions to be geven to C. Furbysher, And in this meane tyme the Commissioners dealt with Jonas apart in conference for the erection of the workehowsses for the great works, to whome Jonas gave diuers platts, and Instructions, for the buildings howe and wheare he woold have them, to all the which dooings, C. Furbysher was of Councell as in Commission / And he as messinger putt in trust for the Companye, dealt apart with D. Burcott to the ende to knowe the cunninge of them boeth, to whome he reveled all the dooings of Jonas, without the knowledge of Jonas, and contrary to the will of the Comissioners, from tyme to tyme, as apeared evidently for the buildings by the twoo seuerall platts of the workehowses browght from burcott, which are to be seene, The first of D. Burcotts owne device strangely made, The second which he woold followe, which was iust the Coppie of Jonas drawinge, and by the desire that Burcott had to see the Furnace of Jonas at Tower hill, before he woold shewe anye platt of his owne makinge, whiche was not shewed him, but was denied by Sir William Wintar. Whereuppon followed great contencion and evill dealings betwene C. Furbysher and him, And for the worke of Dr Burcott in the Ewre, it appeared by the venturers valewe thereof which he promised to yeld, to thintent to have the Mastershipp of the works and benyfitt of the lyvinge by his patent, and afterwards it was playnely fownd and proved, by the meanes of Robert Denhame as followeth/[2]

---

[1] Margin note: 'C. furbusher drewe his dagger upon Jonas to hast his works for a third voyag'.

[2] Margin note: 'he practiseth with Dr burcott to worke for his theird voyage'. For the details of these events, Lok (here, and in his deposition *A Little bundle of the tryeing of ye Northwest Ewre*: PRO SP/12/122, 62) is our only authority. However, the eventual denouement regarding Kranich's apparent deceptions was indeed so public (being played out, as Lok claimed, at Burghley's house, in the presence of he, Sir Walter

When Dr Burcott was preferred to a patent of great lyving he was willed to make a tryall of the weight of the Ewre in suche manner as he woold stand to it in the great works, and to worke it after his owne order, where and how he lyst himselfe, to the intent some more certainty might be had of the valew of the Ewre, before the great cost weare bestowed one the buyldings or workehowses, and that the theird voyadge which C. Furbusher so muche solicited might have the better foundacion, whereuppon D. Burcott desired to worke his proffe in his owne howsse, and to have Robert Denham to helpe him therein, which was graunted and one the xxiiii of Januarye was delyvered him CC weight of the Ewre, and xli of mooney to build his furnace, and Robert Denham went to helpe him therein, whom he swore with an oathe not to

[f. 4v] reveale his secrets, and he did as Burcott commaunded him in all the worke, and one the xxj daye of Februarye all the Commissioners went to the howsse of D. Burcott at his request, where he sayd unto them, that he had molton a C. weight of that Ewre, & he shewed unto them the gold and siluer which he sayd cam owtt of that Ewre by his worke, which was founde too be after the rate of xiii ounces and a halfe of fyne golde, and xxxviii ounces of fyne siluer in every ton of the Ewre, which is worth fyftie pounds of mooney every ton Ewre, and soo mutch he promised them to make good in the great works, and sayd that for the performaunce thereof he had alredy bounde him selfe and gaged unto the right honorable the Lorde Highe Tresorer of England, with his lyef, his lands and all his goods by writinge, the Coppie whereof he shewed to the Commissioners, and the same he woold performe in the great workes, with onely one Condycion, that is that he might have delyvered to him a quantitie of a certaine Markesit mynerall which he shewed to the Commissioners and namyd it to be Antemoni and sayd that it held no manner of mettall at all, and that thereof there was quantitye Inoughe to be had in the grownd of Master Edgcome gentilman in Devonshire/And also at that same instant, he shewed unto the Commissioners divers papers of the platts of workhowses, that he woold have to be builded which weare most like those that Jonas had made before/And then after a little talke imedyately he resumed agayne into his owne hands boethe the gold and siluer, and the platts of the buildings, and therewithall required the Commissioners to goo with him to the howsse of the right honnorable the Lorde Highe Treserer afore sayd who was then at home at his howsse, and so in the Strand they went all togethers, to his honnor, and with him was Sir Walter Myldmaye Chauncelor of thexchequor and others, and in their presents D. Burcott did repeate all that he had sayd before the Commisioners and shewed all that he had shewed before to them and did confirme the same promes unto their honnors, that he had made unto the Commissioners, and deliuered to his honnor the gold and siluer and Antemonye stones and so rested concludinge with his honnor upon these iiii poynts, to saye/

That the Antimony Ewre shoold be delyvered hym/
That the great works shoold be builded presently/
That the Ewre at Brystowe shoold be brought hether/

Mildmay and all the commissioners) that it is unlikely that Lok would perjure himself in this, his deposition to the Privy Council.

That Captaine Furbysher shoold be dispatched with all spead one this third newe voyagde/

Unto the which his honnor added the vth point, sayenge that he shoold be well recompenced for his paynes and service, yf his sayengs and his shewes prove trewe, and his honner sayd that he woold enforme her Majestie of all his doings and therewithall they departed. [1]

And nowe forasmuche as Dr burcott did stand so muche upon the havinge of the Antimonye markesite, and so vehemently affirminge it to hold no manner of metall, Master Richard Younge desired my Lord Tresorer to geve him a pece thereof, to make a smale saye, which his honour did give him, and the next daye Robert Denhame made a saye thereof in presens of Master Dier, Master Dee, Master Younge, and other the Comissioners, and thereby founde that the same doath hold a good quantitie of lead, & some siluer, and a little Copper, the which was allso confirmid to them by Robert Denham who then declared unto them, that him selfe had made divers sayes thereof a moneth before, of a pece which he had at Doctor Burcotts howsse, unknowen to D. Burcott / And heareuppon the dooings of D. Burcott grewe in great suspition amongest the Commissioners, and therefore one the xxvj day of Februarye at the howsse of Master Secritarye Walsingham in London his

[f. 5r] honour did call before him all the Commissioners, and allso the sayd Robert Denham, and thear did chardge him uppon his allegeans and dewtye to[2] towards her Majestie, to tell the trewth of the dooings of D. burcott in his worke made of the C. weight of Ewre, whereof the gold and siluer was there presently shewed to him by Master Secritarye,[3] And therewithall Robert Denham kneled downe and craved pardon, alleaged his oathe made to Dr burcott not to reveale his secrets / and acknowleged his dewty to her Majestie, and afterwards uppon his allegeaunce sayd thus, that he did not know what addittaments D. burcott did use to the meltinge of the Ewre and that D. burcott made proffe but of one pounde of the Ewre accordinge to the order of the smale sayes, and that accordinge to the proporcion of goold and siluer fownd therein, he did make uppe the rest of the pece of gold and the silver delyvered to the Commissioners with angell Gold and daller Siluer of his owne / And that Denham did melt onely xxvl^i of this Ewre, and did melt it in pottes and skarvells by poundes, and halfe poundes, with the addittaments which D. burcott did putt in, which worke had evill Successe, and made evill proffe, and that afterwards he melted some Ewre with his owne addittaments which proved well, which remayneth still with D. burcott and that the rest of the C. weight of Ewre was melted and handeled by D. burcott and his to little purpose before he cam to him / And that D. burcott knewe not the valewe nor content of the Antimonye Ewre to hold anye mettall therein, nor to be good to worke with this Ewre brought home, untill Thursdaye last beinge the xxth of Februarye at which daye he Robert Denham did reveale the same unto him / And thus was revealed the Ignoraunce of the workemanshippe, and the falshoode of the practises of this famous connynge great Master D. burcott,

---

[1] Margin note: 'Dr burcotts false works'.
[2] *Sic.*
[3] Walsingham.

uppon whose great promises and great gages, so great a Captaine Furbysher was exalted to so great a dominion in his theird voyadge to so great chardge of the Company /[1]

In this Secound voyadge weare discovered certaine ritche mines, of Redd Ewre & yellowe Ewre at a place namyd Jonas Mount, whereof diuers stounes weare browght home, and mutch was digged as they said, but was not laded into the Shipps, because the Shipps weare alredye loden with the black Ewre, and as they sayd the tyme was come for them to depart owt of that Countrye, and this redd Ewre was discoveryd but even at their departure thence, So as they coold not tarrye to change their ladinge / And off this redd Ewre were made divers small sayes, by Jonas and Denham, and fownd verrye ritche of gold, and by Dr burcott who vowched the same to be worthe more than Cxx[li] a ton, and some of those stoones are yet to be sene, and C. Furbysher did vowche with oathes openly, and often tymes that there was to be had aboundant quantitie thereof, and did promis to the Commissioners and to Dr burcott too lade the most parte of the Shipps in the theird voyadge with the same Ewre, and for that purpose would neds have Gregorie with him because he knewe the place and to that purpose and end he had diuers notes and Instructions of D. burcott for the choyce thereof, for that redd Ewre was the thinge whereuppon D. burcott did make his foundacions of performaunce at the theird voyadge of great promises and gages that he had made for his great mastershippe of the Workes of the Ewre of this second voyadge, whereby he hoaped in the theirde voyadge to make a mends for his faultes of the Second voyadge / And yet for conclusion of this great matter and parformeaunce of this greate promises, this great C. Furbysher hathe not browght home in the theird voyadge, one tonne of this ritche redd Ewre that can be yet fownde /[2]

There was fownd by chaunce in this voyage one a little Ilande in Jackmans sownde A Sea beast like a verrye great porpos fyshe, being dead, havinge in the heade a great horne of five fotte longe or thereabout

[f. 5v] wrethed like an unicornes horne, and is judged to be a right unicornes horne estemed worthe iii[li] of mooney, this Jewell is mete for a present to her Majestie to whome Captaine Furbysher did present it in his owne name and not in the Companyes name to whome it did belonge. [3]

There was fownde in this voyadge by Jonas amongest the Rocks, a great Rubie stoune of

---

[1] Margin note: 'Robert Denham openeth Dr burcotts false woorke'.

[2] Margin note: 'He browght a stone of ritche redd Ewre and in second voyage promiseth to lade the shipps therewithall in theird voyage but laded nothing at all'. As all accounts of the voyage make clear, the red ore proved to be extremely elusive, though some samples of a superficially similar composition were discovered at Countess of Sussex mine.

[3] Margin note: 'An unicornes horne presented to her Majestie in his owne name'. This 'unicornes horne' was a narwhal's tusk. George Best, in his account of the 1577 voyage, stated that the creature from which it came 'maye truly be thoughte to be the sea Unicorne', but he was indicating what to him was an obvious comparison, not surmising its true nature. Clearly, the mariners who found the dead creature understood it to be a variety of whale, as Best's sketch thereof confirms. The fact that the tusk was presented to the Queen indicates the widespread contemporary appreciation of the horn's rarity and value, though it is not known whether Englishmen were aware of the pharmaceutical properties attributed to it by eastern cultures. According to Best, the tusk was subsequently displayed at the Wardrobe, 'to be seene and reserved as a Jewel.'

more than one ynche square, a present meat for A prince / this Jewell did Jonas delyver to C. Furbusher at his departure from Mildford Haven, towardes the Coorte whoe promised him to present the same to her Majestie in Jonas name, which Jonas doeth not yet heare of nor cannot learne what is become of it. [1]

There was fownd and brought home in this Second voyadge manye smalle Jewell stoones, Diamants, Rubies, Saphiers and others by diuers persons which are put upp privatly, and so none accompt to be taken of them thoughe they be of vallewe.[2]

At retorne home of this Seconde voyadge, Captaine Furbysher made so good report thereof to her Majestie of the great ritches that he had browght home and so great promises of the infynit Treasor of this newe land, whereof he woold posses her Majestie surmounting the Treasor of the Indias of the kinge of Spaine, whereby he woold make her Majestie the richest prince in all Europe,[3] and withall so shewed the great dangers of the yse and Shippewrake and sore labors, that he and his Companye had passed & Indured in her Majestis Service in this voyadge, that he hathe obteyned of her Majestie a leasse of a good lyvinge, for him selfe which he keapethe[4] / and allso C. pounds of mooney of her Majesties benevolente gyft to be distributed amongest the maryners which served in that voyadge / which C. pounds he keapeth allso to him selfe, and hathe not yet made distrybucion thereof as the Shipps Masters and men do saye /[5]

When the Shippe Ayde and Gabriel weare arryved in this Seconde voyadge at Brystowe, and the Ewre of their ladings theire dischardged one land he was sent thether by the Commissioners too paye the mans wages and laye uppe the Shipps furniture untill the next yeare, at which tyme he lefte xiii men in chardge of the Companye at meat and wages all the winter to keape the Shipps, which woold have benn doonn with iii men and allsoo toke liberty to retaine xx men of this voyadge at his lykinge at vj^d a daye wages to be reddy too serve in the next voyadge, which togethers cost the Companye C. pounds superfluous.[6]

And althoughe he had specyall Commission in writing to cause dewe Inventaries to be made of all the goods and merchandizes remayninge in the Shipps at their arryvall at Brystowe, and in whose custody they weare least at Brystowe, and for that purpose had ii of the Companyes servaunts Edward Sellman and Thomas Mershe, yet when he had payed the mens wages ther he retorned to London with his great band of men and left the chiefe chardge of all things there with a false Ruffyanly boye of his owne namyd John Commings whoe is nowe gone a rovinge and left the Inventaries to be made at the discression of other men; and left the merchandizes in the howsse of an honest merchant namyd

---

[1] Margin note: 'he had of Jonas a great Rubie stoune for her Majestie'.

[2] Again, this opinion is contradicted by that of Bernadino de Mendoza (document 13, p. 250).

[3] Margin note: 'his great vaunte of treasor brought home hathe gotten him a good leasse of her Majestie'.

[4] Unidentified, though possibly this was the lease regarding whose title Frobisher was later (1580) to petition the Queen, claiming that he had been some expense at law in attempting – and failing – to obtain it (PRO SP/12/151, 16).

[5] Margin note: 'he hathe a C.^{li} of her Majesties to distribut amonge the men which is nott donne'.

[6] Margin note: 'he made great chardgs to keape the Ayde at brystowe'. Thirteen men employed to guard and maintain two ships in dock was not an excessive number, particularly as there was no rudimentary naval establishment at Bristol that might otherwise have supervised the ships' 'grounding'. Wages of sixpence per day would have represented the men's victualling, and no more.

Master Kitchen, but the keye thereof with his owne mane John Commings and browght no Inventarye at all thereof and afterwards when the Commissioners woold have sente Edward Sellman to Brystowe to take the Inventarye and see all things he woold not suffer it, sayenge that all things is salfe and he woold warrant and answer for all / And so when the Shipp Ayde shoold bee furnished owt one the theird voyadg, newe Inventaries were made. And thereuppon conference made of the Inventarye of the second voyadg furniture & goods laden in her owtwards, ther was fownd lacking a nomber of things of the Shipps Furniture & merchandizes, apperinge in a writinge to the valew of iiii^c pounds, which are confirmed wasted & pilfered in the second viadge, by evill men and officers placed by evill government.[1]

[f. 6r] The theird voyadge of Captaine Furbysher was sett forthe uppon manyfest conjecture of great honnor to her Majestie likely to ensewe thereby, as allsoo of great hoape conceaved of great Comoditie to grow, aswell to the whole Realme as to the venturers therein, by diuers arguments and matters layed owte before the Commissioners, which cheifly consisted in these ii points, to saye [2]/ The great ritches of the mynes of gold fownd in the newe Contries which was certified by the workemen Jonas and Robert Denham, and doctor Burcott and others which had made tryall thereof / And the open passage by Sea to Cathay, which Captaine Furbusher vowched to be by him discoveryd and made plaine /[3] which matters beinge certified to her Majesties honnorable pryvie Councell by the Commissioners writings, Their honnors thowght it good to proced with a theird voyadge / whereuppon they directed their lettres of Commission unto Sir William Wintar, Edward dier, John dee, Martine furbysher, Richard younge, Mathew Feild, Edmund hogan, Michael Lok, Andrew palmer, dated the xii daye of Marche 1577(8) willinge them to see all things provided, and the voyadge dispatched with expedicion / And nowe Captaine Furbysher havinge the thinge that he so mutch hunted for, grewe into such a monsterous minde, that a whole Kingdome coold not conteyne it, but as alredy by discoverye of a new worlde, he was become another Columbus so allso nowe by conquest of a new world he woold become another Cortes / And for this purpose he enforced unto the Commissioners manye arguments and reasons, howe requisite and needful it was to fortifie and to inhabit in that newe Countrye / And for to vrge the same to a greater furniture of Shippinge for his dominion, he vowched with oathes unto the Commissioners, and withall shewed a lettre (but redd it not) which he sayd cam owtt of Fraunce, by a messenger of his owne, how that the Frenche kinge did arme presently xii Shipps, to passe to the same newe Countrye, to take possession of the straightes and to fortyfie at the mynes there, before he shoold come thether /[4] whereuppon after manye tymes conferens had by

---

[1] Margin note: 'he woold not make Inventarie of goods at brystowe and his evill men mad muche wast & pilferye of goods in the voyadg contrarie to Commission'.

[2] Margin note: 'Captaine Furbushers great pride'.

[3] Margin note: 'The cause of the theird voyage'.

[4] Margin note: 'he forgethe newes of the french kings navye to advaunce his owne kingdom'. See also p. 252, n. 5. Did Frobisher have advanced notice of Troilus de la Roche's voyage? He had several Huguenot contacts dating from his privateering days, when he had been employed by both Cardinal Châtillon and count Montgomery. It is not unlikely that these remained intact, if inactive, by the late 1570s (cf. McDermott, *Frobisher*, pp. 67, 74–5, 85–7).

the Commissioners of manye matters appertayninge to the voyadge, they concluded and did sett forwarde this theird voyage with xj ships verrye well furnished and provided, under the generall conduct of C. Furbysher,[1] And with C. men verry well furnished & provided to fortifie and inhabit in that newe contry for one yeare or twayne yf neede weare, under the cheife chardge & guide of Captaine Fenton as lyuetenaunt generall of C. Furbysher where-withall. C. Furbussher was nowe in great jolitie, and coolde take no rest, untill he weare gonn one the waye to his newe Empier, and so he departed with this navie from London the 26. daye of Maye 1578 one this theird voyage which cost the Companye xiii^m poundes of mooney / But betwene this tyme of his goinge foreward, and the tyme of his retorne home agayne which was the 28. daye of September 1578 manye alteracions and disorders hathe happened, boeth in hymselfe & in his newe Empier, which hathe donne great hurte too manye, as presently heareunder shall appeare /[2]

At the beginninge of this theird voyage C. Furbisher was sent by the Commissioners from London to Brystowe to Furnishe and dispatche from thence the Shipps Ayde and Gabriell for this voyage, wherein he was mad victuler of the Shippe Ayde, for the whiche victualls he had v^c pounds of mooney delyvered him before hande, but he did so evill victuall the same Shippe, that whereas the Companye allowed him mooney for to victuall her with fleshe iiii dayes in the weake, he served the men onely iii dayes and ii dayes in the weake therwith and the rest of the weeke with fyshe and that so evill and so scarse, that thereby mutch sickenes grewe, and diuers of them dyed, as the men do reporte /[3]

[f. 6v] He was sent into the west Countrye to provide cxx men myners, for this voyadge, for whose furniture he had mooney of the Companye before hande for their wages, ccxl. poundes, which is xl.^s for eche man, but thereof he payed theis men to some xx^s. to some xiii^s iiii^d. and to some nothinge the man, as his accoumpts declares, allsoo he had cxx^li. of mooney for their weapons & furniture, which is xx^s. for everye man to provide his weaponnes withall, but what weapons they had, or he for them is yet unknowen, for none doeth appeare anye wheare, but in the west Countrye is spread a Rumor that those myners beinge prest by Commission in her Majesties name, manye of them afterwards wear chardged by favour, for showemakers, taylors musitians, gardeners, and other artyfycers not woorkemen / And they weare furnished to Sea, at the chardges of the Townes and villadgs in manner of a subsidie, as it is reported openly/[4]

When Captaine Furbusher was in the west Country in this greate Jolitie with his Commission generall under broad seale, to presse men and Shipps as he thowght requisite

---

[1] Lok here includes his own vessel, the *Beare Leicester*, as one of the intended vessels, though it was allowed to participate only by concession.

[2] Margin note: 'the furniture of the theird voyage which cost xiii^m pounds'.

[3] Margin note: 'he did vittle the shippe ayde evill'. In view of the strikingly similar accusations made against Frobisher during the 1582 Moluccas voyage, this appears to be one of Lok's more sustainable charges (cf. Donno, *Madox*, pp. 185, 211–12).

[4] Margin note: 'his great abuse in provydinge of cxx myners in the west Countrye'. Given the appalling quality of Frobisher's accounting methods (PRO EKR E164/35, pp. 283–305, with numerous disal-lowances by the auditors of items therein), it is impossible to assess the justice of Lok's claims. However, it seems unlikely that he was immune to the temptations that habitually supplemented the incomes of sea-captains, both then and later.

for service of this voyadge, he remembred the greatnes of the matter apperteyninge to the Conquest of his Empier, and therefore thinkinge that the xj Ships and furniture appointed by the Commissioners was to little for his secreat purpose, he boldly toke upp thear in her Majesties name, and caried with him in the voyadge by his owne authoritie without anye consent or knowledge of the Commissioners, iiii Shipps and C. men more then was appointed by the Commissioners, as is evident by the fact, and by his owne lettre written thereof from Plymouthe, to the which Shipps he promised to deliuer victualls at Harewiche, and so he did in deade, of the victualls which was appointed for the provision of the C. men which weare to remaine in the newe Countrye under Captaine Fenton, which afterwards torned to the whole overthrowe of that purpose, and theis Shipps and men of his owne do cost the Companye iiiᵐ. pounds of mooney unloked for /[1]

After that Captaine Furbusher had obteyned of the Commissioners their consent for C. men to remaine and fortyfie in the straights and that Captaine Fenton was chosen to be their head, and that he sawe so great a preparacion for his furniture, and so greate a fame and Credite growinge towards him for this his willinge enterprise of so difficult and strange matter, and sawe so manye good gentillmen so desirous to goe with him, & hard a broad so greate Comendacions of his wisdome and habillitie to performe this enterprice, and that greater fame was nowe spredd of this enterprice, then was of his owne enterprice before, he begane then to suspect the yssue of this matter, and to feare that the fame of this enterprice of Captaine Fenton woold dashe the glorye and fame of his former dooings / And therefore he sittenge amongst the Commissioners after his retorne owte of the west Countrye, where he had secretly provyded his iiii Shipps, divers tymes with hevie Countenaunce he woolde cast owte speaches cullerably, sometymes sayenge that this great furniture of buildings for Captaine Fenton woold be to little purpose, Sometymes that they shoold hardely be able to plant them selues there, & dangerously to live there, and plainly sayd to Charles Jackeman at harwiche that they shoold not inhabit there, and divers tymes swering and staringe that he woold not be bound to his promes to plant Captaine Fenton there, and to lade the Shipps home, except he might depart by maye daye from hence, and othertimes that he woold not goo at all one the voyage, except he might be dispatched hence by maye daye, which thinge he knewe well coold not be doone, and so woold have forced Captaine Fentons dispatch without his full furniture whereby he[2]

[**f. 7r**] might have had some culler of excuse, that when he weare in that Country he might not remaine there, but at the last when Captaine Fenton was full furnished and must goo, and that Captaine Furbyshers unwillingnes therein did appeare unto the Commissioners, and that the matter rested yet in the will and aucthoritie of Captaine Furbysher, whether that Captaine Fenton when he weare in the newe Countrye shoold

---

[1] Margin note: 'he taketh iiii shipps & C. men more then Comission in this third voyage / contrarie to Commission'. Fenton, who as general of the intended colony would have had an intimate understanding of what victuals might have 'gone missing', makes no such claims regarding Frobisher and his unauthorized ships. He was instead exercised by the failure of the officially-hired vessels – principally the *Denys*, *Thomas of Ipswich* and *Anne Frances* – to deliver supplies ear-marked for his men's use (document 8, pp. 159, 166).

[2] Margin note: 'after that C. Fenton was appointed too inhabitt Captaine furbusher disliked it, and hindereth it and in thend cleane overthroweth it thoroughe pryde'.

yet remayne theare yea or noe, by reason of the generall power geven to him by her Majesties lettres patents under broad seale, which he might abuse by the helpe of his marryners uppon Indignacion or displeasure, Then the Commissioners required C. Furbusher to sett his Seale to a writinge Autenticke of Deputacion unto C. Fenton to be his Lyuetennaunte generall, and too remaine theare as cheife of the C. men appointed untoo him, which he verrye unwillingly dyd consent unto, yet at the very last ower of his departure he did it, and verry shortly afterwards and manye tymes synce he repentid him thereof, as appeared openly uppon heynous contention which afterwards passed betwen then on land in the newe Contrye concerninge their aucthorities, where Captaine Furbusher sayd to Captaine Fenton that he had none Aucthoritye at all in anye matter but by him, [1] whereto Captaine Fenton pleaded and opened his aucthoritie by deputacion as good as his owne, which C. Furbusher wisshed to have toke againe from him, and therewithall sayd to C. Fenton that he had browght him intoo this Creditt and had preferred intoo Service of her Majestie and manye other speches of reproche passed betwen them, which C. Fenton did wisely beare and putt them uppe for the tyme, consideringe the Service he had in hande, thoughe afterwards this matter grewe to mutch murmuringe & danger of mutenye amongest the men of boeth parts, whereby mutche evill Service followed /[2]

And nowe it is evident that this seed of discorde beinge spronge owte of the rootte of Ambicion planted in the mind of C. Furbusher was the verrye cheife cause that moved him to neglect and so mutche forgett his dewtye towards her Majestie in this one princyple article of his Commission geven him in writinge, by her Majesties pryvie Councell, to saye, that at his arryvall in Meta incognita, he shoold helpe and assist with all that he coold too plant Captaine Fenton and his Companye for to inhabitt there, beinge a matter of so great importaunce in expectacion of the cheife intent and purpose of the Companye in all theise voyages, and soo great a chardge and cost to them as more then vj^m pounds of mooney in this one voyadge alone, which he altogether hathe neglected and soo little regarded, that he woold not once make offer of anye good will to further that Service but employed him selfe onely to lade the Shipps, nor when C. Fenton offered to remaine there with lx. men or l. men or lesse, he woold not showe anye manner good will nor encorragement thereunto, but contrarye called a Councell to enquire what things of his provision was lackinge, and asked the simple oppynion of the unwillinge Artificers to erect the howsse, whoe disliked thereof / And therewithall he contented him selfe as with sufficient cloke to cover his evill minde. Wheareby he hathe utterlye overthrowen this service wherein did depend a greater matter then he is able to comprehend / And by this meanes and Culler he had victualls ynoughe to furnishe his owne iiii Shipps and C. men which he toke with him contrarye to Commission, whoe els had famished in their retorne homewards, as the men will wittnes; and the thing doethe prove /[3]

He had placed Androwe Dier his owld Companyon for chiefe Master and pilott with

---

[1] Margin note: 'Contencion betwen C. furbusher & C. fenton in Meta Incognita'.

[2] Margin note: 'wherto C. Fenton answered that he did great wronge to their Lord & Master therle of Warwick, whoe did preferr them boeth together unto her Majestie'.

[3] Margin note: 'Captaine Furbusher did overthrowe the purpose for Captaine Fentons habitacion, which cost vj^c pounds to victuell his owne iiii Shipps'.

Captaine Fenton in this theird voyadge too inhabitt theare, for to make discoverye of the Countrye, where

[f. 7v] they shoold inhabit, and seeke owt the waye to Cathay, he beinge fitt for nothinge but to hinder the enterprise of Captaine Fenton And with to highe speches exalted him to the Commissioners, for the fittest man for that Service, boeth for his honestye, and trewth, his valor, his skillfullnes, and experience, who hathe benn a verye costly man to the Companye. And yet the same Androwe is a man so impotent and criple of his leggs as he can verye evill goe, so unskillfull as he can neither wright nor redde so unexpert of the Sea, as he was never further from England then Fraunce, and Ireland, so honest and so trewe that syns his retorne home he is gonne owt with his Fellowes to Sea in evill ventures, but the Commissioners did displace him and putt Charles Jackeman in that voyadge /[1]

He had speciall Commission in writing in this theird voyadge to have great care and regarde to the maintenaunce of Concord amongest his men, and to receive no mutinus and disordered persons, but to putt them awaye, but contrarye he placed Allexander Creeke his kinesman for boateswayne of the Ayde in the theird voyadge who is butt a younge mane unskillfull and farr unfitt for that office of sutch chardge, and is of great disordered lyef, who syns his retorne home is gonne to Sea with others his like fellowes one evill ventures,[2] And allsoo he woold not punishe the disorders of hym and of Edward Robinson and others for anye complaynt mad too him, but rather maynetayned their disobediences against the Masters Christofer Hawle and Robert Davies and alsoo against Captaine Fenton beinge in that newe Countrye whereby followed in that voyadge great spoyle and pilferye of the Ships takle and furniture as will appeare by Inventarye thereof. And through their disobedience to the Masters Commaundements and careles service in the Shipps busines the Shippe the Ayde was bilged with her owne Anker stroken into the bowe of her with a rocke of yse, whereby verrye hardly she escaped synkynge presently beinge within the Countes sownde / And throughe there disordered and mutinus dealings amongest the men great evill Service followed in the Companies busynes, and great contencion and stryff grewe amonge then men in that newe Countrye betwene the marryners one thone parte and the gentillmen one thother parte, that they weare with their weapons to have joyned togethers, had not Captaine Fenton wisely pacyfied that Stryffe by quiett puttinge uppe of the Injuryes /[3]

He had speciall Commission in writing that in matters of difficulty happeninge in this voyadge, he shoold have conference and Councell with the Captaines Yorke and Best, and others, and with the Masters Hawlle, Jackemane and others, but he refused their conference and Councell, And sayd that his Commission of Instructions geven by her

---

[1] Margin note: 'he placed Androw dier unworthy man to discover Cathay'.

[2] Cf. Lok's implications regarding Andrew Diar in the paragraph immediately preceeding. However coloured, Lok's testimony is invaluable in confirming the privateering profession to have been a rich source of recruitment for this and other contemporary enterprises.

[3] Margin note: 'he placed Allexander Creeke his kinesman boateswaine of the Ayde, whereby followed muche contention amongest the men and wast of goods in the Shippe / contrarie to Commission'. Creake's precise relationship to Frobisher is not known; he was one of only four men (the others being Frobisher himself, Christopher Hall and Luke Warde) to sail in all three northwest voyages. In view of this and other charges against him (cf. document 9, p. 185), it appears that his contribution thereto was almost unremittingly malign.

Majesties Honorable pryvie Councell weare but the devise of Fenton and Lok and weare never redde by their honnors thoughe their handes had subscrybed the same /[1]

And when as he and all the navie of Shipps weare arryved in sight of the head land, named the Queenes Foreland, and weare entred within the straightes the first daye of July, beinge the first tyme of their entrye in this voyadge, they weare putt backe againe owt of the sight thereof by stormes and by Ise and within vj or vii dayes after that commynge againe to the sight of the northe syde thereof they weare putt backe againe to the sowthe side thereof, which land was to them unknowen/ And this uppon Conference Christofer Hawlle and Robert Davies Masters affirmed it like to be soo, and Captaine Furbysher with Jeames Beare affirmed it to be the northe lande by Hawlls Iland, which is xx leages from this place, with outragious oathes of affirmacion and woords of reproche against Hawlle, whereuppon Hawlle with iii Shipps trustinge his

[f. 8r] knowledge retorned backe againe, [2] but Captaine Furbusher with ix Shipps that trusted his knowledge followed one their waye still forwardes takinge him selfe to be within the right straight leadinge to the Countes Sownd wheare is their porte of ladinge, and so thorowghe his obstinat ignoraunce he lede that flett of Shipps lx leages alongest a Coast of land unknowen, enduringe manye stormes in extreeme danger oftetymes of perrishinge amongest rocks and Ise, by the space of xviii dayes and so by the great favour of god escaped and retorned backe againe to the head land of the Queenes foreland, and from thence about into the right Straights passinge by Jackemans Sownde in a verrye cleare daye, which he did not knowe unto their right porte in the Countes Sownd, which place also when he came to the sight of it he did not knowe but woold have gonne to Gabriels Ilande which is 20. leages beyonnd it, had not one Christofer Jackesone trompeter perswaded him of his error therein. [3]

He had specyall Commission in writinge and great charge in this theird voyage to cause to be made some further discoverye of that Countrye, beyonde the place where he lost his v. men in the first yeare, and otherwise whereby to have some better knowledg of the passadge into the Sowthe Sea, which with one of the smalle barkes and pynnasses he might have caused to be doonne, betwen the tyme of his arryvall at the Countes Sownd which was the xxx[th] of July and his departure from thence, beinge the seconde daye of September, for the doinge whereof he was put in minde sundrye tymes by Christofer Hawlle, and Charles Jackeman Shipemasters who offered their service therein, which service he did putt of from tyme too tyme, sayenge that he woold fynde a tyme for it, but he employed all his tyme onely to the seakinge and digginge of mynes, for Ewre to lade so in anye Shipps wherewith-all he had encombred him selfe, that him selfe had no tyme to do anye thinge els / And his mind beinge so vayne glorious, that he will not suffer anye discoverye to bee made

---

[1] Margin note: 'he sayd that his Commission was but the device of Fenton and Lok'.

[2] Margin note: 'he woold not take consaile but obstinatly carried the shipps to a wrong place in extreme perill throughe his ignorans contrarie to Commission'. Hall's own account of the encounter (document 6, p. 116) largely bears out Lok.

[3] Parenthesis crowded into text: 'where he would haue caried all the ships to harbour into an unknowen place amonge the Rockes, sweringe that it was the Countes sound, yf two mariners named stuborn & Lunt had not shewed hym his errour'. Clearly, Lok's account here is drawn from that of his 'servant', Edward Selman (document 9, p. 181).

without his owne presens, so much tyme was putt of that nothinge at all is doon therein / And so that Service which was the cheife entent of the Companye and first cause of the begininge of all these costly voyags is utterly frustrated and deade /[1]

He had speciall Commission in writinge to sett downe Articles and orders in writinge, to be deliuered amongest the fleet of shipps at the departure owtewards from hence in this theird voyadge, whereby all the Fleet of Shipps might keape them selues togethers at Sea and aswell for their saftye against Enemyes, and other misfortune as alsoo for salfe comminge to their place appointed for their ladinge and like for salfe passage in retorninge with their ladinge from thence homewards againe / And nowe when as the Shipps weare mored salfe[2] in harbor in the Countes of Warwicks Sownd, wher they shoold lade and from thence orderly shoold have departed with their ladinge home-wards againe he beinge then with the myners at beares Sownd, wheare most of their ladinge was had, which is 7. leages from the Counts Sownd, and having now but ii boates ladinge of Ewre to send thether to make full the Aydes ladinge which he might have sent thether and havinge with him 80. men and their furnitur to Shippe and bestowe in the shipps, he sent woord to the Countes sownd, Commandinge all the Shipps to com to beares sownd to take in him with his men and their furniture, which place beinge no harbour but wild open Sea uppon Rocks straight uppon their Comminge to an Anker, ther happened a gale of winde verry strong with storme which putt all their Shipps from their Ankers and drove the to sea to save them selves with losse of all their boats and pynnasses and some men and other spoyle whereby they were forced to leave behinde them one land their generall Captaine and all his men to helpe them selfes as they coold, with the barke Gabriel and pynnasse boate, wherewithall they went to Sea and by good fortune[3]

[f. 8v] mette with the Shipps Anne Fraunces, Judeth and Michael, which toke in the men, and the generall Captaine remayned still in the Gabriell, wherewithall he cam into Englande. And by this meanes all the whole fleet of Shipps weare scattered and seperated a sunder and cam home straglinge by one alone and ii togethers a longe tyme and a farre waye a sunder one not knowing of another but euery one as they coold shifte and helpe them selfes, throwghe all dangers in suche disorders as is openly knowen and so they arryved at home by Gods providence more then by this mans pollicy.

Abowt a moneth before the retorne home of anye of all these Shipps here arryved at Har-wiche one of the fraighted shipps named the Thomas of ypswiche *Master* [blank] Stam-ford, who had neuer benn in that Countrye, whereof was for pylott Richard Cox gonner

---

[1] Margin note: 'he woold not suffer anye further discouere to be made of the passage contrarie to Com-*mission*'. Lok's accusation is not supported by the letter of Frobisher's instructions (document 2, p. 60), which required him to undertake these tasks only 'yf Leasure and tyme wille *permitt* the same'. Being four weeks overdue at his destination, Frobisher had every reason to consider the qualification redundant.

[2] Safely.

[3] Margin note: 'he com*m*aundethe the shipps owt of salfe porte to a dangerous roade, wheareby they cam home in suche disorder with soo great spoile, contrarie to Com*mission*'. In fact, Fenton (document 8, p. 189) stated that Frobisher took only those five ships which still had room for further lading to Beare Sound on 1 September; the other vessels (other than *Anne Frances* and *Judith*) remained at anchor at Corbett's Point until the following day, and then came on after to rendezvous with the fleet

who had benn in that newe Countrye for *Master* Gonner of the Ayde in the Second voyadge, this Shipp beinge entered intoo the straights in Companye of all the Fleete of Shipps, the first of July was putt backe againe *with* yse as all the rest weare, which putt them in great feare and yet they remayned still *with* other of the Shipps uppon the Coast to and from untill the 8 August having susteyned great dangers of yse and rocks as they sayd, *which* discoraged them from attemptinge anye more to enter intoo the straights, and therefore beinge then gonn owte of sight of the other Shipps the pilott was cleane discoraged to tarrye anye longer in that Country, and soo at that daye made hid Course homewards againe for England against the will of the Captaine william Tandfield and so beinge arryved at Harwiche one the (blank) daye of September, *with*out havinge anye lycens of the generall Captaine Furbysher to de*part* and *with*out havinge ben aland at the place appointed for their ladinge but retorned as she went / to excuse this theire owne Feare and to shewe some just cause of their retorne home so disorderly the pilott alleged terrible dangers of yse not possible to be passed thorowghe that drove them home, and gave reporte of the rest of the Shipps to be almost perished amongst the yse or extreame dangerouslye escaped, and so as they coold not come to their porte to have anye ladinge at all, the *which* proved false tales, in fewe dayes after, uppon the salfe retorne home of all the xv Shipps that went owt in this voyadge, except one Shipp named the barke Dennys who suncke their amongst the Rocks of yse by negligent regard of their owne men.[1]

Nowe Captaine Furbusher beinge retorned home againe one this third voyadge in the barke Gabriell he arryved at Foye in Cornewall the 25 daye of September 1578[2] / *which* was the first newes that was hard of his salftye. And shortly after him weare hard of other Shipps, and longe tyme after all the rest allsoo arryved in sondrye places of the Realme north & sowthe / And imedyatly uppon his arryvall he repaired to the Coort at Richemond to her Ma*jes*tie and from thens to London whereuppo*n* was no smale Joye conceaved on all *partes* cheifly of the salftie of the men, thoughe manye of them died of sicknes by the waye at their retorne, but specyally for the treaser he brough*te with* him having laden all the Shipps *with* suche ritche Ewre of gold worthe lx[li] and lxx[li] a tonn as he sayd, sweared and published in all the Courte the Citie and so in the Country, thoughe it be not so found, but whatsoeuer it be it must be thankefully accepted, for hathe donne his good will to bringe the best that he coold fynd, besyds sutch number of Gewells and precious stonnes, as he talked of and *perchance* secretly hathe fownd and selt.[3]

[f. 9r] And as all these Shipps in the moneth of October and Novemb*er* did arryve in the Thamis, their ladinge of the Ewre was dischardged aland at Dartford, and bestowed in her Ma*jes*ties howsse theire / And by this tyme off their arryvall, the great buildings of the workehowses made there at Dartford by the order and direction of Jonas him selfe for the

---

[1] Margin note: 'the shippe thomas of ypswich retorned home *with*owt ladinge with false newes that all the shipps were lost'.

[2] This is the only account to identify Frobisher's first landfall upon his return to England.

[3] Margin note: 'Captaine Furbusher retorned home the theird voyage with great glorie of gold and Jewells'. Cf. Mendoza's comments (document 13, p. 251) regarding 'white sapphires' and 'mediocre rubies'.

melting and refyninge and workinge of this Ewre, was at appoint of redynes to worke the same Ewre / And allso weare nowe come iiii workemen which he had sennt for owt of Saxonye and Germanye and allso was come certaine Mynerall Markesit of seacolle which he had sent for from New Castell by Humfrye Colle /[1]

And heareuppon Commission was directed from her Majesties pryvie Councell unto Sir Thomas Gresham, Sir Leonell Duckett, William Pelham, Thomas Randolphe and the rest of the Commissioners appointed, dated the xxx of October 1578 willinge them to see good proffe and tryall made of the valewe of this Ewre brought home this theird voyadge / Whereuppon the Commissioners called before them Jonas and the other workemen, and toke order with him for the workeinge of some quantitie of Ewre in the great works, And for his first proffe thereof he with the helpe of his iiii men workemen which weare broughte owte of Germanye did melt down at Dartford one the 8. daye of November twoo tonnes of Ewre of the Second voyage in the iii Furnaces putting thereto for addittament certaine of the markesite of seacole brought from New Castell and other things, which woorke proved verye evill woorke, by reason as he sayd of that seacole Markesit beinge but a boddye of Sulfer / And allso of the evill frame of the bellowes made by the Carpenter / And after one the xii[th] and xiii[th] daye of november, he melted other twoo tonnes of the Ewre of the theird voyadge in the presens of Sir Thomas Gresham and the rest of the Commissioners which proved somewhat reasonable, but was farr from the ritches looked for / wherewithall the Commissioners departed to London, and hereby the Ewre brought home by Captaine Furbusher grewe into great discredit / whereuppon followed muche hurte unto manye that had dooings in these voyages /[2]

In this meane tyme of these evill works at Darteford and allso longe tyme after Captaine Furbysher was there contynually solyciting the furtherauns of the works, that he might have some good newes to carrye to her Majestie, for a knighthood which hee hoaped for, but the matter happened farr contrary to his expectacion / And whiles he was there at Dartford, he shewed him selfe like a generall misrewlar in manye matters following as he had donne in manye others before, thoughe he coold not there have rulle and Commaund all things as he lyst him selfe a lone as he had done at Sea and abroade/[3]

Uppon the arryvall of the Shipp the Judethe at Dartford Creek The Captaine Fenton went to the Towne of Dartford to have order to unlade the Shipps and to visit Captaine Furbysher who was there longe before, And at their meatinge Captaine Furbysher uppon his former quarrelous humor which he had uttered before at Meta incognita entered nowe agayne into quarrelous speache with Captaine Fenton, and uppon the sodaine drewe his dagger at him, and woold have mischeved him yf Master william pelham and others had not ben present & pacyfied that stryffe /[4]

[f. 9v] When the Shippe Ayde was arryved at Dartford Creeke and remayned longe tyme there before she coold be unladen he Captaine Furbysher remayned one land with jonas

---

[1] Margin note: 'the shipps dischardged their Ewre at Dartford'.
[2] Margin note: 'Jonas first proffe of great works at Darteforde'.
[3] Margin note: 'Captaine Furbusher at darteford works with evill rule'.
[4] Margin note: 'Captaine Furbusher abuseth C. Fenton at Darteford'.

and the workemen of the Ewre at the mills and left the Shipps goods at discretion of the evill boateswaine named Alexander Creeke, and of his owne men because he was vitteler of the Shippe, and sayd that he had muche goods of his owne in the Shippe / And woold not cause to be sent owt of the Shippe intoo the Storehowsse at London, suche takle munition merchandizes and goods as weare in the Shippe superfluous, but suffered the same to lie there still without purpose comberinge the Shipp of her unladinge, and at Bandon[1] to the pilferinge of manye evill men in the Shippe / neither woold he cause to be made anye Inventorie thereof at their arryvall, thoughe he had one speciall article in his Commission so to doo, whereuppon the Commissioners gave order to the master Christofer Hawlle to send the same goods one land by Inventorie, which he did soo,[2] And because the master did so when he Captaine Furbysher was absent at Dartford, he made great storme and radge thereat sayenge the master and Master Lok ought not to medle in that matter beinge his office and chardge, And that it was the Gonners Fees to have so mutch powder as woold chardg all the ordenaunce in the Shippe, And the boateswayne Fees to have manye parcells of the tackelinge, which in deede they had not at that tyme, whatsoeuer they had before of a great nomber of things, that are pilfered and consumed to the valewe of CCC. pounds appearinge by Inventarye made thereof /[3]

Mychaell Lok beinge Treasorer and havinge the cheife chardge of the workehowses and goods therein at Dartford, for the which he was to giue accompt to the Companye, And having placed there Edward Casteline as his deputie, who then was soo occupied in providinge of Carts, lighters, laborers, and things necessarye for the unladinge of the Ewre owt of the Shipps into the Storehowsse in her Majesties howsse at Darteford, that he coold not as yet be present at the works of the Mills, hee thought good for a tyme untill other order weare considered, to geve the keyes of the workehowes dores at the mills to the keapinge of Richard Rawson host of the Bull at Dartford & post of her Majestie, in whose howsse Michael Lok was still lodged beinge well knowen unto Master Thomas Randolphe for a verye honest mane, and one who had byn and daylie was greatly furtheringe to the buyldings of the workhowses, and other busines daylye happeninge there, which thinge Captaine Furbysher greatly mislyked uppon a pryvat Quarrell against him, for mallice betwene hym and one parker the host of Captaine Furbysher whereuppon with great oathes and rages he flewe uppon Rawson revyling him and plucked the keyes from hym and bracke his head with them, and gave them to his owne Cossyn and Servinge man william hawks,[4] A man not to be trusted by M. Lok and swore noe smale oathes that M. Lok nor no man ells shoold be porter of that howsse nor command anye thinge in the worke there without his good will and likinge, this was donn openly in the workehowsse when the

---

[1] i.e. Abandoned.

[2] On 23 February 1578(9), Sir William Winter and Sir William Holstock (in their respective capacities as Surveyor and Controller of the Queen's ships) conducted a full inventory of the *Ayde* (PRO SP/12/129, 36). They make no mention in their very detailed report of any missing equipment.

[3] Margin note: 'he abuseth the Commissioners for unlading the goods owt of the Ayde withowt his commaund'.

[4] Hawkes appears to have been Frobisher's personal servant for many years. He received an annuity of £6. 13s. 4d. in Frobisher's will, though subsequently he failed to secure this from the heir at law, Peter Frobisher (PRO PCC 2 Scott; REQ/2/221, 25).

men weare at worke in presens of the Commissioners the 12. november, the which hurte Rawson did quietly beare, and this Insolency M. Lok did

[f. 10r] quietly putt uppe having respect to the works in hand /And so the keyes remayned with Captaine Furbushers man at his masters Commaund of all things in the workehowses he beinge then lodged at the Farme of the Mills withowt anye a ccoumpt to be geven for that no Inventorie was then made thereof whereby followed great wast and pilferye of the Cooles, woode and other things of the Companye as will appeare.

After this that[1] he had remayned at Darteford this longe tyme, and no good works coold be made there, whiche caused the cheife venturers to withoold their mooney dewe for the payment of the Shipps fraight and mens wages, nowe retorned home to the some of more then vj.^m pounds / And the marryners and men callinge and cryenge on him daylie for the same, he retorned to London, with minde to goo to the Court him selfe to solicit the venturars to paye their mooney / And when he had doone there what he coold and fownd there that coold sute that M. Lok had fownd amongest them for the space of iii weeks before wherein no mooney cowld be had of no venturer, but oneley her Majesties parte beinge xj^c l.^li /And Master Secretarye Willsones parte beinge lv^li / which was payed to M. Lok which he likewise payd owte againe for fraight of the Shipps and wages of men and other nedefull busynes of the Companies appearinge in his accoumpts, whereby was no more mooney to be had for to paye the rest of the mens wages and the fraights dewe to the twoo Shipps nowe retorned and unladen at Dartford, for the pryvat accoumpt of Captaine Furbusher which had no assuraunce for their mooney, but onely the bare Creedit and promis of Captaine Furbusher, and he beinge now cleane owte of all Creditt by occasion of the discreditt of the works don at Dartford he nowe cameth to Michael Lok for mooney of whome he was wonnt allwaies to be holpen at his request, but nowe Michael Lok beinge not able to salve this sore, by reason that he coold gett no more mooney amonge the venturers / And his owne Creditt allsoo utterly fayllinge uppon the discredit of the works at Darteford, wherein he had for his parte more then xxiiii^c pounds well knowen to his Creditors which woold be his undoinge yf the Ewre at Dartford shoold prove naught / And so Captaine Furbusher beinge now utterly destitute of mooney he cometh to the howsse of M. Lok one the xx^th daye of November, with a band of xl. men at his heeles, and there openly in great radge and furye exclaimed one M. Lok, in this wise, sayenge thow hast cossyned my Lorde of Oxford of m.^li / thow haste made false accompts and deceavyd the Companye of iii.^m pounds, thow hast not one groat venture in all theis voyages, thow art A bankeroot knaive, and swore by gods bludd he woold pull him owtt of his howsse by the eares, All which villanus reproches M. Lok did beare quietly for that tyme, knowinge them to be false, and thinkinge C. Furbusher to be either dronke or made / And so C. Furbusher departed, and proclaymed all theis Sclaunders against him, in the Coorte, and in the Royall Exchange and everywhere in London and others (sic) places where he came / And withall gave Informacion to her Majesties honorable pryvie Councell and procured new Commissioners and newe Awditors of Michael Loks accoumpts which had ben awdited before by others, which sayd newe Commissioners and Awditors have fownd

---

[1] *Sic.*

the accompts and dooings of Michael Lok to be trewe and the sayengs of C. Furbusher to be false / And so Michael Lok is then satisfied of this great Iniurye against Captaine Furbusher, and hathe troden it all under footte at the intreatye of the sayd Commissioners of late, reseruinge his dewtye towards the Companye.[1]

[f. 10v] Wheareas the Shippe Thomas of ypeswiche retorned home from Meta incognita without lycence and emptie without any ladinge, because they cowld not or wold not goe to their ladinge place for it, and arryved at millford in wales the 6. September And the Commissioners ordeyned to paye the myners of that Shippe beinge xv men but for iiii monethes wages, he Captaine Furbusher of his owne awthoritye did paye them v. moneths wages/[2]

He hathe browght into wages of the Companye, so manye men and suche manner men as he lyst and manye of them at suche great wages as he lyst, under name of valliant men, tale men, and proper men, withowt regard of their sarvice of defects, but for frendshipp whereof manye of them rone awaye, with great payes, to the great chardgs of the Companye /[3]

The Shippe Ayde beinge dischardged of her ladinge at Dartford and remaining in the Thamis at London, he did place in her against the Commaundment of the Commissioners a number of men at the Companyes Chardgs without cause or dewtye, whereof manye weare suche disordered men of their hands as made great pilferye and spoyle of the goods in the Shippe and allso of their toongs as raysed great sclaunder to the Companye, by their false clamours and exclamacions made for their wages, and yet had but smale dewtye of wages owing to them when their accompts weare examyned perticulerly /[4]

He sayd at Darteford and other places that him selfe is the greateste venturer in all theise voyages, except the Queene and thearle of Oxford / And yet him selfe hathe not one pennye venture therein but C. poundes which the Companye gave him in parte of viii[c] pounds which he hathe had of them for his owne wages and sarvice in thes voyadgs / besides the Enterteynment of xv. of his Sarvinge men & Followers in twoo years voyags, in the name of Soldiers, marryners & myners, which have cost the Companye iiii[c] pounds, and besids v[c] pounds of mooney which remayneth still in his hands, at this daye dewe to the Companye, upon his accoumpt, not yet awdited, and perchaunce never wilbe payd them. And yet he reporteth dayly that he hathe had nothing at all of the Companye for all his service /[5]

He had specyall Commission in writinge boeth in his second voyadge and allso in his theird voyage, to keape good accoumpt in a booke in writinge of his doings in the gouerment of the same voyadges and of suche matters as shoold happen therein, boeth at Sea and

---

[1] Margin note: 'he abuseth M. Lok with sclaunderous reports and false tales'. This, perhaps the most colourful passage of the 'Doinges', is also one of the most credible. The occasion of Frobisher's visit, together with his assiduous promotion of the same accusations around the city, was almost certainly the catalyst for Lok's removal as treasurer of the 'company' some days later.

[2] Margin note: 'he payeth men more wages then is dewe to them'.

[3] Margin note: 'he chardgethe the Companye with what and how he lyst'.

[4] Margin note: 'he chargeth the Companye with men in the Ayde against the Commissioners'.

[5] Margin note: 'his smale venture in the voyages and his great wagis for his service'.

one land / And at his retorne home to delyver the same booke, to remayne for Instruction of those that thereafter shoold take chardge in these voyags for the Companye / And allso for that purpose her Majesties honorable pryvye Counsell have written their lettres unto the Commissioners, willinge them to calle into their hands from all men, that tooke chardge in these voyages, all suche books, Cartes, and writings, as they had made thereof, whereuppon divers of them have browght in the same, which remaine with Michael Lok for the Companye / aperinge in a book of regester kept thereof / And he Captaine Furbusher beinge requested divers tymes to bringe in his and to shewe his owne dooings therein, he doeth hetherto refuse to doo the same, whereby it semeth he hath not keapt anye accompt at all thereof in neither of boeth these voyages, contrarye to his Commission and contrarye to the dewtye of a carefull Gouernor /[1]

[f. 11r] He had specyall Comission in writinge in this theird voyadge to cause to bee made smale Sayes perticulerly of all the seuerall Mynes, that should be fownde and the same to be regestered in a booke, and allso of the same mynes to be keapt smale peces of Ewre for Samples, with marks writen whereby to knowe the places where they weare fownd, And the same at his retorne home to be delyvered to the Commissioners whereby to knowe the good from the badd, and what to do best heareafter / but of this matter he hath not shewed anye accompt at all of his dooings therein, but sayd that he had layed upp divers peces of the seuerall mynes fownd, which he putt into a benche in his Cabyn of the Shippe the Ayde, and sayd that at the sea in a storme of wether that Cabbyn was brast open and so all is gonn which is to be examyned better of Robert Denham, and of the Master and men that weare in the Shippe for that as yet the same is not so fownd to be doon.[2]

Her Majestis honorable pryvie Councell wrotte their lettres to the Commissioners at the retorne home of the Shipps in the theird voyadg, willing them amongest other matters to cause all the Captaines and Masters of Shipps to cause to be brought unto the Commissioners all peces of Ewre and Stoones thought or named to be diamants, Saphires Rubies and other like things which the men of the Shipps had fownd and did conceale and hyde, whereuppon divers things weare brought in by divers men appearinge in a Booke of Register remayninge with Michael Lok and Christofer Hawle Master of the ayde had collected a great quantity of a Busshell of divers men of that Shippe and others, which he delyvered to Captaine Furbusher who keapeth them still from knowledge of the Commissioners /[3]

For the better sarvice of the Companye in their desire of discoverye of Countries to Cathay in these voyages weare provided divers Instruments of mettall for navigacon, Globes, spheres, astrolabes and others which cost L. pounds of mooney which nowe do

---

[1] Margin note: 'he givethe none Accompt of his Governement in the voiage, nor of what has happened therein'.

[2] Margin note: 'he hath not brought samples nor sayes of the mines fownd in their places'. The occasion was probably that of 4 o'clock of the morning of 14 September, when the sea had burst into Frobisher's cabin and almost swept away the helmsman of the *Ayde*, Francis Austen (document 6, p. 127). As Frobisher was elsewhere in the Atlantic at that moment, struggling to bring an overloaded *Gabriel* safely back to England, blame for the loss can hardly be laid at his door.

[3] Margin note: 'he deteyned the minerall Ewre and Jewell stones had of men of the Ayde'.

remayne in possessyon of Captaine Furbusher who is not willinge too restore them and therefore must paye for them /[1]

And whereas for the furniture of the C. men to Inhabit in Meta incognita under Captaine Fenton an infinit number of things and Implements weare provided and sent with them for their relief and service / it hathe come to passe throwghe the overthrowe of that purpose of habitacion which cost the Companye vj^m pounds, that great havocke and waste hathe benn made of things provyded, throughe the choppinge and changinge of those men from one shipp too an other in the voyadge, and stowinge of those goods from one shippe to an other, whereby the chardge thereof hathe come to sondrye mens hands withowt care or dewe accoumpt, that of the victualls provided, the most parte of them are eaten and wasted to the valewe of xii^c pounds, and the rest buryed there in Meta incognita under grownd and also of the implementes the which is lost, to the valewe of vj^c pounds, besydes a nomber of Implements pillfered, stolen, consumed and wasted in the voyadge, without anye accoumpt to the valewe of v^c pounds appearinge by Inventarye thereof collected at home /[2]

Forasmuche as the former works made by jonas with the Ewre at Dartford in November last had suche evill successe as cowld not be worse / muche enquirye was madd by the Commissioners of the cawse and fawlt thereof / whereunto Jonas answered the fawlt

[f. 11v] to be in the seacole markesite / whereuppon was provided from Keswicke Copper mines, certaine mineralls of his owne chose uppon a smale saye thereof which he had mad, one tonn of lead Ewre and one tonn of a Copper markesite, which was browght by land from thens to darteford by conduct of Robert Denham / So as one the 29 daye of December Jonas made at dartford a great proffe of a tonn of the Ewre of the Second voyadge with the addittaments of lead Ewre and markesite browght from Keswicke which worke was donn in presens of Captaine Furbusher who made a greate hast thereof to have presented it unto her Majestie for a newe years gifte to bringe him a knighthoode / but this worke also succeaded but evill, throwghe his hast made thereof / whereuppon Jonas did translate one of the Furnaces and made an other great proofe of halfe a ton of the Ewre of the Judeths ladinge with the fore sayde addittaments of lead Ewre and markesit browght from Keswicke which was molten the 20 Januarye in presens of Captaine Furbusher alone by the Commissioners order which worke was as the Ewre of the Judeth was fownd to bee worthe x^{li} of mooney the tonn which was somewhat comfortable and that great fault was yet still remaininge in the workemanship which Jonas promised to mend the next tyme /[3]

At this meane tyme of these works at Darteford, Captaine Furbusher was there alone[4] to Commission where he played his parte of generall misrule, he spake his evill pleasure

---

[1] Margin note: 'he deteyneth the Instruments of navigacon of the Companye'.

[2] Margin note: the great provicion for the C. men to inhabitt with Capten Fenton is consumed and gonne'.

[3] Margin note: 'Jonas second proffe of great workes at dartford, which is with minerall additament of Keswyke mynes'.

[4] Supply 'according'.

against Master Lok, who had the chardge as accountant to the Companye for all the Goods at Darteford, he took the keyes of the workehowses from Edward Castelyne, there beinge in Chardge under Master Lok and reviled him, with villanous speach & thratenings and the like did he to one of Master Loks servaunts named Charles Sledd / All which Injuryes was borne quietlye for the Commissioners to reforme which they did not /[1]

Allso the Commissioners made him Captaine Furbusher Surveyor of these twoo great meltinge works of Jonas at Dartford to thend the same workes might be donne withall perfection and secretly & thriftelye with little cost, which he promised to performe with xl.ˢ chardgs, yet was yet requisite to build a little rostinge furnace which Jonas required to have donne, and for the dooings thereof C. Furbusher receaved of Master Allyn v.ˡⁱ of mooney by the Commissioners appointment / And nowe hathe he donne this busynes there so well and so secretly that none accoumpt at all is keapt of all his dooings therein that tyme, neither what tymbers woode and other stuffe, he toke uppe and provided for those works, neither what nomber of workemen weare in wages in these works / but by that which longe afterwards is inquired at Dartforde, it is verye like that the same smale worke which he sayd woold cost v.ˡⁱ will not be cleared with xl.ˡⁱ which is wages to divers men at Darteford for the same / And therefore noe account at all is kept by Captaine Furbusher nor by anye other man for that he woold not suffer Master Castelyn nor anye man but hym selfe and his men to see nor knowe what was donne there neither woold he suffer anye accountt to be taken by Master Loks men of the weight of the lead and other stuffe of the Companyes, which apperteyned unto that worke but sayd that him selfe woold accountt for all, and no man but him selfe shoold meddle anye more there, for the which he is to be called to accoumpt that eache man maye have his dewtye /[2]

[f. 12r] These works beinge thus doone at Darteford, they did not please the new Commissioners , nor yet did like the cheife Venturers for any fowndacyone / Whereuppon to be at chardgs to provid addittaments for the great works to be done with the Ewre at Darteford, but great blame was layed one Jonas for his evill worke at Dartford and whye he cowld not make that worke nowe as good as he had mad his worke the last yeare, at Tower hill of CC. weight of the same Ewre, and thereuppon muche suspicion grewe of some false dealings to have benn usyd the last yeare in the works at Tower hill either by Jonas or by Robert Denham or by Captayne Furbusher or by Master Lok or by some other man / And therefore the newe Commissioners to saye Sir Thomas Gresham, Sir Leonell Duckett, Captaine Fenton, Captaine Yorke, Thomas Allyn, Christofer Huddesdon, who had seen nothing of the works donne the last yeare at the Tower hill, they woold nowe be satisfied them selves in the dooings thereof / And soo commanded Jonas to worke and melt CC. weight of the Ewre at the Tower hill, even of the same Ewre, and in the same order as they had donne the yeare before, which Jonas willingly did graunt and in their presens one the xxiiᵗʰ daye of Marche 1578(9) he did so whereby was fownde the same Ewre to be

---

[1] Margin note: 'C. furbusher abuseth Ed. Castelin at dartford'. For this injury, Castelin may have had his revenge upon Frobisher some four years later, when his brother John, one of three Muscovy merchants appointed by Burghley to oversee preparations for the projected Moluccas voyage (of which Frobisher had been appointed commander), led moves to limit the influence of Drake and Frobisher in selecting personnel – one of the principal reasons, it was then inferred, for Frobisher's withdrawal from the project (Donno, *Madox*, p. 25; further discussion in McDermott, *Frobisher*, p. 278).

[2] Margin note: 'his disorder in the workes at dartford without Accoumpt of Jonas third proffe'.

worthe xv^{li} a ton, which these Commissioners did well like and judged the same to be with-owte anye falsehoode, beinge donne without the presens of anye of the owld Commission-ers, or parties aforesaid / And so these works rest for this tyme / which god graunt maye procead with good Successe /[1]

Captayne furbusher being yet not quiett that Master Castelyn or any man for Master Lok shoold remayne at Darteford sowght all meanes to thrust them owtt and to thrust in him selfe because he had geven suche great speaches at Darteford that he woold soo doo / and because he and his men when they weare there had warme, beinge by the Companyes Fier / And therefore sowght meanes amongest the Commissioners that some more proffes might be made at Darteforde, by water works of Cornishe men or by Fier worke of Jonas / and that he might have the chardge thereof and Master Castelyn to be putt owt of the place but the Commissioners lokinge to the Companyes proffitt in savinge wages, thowght it good to sent to Dartford one of their Sarvaunts named Edward Selman, who went thether the xvth of Aprill 1579 and toke the Chardge at the hands of Master Castelyn of all things thereby Inventorye, and allso the keyes of all the workehowses aswell of Master Castelyn as allsoo of William Hawks Captaine Furbushers kinesman whoe with heavie harte delivered them owt of his possessyon and within fower dayes afterward Captaine Furbisher himselfe wente to dartford and uppon his owld braberinge humor revyled Master Castelyn, and bete Edward Selman abowt the head and with his dagger had almost cloven his head, which Edward Selman hathe complayned to the Commissioners and so the matter restethe as it is/[2]

Now after all these many sayes, proffes, and trialls made of the Ewre of Meta incognita, in smale, and in great, at Tower hill, at Dartford, and other places, by Jonas, Robert Denham, Baptista Angello,[3] william Humfrey and manye other workemen professinge still in the Arte whereby the goodnes and ritchnes of this Ewre did satisfie the woorkemen & some of the venturers to procead to provid the Mynerall additaments requisitt for the workinge of all the Ewre in the great woorks at Darteford;[4]

[f. 12v] which Jonas had longe tyme before and oftentymes declared to the Com-missioners that it must be had before the Ewre can be wrought to the perfection desired / yet neverthelesse the cheife of the venturers weare not yet satisfied in the goodnes of this matter, nor woold consent to provid these additaments / Whereuppon Jonas and Denham and the Dutche workemen seinge them selves destitute of their wages, and discredited in all that they had donn, and they knowinge the goodnes of the Ewre, and what was to be done in the woorks / They determined to make offer unto the Companye of a bargaine and to buye all the xiii^c tonn of Ewre at Darteford, at xx marks mooney for the tonn / and to woorke it them selues at their owne chardgs / which offer was deliuered in writinge by Michael Lok the 18 Aprill 1579 unto the right honorable the Lord Highe Tresorer and to Master Secretarie Walsingham, togethers with an other writinge of nottes for officers requisite for the proceadinge in the great works of the Ewre at Darteford for the Companyes owne behalfe / and allsoo with an other writinge, wherein Michael Lok

---

[1] Margin note: 'the new Commyssioners cause Jonas to make a new proff of CC. of ewre at Tower hill'.
[2] Margin note: 'C. furbusher beatethe Ed. sellman att dartford, havinge charge of all there by the Com-missioners'.
[3] Sic.
[4] Margin note: Jonas offerethe a bargayne to buy all the Ewre at Dartford'.

desired to have owte his parte of the Ewre beinge Cl. tonn to woorke the same at his owne cost and chargs, for a tryall and example to the rest, the which sayd offer of bargaine to buye the Ewre, there honors did them selves like well / but shortely afterwards Captaine Furbusher hearinge thereof, and perceavinge that he was lefte owte of the bargaine and busynes, and was not made of Councell therein, which he thowght a disgrace unto him, especially at Darteford, he enformed her Majesties honorable pryvie Councell that the Ewre was worthe xl. pounds the tonn, and insenced their honors that this bargaine was a practise betwen Lok and Jonas, whereby to gett all the Ewre intoo their owne hands at that lowe price of xxtie marks the tonn, and soo to deceave the Companye, and keape from them the knowledge of the trewe vallewe of the Ewre / And likewise informed the Commissioners of the same matter / whereuppon great Stormes weare raysed in the Court and in the Cittie, bothe against M. Lok and against Jonas and the workemen / And theruppon the Commissioners sent for them at the theird daye of Maye to understand of the bargaine offered by Jonas, which M. Lok deliuered then to them in writinge / A Coppie of that deliueryd before to there honnors foresayd, the which sayd bargaine Sir Thomas Greshame and other the Commissioners did utterly dislike and sayd that it would be a greate dishonor unto her Majestie to make anye bargaine to sell awaye the Ewre, and therefore the Companye them selves showld procead in the great woorks thereof / And nowe uppon this determynacon of the Commissioners, Captaine Furbusher bestired hym selfe againe to gett some place and Awcthoritie in the works at darteforde and in this meane tyme he happened to Receave a lettre from the Duke Casimirus whome he had passed ouer Sea owt of England, wherein (as he sayed) the Duke writethe to him that he would send hym shortely owt of Germanye vj verye good workemen for the Ewre[1] / And hereof Captaine Furbusher geveth knowledge to her Majestis pryvie Councell, and condemeth Jonas to be but a knave, and boethe he & his workemen to be but fooles and Ignoraunt in the works / And so causes the

[f. 13r] works entirely to staye from proceadinge / And yet in the meane tyme him selfe practised with Jonas and Denham to have them joyne with him and his parteners, to procead to woorke the Ewre, for theire owne accoumpts accordinge to the bargayne offered by them, but Jonas and Denham utterly refused to joyne with hym in the works or anye other busynes of theires / but for the Companye do offer their Service to the best of their powre and by this meanes this bargaine and offer of the woorkemen was overthrowen / And allsoo the request of M. Lok for to worke his owne parte of the Ewre was refused / And yet the Companye them selves have not proceaded anye thinge at all in the woorks at Darteforde, but all lyethe still dead as yet to no smale damage of them selves and manye others, and greate discreditt of the matter withowt cause /[2]

[1] From 11 February – 3 March 1579, Frobisher had been at sea, transporting Duke Casimir and his men into the Low Countries in the ship *Foresight* (PRO E351/2215); it was probably during these days that he broached the subject of the Dartford works to the Duke. The timing of this sea commission, arising in the middle of a period of intense negotiations regarding the ore, seems unusual, unless it was intended to keep Frobisher from exercising his rather robust influence thereupon. The temptation that lured him away was a paltry 10 shillings per day board diet: an indication of his parlous financial situation by this time.

[2] Margin note: 'C. furbusher overthrowethe Jonas bargaine offered & hindreth the great works procedinges'.

And nowe to conclude these dooings of Captaine Furbusher / he is soo arrogaunt and obstinat in his government at Sea, as the Shippemasters Hawlle, Jackeman, Davis, Gibbes, and others will no more be under his government / And so insolent in his dooings amonge the Commissioners, as they are werye of his Companye / And soo prodigall and disordered in the Companyes busines, as manye of the venturers are minded to meddle no more with hym / And so full of lyenge talke as no man maye creditt hym in anye thinge that he doethe speake / And so impudent of his townge as his best frynds are most of all sclandered of hym when he cannott have his waie / And fynnally yf his dooings in these iii voyags bee well looked into, perchaunce he wilbe founde the most unprofitable Servaunt of all that have servid the Companye therein, as his Accoumpts will appeare /[1]

[f. 14r] Thaccompt of Captaine Furbussher.

Captayn furbusher is Debtor to the Company as FollowIth/
For the rest of his accompt of li. 1600 paid hym in monney
To furnishe the Ayd at bristowe, and to presse the Myners,
Wherof remayned in his handes uppon that accompt at his
Departure owt of England on this third voyage in monye

1578	Summ	li 645. 18.	0.
for monney he Receaved of the venturers in december 1578		li 262. 6.	8.
For his owne stock and venture in third voyag not yet paid		li 270. 0.	0.
	Summ	li 1178. 4.	8.
Whereof receaved as hereagaynst –		li 701. 5.	8.
And so he resteth debtor –		li 476. 19.	0.

More for Instrumenes of navigacion which he hathe, cost

50 li, but estemed at nowe, summ	li 40. 0.	0.
for marchaundiz and victualles he had in the voiage	li 46. 18.	8.
And so he owethe to the Companie	li 563. 17.	8.

And nowe he hath had of the Companye in monney for his own
Wages and Sarvice as Followeth

for the First voiag, Summ	li 80. 0.	0.
for the Second voiag, Summ	li 250. 0.	0.
For the Third voiag, Summ	li 428. 0.	0.
Summ	li 758. 0.	0.

Bysides the wages and victualles of all his sarving men
And followars, 18. men in two yeres, placed in the name of
Soldiars, maryners and mynars, which have cost the

Companye more then the somme of	li 400. 0.	0.
	li 1158. 0.	0.

---

[1] Margin note: 'C. furbushers general disordered dealynges'.

And more he hathe Endamagged the Company by his evill
Sarvice, and prodigallitie, as Followith –
For the Chardge of 28. Men taken with hym in the second
Voyag, above nomber, and contrarie to comission, and 50.
more Entertayned for a tyme, sum*m*   li   400. 0. 0.
For the Chardge of C. men taken with hym in the third
Voiag above nomber and contrarie to Comission –   li 1600. 0. 0.
For the fraight of two Shippes retorned home, of the 4.
Shipps taken with hym in the third voiag, above
nomber, and contrarie to Comission, sum*m*   li 1000. 0. 0.
For the takell, Implemente*s*, and goode*s* of the Shipps
In these voiages wasted, pilfered, and consumed, by evell
Officers and men in the Shipps, & evell governem(en)t therin   li 1200. 0. 0.
For the furniture provided for the C. men under Captayn
Fenton, to fortifie and inhabit there, w*h*ich vayne
Gloriouslie he caused to be provided, and afterwarde*s*
In that countrie utterlie did overthrowe the same, which cost   li 6000. 0. 0.
                                    Sum*m* of this damage   li10200. 0. 0.

[f. 14v] Captayn furbusher ys Creditor as followith/
For in Accoumpt he delivered in Aprill 1579 to the
Com*m*issioners, wh*i*ch is not yet Awdited, wherin he
Maketh paid li. 842. 11. 8. for wage*s* and victualle*s*
Of men and other matters, Lacking li. 316. 6. 0. of
Errors therin, so resteth li. 526. 5. 8. W*h*ich must
be Awdited -   li   526. 5. 8.
For his wages from the – of June 1578 to the last of
december 1578 is 7 monthes at li. 25 the month by
agreement of the Com*m*issioners –   li   175. 0. 0.
                                                                  li   701. 5. 8. [1]

---

[1] Clearly, Frobisher may only be regarded as substantially guilty of these charges if every misadventure to befall the three voyages, and the supremely flawed assumptions upon which they were despatched, were entirely the result of his 'doinges'. Insofar as Lok himself was one of the principal movers behind attempts to find value in the sample of ore returned from the first voyage, he must be regarded as at least as – and probably more – culpable than Frobisher himself for the expensive perpetuation of the enterprise beyond its failure to establish a sea-route to the East.

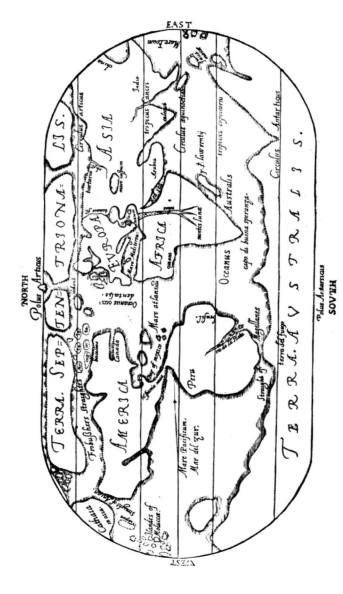

Plate IV: World map, from George Best's *Discourse*. Usually attributed to James Beare, master of Best's command, the ship *Anne Frances*, during the 1578 voyage. This is undoubtedly the most optimistic rendering of Frobisher's 'strait' – a passage of near oceanic dimensions in which only the fractured archipelago of Meta Incognita offers the slightest impediment to fleets making for the Far East. The Strait of Anian has been relegated to represent a mere western outflow of this vast feature.

By permission of the James Ford Bell Library, University of Minnesota.

DOCUMENT 6

Christopher Hall's ship's log[1]

In the Name of God Amen, this third voyage
of discovery and second voyage in the ayd Ayde[2]
begonne from *BRISTOW* the second day of May
this good Voyage pretended, w*hic*h I pray God
blesse in Anno 1578: by me Christopher Hawle.

The second of May 1578. friday, at 12. of clock at none we wayed our Ankers
in the Ayde in *King rode* the winde at North little winde, we hired 2. men
& 24. Oxen to draw owt *our* ship into the river mowth and there set sayle
into *King rode*, and there ankered being little winde.

The third of the said May, Saturday morning at 4. of the clock, the winde at
Nor east, a pretty gale, we wayed *our* anker & set sayle owt of *King rode*, and
sayled down to *Kettels Wood* and so down the channell betwene the 2. Sands
†[3] is *Posset* point and *Blackenor* point the one in the other in this order.

said not, that
the leading
marke between
Blackenor the
two sands

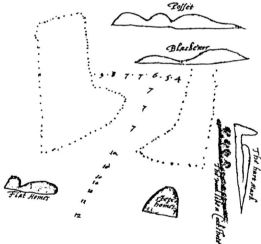

[1] Ship's log of the *Thomas Allen* (outward passage) and *Ayde* (return passage). The document is foliated,
with folio marks on the recto sheet only. As with document 8, the log format has been retained as far as possible. Although Hall (or John Dee, when copying his log) italicized some of his marginalia, for the sake of
clarity all such entries have been presented here in roman. Hall headed each page with the relevant month;
for September, however, several pages were wrongly marked 'August' and subsequently scored through. His
sketches, with annotations, have been retained.
[2] *Sic.*   [3] Insertion mark for adjacent margin note.

May 1578

In the Ayde

The 4. day of May 1578. Sunday the winde at West, S. West, I wayed and turned down of *Ellford come*[1] and there stopped the flud & set my Generall a shore, and so waye agayn, the winde as before.

The 5. day, Monday, the winde at W. Nor.W. a fayre gale being thwart of land to stop the flud I wayed & sayled S.W. & by W. to 12. of clock at None & then the winde viered with fog & rayne to the Nor.West, & there the ship sayled from 12. of clock at None to 5. of clock in the Morning S.W. & by S. and at that 5. of clock in the Morning, the Lands end East from me.

The 6. day, Tusday, the winde at Nor.West, the ship sayled from 5. of clock in the Morning, to 12. of clock at None, N.E. at that present beinge a Sowth sunn I did observe Latitude one myle from the *Lezard*

ID – 59   And fownd my elevation to be _____ *49.* grad.
     40   my aquinoctiall _____ *41.*
ID   my declination _____ *09.*
     19   my Latitude to be _____ *50.* truely observed
                                                     being a myle
                                                     from the
                                                     Lezard.[2]

In the Ayde

Note that the longest marke to go clere of the manickles,[3] is to kepe the *Lezard* a sayles bredth open of *Blackhed* to go clere withowt them & allso a sharp Steple with a broche to be pepte open over the land which serveth for the Lecke, that present day at 8. of clock at Night at anker in *Plymouth sownde.*

Thursday the 8. day of May 1578. I set sayle from *Plymouth sownd* in the *Gabriell*, the winde at Nor.West a fayre gale at 12 of clock at None and sayled Estward as hye as *Portland*, the winde at S.S.E. & then cam to anker till friday 6. of clock in the morning, & then the winde was as[4] S.S.W., I wayed & set sayle & plyed to the E.warde till yt was the 10. day at night and there ankered till the 11. day.

owt of the Gabriel

The 11. day, Sunday, in the morning, the winde then at S.E. & put rome with *Portchemowth* & there I landed & rode to *London*.

May 1578   [185]

In the Gabriel   The 26. day Monday, I set sayle in the *Gabriel* from *Blackwall* at 6. of clock in the morning the winde at W.S.W. and ankered at *Gravesend*.

[1] Ilfracombe.
[2] An interesting early illustration of the calculation of latitude, though Hall incorrectly states the equinoctial, which should be 40 degrees.
[3] The Manacle rocks, off Dean Point, Cornwall.   [4] *Sic.*

106

The 27. day of May 1578. Tuseday, I set sayle in the *Thomas Allin* from *Gravesend* at 5. of the clock in the morning, the winde at S.W. a fayre gale and ankered at the *Lade holland*, the cause was yt was a quarter to of the Nas[1] & not water to go over.

The 28. day, Wensday, I wayed & set sayle at 3 of clock in the morning & sayled over the Nas, the winde at S.W. a fayre gale & sayled into *Harwich* haven & there ankered.

The 30. day, friday, I wayed with the *Ayde* and towed down towards the havens mowth to a place called the *Altor*, & there ankered at 10. of clock in the forenone, & the same day at 8. of clock at night, the winde at N.E. I wayed in the *Ayde* & set sayle & sayled into the *Rolling growndes*, & there ankered all night.

The 31. day, Saturday, I set sayle at 8. of clock in the morning, owt of the *Rowling grownd* the winde at N.E. and turned down with the *Ayde* in the marks of the Slade of balesse & so launched hens to say, Sowth East, I sounded going owt at the Slade & fownd 5.6.7.8.9.10.11. 8.7.7.8.9.9.10.13.17.18.19.20.15.14. faddom, and whether I got 20. faddom, I sayled S. to go clere of the East side of the Goodione[2] & when I had 24. faddom, I sayled S. beinge (clere of the East)[3] S.W. to go with the master.

June 1578

chase of a
french man of
warr.

The 1. of June 1578. Sunday, the winde at N.E. & at 4. of clock in the morning, I was thwart of *Follstone*, & there we had sight of a french man-of warr which we gave chase to, & he sayled toward some of the coast of *Fraunce*, & the yt fell callme, & so we gave over the chase.

The second of June 1578, Monday, the winde at N.W. a fayre gale, the ship Sowth of Wight at 4. of clock in the morning.

In tho. Allin

The 3. of June, Tuseday, the winde at East a good gale of winde, the ship being thwart of *Plymouth sownd* at 3. of clock in the afternone, my Generall went a shore at Mount Edgcome, and all the flete sayled into the sownd, saving the Ayde & Thomas Allin, & there we lay a hull from tuseday 3. of clock to wensday 3. of clock the morning, & then set sayle & sayled Sowth West, & at 8. of clock that present day, I entred a bord the Thomas Allin.

The 4. day of June 1578, wensday at 8. of clock at night, the winde at South East, little winde and at that present 8. of clock at night the ship was from Lands end of England – 9.L.

[1] The Naze.
[2] Goodwin Sands.
[3] Erased.

The 5. day, thursday, from 8. of clock wensday at night till Thursday 8. of clock at night the ship sayled west – 41.L.

The 6. day friday, the winde at East a good gale the ship sayled west nor.west and at 8. of clock in the afternone I had sight of *Ireland* of the old head of *kensayl*.

The 7. day saturday, in the morning the winde at East S.E. (& by S. a fayre gale)[1], the ship was W.N.W. (& by W.)[2] from *Cap Clere* 8. leages at 4. of clock in the morning – 8.L.
from 4. of clock to 8. of clock at None[3] the wind at S.E. & by S. a fayre gale the ship sayled N.W. & by W. – 4.L.
from 8. to 12. of clock at None, the winde at S.E. & by S. a fayre gale the ship sailed N.W. & by W. – 4.L.
from 12. to 4. of clock at afternone the winde at S.E. & by S. a faire gale the ship sailed N.W. & by W. – 4.L.
from 4. to 8. of clock at night the winde at S.E. & by S. a fayre gale, the ship sayled N.W. & by W. – 4.L.

(The 8. day Sonday, from 4. to 8. of clock the forenone, the winde at S.E. & by E. a good gale)[4]
from 8 to mydnight the winde at E.S.E. a fayre gale, the ship sayled N.W. & by West – 4.L.
From Mydnight to 4. of clock in the morning [186] the winde at E.S.E. a good gale the ship sailed N.W. & by W. – 5.L.

The 8. day, Sonday, from 4. to 8. of clock the forenone the winde at S.E. & by E. a good gale, the ship sailed North West & by West – 6.L.
from 8. to 12. at None, the winde at S.E. a good gale the ship sayled N.W. and by W. – 8.L.
from 12. to 4. of clock at afternone the winde at S.W. the ship sayled N.W. & by West – 5.L.
from 4. to 8. of clock at night the winde at S.S.E. a fayre gale the ship sayled N.W. & by W. – 5.L.
from 8. to mydnight, the winde at S.S.E. a good gale, the ship sayled N.W. & by W. – 8.L.
from mydnight to 4. of clock in the morning, the winde at S.S.E. a good gayle the ship sayled N.W. & by W. – 7.L.
The 9. of June Monday from 4. to 8. in the forenone the winde at S.S.E. a fayre gale the ship sailed N.W. & by W. – 6.L.
from 8. to 12. at None the winde at S.S.E. a good gale the ship sayled N.W. & by West – 6.L.

---

[1] Erased.
[2] Erased.
[3] *Sic.*
[4] Erased.

from 12. to 4. of clock at afternone the winde at S.S.E. a fayre gale, the ship sailed N.W. and by W. – 6.L.

from 4. to 8. of clock the winde at S.S.E. little winde, the ship sayled North West & by West – 4.L.

from 8. to mydnight, the winde at S.E. a fayre gale, the ship sayled N.W. & by W. – 4.L.

from mydnight to 4. of clock in the morning, the winde at S.E. a fayre gale, the ship sayled North West & by West – 4.L.

The 10. of June, tuseday, from 4. to 8. of clock, the winde at S.E. a fayre gale, the ship sayled N.W. & by W. – 4.L.

from 8. to 12. at None, the winde at S.E. a fayre gale, the ship sayled N.W. & by W. – 4.L.

from 12. to 4. of clock at afternone, the winde at S.E. a fayre gale, the ship sayled N.W. & by W. – 4.L.

from 4. to 8. of clock at night, the winde at S.E. a fayre gale, the ship sayled N.W. & by W. – 5.L.

from 8. to Mydnight, the winde at S.W. little winde, the ship sailed N.W. & by W. – 3.L.

from Mydnight to 4. of clock, the winde calme, the ship sayled North West and by West – 1.L.

pricket Ø[1] The 11 of June, wensday, from 4. to 8. the forenone, calme from 8. to 12. at none, calme. Latitude 55 degr. 58 min. from 12. to 4. of clock at afternone calme. from 4 of clock, wensday at afternone to thursday 6. of clock at night calme.

The 12 of June, thursday, from 6. to 8. of clock at night the winde at S.S.E., a fayre gale, the ship sayled Nor.West & by West 3.L.

from 8. to mydnight, the winde at East a good gale, the ship sayled N.West & by West – 6.L.

from mydnight to 4. of clock, the winde at East a good gale, the ship sayled N.W. & by West – 8.L.

The 13 of June friday, from 4. to 8. the winde E. a good gale, the ship sayled N.W. & by West – 5.L.

from 8. to 12. of clock at None, the winde at East a good gale, the ship sayled N.W. & by West – 5½. L.

from 12. to 4. at afternone, the winde at E.N.E., a fayre gale, the ship sayled N.W. & by W. – 4½.L.

ID
forte, N.W.
and by West.
from 4. to 8. of clock, the winde at N.N.E., a fayre gale, the ship sailed W, and by West – 3.L.

from 8. to mydnight, the winde at N.E. a fayre gale, the ship sayled N.W. & by West – 4.L.

[1] That is, made no way in the sea.

from mydnight the winde at N.E. a fayre gale, the ship sayled N.W. & by W. – 4½.L.

The 14. day, Saturday, from 4. to 8. the winde at N.E. a fayre gale, the ship sayled N.W. & by W. – 5.L.

from 8. to 12. at None the winde at N.E. & by N. the ship sayled N.W. & by West – 5.L.

Pricket 4.

from 12. to 4. of clock at afternone, the winde at N.E. & by N, the ship sayled N.W. – 4½.L.

from 4. to 8. of clock, the winde at N. & by E, a fayre gale the ship sayled W.N.W. – 3.L.

from 8. to mydnight, the winde at North a fayre gale, the ship sayled W.N.W. – 4.L.

from mydnight to 4. of clock, the winde at North a fayre gale, the ship sayled W.N.W. – 4.L.

The 15 day Sunday, from 4. to 8. of clock in the forenone, the winde at N. a fayre gale, the ship sayled W.N.W. – 4.L. [187] from 8. to 12. of the clock at none, the winde at North little winde, the ship sayled West, N.W. – 3.L.

Latitude 58de–6^{m}

pricket 0.

from 12. at none, to 8. at night, little winde, the ship sayled West Sowth West – 2.L.

from 8. to mydnight, the winde at West S.W. a fayre gale, the ship sayled N.W. and by W. – 4.L.

from mydnight to 4. of clock in the morning, the winde at W.S.W. a fayre gale the ship sayled N.W. – 4.L.

The 16. day Munday, from 4. to 8. the winde at W.S.W. a fayre gale, the ship sayled N.W. & by W. – 4.L.

from 8. to 12. the winde W.S.W. a fayre gale the ship sayled N.W. & by W. – 3.L.

from 12. to 4. of clock at afternone, the winde at West, little winde, the ship sayled N.N.W. – 3.L.

from 4. to 8. the winde at West, little winde, the ship sayled N.N.W. – 2.L.

from 8. to mydnight callme.

from Mydnight to 4. of clock the winde at West S.W. little winde, the ship sayled N.W. & by W. – 1.L.

The 17. day, Tusday from 4. to 8. the winde at sowth S.W. a prety gale, the ship sailed S.S.W. – 3.L.

Latitude. 58de–44^{m}

pricket 0.

from 8. to 12. at None, the winde at S.E. a fayre gale, the ship sayled North West & by West – 5½.L.

from 12. to 4. of clock at afternone, the winde at Sowth E. a good gale, the ship sayled N.W. & by W. – 7.L.

from 4. to 8, the winde at S.E. a good gale the ship sayled N.W. & by W. – 8.L.

from 8. to Mydnight the winde at S.E. a good gale, the ship sayled N.W. & by W. – 8.L.

from mydnight to 4. of clock in the morning the winde at S.E. a good stout gale, the ship sailed N.W. & by W. – 9.L.

The 18 day Wensday from 4. to 8. in the fornone the winde at S.E. a stiff gale, the ship sayled N.W. & by W. – 9.L.

from 8. to 12. at None, the winde at S.E. a good gale, the ship sayled N.W. & by West – 8.L.

from 12. to 4. of clock at afternone the winde at East a good gale, the ship sailed North West – 8.L.

from 4. to 8. the winde at East N.E. a good gale the ship sayled N.W. – 9.L.

from 8. to mydnight the winde at E.N.E. a fayre gale, the ship sayled North West – 6.L.

from mydnight to 4. of clock in the morning, the winde at N.E. & by E. a fayre gale the ship sailed N.W. – 6.L.

The 19. day thursday, from 4. to 8., the winde at N.E. & by E, a fayre gale, the ship sailed N.W. – 6.L.

Latitude: 60.–06.

pricket 4.

from 8. to 12. at none, the winde at N.E. & by E. a fayre gale, the ship sayled N.W. – 6.L.

from 12. to 4. of clock, the winde at E.N.E. a faire gale, the ship sayled W.N.W. – 6.L.

from 4. to 8, the winde at E.N.E. a fayre gale, the ship sayled W.N.W. – 6.L.

The 20. friday from 8. to mydnight the winde at E.N.E. a good gale, the ship sayled W.N.W. – 8.L.

And at that present being 2. of clock in the morning, I had sight of *Friseland* being from me 5. leages in this forme

[1]

from *Dee's Pinacles*, being the Sowth hed to *Mount Edgcombe*, being the North point in sight, this Land by the S.S.W. & N.N.E. being the S.E. parte of *Friseland*. And note that from the Sowth Pinacles westerly, from the said *Dee's pinacles* to *frobushers Cape*, the land lyeth S.W. and by W, N.E. and by E. 5.L. And from *Frobushers Cape* to *Borowe's* point, is W. & by S, E. & by N. 5.L./ geving respect to *Hawles needels* by the way, which be certain Rocks, ther is 16. of them lyeth in sight./ from *Master William Borowe's point*, to *Master Michael Locks foreland*, is N.W. & S.E, 5.L, so that the land falleth & turneth Northerly./[2]

[1] Hall's annotations as follows: (top left) 'Mr Dee his Pinacles' (top centre) 'N.N.E. in this forme' (top right) 'Mownt Edgecombe' (bottom left) 'West and by north in this forme.

[2] This is the most detailed contemporary description of the coastline of southern Greenland, though inevitably, the location of these place names has been lost.

[188] The 20. of June 1578. friday, being under *Friseland*, at 5 of the clock in the morning, my Generall caused the ship *Ayde* to be layd by the Lee, and hoised owt his pinas, and the tyme the ship lay by the Lee, I came up under his Lee, and bed him good morrow, & then my Generall axed me whether I wold go a shore with him, and I said I wold, & yt pleased him./ presently he toke the Pinas & came a boord the *Thomas Allin*, and toke me in, & so he and I departed from the ships, to[1] we came abord the *Gabriell*, & then we sayled toward the shore, and so nere the shore as the yse wold give us leave, and sayled from the Sowth East side, to the S. side of Friseland, to we came to the westward of *Frobushers cape*, and that the yse was scattered abrode / and then we left the *Gabriel*, & toke the Pinas, & rowed in toward the shore, and as we rowed in, one of our men spyed men ronning a shore, as sone as they had spyed us, they ronne from their tents.[2]/ So we rowed toward the shore, & nere unto that place, where we iudged them to go from, and when we came a shore, there we fownd theire tents, covered with Seales skinnes, very hansomly made, & two great botes, & one smal boate, made in the same order that the mens botetes[3] be made in *Meta incognita*, & allso their apparell be all one, for they left all their things behinde them, as boates, oares, apparell, & meate, and 12. white dogs yong & old, & 4. whole Seales, the skinnes not taken of, & all their other provision, so that we left all their things, saving one White dog that my Generall toke, & the Trompeter *Jackson* stoll an other, unknown to my Generall, or to any man there[4] / or ells there was not diminished not the value of a point from them; And so we serched for a harbour for our ships & fownd a very good one where there may ryde a hundreth sayle, at 12. or 20. faddom & streamy grownd./

The 21. day of June, satterday, being little winde, at N.W. & fog, we lay of & on, a little from the shore, thinking yt wold have byn clere, to discover more, & then thinking to a stand into the shore, we myst 4 of our shipps when yt was clere which did stand into the shore, and then we cast offward to the westward, lying then North West, & by West, & the land in sight 6. leages from us, & the Northermost land, North from us.
from 11. of clock at night to 4. in the morning the winde at E.N.E. a fayre gale, the ship sailed N.W. & by W. – 8.L.

The 22. day, sunday from 4. to 8. in the forenone, the winde at E.N.E. a fayre gale, the ship sailed N.W. & by W. – 6.L.
from 8. to 12. at none, the winde at E. a good gale, the ship sayled North West & by West – 6.L.
from 12. to 4, the winde at E.S.E. a good gale, the ship sayled S.S.W. 4. glasses 3.L, bycause of the yce, & when we were clere of the yse, the ship sayled N.W. & by W. 4. glasses[5] – 3.L.

[1] Hall's repeated use of 'to' for 'till' may be indicative of contemporary Essex/Middlesex practice (he was a native of Limehouse).
[2] Cf. Mendoza's account, document 13, p. 249.
[3] *Sic.*
[4] Hall's is the only account to identify the thief.
[5] Repetition of word 'glasses'.

from 4. to 8. the winde at South E. a good gale the ship sayled West North West – 8.L.

from 8. to mydnight, the winde at Sowth Est a good gale, the ship sayled West Nor.West – 8.L.

Lost Company of the Michael.

from mydnight to 4. of clock, the winde at South Est a good gale, the ship sponed W.N.W. afore the sea – 4.L.

The 23. day Monday from 4. to 8. the winde at S.E. a good gale, the ship sayled West North West – 4.L.

from 8. to 12. at None, the winde at S.E. a faire gale, the ship sayled N.W. & by West – 5.L.

from 12. to 4. of clock at afternone the winde at S.E. a fayre gale, the ship sayled North West & by W. – 5.L.

from 4. of clock to 8. of clock at night, the winde at South E. a fayre gale the ship sayled N.W. & by W. – 5.L.

from 8. to mydnight, the winde at S.E. a fayre gale the ship sayled North West & by West – 5.L.

from mydnight to 4. in the morning, the winde at S.E. a fayre gale the ship sayled N.W. & by W. – 5.L.

The 24. day of June Tuseday from 4. to 8. the winde at [189] E.N.E. Little winde, the ship sayled N.W. & by W. – 4.L.

from 8. to 12. callme./

from 12. to 4. of clock, the winde at W. a fayre gale the ship sayled North North West – 3.L.

from 4. to 8. the winde at the West the ship sayled N.N.W. – 3.L.

from 8. to mydnight the winde at West a fayre gale, the ship sayled North North West – 5.L.

from mydnight to 4. of clock in the morning the winde at W.S.W. the ship sayled N.W. & by N. – 3.L.

The 25. day Wensday from 4. to 8, the winde at W. & by N. a prety gale, the ship sayled N. & by W. – 2.L.

Latitude 61de–24^m [1]

from 8. to 12. at none, the winde at West & by S. the ship sayled North North West – 4.L.

from 12. to 4. the winde at West a fayre gale the ship sailed North N.E. to go rome with the flete 8. Glasses – 4.L.[2]

pricket 0./

from 4. to 8. the winde at W. a fayre gale the ship sailed North North West – 3.L.

from 8. to mydnight, the winde at West a fayre gale the ship sayled North North West – 3.L.

from mydnight to 4. of clock in the morning the winde at W. a fayre gale, the ship sayled N.N.W. – 3.L.

[1] Cf. Fenton's observation of latitude only twenty four hours later.

[2] A course correction. Presumably, the *Thomas Allen* had put distance between herself and the rest of the fleet.

The 26. day thursday from 4. to 8. the winde at West a fayre gale, the ship sayled North North West – 4.L.

from 8. to 12. at none, the winde at West a fayre gale, the ship sayled North North West – 4.L.

from 12. to 4. of clock, the winde at W.S.W. a fayre gale, the ship sayled North North West – 5.L.

pricket 0./

from 4. to 8. the winde as before, the ship sailed N.W. & by W. – 5.L.

from 8. to mydnight, the winde at W.S.W. little winde, the ship sayled N.W. and by N. – 2.L.

from mydnight to 12. of clock at None little winde, the ship sayled North West & by North – 3.L.

The 27. day of June, friday from 12. to 4. at afternone the winde at S.W. a fayre gale the ship sailed W.N.W. – 2.L.

from 4. of clock friday at afternone to 8. of clock satterday at night callme, being in betwene 2. lands of yse, & the land in sight

From Satterday 8. of clock at night to sunday 8&d. [i.e. 8.30] of clock at night, the winde shifting the ships sayles S.E. & by S. little winde 16. glasses – 4.L.

The ship sayled S.S.E. 16. glasses 8. leges – 8.L.

The ship sailed S.W. a good gale of winde a hed saye – 5.L.

The 30. day of June, Monday, from Sunday 8. of clock at night to Monday 8. of clock at night the winde at W. a fayre gale the ship sayled N.N.W. – 20.L.

The first of July *Meta incognita* sene

Latitude 62de-14^{m}

The fyrst of July 1578. tuseday the winde at W.N.W. a fayre gale at 4. of clock in the morning (and at that present 4. of clock in the morning)[2] had sight of *Master Locks Land*, and *Hawles Iland*, and at 8. of clock at night the same day, I had sight of *Quene Elizabeths Foreland*, and two howres after that I had sight of the land, then came a great cumpany of willmots & sea pyes, flocking abowt our maintop mast, & top sayle yard, that one of our men went to the hed of our top mast, & toke 3. willmots with his hand, as they did flye about his hed, and so I stode into the land, to I did se a whole land of yse & then stood ofward agayn, all night to the next morning, to mete the flete that was at sea, and had not sene nor made the land./[3]

Locks Land.
Hawles Iland.
Quenes
foreland

The 2. day of July 1578. wensday, the winde at S.S.W. in the morning fayre

[1] Hall's annotations: (i) The land in sight in this order Satterday The 28. (ii) Sunday the 29 day the Michael in sight agayne.

[2] Words in editor's parenthesis crowded into text.

[3] This reconnaissance, and the *Thomas Allen*'s earlier distancing from the fleet on 25 June, was against the letter of the instructions issued prior to the voyage (document 2, p. 59). However, her movements, and the presence of the expedition's chief pilot on board, may indicate that she was the designated 'scout' for the other vessels.

weather, I had byn hard aborde the yse, and cam of to tell my Amberall & the rest of the flete, that there was no way into the straightes, bycause the yse was so thick, so at my comming of, I met first with the Master of the Barke *Dennis*, whose name was Dabney, & told him, and he was partely perswaded, and so from him I spoke with Androw Diar, Master of the *Hopewell*, and perswaded him, so that the rest of the ships were to winde-ward, that I could not speake with them, so that Richard [190] Cockes[1] came sayling up being to windewardes, and I could not speake to him, he presently set up his Mainetop sayle, and fortop sayle, and sayled in among the yse, and the bark *Denis* after him, the *Salamon* after him, the *Fraunces of Foye* after him, and one after another, to[2] yt came to the 11. sayle and that was the Amrall, I next to him, and the *Hopewell* last of all, so that we ronne so far in among them that we were inclosed of every side, that we could nei-ther get out nor in no way, so we layde yt a hull, being then fayre weather, and a pretty *plasser*[3] to ply up and down with a sayle, so that we set sayle agayn & plyed up / and in setting of sayle, the Bark *Dennis*, with flatting of her foresayle chaunced to hyt an yse, and within an howre after she was sonk, and nothing to be sene of her, so that my Amralls pinas saved all the men[4] / so at that present, the winde was at S.S.E. and did increase much winde, and the yse cam so thick uppon us, that we could not sayle, but drive among the yse, ready to sink us, yf the mighty power of *God* had not bin great, for we put a whole cable all abowt the side as thick as yt wold lye of the one syde of the ship, and for all that cable, the sea was so growne, that yt was like to beat in the ships sydes, yf he had not byn a strong ship, nor none of the rest of the ships, that there was, but were in as great danger as we were, and there we tarryed in the yse in this trouble, from wensday 8. of clock at night to thursday 9. of clock in the forenone, that the winde came to the west, and so we drived furth from the yse, and then set sayle which I thank *God* for yt, & sayled S.E., clere of the yse, a fayre bredth of. And then layde yt a hull, to the Ayde, and the rest was gone owt of the yse, yt was the very mighty hand of *God*, that any ship that was in the yse did skape and come clere withowt a misfortune.

The 3. of July, thursday, the winde at west the ship sayled from thursday 8. of clock at night to friday at 4. of clock at afternone to go clere of the yse – 15.L.[5]

The 4. day friday at 4. of clock at afternone we layd it a hull, the winde at North West, the ship caped S.W. & by Sowth, the drift S.E. & by S. – 5.L.

Lost the cumpany of the Judith and Michael.

The bark Denis sonk

---

[1] Master of the *Thomas of Ipswich*; later ringleader of that vessel's mutineers.
[2] Until.
[3] Pleasure.
[4] Fenton claims that it was a boat from the *Beare Leicester* which picked up the crew of the *Denys*.
[5] If the fleet was indeed obliged to pass so far into the Atlantic to evade the hazard of ice, it explains why the *Judith*, moving southeastwards towards the Queen's Foreland in an attempt to rejoin the other vessels that day, missed them entirely.

The 5. day Satterday at 12 of clock we set sayle, the winde at W.N.W. the ship sayled with her foresayle and messen from 12. of clock to 8, Sowth West.

The 6. day sunday the winde at W.N.W. a fayre gale we being to the South-ward of the Straits I sayled N.E. & by E. alongst by the shore, to I came open of the *Quenes foreland*, being the S.W. parte of the streictes, & there laye it a hull.

The 7. day Monday the winde at S.S.E. a good gale I set sayle in the morning at 4. of clock & sayled N.E. and by E. towards *Halles Iland* & there layd yt a drift.

The 8. day tuseday I set sayle being little winde at W. and lay to the sowth-ward being thick.

The 9. day, wensday the winde at E.N.E. a prety gale of winde sometymes thick & sometimes clere, we sayled N.N.W. and N.W. being hassye not clere, and shot to the westward of the *Quenes Foreland*, and at one of clock at after-none yt clered up very fayre, that all we see the land, & that my Gen*er*all made yt to be in the straits, & all the rest of the cumpany being the Masters & Pilates of the ships made yt the streits, as the generall sayd, and I stode against them all, and sayd yt was not yt, And then I toke my Pinas & rowed a bord (the)[1] my generall, I told him that yt was not the streits, and told him all the marks of both the lands, that yt was not the Streicts, and he presently was in a great rage & sware by *Gods wounds* that yt was yt, or els take his life, so I see him in such a rage, I toke my pinas & came abord the Thomas Allin againe, & kept him cumpany, to perswade him, to it was thursday 4. of clock in the morning, & then yt fell thick, & I lay a hull, bycause I knew not the place, & he bore sayle, & I lost company one of an other.[2]

[191]   The 11. day of July 1578. friday from 12. of clock at none unto satterday 12. of clock at none, the winde at S.E. & at S. the ship sayled S. & by W. and sometyme S.S.E. and at S. for that the winde was shifting S. 10.L. of the shore, to the sowthward of the streicts.

The 12. satterday from 10. of clock at night to 12. at None satterday the ship sayled E.N.E. fog & thick – 12.L.

The 13. day Sunday, from satterday 12. of clock to sunday at 8. of clock at night, the winde Easterly thick, the shore in sight, we plyed to the East-ward the ship sayled S.E. & by Sowth, & East S.E. – 12.L.

---

[1] Erased.

[2] Cf. Best's account of this confrontation, document 10, p. 215. For the next nine days, Hall and his cap-tain Gilbert Yorke made no attempt to make their appointed landfall. Indeed, the *Thomas Allen*'s move-ments during this time indicate that having abandoned the fleet, they were content to await its reappearance from out of what Frobisher would name the Mistaken Strait.

The 14. day Monday from sunday 8. of clock at night to Monday 4. of clock in the morning the winde at N.N.E. little winde the ship sayled E. & by S. & East – 5.L.

from 4. of clock in the morning to 4. at afternone callme.

from 4. of clock at afternone to 8. of clock the winde at East S.E. the ship sayled N.E. and N.N.E. – 4.L.

from 8. to 4. a hull, the ships way North West – 2.L.

The 15. day tuseday from 4. of clock in the morning to 12. at none the winde at E.S.E. a fayre gale the ship sayled North East, her way N.N.E. – 5.L.

thick

from 12. to 8. at night the winde at E.N.E. the ship sayed S.E. and by S., her way S.S.E. – 6.L.

The 16. day wensday, in the morning at 4. of clock the winde at S.S.E.a prety gale of winde clere a little, we stode into the shore N.N.W. being a litle clere & a great fog of the Land, having sight of the shore & then the winde varied to the N.E. and then I stode of E.S.E. & S.E. being foggy to yt was clere.

Latitude.
61de–17^{m}

The 17. day thursday in the morning the winde at S.E. a fayre gale the ship sayled N.E. to 4. of clock at afternone, being then before fog, and then at that present 4. of clock clere, I had sight of the Land being to the sowth-ward of the *Quenes foreland* & then I stode to the Northward all that night.

The 18. of July, friday in the morning the winde at S.S.W. a fayre gale, I had sight of the *Quenes Foreland* and sayled from the Sowthward N.N.E. along by the land, and let Captayn York and Master Gibbes see all the markes of the same land, that I had told them before, when my Generall and I stode in controversy.

The 19. of July satterday in the morning, the winde Easterly, being a prety lin-gering gale & very thick thinking the streicts had byn clere, as the night before was, being clere, I could see no yse, I bore up all satterday N.W. to yt was night, & then I had a clere of one howre long, & I was shot up betwene 2. lands of yse that both the sides of the straicts as far as I did see was full, & so I turned owt againe that night, to yt was day the next morning.

The 20. of July, sunday the winde at N. a prety gale of winde, I sayled E.N.E. to the east syde of the streicts to go in, (the *Quenes foreland* being S. & by W. from me 4. leags), but when I came there the streicts was so full of yse that there was no going in, & allso I let Capteyn York & Master Gibbes see all the markes of the North side to, according to promyse.

Latitude
61de–42^{m}

The 21 of July Monday, the winde at North a fayre gale, the yse somwhat broke, I turned up in a slade betwene the yse being fayre weather, and hoping to get up, but the yse was so thick, I durst not put up amongst them but put rome with the *Quenes foreland* agayne, & there laid yt adrift, & hoyssed owt the pinas & I went a shore to seke a harbour, but I fownd one, but yt was not very good, besides that, I fownd a little black oare of one of the Ilands.

The 22. July, tuseday, the winde at W.S.W. I plyed up by the *Quenes foreland*, where there was a clere place with owt yse, to I came in the middes of the bay betwene the *Quenes foreland* and *Cape Hopewell*,[1]and there I espyed the *Gabriell*, comming owt of the yse to the clere place where I was, and they told me that my Generall in the *Ayde* was at the sea, and there was in cumpany with him, the *Hopewell*, the *Beare*, the *Salamon*, the *Thomas of Ipswiche*, the *Armonell*, & the *Mone* & there was with me the *Fraunces of Foy*.

[192] The 23. of July wensday the winde at S.W. a fayre gale and clere weather, I sayled from *Mount Oxford* to *Jackmanne's Sound*, (the yse being so thick over the streicts no sea to be sene about Jackmans sownd) & when I came there to go in, there was so much yse I could not get in so that I was glad to turn owt agayn, & so plyed up betwene *Mount Oxford* & *Cape Hopewell* where the yse was gon and that night the *Gabriel* sought harbour and came to anker.

The 24. of July thursday, the winde at S.W. a fayre gale I plyed up & down alongst *Q. Elizabeths Iland*[2] & sent my pinas a shore, to see a harbour, but they could finde none, so comming down where the *Gabriel* was, I sounded my trumpet, and then the *Gabriells* pinas & 4. men came furth, and told me there was a good harbour, and so I sayled in, and there ankered in 11. faddom & fayre white sand.

The 25. of July, friday, the winde at N. a good gale of winde, the yse came in & shot up the harbour, but of the ere they were all gon.

The 26. of July satterday the winde at N.E. a good gale of winde with thick & ded snow, half a fote thick of the hatches.

The 27. of July, sunday in the morning the winde at N.N.E. a pretty gale of winde; the water frosen abowt the ship half a quarter of an inche thick, but ere yt was 12. of clock at none the yse was gon.

The 28. day of July Monday in the morning the winde at W.N.W. and fayre weather, I toke my boate to row to *Mount Oxford*, to see the ships & when I cam there I see 7. sayles a hull under the shoare, & then yt increased so much winde, that I durst not put rome with them for putting to the Leward of all together in the shore.

The 29. of July tuseday the winde at W.N.W. a styf gale & a fog.

The 30. of July wensday in the morning I departed from the Thomas Allin,

---

[1] Not identified; but the context of the entry suggests that the feature was a promonotory on Edgell Island.

[2] Possibly to be identified with either Gross or Potter Islands.

byding in *Gibbes sound* , and I went abord the *Gabriell*, to seke the Ayd & the rest of the flete, the winde then at W. a fayre gale, I directed my way towards the *Quene's foreland* & ere I came at *Mount Oxford*, yt was callme & at 8. of clock I sent 4. men to *Mount Oxford* to loke for the flete, and they cam abord agayne & told me that they had sene 5. sayles, sayling towards *Jackmans sownd*, so that presently I set sayle after them, the winde at S.W. & at night yt fell callme, I being thwart of *Jackmans* sound.

The 31. of July, thursday in the morning the winde at N.E. with fog and rayn, & a styf gale of winde being but 4. Leages from Yorks sownd, I put rome withall & ryd of the N. side in 7. and 8. faddom & fayre white sand, & I had coming in 20.15.10.9.8.7. & there ankered.

August

The 1. day of *August* 1578. friday in the Morning the winde at N.W. a fayre gale I wayed & set sayle from *Yorks sound* & sayled N.E. & by E. clere of the land & then came the winde at E.N.E. a styf gale & thick, I put rome againe in the same sownd & ryd of the N.W. side, & ankered in 11. faddom & fayre sand, & I toke my boate & sownded another place that I rowed up N. & found a good harbour where 20. sayls of ships may ride, & the land locked abowt them, & at low water 4. faddom water, & fyne white sand.

The 2. of August, satterday the winde at N.W. & a fayre weather in the morning, I set sayle being fayre weather & came over to the Countes sownd, & there came to Anker at 10. of clock at night & then I found some of the flete, as my Generall in the Ayde, the Hopewell, the Fraunces of Foye, the Armenall, the Judith, the *Salomon*, the *Manuel*, the Bear & Michael.

The 3. of August 1578 sonday callme & no winde, I went a shore to my generall, & to Captayn fenton, uppon the Countes Iland.

The 4. of August Monday in the morning I wayed being callme, and towed owt of the Countes sound to fetch the *Thomas Allyn*, and at 10. of clock the forenone the winde come to the N.W., I sayled over toward *Gibbes* sound where the Thomas rode, & before I could get thither yt was night & so lay to seaward.

The 5. of August, Tuseday in the morning very thick & no winde, & dreff[1] as the tyde set.

The 6. day of August, wensday in the morning very thick & no winde to 12. of clock at none, & then [**193**] the winde came to the S.E. & then I being driven to the westward owt at *Harves goulf*, I set sayle & sayled N.E. with Pamors poynt, & at that night yt fell callme and thick, & I lay thwart of *Gibbes sound* all night.

---

[1] I.e., drift.

The 7. of August thursday in the morning the winde at E. I sailed S. & by E. to *Gibbes sound*, and when I came within a myle of the sound, the *Thomas Allins* bote fet[1] me from the *Gabriell* and rowed me a bord the Thomas Allin, & then presently I wayed & set sayle and sayled N.N.E. to the *Countes of Warwiks sound* and that night being thick & much winde, I kept yt of and on with my foresayle & messen & kept my hed allnight ofward to 45. faddom & to the shore in 30.20.15. & fayre grownd, white shells & sand.

The 8. of August friday in the morning the winde at S.E. a fayre gale, I sayled into the Countes sownd & there ankered in the *Thomas Allin*, at 10. faddom.

The 9. of August satterday at 10. of clock in the forenone the winde at S. little winde: my Generall & I determined to go to *Beare's sound*, & willed me to carry 100. men to be set on work, & I presently wayed in the *Gabriell*, & towed owt & then the said men & night came, & ankered at *Corbet's point* all night.

The 10. of August sunday at 2. of clock in the morning, callme, I wayed & towed to *Beare's sound* & came to anker in 7. faddom and fayre ground & set all my Myners a shore.

The 11. of August Monday in the morning the winde at S.W. fayre wether, the *Gabriel* & *Michael* did heave owt their balest.[2]

The 12. of August in the morning the winde at N.N.E. fayre weather, little winde, the *Gabriell* toke 4. pinasses in & laded her.

The 13. of August in the morning the winde at N.W. a fayre gale of winde & the eb in hand & at 12. of clock at none the flud came, I wayed in the *Gabriell*, & set sayle towarde the Ayde & plyed up all the flud, being fayre weather, & ankered all the eb, & at that present being halfes, there came so muche winde at N.W. that I was glad to way & set sayle to sea & kepe yt to windeward with both my courses all that night.

The 14. of August, thursday in the morning the winde at N.W. a fayre styf gale of winde, I put rome with *Beare sound* againe, & there rid all that day much winde.

A new land to the N.E. of Locks Land

The 15. of August friday in the morning the winde at S.W. the eb in hand, my Generall & I toke a pinas & rowed through *Beares sound*,[3] and went to the top of a mowntayn[4] & saw the N.E. sea & allso the land bearing from us N.N.E. the vttermost land in sight from *Locks Land*, and at the flud we rowed to my Lord Hayward's Ilande[5] & the barkes was gon & we followed

---

[1] I.e., fetched.
[2] To provide storage space for the ore they would carry between the sound and the waiting freight ships.
[3] Hall emphasizes the name with underscoring here, rather than italics.
[4] This was possibly a high point on Scott's Fortress.
[5] Unidentified.

in the pinas, & that night, the barkes was got a bord, & we in the Pinas allso aborde the Ayde.

The 16. of August satterday the barks did unlade abord the Ayde.

The 17. of August sonday, my Generall & I went to divers sounds, to se what store of owr was there.

The 18. of August Monday, the winde at North E. & much rayne all day.

The 19. of August, tuseday, the barkes departed from *Cownte's Sound*, and sayled to *Beare's sound*, & I went with them, in the *Salomon*, & laded hers there.

The 20. of August wensday the barks & the *Salomon* did lade.[1]

The 21. of August thursday; the Gabriell was laded, the winde at S.S.W. I set sayle & came in her to *Corbet's point*, and there ankered being callme.

The 22. of August friday the winde at N.W. I turned[2] with the Gabriel from Corbets point abord the Ayde, & so discharged her.

The 23. of August satterday callme & no winde.

The 24. of August, sunday, fayre wether, I toke my pinas & rowed to the Cowntes of Sussex myne.

The 25. of August Monday the winde at N.W. a fayre gale, I wayed & set sayle & carried her from the Cowntes sound to Beares sownd & there ankered, & ther laded her.[3]

The 26. day of August tuseday, the winde at N.N.W. my Generall and I rowed through *Beare's sound* [194] to the Eastward to see yf we could se any people but we could se none.

The 27. of August wensday, my Generall went away from *Beare's sound* & left me there to see the lading of the Thomas Allin.

The 28. of August (friday)[4] thursday the winde at S.W. & S.S.W. I turned owt of Beares sound with the Thomas Allin & that night ankered in the Countes sownd.

The 29. of August friday, the winde N.E. a styf gale of winde with great stormes of snow.

The 30. of August, satterday the winde at N.E. a styf gale of winde, with

---

[1] Captain Randall's early return to Countess of Warwick's Sound from this lading was to earn him a dressing down from Frobisher (document 8, p. 164).

[2] I.e., returned.

[3] The *Thomas Allen*. Hall's peripatetic habits during these days indicates that he was supervising much of the lading into the ships' holds; probably to ensure the ore's stable distribution.

[4] Erased.

snow, the *An fraunces* came to us where we rod in the Cowntes sownd, & there ankered & haled agrownde & stopped his leakes.[1]

The 31. of August sunday at 8. of clock in the morning the winde at W. a prety gale, I wayed in the Ayde and set sayle from the Countes of Warwicks sound, & at 12. of clock yt fell callme, I towed owt to *Corbets point*, the flud in hand, & there ankered all night, (before)[2] being as before calme.

September 1578.

The 1. of September 1578 Monday, the winde at N. a prety gale, I wayed at *Corbets point*, and set both my topsailes & sayled thwart of *Beare's sound* being little winde, & there ankered, to take in my Miners & 2. pinases lading of owr, my Generall being there to lade the barkes *Gabriel* & *Michael* & two pinases to bring abord the Ayde, at that present being callme & no winde, but a great sea ronning in, that we shold have much winde, as yt did appere afterward, and so he told me that he wold be a bord afore night, so that I left him, & came abord in *Andrew Dyer's* pinas, & by that tyme, that I was a bord, & had taken in the gondolos lading, & the pinas lading, the winde came to the west, and a good gale of winde, we ryding upon the Lee shore, so that I sent the pinas a shore to my Generall, & got the ship under sayle with great danger, & within 2. howres yt fell starke callme, & afore eb in hand, I ankered againe, and hong owt a light, that my Generall might come abord, and at mydnight there came down so much winde at North that broke my anker in the shank, so I set sayle, & stode under my foresayle, to get of the shore, & when I was half the channell over, I toke in my sayles and layd yt a hull, to yt was day light to se the rest of the flete & my Generall to come with 2. Barks.[3]

The 2. of *September* tuseday in the morning, I set sayle at 2. of the clock, and I did see at that present the hopewell the fraunces of foy, the Salomon of Waymoth, all of hed me being to Leward, the sea being grown & much wynde, I set my fore course to halle in the weather shore, to take in my boate, & in towing after the ship, she sepletted[4] & sonk & so lost her, & at that present 10. of clock. I scryed 2. sayles comming after, I toke in my fore corse & layd the ship a drift, & that 2. ships came up by my & spoke with me, whose names were the *Beare*, and the *Armonell*, I axed for my

---

[1] The *Anne Frances*'s mariners probably utilized the large wooden crabs intended for the colony's use to bring her on-shore.

[2] Erased.

[3] If Hall's description of his travails this day is accurate, it is hardly to be wondered that he abandoned his anchorage (though it is also possible that he was attempting to excuse his desertion of Frobisher the following day).

[4] I.e., her hull-timbers separated

Generall & the rest of the flete & they could tell me of none, but that fayr-weather Master of the Beare told me of a Pinas that was alongst the shore so that I lay a drift withowt sayle, & they 5.[1] went hence under their fore-sailes & at 5. of clock at night I spied 2. sayles, the one of them was the pinas that I sent to my Generall the night before, for him to come aboord, and the men that came in that pynnas told me that my Generall came after in the *Gabriell*, And that there was in cumpany with him the *An fraunces*, the *Judith* & *Michael*, & so that present 6. of clock [195] at night I was of the *Quenes foreland* S.E, the *foreland* of me N.W. 4. leages of, I layd yt a hull & there came the *Thomas Allin* & the *Mone of foy* & lay a hull by me all night, & so I kept a duble light all night, half shroudes hye, bycause they might see yt that came after, but as yet I could not see them, nor here from them.

The 3. of September wensday, the Thomas Allin & Mone in cumpany with me in the morning, the winde at N.W. a styf gale of winde, I set sayle at 7. of clock in the morning & sayled S.S.E. from 7. to 12. of clock at none – 7.L.

from 12. to 4. the winde at N.W. a fayre gale the ship sayled S.S.E. – 4.L.

from 4. to 8. the winde at W. a fayre gale the ship sayled *South South East* – 6.L.

from 8. to mydnight the winde at W. a fayre gale the ship sayled Sowth Sowth East – 5.L.

from mydnight to 4. of clock in the morning the winde at W. a styf gale the ship sailed South S.E. – 5½.L.

The 4. of September thursday from 4. to 8. the winde at N.W. a stout gale of winde the ship sailed S.S.E. – 6½.L.

our Pynas lost.
Latitude
60de–15^m
pricked 45L.
N.N.W. from
the Queenes
foreland

and at that present the watche being owt, being water in our pynnas, we haled her over to fre the water owt of her, & the sea being growen, the sea toke her in the sterne & threw her against the ship & splet her all to peces.[2]

from 8. to 12. at none the winde at N.W. a styf gale of winde with fog & small rayn the ship sayled Sowth South East – 6.L.

from 12. to 4. of clock at afternone the winde at N.N.E. a fayre gale, the ship sayled S.E. – 4.L.

from 4. to 8. the winde at N.N.E. little winde the ship sayled Sowth East – 2.L.

from 8. to mydnight, the winde at S.W. a fayre gale of winde, the ship standing under a course & bonet of eache maste & the fore top sayle abroad the ship sayled Sowth East – 6.L.

from mydnight to 4. of clock the winde at S.W. a fayre gale the ship sayled Sowth East – 4.L.

---

[1] *Sic.*
[2] Cf. Fenton's similar losses (document 8, p. 168). The entire fleet, according to Best, lost more than 20 pinnaces in the space of twenty-four hours in this manner.

Latitude 59ᵈᵉ–13ᵐ pricked Freseland. E. & by N. from me 100L.

The 5. of September friday from 4. to 8. the winde at S.W. a good gale the ship sayled S. East – 5.L.

from 8. to 12. at None the winde at S.W., a good gale the ship sayled Sowth Sowth East – 6.L.

from 12. to 4. at afternone the winde at S.W. a good gale the ship sayled Sowth Sowth East – 6.L.

from 4. to 8. the winde at S.W. with thick & rayn a good gale the ship sailed Sowth East – 5.L.

from 8. to mydnight the winde at S.W. a fayre gale with much rayn the ship sayled Sowth East – 5.L.

from mydnight to 4. of clock in the morning lost the cumpany of the Mone the winde at N.N.W. a fayre gale of winde with rayne the ship sayled S.E. – 4.L.

put a dead man overbord whose name was Tho Batters sayller.[1]

The 6. of September satterday from 4. to 8. the winde at N.N.W. & dry & stowt storme the ship sailed S.E. – 7.L.

from 8. to 12. of clock at None the winde at N.N.W. a stout storme, I toke in all my sayles & sponed a fore the sea, for to tarry the Thomas Allin the ship sayled Sowth East – 6.L.

from 12. to 4. of clock at afternone the winde at N.W. a stowt storme the ship sayled with her fore course Sowth East – 8L.

from 4. to 8. the winde as before a stout storme the ship sayled with her fore course Sowth East – 8.L.

from 8. to mydnight the winde at N.W. a stout gale of winde the ship sayled with her fore course S.E. – 8.L.

from mydnight to 4. of clock the winde at N.W. a stout gale of winde, by the fore course the ship sayled S.E. – 8.L.

The 7. of September sunday from 4. to 8. the winde at W.N.W. a fayre gale I put on my foresayle bonet & set my manesayle then the ship sayled Sowth E. – 9.L.[2]

Latitude 57ᵈᵉ–26ᵐ pricked O.

from 8. to 12. at None the winde at N.W. veried with snow & hayle a stowt gale the ship sayled S.E. – 9.L.

from 12. to 4. of clock at afternone the winde at N.W. a stif gale of winde I toke in my maynesaile to tarry the Thomas Allin & sayled S.E. with my foresayle – 6.L.

[196]

from 4. to 8. the winde as before a stout storme N.W. a styf gale, the ship sailed with her foresayle being attaint Sowth East – 7.L.

from 8. to mydnight the winde at N.W. the foresaill atant & and the fore-top sayle half mast high the ship sayled Sowth East – 8.L.

[1] By 17 September, the description of the preferred method of disposing of the dead had degenerated from 'put' to 'heaved' overboard: Hall's looseness of terminology, or an indication of creeping callousness brought on by exhaustion? 'Batters' was also referred to as Batterby (p. 193) and Batterick (HM 715, fo 20). Cf. also p. 16 n. 4.

[2] This, and subsequent log entries by Hall, constitute by far the most detailed extant exposition of six-teenth-century sail-setting in adverse weather conditions.

from mydnight to 4. of clock the winde at (styf)[1] N.W. a styf gale, the foresayle as before, & all the foretop sayle the ship sayled Sowth East – 8.L.

The 8. of September Monday from 4. to 8. in the forenone the winde at N.W. & by west a fayre gale the foresayle & foretopsaile attant the ship sayled S.E. – 5.L.

4.C. set S.E. & by East in the Latitude 56.–30.

from 8. to 12. of clock at none, the winde at N.W. & by W. a fayre gale of winde & fayre weather the foresayle & the topsayle & Maye sayle abrode the ship sayled Sowth East & by East – 9L.

from 12. to 4. of clock at afternone the winde at N.W. & by W. a fayre gale, the ship sayled with the sayles aforesaid, Sowth East & by East – 9.L.

from 4. to 8. the winde at west a good fresh gale the ship sayled with a corse[2] & a bonnet of eche maste and spret sayle, Sowth East & by East – 9.L.

from 8. to mydnight, the winde at W. a fresh gale the ship sayled with a corse & a bonnet of eche mast & spret sayle Sowth East & by East – 10.L.

from mydnight to 4. of clock in the morning the winde at W. a styf gale the ship sayled with a corse & a bonnet of eche mast & sprite sayle S.E. & by E – 10.L.

The 9. of September tuseday from 4. to 8. the winde at W. a meane gale she sayled with her sayles aforesaid S.E. & by E. – 8.L.

Latitude 55de–42^m

from 8. to 12. of clock at None the winde at West a meane gale the ship sayled *Sowth East & by East* – 8.L.

from 12. to 4. at afternone the winde at W.N.W. a meane gale the ship sayled *East & by East* – 8.L.

from 4. to 8. the winde at W.N.W. a fayre gale the ship sayled *East & by East* – 7.L.

from 8. to mydnight the winde at W.N.W. a fayre gale the ship sayled with a corse & a bonnet on the mast with spritte sayle & fortopsayle the ship sayled S.E. & by E. – 8.L.

from mydnight to 4. of clock in the morning the winde at W.N.W. a fayre gale the ship sayled S.E. & by E. – 8.L.

The 10. of September wensday from 4. to 8. in the forenone the winde at W. a fayre gale of winde the ship sayled with mayne sayle & 2. top sayles, & spritte sayle, Sowth East & by East – 9.L.

Latitude 54de–00^m
pricked 0.

from 8. to 12. at none the winde at S.W. a fayre gale of winde, all the sayles attaint, saving the foretop saile, the ship sayled Sowth East & by East – 8.L.

from 12. to 4. at afternone the winde at S.W. a fayre gale all the sayles attaint to the hard top, the ship sayled South East & by East – 9.L.

from 4. to 8. the winde at S.W. a fayre gale the ship sayled Sowth East & by East – 8.L.

[1] Erased.
[2] 'Crosse' erased.

from 8. to mydnight, the winde at S.W. a fayre gale the ship sayled Sowth East & by East – 8.L.

from mydnight to 4. of clock in the morning the winde at S.S.W. a good hard gale my foresaill & Maynsayle & topsaile & spritt sayle abroade, being but a reasonable gale of winde at the end of this sterbord watche I broke my mayn yard 2 howres afore day & allso I left the company of the Thomas Allin the ship sailed S.E. & by E. – 6.L.

The 11. of September thursday from 4. to 8. the winde at S.S.W. a good gayle the ship sayled with her foresaile & spritte sayle East S.E. – 5.L.

from 8. to 12. at none the winde at S.S.W. a good gale with rayne & fog, the ship sailed E.S.E. – 4.L.

I.D.
S.E. and by
E.

from 12. to 4. of clock at afternone the winde at S.W. the ship sailed *East* & by East the foresayle & foretopsaile over the top reame – 6.L.

from 4. to 8. at night the winde at W.S.W. a fayre gale, the ship sayled E.S.E. set our corse upon our yards & they broke againe after yt was mended – 6.L.

from 8. to mydnight the winde at W.S.W. a fayre gale the ship sailed South Sowth East – 5.L.

[197]

from mydnight to 4. in the morning the winde at W.S.W. a prety gale the ship sayled with foresaile & messen South East – 4.L.

The 12. of September friday from 4. to 8. in the forenone the winde at W. a faire gale, the ship sailed S.E. & at that present we fell in hand to mend our mayne yarde – 5.L.

from 8. to 12. at none, the winde callme & fayre weather.

from 12. to 4. callme.

from 4. to 8. of clock at night callme & at that present 6. of clock in the afternone our yarde was mended & then I pot to my new mayne saile & wonde my mayne yarde across & at 8. of clock the winde came to S.S.W.

from 8. to mydnight the winde at Sowth sowth west a fayre gale the ship sayled East Sowth East – 5.L.

from mydnight to 4. of clock the winde at S. & by W, the ship sayled East Sowth East & at that present being a styf gale of winde we toke of our bonnet & sayled in our corses – 4.L.

The 13. of September satterday from 4. to 8. the winde at S. & by W. the ship sayled E.S.E. – 2½.L.

pricked 0.

from 8. to 12. at none the winde at S. the ship sayled East Sowth East, East – 2½.L.

from 12. to 4. the winde at S. a stoute gale of winde, the ship sayled East Sowth East, East – 2½.L.

from 4. to 8. of clock at night the winde at S. a good gale the ship sayled East Sowth East, East – 2½.L.

from 8. to mydnight the winde at S. a fayre gale the ship sayled; East Sowth East – 2½.L.

from Mydnight to 4. of clock in the morning, the winde at S.S.W. a fayre gale the ship sailed S.E. & by E – 2.L.

The 14. of September Sunday, from 4. to 8, the winde at S.W. a prety gale I put owt my bonnet the ship sayled S.S.E. – 2.L.
from 8. to 12. at none callme.
from 12. of clock to 4. at afternone the winde at E.S.E. a stout gale we toke of our bonnets, & sayle by the corses S.S.W. her way S.W. – 3.L. from 4. to 8. of clock at night the winde at E.S.E. a stout storme I toke in my sailes & laide a hull, the ship caped S.S.W. her way W.N.W. – 4 myles[1]
from 8. of clock at night sunday to 4. of clock monday morning the winde at East, S.S.E. & shifting to yt came to the West S.W. & a great storme, the ship sponned afore the sea withowt any saile N.N.E. & at that present 4. of clock, the sea let in at my Generalls cabban; & burst from the Cabban floors to the windows all the Timber & bords into him who was at the helme his name is fraunces Austen. – 8.L.[2]
from 4. to 8. the winde at W.S.W. a good gale the ship sponed East North East – 4.L.

The 15. of September Monday from 8. to 12. the winde at W.S.W. the weather somwhat fayre, I set my forecorse under the sea & sayled E.S.E. – 5.L.
from 12. to 4. at afternone the winde at W.S.W. a fayre gale, the ship sailed S.E. & by E. – 6.L.
from 4. to 8. the winde as before a fayre gale the ship sailed S.E. and by East – 6.L.
from 8. to mydnight the winde at W.S.W. a fayre gale, the ship sayled S.E. & by E. – 5.L.
from mydnight to 4. of clock in the morning the winde at S.S.W. a fayre gale the ship sailed S.E. & by E. – 4.L.

The 16. of September tuseday from 4. to 8. of clock in the fornone, the winde at S. & by W. & S. the ship sailed East Sowth East – 3.L.

all pricked 0. saving Easterly way

from 8. to 12. of clock at none, the winde at S.S.E. I stode to the westward the ship sayled S.W. – 3.L.
from 12. to 4. of clock at afternone, callme.
from 4. to 8. the winde at E.S.E. a fayre gale the ship sayled Sowth – 3.L.
from 8. to mydnight the winde at N.E. a good gale the ship sayled S.E. & by East – 3.L.
from mydnight to 4. of clock in the morning the winde at South, the ship sayled W.S.W. – 4½.L.

---

[1] *Sic.*

[2] The accounts for discharging of mariners following the return of the voyage indicate that Austen survived the experience (PRO EKR E164/36, p. 55). According to Lok (document 5, p. 96), Frobisher later claimed that this was the incident in which the register books containing all data on assays carried out in Meta Incognita were lost.

The 17. of September wensday from 4. to 8. in the forenone the winde at Sowth
a good gale the ship sailed W.S.W. – 4.L.

[198]

from 8. to 12. at none the winde at S.S.W. a good gale I toke of my bonnets, the ship sailed west 4. glasses 2.L. & at that present I stant about to the West Eastward[1] the ship sailed Sowth East & by East – 1½.L.

from 12. to 4. of clock at afternoone the winde at S.W. & by S. the ship sailed S.E. & by E. – 3.L.

w. bett
a myner
being dead,
heved
ouerboord

from 4. to 8. of clock at night, the winde at N.W. a fayre gale, the ship sayled S.E. & by E. – 3.L.

from 8. to mydnight the winde at N.N.W. a fayre gale, the ship sayled S.E. & by E. – 6.L.

from mydnight to 4. of clock in the morning the winde at N.E. a fayre gale, the ship sailed S.E. & by E. – 5.L.

The 18. of September thursday, from 4. to 8. of clock in the forenone the winde at E. a fayre gale the ship sayled Sowth Sowth East – 5.L.

from 8. to 12. at none the winde at E.S.E. a fayre gale, the ship sayled S. and by West – 5.L.

from 12. to 4. of clock the winde at E.S.E. the ship sailed S. and by W. – 5.L.

from 4. to 8. the winde at S.S.E. a prety gale the ship sailed Sowth West – 3.L.

from 8. to mydnight, the winde at S.S.E. a fayre gale, the ship sayled Sowth west – 4.L.

from mydnight to 4. of clock in the morning, the winde at South & by East the ship sailed S.W. & by W. – 4.L.

The 19. of September friday from 4. to 8. the winde at S. a fayre gale the ship sayled E.S.E. – 3.L.

from 8. to 12. at none, the winde at S. a fayre gale I had sight of a ship to the Leward of me, I layd rome to her North East & when I came to hale her, I fownd yt to be the *Hopewell* & kept her company – 6.L.

Latitude
52de–00m

from 12. to 4. of clock at afternone the winde at S.E. a fayre gale, the ship sailed S.S.W. – 5.L.

from 4. to 8. of clock the winde at S.S.E. a fayre gale, the ship sayled Sowth West – 5.L.

from 8. of clock friday at night to satterday 4. of clock in the morning callme & withowt accownt.

The 20. of September satterday, from 4. of clock to 8. of clock in the forenone the winde at S.W. a prety gale, the ship sayled S.E. & by E. – 2.L.

from 8. to 12. at none, the winde at S.W. a prety gale, the ship sailed S.E. & by E. – 3.L.

[1] *Sic.*

from 12. to 4. of clock at afternone, the winde at S.W, little winde, the ship sayled S.E. & by E. – 2.L.

from 4. to 8. the winde at S.W. a fayre gale the ship sailed S.E. & by E. – 4.L.

from 8. to mydnight, the winde at W.S.W. a fayre gale the ship sailed Sowth East & by East – 5.L.

from mydnight to 4. of clock in the morning the winde at W.S.W. a fayre gale, the ship sayled S.E. & by E. – 6.L.

The 21. of September sunday from 4. to 8. the winde at W. a pretty gale, the ship sailed S.E. & by E. – 4.L.

Latitude
52de–00^m
pricked 3.

from 8. to 12. of clock at none the winde at W. a pretty gale, the ship sailed Sowth East & by East – 4.L.

from 12. to 4. of clock at afternone, the winde at W. a pretty gale, the ship sayled S.E. & by E. – 3.L.

from 4. to 8. the winde at W. a pretty gale the ship sayled S.E. & by E. 2.L. S. & by W. 2.L. – 5.L.[1]

and at that present I tarried for the *An fraunces* to she came up & spoke with her & the Capteyn of the An fraunces told me that my Generall was in a great coller against me, and allso the *Master* of the Anne fraunces toke me up very short & wold haue had me to have gone East & by Sowth, & the land being Sowth of me, & I aunswered him I wold not.

from 8. to mydnight, the winde at W.S.W. a faire gale, the ship sailed S.E. & by E. – 6.L.

from mydnight to 4. of clock in the morning, the winde at W. a pretty gale, the ship sayled S.E. & by E. – 6.L.

[199]

The 22. of September monday, from 4. to 8. in the forenone, the winde at W.N.W. a pretty gale, the ship sailed Sowth East & by East – 4.L.

from 8. to 12. at none, the winde at S.W. a pretty gale of winde the ship sayled Sowth East & by East – 3.L.

from 12. to 4. of clock at afternone the winde at S.W. a pretty gale, the ship sailed E.S.E. – 2.L.

from 4. to 8. the winde at S.S.W. a good gale, the ship sayled East Sowth East – 6.L.

from 8. to mydnight, the winde at S.S.W. a styf gale, the ship in her corses, the ship sayled E.S.E. – 7.L.[2]

The 23. of September tuseday from 4. to 8. the winde at W. a styf gale, the ship sailed E. & by S. – 8.L.

Latitude 49^de

from 8. to 12. of clock at none, the winde at W. a styf gale the ship sayled East and by Sowth – 8.L.

from 12. to 4. of clock at afternone, the winde at W. a stout storme I toke in my Mayne corse to tarry the *Hopewell* and the *An fraunces*, they being both a sterne the ship sayled East – 7.L.

---

[1] *Sic.*

[2] Missing entry crowded into margin: 'from mydnight to 4. of the clock in the morning, the winde at S.W. a styf gale, the ship sayled E.S.E – 7.L'.

from 4. to 8. the winde at W. a stout storme, the ship sayled by the forecorse East. lost company of the *Hopewell* & the *An fraunces* – 7.L.

from 8. to mydnight the winde at N.W. a stout storme, the ship sayled E. & by S. the sea grew – 6.L.

from Mydnight to 4. of clock in the morning, the winde at N.W. a stout storme, the sea grew the ship sayled East & by Sowth – 6.L.

The 24. of Septemb*er* wensday, from 4. to 8. of clock in the forenone, the winde at N.W. a styf gale, & somwhat lesse winde, the ship sayled East – 6.L.

from 8. to 12. of clock the winde at N.W. & began somwhat to be fayre I set my Mayne corse, the ship sayled East and by North – 7.L.

from 12. to 4. of clock at afternone the winde at W.N.W. a fayre gale I sounded & could get no ground at 150. faddom, and then I did hoyst over bord 2. Mariners that did dye the night before the ship sayled E.N.E. – 4.L.

from 4. to 8, the winde at W. little winde the ship sayled East North East – 1½.L.

from 8. to Mydnight the winde at N.N.W. a good gale the ship sayled East North East – 5.L.

from Mydnight to 4. in the morning the winde at N.N.W. by the 2. corses the ship sayled E.N.E. – 6.L.

The 25. of Septemb*er* thursday, from 4. to 8. the winde at N.W. & by N. a stout gale the ship sayled by the 2. corses East and by North – 6.L.

from 8. to 12. of clock at None, the winde at North west & by N. a stout gale, the ship sailed E. & by N. – 6.L.

from 12. to 4. of clock at afternone the winde at N.W. & by N. a stif gale of winde the ship sailed E.N.E. – 4.L.

Tho. Coningham dyed & heaued ouerbord, sayler. 3L.

And at the ende of this watche I toke in my forecorse, & sounded & had 70. faddom & fyne oosey sand with 3. blackes amongst & some white sand about the red cloth Scilly being from me 8. leages East and by Sowth.[1]

from 4. to 8. the winde at N.W. & by N. the ship sayled East Sowth East, & in the myddest of this watche I sounded & found 70. faddom and fyne oose sand and then I set my forecorse and sayled Sowth East from 6. to 12. of clock at Mydnight – 8.L.

from 12. to 4. in the morning, the winde at N.N.W. the ship sailed East – 4.L.

The 26. of Septemb*er* friday, from 4. to 8. the winde as before , the ship sayled East N.E. – 5.L.

from 8. to 12. at none, the winde at N & by N. a styf gale, the ship sayled East North East – 5.L.

from 12. to 4. of clock, the winde at N.W. a fayre gale, the ship sayled N.E. – 5.L.

from 4. to 8. the winde at N.W. a fayre gale the ship sayled North East – 5.L.

---

[1] The *Ayde* had entered the Soundings.

[200]   from 8. to mydnight the winde at North west a (prety)[1] fayre gale the ship sayled North East and at the end of this watche, I sounded & found 50. faddom, stern grownd white, black stones & white stones amongst – 5.L. from mydnight to 4. the winde at North West a fayre gale, I layde yt a hull the Mone rose, & that was at 4. of clock in the Morning and then I sounded agayne, & found 50. faddom & fyne red shells & white shells & one masse.

The 27. September satterday, from 4. to 8. the winde at North West a styf gale of winde the ship sayled N.E. & at that present the watche being owt I had sight of the Bollt, & at 12. of clock I had the *start*[2] N.W. of me.

The 28. September, sunday in the morning at 4. of clock, the winde at N.N.W. little winde, being thwart of *Donoze*,[3] and at 12. of clock at none, the winde came to the Sowth & Sowth East, I being thwart of Sainct Helleinges, I put rome with *Portchemouth* and there ankered.

[1] Erased.
[2] Name underscored.
[3] Dunnose, Isle of Wight.

DOCUMENT 7

Fragmentary journal of the ship *Judith*, usually attributed to Charles Jackman[1]

[181] **FROM** London vppon *o*ur voyage towardes Meta incognita in *th*e Judith whos bur-then is 90 tones over home master Edwar*d* Fenton is captayne Charles Jackman master.
FROM blake wall *th*e 25 of may and so to grauesend from thenc *th*e 27th to harwich beinge of us .6. sayle so we came to anker in *th*e rode wher we fownde .9. sayle more of (shi)ppes well apoynted attendinge *o*ur cuminge ther. when *th*e generall had mustred the (sol)diers and furnished *th*e fleet of such nessesarys as war laking he weed[2] thenc *th*e laste (of May) with 13 sayle of tale shippes and .2. barkes, the wynd beinge at northest. the 3 at plymouth (wher) we stayed .4. howers for fresh water, and weed thenc by night. the .4. we passed by saynt (Micha)eles mownt in cornewall and sertayne rokes ther caled the longe shippes beinge the fyr(thest point) of Ingland wher the generall sent his letters to *th*e captaynes and masters *tha*t ther sh(old atten)d vpon hyme .4. sayle vidiliset the francis of foy *th*e mowne *th*e barke denis and *th*e gab(riell. To) Captayne Fenton his leftenant generall, in *th*e Judith he appoynted the hopwell *th*e beare *th*e Arminall and the Salomone and vpon captaine yorke his vise admirall in *th*e (Tho)m*a*s allyne he appoynted *th*e An francis the Thomas of Ipswhych the Emanuell and *th*e m(ichaell) to attend in ther places aforesaid yf per*a*duen-ture we shold com to a fight by sea (which than)kes be to god we did not, the .6. we felt to felt[3] with a place of Ireland caled cape (cl)oynd[4] beinge est and by north and passing by belthamore[5] and .3. lyttell Ilandes nearby (yt) we left Ireland divertinge our course to fres-land the wynde beinge south est and by est. the .20 of June we felt with fresland at one of the cloke in the morninge fyndinge it very fu(ll of r)ough mowntaynes well neare covered with snow. beinge so exceedinge cowld as in Ingland at (Christ)mas I haue not felt the lyke. moreover ther was flotinge rownd in *th*e sownde about (much) thyke monsteros great Ise

---

[1] The document is in poor condition, particularly at the edges, where significant fall-off occurs. Words in parenthesis are the editor's reconstruction. The attribution remains uncertain; if the journal was indeed that of Jackman, it is unusual in being written in the third person (there are several references to the 'master' therein). It is possible that the work is rather that of one of the gentleman soldiers, carried in the *Judith*, who were to have remained in Baffin Island to protect Fenton's colony. Certainly, there is no hint in the fragmentary text of the technical minutiae that one would expect of someone with experience of keep-ing a formal ship's log. However, the present work will refer to 'Jackman' as the recognized provenance in the absence of firm evidence to controvert this.
[2] Weighed.
[3] *Sic.*
[4] Cloyne, or possibly Cape Clogh (Galley Head).
[5] Baltimore Bay.

which the generall and captayne Fentone hauinge (in) ther .2. litle botes passed through in great daunger and peryll this when thay had arriued beinge after (h)evy toyle rested and refreshed they marched alongest the shower ther bote rowinge by them (and goi)nge aboute the corner of a hey[1] stoney and raged mountayne they found a fayr bay afor (them at the) vpper end therof sertaine tentes of seales skynes which beinge espyed he with his company ent(red ther) botes and made thether with great speed but cominge ashower we fownd the people fled which we (supp)ose ware forewarned by the sownd of a trumpet at our first arivall the strange and vnacu(stomed noise) wherof together with the sodane sight of our people forced ther flight in such spedy (fear)full sorte that they left all ther prouision and furniture behinde them which in resp(ect) of valu or goodnes therof we estemed as nothinge but for the strangnes (of) sundry ware (being less de)sirous of them as of Jueles of greter pryse But our generall rather seekinge by tru(st to det)ayne them then otherwyse to offend them woold in no wyse permit or suffer any man to take (awaie) anythinge sauinge .2. white whelpes very like to woluues in shape moreover ther tentes to(ols) botes owers dartes and vitales we fownde in all respectes agreable to the order and m(anner lyke the) people at Meta incognita and although they for asmuch as as[2] the generall and master (haue) deserne by .2. sevirall meanes as also sertaynly knowen from the south shower of fre(sland that the) queenes forland lyinge in the mough[3] of the strates be onely .100. & .50. leages in distance so they was coniecture[4] otherwyse of them by reasones aforesaide but to be allowed in thyer diet and order of lyfe which yf they be it passeth manes reasone for asmuch as yet (we can not) desern how they cam (to) haue skill to conducte them selues (over) so large and wyde a passage or therfrom (be) able to brooke such hyswellinge seas which we haue founde very dangerous to our gr(eat ship)ps but to seas this coniectory to such as further tryall may be made they shall (under)stand yt. the generall and captayne Fenton, after this ven(ture) taken departing (we) went aborde and hoysed sayle the same day toward Meta Incognita.

[182] **THE** 22 we lost the company of the Barke michell the 28 the generall and the master then accompte supposed them in the high of furbusher freet or strate which had fallen owte (acc)ordinge to ther computation But that contrary wyndes drawe them overmuch to the east (wh)ar we ware intangled amongest many and great Ise, the j of July we felt with the (bar)kes then the generall with .13. sayle plyed for the west parte of the strates cauld the quee(nes fore)land which he supposed to be les incumbred with Ise then the other partes by occasion of westerlie wyndes, Master Fentone Captayne of the Judith entred now into the myddell of the strates. The .2. of July being very fayre and the wynd prosperous the generall with .13. shippes (in)tended therby notwithstandinge the monsterous thyknes of Ise to pase vp the strates hopinge to (find)e that the further in the more owere But contrary to his expectation this fayre changed to fowle and thyke foges and boysteros winde which inclosed and buffited them so (grievously) that to deffend themselues from the beatinge of the Ise they ware forsed to hange over (owe)rs plankes Ankerstockes and great peases of mastes in ropes hausers which seuerally by godes (mercy) was the safegarde of all ther liues savinge one shipp cauld the barke denise which notwith(stan)dinge all defences aforesaid

---

[1] High.
[2] *Sic.*
[3] *Sic.*
[4] Conjecture.

was so brused and crused[1] with Ise in *the* soden storme *tha*t in one half hower she sanke before ther faces with all that was in her sauinge *that* which by god*es* (mercy) with captaines filpot*es* bote was the safegard of all ther liues. Thus sesinge (l)eave of the generall I retorne to captayn Fenton in the Judith who the .2. of (July) was lykewyse alured by the beuty of *the* day and fayrnes of the gole to enter the strat*es* fyrth*er* by .5. leages then the generall and his company war vpone when this (fayr)e lykwyse changed to fowle, and the further vp the thyker the Ise so he therby (de)fied sought by all meanes to the sea again but the storme so tossed the Ise rownd and vpon us that it preuayled not to beare any sayle amongest them then in (vnder) holl driuinge whether wynd and tyde wold carry us abydinge for that night (in) furious and stormes of Ise. Thus with great labor and danger the night beinge fled the morninge followinge at .3. of the cloke being *the* .3. of July we ware fastned all abowt with Ise then the storm again growinge then the Ise so vehement (aga)inst the side of the shipp that notwithstandinge all defences aforesaid was so brused (and) crused that we supposed ourself lost forlorn hope then M*aste*r Woolfall a good (and) godly precher who for his zelowes and godly lyffe was chosen to haue remained with us the (pre)cher moved us to prayer layinge befor us our *present* danger and how we ought to behave (our)selues to god-ward in this distres wo whom as it semed from this woorld we ware redy (se)singe this his comfortable exhortation so quietned and reviued o*u*r *present* estate that the dangers wherin we ware was therby relented and made the more tollerable in *the* hope (we) had in god*es* mersis. This his exortation fynished o*u*r captayn and m*aste*r by god apoynted our safegard incoraged *the* gentelmen and soldiers with pikes and owers to beare *the* Ise (from) the side of the shipp, the other with lyke diligenc chered his saylors with great currage (and) man-lynes to stand to ther labor and taklinge. then every man imployed hymself to labore he cold best skyll of and as the spech goeth we laboringe for lyffe it (ples)ed god to send by .9. aclocke to apeas the storme and open a glad[2] in *the* Ise and therwith (the) myst clered vp that we might see in what parte of the strat*es* we ware in as allso (cor)rect our course then our captayn and m*aste*r toke cownsell what was best to be done fyndinge so thyke both at the enteraunce and also alangth in ye strat*es* that ether to passe out or vpward (se)med vnpossible they therfor concluded to beare vp the glad toward*es* the queenes forland ther to enter some harbore. thus cominge to the said forland we fownd a fayre bay (or) sownd which deuided it in to sundry Iland*es* then the m*aste*r sownded with lyne & led (in) great diligenc who fyndinge it very deep and rokey at the bottom was forced to retorne to *the* enter(aunce) (ther) fownde a rode for the tyme at .3. fathom the shipp ryding ther toke in fresh water with

[The manuscript ends here]

---

[1] Crushed.
[2] Glade; clearing.

The page which immediately precedes Fenton's journal in the Pepys MSS, showing the two extremities of the entrance to Frobisher Bay. The descriptive text for the sketches is as follows: (top) 'Warwicke forland, This Lande lieth betwene northwest & by north, and north northest in this sorte going into the Straites called Forbishers straites, being 8 Leagues of.' (bottom) 'The Quenes forelande lieth in this sorte Southwest and by south and west and by north, going into Frobushers straites, being vii Leagues of. Having brought thes landes together, they lie nearest hande northest and southwest. When you have brought Oxfordes mounte and Leicesters Cape going into the Straites, southest and southest (*sic*) from you layding to Jackman sownde, you shall open twoo great sowndes, the one lying south, and by west and the other southwest and by west. From Warwikes Cape at Fryzeland to Leicesters Cape the lande lieth west and by north and est and by north; from Cape Warwik to the next Cape of lande trendes northwest & by west and northest and by est.'

DOCUMENT 8

Edward Fenton's log for the ship *Judith*[1]

[17]   Emanuell 1578

May 25.   Sonndaie being the xxv[th] daie of Maye at iiii of the clock in the afternoone, the winde was west northwest, and cam to Gravesende at vii of the clock in the eveninge ankering there all night.

26.   Monndaye the xxvi[th] daye we did ride at Gravesende with the tide att westerlie.

27.   Tewesdaye the xxvii[th] daye we waighed our ancour at v. of the clock in the morninge and sett sayle towardes Harwich, the winde south southweste / we did ancour at the Naze becawse the tyde was spente, having harwich Nis open, and did ride there all night /

28.   Wedensdaye the xxviii[th] daye, We did weigh ancour at iii of the clocke in the morninge and wente over the Naze, it became calme at viii of the clocke, and we cam to an ancour at the polle heade of Orwell. And weighing ancour at xii of the clocke did goo into Orwell, where we founde the Ayde and the rest of the Shipps, being in the whole xv sayles / the winde south southwest /

29.   Thursdaye the xxix[th] daye, we rode still at Orwell, staying till the rest of the Shipps had taken in such provicion as was not Shipped at London. The winde Southest /

30.   Frydaye the xxx[th] daye, we made an ende of taking in our proviccon and water; being then readie to Sett sayle.

31.   Satterdaye the Laste of Maye, We sett sayle in the morninge & went into the rowling grownde, the winde Northest and byrst and ankred there till 10 of the clock, and waighing then did sett saile and turned into the swell, and having brought our markes together, wente thence with the forelande, and at night was as high as the same /

June 1.   Sonndaye the firste daye of June, we were thwart of fayrele,[2] we cam

---

[1] Magdelene College, Pepys Library MS 2133. Original pagination shown in parenthesis.
[2] Fair Isle.

through the sea becawse the winde was northest, and cam on heade beachey the same night.

[18]

Monndaie 2. Monndaye the ii[d] daye we were thwart the wight at vi of the clocke in the morning, at night thwart Portlande /

3. Tewesdaye the iii[d] daye we cam to plymouth in the afternoone and there watred, and sett sayle from thence abowte ix of the clocke in the night; and there reatorned Master Skimton home.[1]

4. Wedensdaye the iiii[th] daie we were thwarte the Lizarde & by 10 of the clock in the morninge thwart of the Landesende, directing our courses the westwardes all the daye till midnight, then it was calme and the winde was westerly and we did lye to the Northe /

n.n.e. 5L.

5. Thursdaye the vth daye, we stood to the northwardes being 10 Leagues west from the Landesende. and sayled from vi of the clock in the morning till 12 at middaye, 5L north northest, then we Layde it abowt to the westwardes, the winde cam north northest, we did rune from 12 of the clock at middaye till vi at night 4L, from thens till midnight 6L, west northwest; Then the winde was northest and to the southwarde from 12 of the clock at midnight till 4 in the morning went 5L west northwest, the winde est northest /

Altitude 51–23.

w.18L.

6. Frydaie the vi[th] daie from 4 of the clock in the morninge we sailed till 12 of the clock at middaye 18L, and we mett at ii of the clock in the afternoone with the olde head of Kinsale or betwene Ballemone and it, from ii of the clock we wente 18L west the winde at est and muche winde, at midnight we were thwart of the dorzes[2] directing our course west northwest and northwest and by west. We mett at Beareshaven the Grechwinde of Bristol robbed by the frenche at Cape St Vincent.[3]

n.w. by w. 35L.

7. Satterdaye the vii[th] daie at 12 of the clock I tooke the sonne and was in 52 degrees beinge 18L northwest and bywest from the dorzes, the winde southest and by est, from 12 of the clock till 4 in the afternoone went 4L, & demi from 4 **[19]** till 8, 4L & northwest and by west, from viii till 12, 4L, from 12 till 4 in the morninge 6L, from 4 till 12 at middaye 16L, the winde est with muche winde Rayne and thick.

n.w. b. n. 45L.

8. Sonndaye the viii[th]. We wente northwest and by west the winde est with muche winde, from 12 of the clock at middaye till 8 at night we wente 16L and the winde cam est southest with a reasonable gale, we wente till viii in the morninge which was 12 howers, 22L northwest and by west, from 8 till 12 at middaye, we wente vi.L in the same point.

[1] Presumably, Skimpton was a harbour pilot of Plymouth.
[2] Dursey Head and Island.
[3] Fenton's is the only account to name the *Grechewinde*, though others mention the incident.

9. Monndaye the ix[th] daye, We wente from 12 of the clock at middaye till 4 in the afternoone 4L northwest and by west, the winde est southest, from 4 till 8, 4L, from viii of the clock till 12, 3L, &d from 12 till 4 in the morninge, 3L, &d from 4 till 8, 4L, from viii till 12 at middaye 5L, on the same point.

n.w.b.w. 24L

The Altitude 54–30.

10. Tewesdaye the xth daie from 12 of the clock till 4 in the afternoone 4L, from 4 till 8, 5L, from 8 till midnight 4L, and from thence till 4 in the morninge 6L, from 4 till 8, 4L northwest and by west, the winde est and by est. At viii of the clock in the morninge it fell calme till 12 of the clocke at middaye that we wente not ii myles.[1]

The Altitude 55–5.[2]

11. Wedensdaye the xj[th] daye. from 12 at middaye we wente 1L, till 4 in the afternoone it was litle winde southest and by est, and from 4 till 4 in the morninge it was so calme we wente nothinge. At 4 there cam a gale of winde so that we wente till 10 of the clock 4L, and then it was calme and no winde, at 2 of the clock the winde was southwest and it cam westerlie /

s.e. b. e. 5L.

12. Thursdaye the xii[th] daye it was calme till 4 in the afternoone, we wente till 8 of the clock 4L. The winde was south southwest and southwest, from viii till 12 at midnight 6L N.W. and bywest then it Rayned with the winde esterlie and [20] muche winde, from 12 till 4, we wente 8L, from 4 till 8, 8L, from 8 till 12 at middaye 8L, northwest and by west. The winde est northest, with Rayne & thick /

n.w. b. w. 34L.

13. Frydaie the xiii[th] daye from 12 of the clock at middaye till 4, we wente iiL, the winde est northest, from 4 till 8, 6L, the winde cam northest and by northe. from 8 till 12 at midnight 4L, from 12 till 4, 5L, from 4 till 8, 5L, from 8 till 12 at middaye 5L, northwest and by west. The winde was from 8 till 12 northest.

n.w. b. w. 32L.

The Altitude 56–47.

14. Satterdaye the xiiii[th] daye from 12 till 4 in the afternoone, 4L, the winde northe. from 4 till 8, 4L, from 8 till midnight 4L, from thence w.n.w. 23L. till 4, 4L, from 4 till 8, 4L, from 8 till 12 at middaye, 3L. West northwest.

w.n.w. 23L.

The Altitude 57.

15. Sonndaye the xv[th] daye, the winde was north with litle winde the weather fayre & cleare, from 12 of the clock at middaye till 8 at night wente litle in

---

[1] There is no margin note to this entry.

[2] Until 7 September, Fenton repeatedly misstates his observation of latitude as that of 'altitude' (the meridional altitude of the sun or Pole Star, one component of the calculation to establish latitude). As far as may be ascertained by cross-referencing these observations with those of Christopher Hall (document 6, *ad finem*), Fenton's observation of latitude (however he referred to it) was broadly accurate. It is not known whether Fenton was conversant with such calculations prior to the voyage, or that they were the fruits of Charles Jackman's tuition.

n.w. 10L.

our course, the michaell farr to the Leawardes, *which* cawsed us to spende the time and gett litle, being in effect calme. At 8 of the clock the winde was southwest and by west. we went northwest till midnight *with* litle winde 2, from thence till 4 in the morni*n*ge 3L, and from 8 till 12 at mid-daye 2L northwest.

The Altitude 57–40.

16. Monnd*a*ye the xvi[th] d*a*ye the winde was westerlie *with* lilte winde, we stoode to the northwestwardes from 12 of the clock at middaye till 4 in the morni*n*ge 7L, north northwest, from 4 till 8, 2L, west northwest the winde

n.n.w.–4L.
n.n.w.–2L.
n.w.b.w.–4L.

est southest. from 8 till 12 at middaye 4L, northwest & by west / the winde southest *with* a good gale.

The Altitude 57–54.

[21]

w.n.w.–46L.

17. Tewesd*a*ye the xvii[th] d*a*ye from 12 of the clock till 12 of the clock the next d*a*ye, we wente 46L west northwest *with* the winde est *with* muche winde thick and Rayne.

18. Wedensd*a*ye the xviii[th] d*a*ye. The winde was esterlie est northest, verie fowle weather *with* thick and Rayne. we went northwest and by west till

n.w.b.w.–34L.

12 of the clock at midnight 18L, from thence till 12 at middaye 16L on the same pointe. The winde northest faire and cleare weather from midnight till middaye.

The Altitude 59–50.

19. Thursd*a*ye the xix[th] d*a*ye, the winde was northest we wente from 12 at mid-daye till midnight northwest and northwest and by north, 15L, from thence till 4 we wente west northwest being in the sight of Fryzelande, from 4 till 8 we bore upp west and westsouthwest being from the shoore 5 or 6L,

n.w. &
n.w.b.w. 15L.

betwixte 8 and 12 at middaye we haled in betwene the ii south Capes named Warwick and Leicestre[1] and then tooke we *our* boate, and I wente to the shoore where I mett *with* the Ge*n*erall who gayned verye litle the shore before me. We fownde there a good sownde *with* xii fathom water & good grownde. we nest[2] fownde ii or iii tentes of the people built in sorte like those of *Meta incognita*, their botes of the same fashion, and all other thinges therof *per*teyninge. The people fled upon *our* coming to lande, so that we had no *per*fect view of them. we tooke nothing of such triffles as we fownde there, saving that the Ge*n*erall brought awaie one of there dogges. Further we founde there the stone *which* yeldes the mother of Rubie like to that in *Meta incognita*, and some greate liklehood of the other oures; the Landes yelding all other sort*es* of grasse & herbes like to the first by us diskovered / The land trendes est and west nearest hande. And, in sayling long the same we might discerne the lande to thende alonge to the north and by west and north northest. Within ii or iii howers we

[1] Unidentified; but Fenton's narrative indicates that this was west of 'Cape Frobisher' (Kap Farvel).
[2] *Sic.*

repaired againe to o*u*r shipps and spente the most p*ar*te of that daye in hull and under o*r* foresaile till I was caried aborde againe.

[22]   20.   Frydaye the xxth daye, I cam aborde at abowt j of the clock in the after-nown being then wi*th*in ii mile of the lande, bearinge then of wi*th* the shipps west southwest, the winde esterly being a freshe gale. We cam together at 7 or 8 of the clock, being viiiL. from the Land, directing o*u*r course to the northwest and by west. The winde then cam northerlie, being calme from midnight till 4 in the morni*n*ge the winde being norther-lie went northwest and by west and west northwest. At 12 of the clock the winde was north and by west. we laye it all abowte to thest wardes beinge 13L from the land and litle winde wente est northest and northest and by est with the lande of Frizelande /

  21.   Satterdaye the xxjth daye the winde was northerlie and litle winde wi*th* thick and fogg. We wente est northest and by est, Laying it abowte to the

w.n.w. 4L.   westwardes. and went west northwest till 8 of the clock wi*th* litle winde 4L from 8 till 12, 5L, northwest and by west and then there showed more

n.w.b.w. 5L.¹   lande to us north northwest w*hich* made us to Loose upp northwest & by
n.w.b.w. 17L.   north 5L wherupon we viewed Low lande & muche ize, the winde southest and by est, at 4 of the clock in the morni*n*ge we wente 6L till 8; then the winde did harle in at southwest wi*th* thick and Rain, we wente from 8 till 12, 6L northwest and by west. Then we sawe muche ize in the southwest did shifte o*u*r tackle aborde and went southwest /

  22.   Sonndaye the xxiith daye, from 12 till 3 in the afternone we went southwest through much ize & at that time cleare of thize, Then we sett o*u*r course

s.w.–5L.   northwest & by west wi*th* the winde southest, with fogg and Rayne went 5L southwest, from 3 of the clock till 8, 8L on the same pointe the winde southest & by est, from 8 till 12 at midnight 8L on the same point wi*th* much winde, thick & rayne; From thence till 4 we spone afore the sea with the sail 2L from 4 till 8, 6L, **[23]** the winde southest & by est, from 8 till 12, 7L northwest and by west. The Michaell dep*ar*ted from us at 4 of the clock in the afternone of the same daie. A shipp did break her forey*ar*de w*hich* cawsed us to spone afore the sea as aforesaid.

  23.   Monndaye the xxiiith daye, the winde was southest and by est wi*th* thick and Rayne we wente from 12 at middaie till 4 in the afternone 6L, from 4

n.w. by w.   till 8 5L, from 8 till 12 at midnight 4L, with litle winde, begyninge then to
23L.   cleare, from thence till 4, 4L, with litle winde esterlie, from 4 till 8, 4L then it fell calme. so that we wente 2L till 12 of the clock at middaie northwest & by weste all this watch, then the winde came westerlie with litle winde / St John daie.

                                           Altitude 60–50.

---

¹ *Sic.*

24. Tewesdaie the xxiiii^th daie, it was calme and the winde westerlie, from 12 at middaie till 4, 1L northe, from 4 till 8, 4 north & by west, from 8 til 12 at midnight, 4L northe, from thence till 4, 4L northe northwest, from 4 till 8, 4L on the same point, from thence till 12 at middaye 4L on the same pointe. The winde westerlie faire and cleare weather /

n.–8L.
n.b.w.–4L.
n.n.w.–12L

25. Wedensdaie the xxv^th the winde was westerlie, we went from 12 at middaie till 4, 4L, from 4 till 8, 3L north northwest and cleare weather, from 8 till 12 at midnight 5L northwest and by west, from thence till 8, 5L in the same pointe, from 8 till 12, 4L northwest, the winde west with faire cleare weather /

n.n.w.–7L.
n.w.b.w.–8L.
n.w.–4L.

26. Thursdaie the xxvi^th daie, the winde west. southwest we wente from 12 at middaie till 4 of the clocke in the afternone, 4L northwest, from 4 till 8, 4L northwest and by north, close by the winde, from 8 till midnight, 4L northwest, from 12 till 4 it was litle winde, 3L on the same pointe, from 4 till 8 it was calme the winde westerlie, making no waie stoode northwardes and were in sight of muche ize, begyninge to drawe nigh the lande it was calme till 12 of the clock then the winde began to blow westerlie. The Altitude 63–3.[1] The sonne sett almost betwexte the north & north & by west.

n.w.–11L.
n.w. by w. 4L.

[24]

Looked for the Straites

27. Frydaie the xxvii^th daie, from 12 at middaie we laye of and on with the winde westerlie with manie short bordes, 5 to the north with faire weather and smoothe water by reason of the ize. Thus we spent the daie and the most parte of the night / In the morning at 4 of the clock being 15L from (Halle Islande)[2] we thought to beare in west and west and by north; the winde was northest and the northlande was northwest & by west and northwest from us. And we were so envyroned with ize that we were faine to Lye owte southest againe to find some waie in. At midnight the winde cam northerlie and northest, we wente from 4 in the morninge till middaie 5L southwest and by south.

s.w.b.s.–5L.

The Altitude 62–36.

28. Satterdaye the xxviii^th daie, at 12 of the clock at middaye it fell calme and the winde cam southe southwest, we laye southest of into the sea to compasse thize to the southwardes. Thinking we sawe the smale Ilandes of the northlande all the morninge being north northwest from us, as we thought 6 or 7L. Wente southest from 4 in the morninge till 8, 4L, (southest),[3] from 8 till 12 at middaie, 5L and at that time the winde was west and by north, we wente southwest & by south /

s.e.–4L.
s.w.b.ws.–3L.

29. Sonndaie the xxix^th daie from 12 at middaie till 6 at night, 4L, southwest

---

[1] The variance between this observation and that of Hall in the *Thomas Allen* only 24 hours earlier (document 6, p. 113) indicates that the *Judith* had become separated from the fleet by now, though Fenton refers to this only obliquely.

[2] This and subsequent real names shown in parenthesis are so placed by Fenton.

[3] Erased by Fenton.

s.w. b s.–11L.

and by south. The winde west and by north with much winde but faire and cleare weather; we tooke of our Bonnettes[1] being much winde and no borde the better:[2] from 6 till 4 in the morninge, 7L, southwest and by south, At 4 of the clock we layde it abowte and went 3L till 12 of the clocke.

The Altitude 61–34.

n.w. b.w.–3L

n.w.–3L.

n.w. b. n.–6 ¬.

30. Monndaye the xxx[th] daie, we wente northwest and by west till 4 of the clock, 3L, The winde westerlie faire weather, from 4 till 8 northwest the winde west southwest 3L, from 8 till midnight northwest & by north 3L, from 12 till 4 in the morninge 4L, northwest & northwest & [25] by north, the winde west southwest.

w.&w.n.w.–2L.

from 4 till 8, 3L northwest and by north, from 8 till 12 of the clock at middaie we went 2L, west and west northwest, Layinge it abowte to the southwardes and westwardes, I thinke we did see the Quenes forelande all the morninge, being from us west northwest and northwest.

The Altitude 60–15

Julie 1. Tewesdaie the first of Julie at 12 of the clock at middaie it was calme and the winde was northerlie and almost rownde abowte. Then at 4 of the clock in the afternone the winde cam northerlie and north northest till betwene 5 and 6 of the clock. We made then the Northlande perfectlie being west and by north and northwest 9L from it. At ix of the clock we fell with much ize and were environed all to the southe, being a good gale of winde north northest.[3] Woulde faine have borne with the other shipps, but coulde not for thize. We turned all night with the winde north northwest and northwest. We gatt through thize at viii of the clocke and the winde was west southwest and at 10 were in them againe, going northwest as we might for thize. We did see bothe the sides of the Straites verie well at the middaie. The Northlande being north & by est from us and the Quenes foreland west southwest.[4]

2. Wedensdaie the ii[de] daie, at Middaie the winde was south southwest. We wente northwest and by west and west northwest, being amongst much ize as possiblie we coulde cleare. The fleete wente then in by the southe side abowt 8 or 9 of the clock at night. The winde cam south southest with so much winde as the sailes could carie in the bolts. And being thus in daunger of it, we did turne in thize all the night, and in the morninge it did shutt upp altogether, and we were fayne to putt into it. And abowte 4 of

[1] Strips of canvas, attached to the bottom of fore and aft sails.
[2] 'Board': the distance made by the ship between tacks when working to windward. 'No borde the better' may have been Fenton's inference that he was struggling to rejoin the fleet and wished to make little headway in a contrary direction.
[3] I.e., the *Judith* was being driven into the ice-field.
[4] The observation indicates that the *Judith* had entered the mouth of the 'strait' by now, earlier than any other ship of the fleet.

the clock in the morninge we were in great daunger to loose Shipp and ourselves (if god of his greate mercie and providence had not wonnderfullie delivered us) after lying thus [26] tossed and shutt upp in the ize with muche winde and a greate fogg, after our hartie prayers made to god, he opened unto us (as to the children of Israell in the brode sea) a litle cleare to the northwest wardes, wherinto we forced our shipp with vyolence. And thus having given our selves to the mercifull handes of god, he of his greate goodnes sente us presentlie faire weather, wherby we gayned some plaine to turne in all the foreparte of the daie.[1]

3. Thursdaye the iii^de daie, at Middaie it was verie foggie and thick the winde westerlie yet faire weather (notwithstanding the thick[2] most daungerous) beinge not well hable to see a bow shoott from us. In the afternoone abowte 1 or 2 of the clock, it cleared upp so that we saw bothe the shoores, being but litle shott into the Straites. And turning upp and downe viewed so much ize as it was ympossible further to gett into the Straites. In thende one in the Topp sawe some waie to the Southwardes and also behelde the Quenes forelande southwest and by southe from us, directing our course with it: the winde being westerlie and west and by north. That night we gayned within 5L of it And the winde beinge west northwest we laye of and on of the Quenes forelande, being (god be thanked) eskaped owt of the ize which were most daungerous. And thus lyinge all night of and on, thinking the nexte daie to find some harbour, bothe to refreshe ourselves, to provide water, and also to make our shipp stiffer, being by reason [of] her lightnes not skarvhable to carie any saile.[3]

4. Frydaie the iiii^th daie we behelde an open great Sounde nigh the Quenes forelande, trusting there to finde some harbour and after the making of manie bordes turned into it.[4] And sawe it go verie farr in, envyroned with a greate sorte of Ilandes: and at night the sea or currunte cam so stronglie owt of the same sownde that we coulde not gett in [27] lying of and on all the night. But in the morninge at the fludd we entred into the same, being verie gladd and in greate hoope to finde therin some good place to ancour And sailing 3L into it, did sownde it over and againe, and founde 100. 60. 40. and 30. fathome til we cam to 15. along the north shoore, being (fladd)[5] flatt grownde and sholde water. But so rockie and hard grownde as it was not to ancour in. And being so 3L into it west northwest and northwest and by west we behelde it iii waies into the sea and into the Straites, so that

---

[1] Cf. Charles Jackman's more colourful account of the *Judith*'s ordeal, document 7.

[2] 'Thick': fog.

[3] Fenton refers here to *Judith*'s lightness of ballast, not to any intrinsic structural weakness. The attrition she absorbed on the night of 2/3 July and during the two further weeks required to make her landfall indicates that she was an extremely robust vessel – possibly, given the known activities of her previous owner, William Borough, a former Muscovy vessel (cf. the damage sustained by the *Anne Frances* during similar travails). Like the *Gabriel*, the *Judith* was one of Matthew Baker's commissions.

[4] Gabriel Strait.   [5] Erased by Fenton.

I judge certeinlie the Quenes forelande but an ilande:[1] But the ize being manie coulde not goo thorow.

5. Satterdaye the vth daie, it did flow 10 of the[2] or thereupon, for it floweth southest and northwest. The tide of fludd beinge spente, we sett saile repairinge owt of harbour againe, and having passed 1L owtwardes, tooke in all our sailes (saving the spritt saile) to amende our foresaile being much dekayed with the fowle weather paste, and thus into the shoore sownding, and founde 34. fathoome stremie grownde and there did ancour. I departed with my boote to the shoore accompanied with certein shott, bothe to view the nature of the grownde and also to seeke for oare, which I there fownde in sorte like that in the Countess of Warwikes Ilande, The land altogether without any earth upon it, or habitaceon that I coulde discerne. Fylled there ii toones of snow water and brought ii botesfull of stone for ballice and so departed to borde againe, being supper time. And being a high water at 2 of the clock in the morninge, sett our sailes from the mouthe of the harbour which was betwene the Quenes forelande and Cape (Fenton)[3] Leicesster The sounde lieth west north-west in and going through, beinge devyded with 3 greate Ilandes, besides so manie smale Ilandes as I coulde not tell them. The winde was westerlie and we wente to the north northwestwardes having runne 4 or 5L the winde cam southest with very [28] fayre weather at Middaie. We sawe much ize in the Straites But viewing a waie to passe amongest theim bare through theim.

6. Sonndaye the vi[th] daie, at 4 of the clock in the afternone we were somwhat troubled with the ize, and all night it was verie calme, the winde was northest In the morninge we were within 3L of Jackmans sownde, but beinge verie calme coulde not gett no nigh it, till it was 12 at middaie, and beinge a tyde of thebb did loose fast to the southwardes againe.

7. Monndaye the vii[th] daie, at Middaie the winde being north and by est with verie litle winde, we were environed with much ize, so that we remayned fast therin to our greate daunger and trouble manie times; But in the after-noone abowt 2 or 3 of the clock there cam a litle gale of winde north and by est, wherby we did borde it upp and downe with a reasonable cleare waie amongest thize, with contynuall and ernest prayer to god for a better harbour. Abowte 11 of the clocke in the night it was a high water being

---

[1] The referrence to 'iii waies into the sea' here indicates that Fenton had become aware of further land-masses – the present-day Edgell and Lower Savage Islands – distinct both from the supposed peninsula and the 'Foreland'.

[2] Blank; presumably 'clock'.

[3] Erased by Fenton. Cape Leicester cannot be identified with certainty, but may be synonymous with the western promontory of Sorry Harbour, opposite Cape Warwick. If this is the case, the 'sound' to which Fenton refers subsequently was in fact Graves Strait; its fragmented topography closely resembles his decription .

within ii miles of (Jackmans)[1] sownde and the winde at southest and calme: we layde it of towardes the northest and by est towing our Shipp a heade with our boote till midnight Then we layde our grapnell upon a greate peice of ize setting a longe the shoore and by the nomber of ize in the eveninge the tide sett into the shoore, that abowt ii or iii of the clock in the morninge we departed from our ancour on thize, and did our best to towe our Shipp from the shoore into the sea, and much ize in the waie to offend and trouble us. So that in thende they shoote us upp, and most vehementlie caried us downe a longe the shoore, being in the laste quarter [29] of thebb driven 4L abowt a pointe of lande from Jackmans sownde[2] And being thus abowt the pointe we were forced with a slake water into a rownde Baye amongest maine Ilandes and sonke rockes which we named the Baye of Distresse, bearing in to the midest therof, bringinge the south pointe est northest to us, and the north pointe, northest and by northe, driving so within a falcon shott of the shoore, being environed with muche ize wherby (as a cheif providence of god) we were kepte from the shoore And being thus in all show without hoope of deliverie, having fullie yelded our selves to the mercie of the most highest, Sounded for grownde finding 30. fathoms, yet not withstandinge, attending death either by thize or Rockes. Laye thus tossed betwixte hoope and feare the space of 4 or 5 howers till it was a high water, wherupon thize openinge and breeking a sownder, there was no other refuge but to comme to ancour or els to drive on the shoore: we espied a cove in one of the Ilandes where determyned to putt in the Shipp or to ancour, and sending our boote furthwith to view the place, ymmediatlie there cam a litle winde at weste southwest, wherupon we called our boote a borde againe, which cam to us againe with greate daunger to be loste, thize shooting theim from us And in the meane time having hoysed our yardes, (and the bote recovered to our shipp) there was one of the foreyarde to cutt the saile, who being not verie readie, the boye goinge upp to helpe and beinge half the shrowdes upp, the saile fell downe and smoote the boye over borde into the sea, who (by godes good providence) gatt holde of the foresail sheathe and was recovered againe with no greate harm, saving his face brooken and his brest brewsed with the block of the sheathe.[3]

[30]   8. Tewesdaie the viii[th] daie, at Middaye the foresaile being cutt as aforesaid, we bare owt of the Baye of Distresse with verie litle winde, and went not half a mile before the winde shifted to the northwest and north northwest that we coulde not laye it owt. But in thende (god sendinge a good freshe gale)[4], we adventred to go owt betwene ii Ilandes where we cam not in

---

[1] Fenton's parenthesis.
[2] Probably Buerger Point, the southeastern extremity of the entrance to Jackman Sound.
[3] This passage, and others in succeeding entries, are extremely interesting; being some of the earliest extant accounts to dwell upon the minutiae of contemporary ship handling – and its hazards.
[4] Editor's closing parenthesis.

more to the southwardes And having obtayned againe the Straites we haled (for Jackmans) sownde & with the (Countess of Warwikes) sownde, with mynde (if god would so permitt) to gaine either of them. But in the eveninge it becam calme and we were at 6 of the clock amongest much ize, the fludd and thebb meeting did cawse thize to meete and shutt us upp that we coulde not steare, wherby we laye all night without winde. In the morninge there cam a litle gale of winde at north northest, we cawsed our men to sett thize from our shipp with pikes and owers, and so in thende (god be praysed) gatt owt to the southwardes with much trouble, putting againe to the sea, for that we coulde gett no harbour for ize, and thus from the morninge till middaie we sailed downe the Straites with the winde at northest, havinge brought the Quenes forelande south and by est from us. In our departing from the Baye of distresse, we viewed discending from the topp an Ilande iii of the countrey people, which (we supposed) cam to view us. These Ilandes within that Baye seamed to be more covered with earth then any erst seen by me, and therfore as well by that occasion as thaptnesse of the place to fishe in (I judged) those Ilandes much inhabited with the people: Being right sorie [31] that the greatnesse of our daunger, forced our departure thence without further view of the same.[1]

9. Wedensdaye the ix^th daie, the winde was at est northest with litle winde. We stoode to the south shoore wardes from Middaie till 4 in the afternoone, and falling calme were amongest much great ize, wherupon we mored our shipp by the grapnell upon a greate peice of ize, wanting winde to chaze her, we rode there all night till the next daie with litle winde est southest, and so extreeme thick and foggie that we coulde not see one mile from us: we abode there still of cleare weather at the Middaie, at what time it cleared a litle wherbie we sawe the South shoore being the Quenes forelande which did beare southest, beinge a driven into a baye and fast locked in with thize that we coulde not gett owt.

10. Thursdaie: the xth daie, from Middaie it fell thick and foggie againe till aboute 2 of the clock in the afternoone, at what time we espyinge a glade to the northwardes, sett our saile, but in one half hower we were shutt upp with thize, were forced to laie our grapnell upon a great peice of flatt ize, to defende the other ize from us, (being verie thick and foggie) were in greate daunger, prayinge to god for mercie and deliveraunce And thus environed with the ize, purposed nothwithstanding to go to the sea, having the winde at southest, a verie harde winde to putt us to the sea withall, yet in respect of our late perill, we rather chewsed to holde our determynacion (if god woulde) then putt any more into the Straites: But the winde beinge

---

[1] This appears to be a reference to Halford Island and its smaller neighbours.

147

at est southest we rode there all night driuinge to the west shoore wardes, and hooped at Middaie for cleare weather but it contynued thick still.

11. Fridaye the xi[th] daie, it was calme at middaie with litle winde esterlie, abowt 2 of the clock we did sett saile having a freshe gale [32] (trustinge) to gett from the shoore to the northwardes. But being environed with much ize we ronne to the north northest, and sailing betwixt ii greate peices of ize, where we saw rowme enough half a quarter of an hower before, the waie was presentlie growen so narow, that thize strake the Shipp on bothe her bowes passing through them, striking a hoole on the larborde (side)[1] bowe a foote longe, were forced to laye our shipp by the lee, and putt a peice therin of 25 ynches longe, and that being amendid used the starborde boo[2] in like sorte having a hoole therin 5 or 6 ynches long and 3 ynches brode, and thus in 4 howers having amended them bothe, the winde beinge at southest and by est. In the eveninge abowt 10 of the clock it was litle winde at est southest. Woulde gladlie have sailed to the northwestwardes but being environed with much ize, espying a greate peice of yze, were forced to caste our grapnell theron, and rode by it all night (hoping) the nexte daie for cleare weather, still it driuinge to the west shoore with litle winde est southest, rode there still to the Middaie, desiering god to sende us a better harbour.

12. Satterdaie: the xii[th] daie, it did cleare upp a litle that we saw the west shoore being within one L. therof, the winde was northe and we were nigh the Baye of Distresse, being 5L from Jackmans sounde. We sett saile to thestwardes, ernestlie desiering of god, to deliver us from the Baie beinge latlie in greate daunger therin, Stoode est and est northest of with litle winde, but reasonable cleare of ize till 5 of the clocke, being calme tooke in our sailes, by reason it was verie foggie, towed with our boote to a greate peice of ize, which we were forced to chewse (as next to god) our chois ancour holde; being for the space of 4 or 5 daies not 2L or litle more from the shoore with greate fogg and no winde at all being abowt 5 or 6 of the clock at night and so contynued all night. In the morninge at 6 of the clock [33] we loosed our shipp from the ize, and towed her est northest 2L Then the winde cam at est and by north and we stoode to the southwardes 2L and then to the northwardes And at Middaie were abowte 5L of from the shoore, which made us right gladd, for the foreparte of the daie it was foggie and at Middaie cleared upp.

13. Sonndaye the xiii[th] daie, the winde was esterlie: and it was cleare on the northe shoore (Halls Ilande beinge est from us, The Countess sownde northest)[3] and thize reasonable cleare, so that we made manie bordes therin. Abowte 2 of the clock in the afternoone we espied the Michaell

---

[1] Erased by Fenton.
[2] I.e., bow.
[3] Editor's closing parenthesis.

beinge southest from us: we made a good saile and fetched her upp abowt 3 of the clock in the afternoone, (being verie glad to see her in saffetie) The winde was northest and by north and some time northest. We stoode to the north northwest till 8 of the clock, and then appeared much ize unto us right on heade, that we layde it abowt to thest southest, and in the latter parte of the night were amongst much ize, being bothe calme and foggie as it coulde be all night with much Raine In the morninge we turned to the northestwardes, and founde a cleare wherin we spente the foreparte of the daie, contynewing foggie with the winde northest.

14. Monndaie the xiiii^th daie, at Middaie we stoode to the north northwest till one of the clock when appeared much ize, that we coulde hardlie passe through theim for the greatnes of the fogg with smale raine, so that we were forced to laye it abowte to thest southest, striving to kepe the cleare we were in for feare of more ize. At 4 of the clock we founde much ize to thest wardes so that we layde it to the northestwardes. The winde being est southest, and finding much ize at 5 of the clock were constrained to ride on an ize by our grapnell and the Michaell also, ridinge there all night, expecting cleare weather in the morninge, being at 8 of the clock somwhar cleare that we [34] behelde the north shoore within 3L of us. But encreasinge presentlie foggie againe, were by the great abowndaunce of ize constrayned to ride there still till middaie being not hable to sett saile for the number of ize which had environed us, having been much troubled befor by them to our great daunger The ize we rode by was in effect 200 yardes broode with a hill in the middest of it.

15. Tewesdaie the xv^th daie. It was so foggie at middaie we were forced to ride there still all the afternoone and all night, and abowt 6 or 7 of the clock in the morninge the sonne did appeare somewhat cleare, so that we sawe bothe the Shoores.[1] The Countess of Warwikes sownde beinge northest and by est from us The winde (though litle) at west southwest, being neither cleare nor thick: We sett saile at 8 of the clock and bare est northest 1L & demi thinking to gett harbour in the (Countess sownde) the winde being west and west southwest And at Middaie the winde cominge at north northest we layde it abowt to the (north northest)[2] northwest with litle winde and foggie.

16. Wedensdaie the xvi^th daie. We wente northwest at Middaie one league or thereabowtes and it becam calme, so that we were forced to take in our sailes and towed with our boote to a greate Ilande of ize, wheron we ancoured with our grapnell and brought the Michaell to the same, being verie calme but reasonable cleare of ize (onelie it was thick with the fogg) were abowte 3 or 4L from the Countess of Warwikes sownde southwest and by west We rode there still till the next daie at Noone, the weather contynewing foggie with no winde: yet nevertheless, the daie clearing upp

---

[1] That is, both sides of the 'strait'.
[2] Erased by Fenton.

we were driven over to the west shoore, which at Middaie we verie well viewed, the est shoore [35] being covered with fogg coulde not verie well see it Jackmans sownde being from us southwest All the night there was but smale stoore of ize abowte us, but Middaie we were so daungerfullie environed therwith, that there appeared no waie for us to gett owt of theim, (till it woulde please god to open the same) The ize were so monstrous that some of theim were by estimacion an acour broode and verie deepe in the water, so that we laie in verie great daunger.

17. Thursdaie the xvii^th daie. The weather at Middaie being verie calme and the winde southerlie we drove northwardes into much ize, so that we saw no waie to cleare theim being verie straunge, for that the last yere on the same daie and monthe, there was litle or no ize to be seen within 8 or 10L of that place And whereas it was suposed we might have gott into the Straites cominge hither in Maie, I see it wilbe much ado to gett in there in the begynninge of August (as this yere we have made daungerfull proofe therof) in thende of which monthe we shoulde reatorne againe home. Wherfore to make any discoverie there, it is not liklie to be performed where a man shalbe bothe in contynuall daunger of thize, and also subiect to Calmes and contynuall fogges, which we have made good proofe of, finding in xvii daies travaill paste (there),[1] but ii of cleare weather, but most daungerous to suche as shall attempt the same.[2] At 4 or 5 of the clock in the afternoone there was litle winde, but it was cleare; so that we might see the weste shoore, and all the north shoore thick with fogg, and contynewed so all night, that we were not hable to sett saile for the nomber of thize, if we had been forced on the shoore And at 5 of the clock in the morninge the winde beinge at southest and by southe, it blew a preetie gale of winde [36] setting us to the west shoore, but unhable to sett saile, by reason we were so environed with the ize, contynewinge so till 10 or 11 of the clock, became calme, and we were almoste within 3L of the west shoore. At Middaie the winde was uncerteine, but enclyned esterlie.

18. Frydaie the xviii^th daie, it was calme at Middaie, and so contynewed till 4 or 5 of the clock in the afternoone and also all night till the next daie at noone with no winde & thick, we rode still at the ize.

19. Satterdaie the xix^th daie, it was calme with a litle cleare at Middaie, it contynued so till night, and then cam a litle winde southerlie, so that abowt 8 or 9 of the clock in the eveninge we sett saile beinge somwhat cleare

---

[1] Erased by Fenton.

[2] Fenton's opinion here reflected that of the commissioners, who had attempted to set out the voyage by 1 May (see p. 19 above). However, from the experience of the previous two voyages, it would appear that the prevalence of ice in the region was unusually heavy in 1578; perhaps the result of a mild spring and heavy calving of icebergs from northwestern Greenland. The danger posed by this threat was undoubtedly exacerbated by the unusually prevalent southeastern winds reported by Fenton and Hall.

weather and the ize not verie thick, standing for the Countess of Warwikes sownde est southest, But before midnight the winde cam about upon manie pointes to thest and est northest and southest: We turned of and on all night, having Gabriells Ilande but 2L north northest from us and manie other Ilandes with much ize abowt them Wherof Gabriells Ilande and an other Ilande lying north and by west from it Laie in this sorte, as we bare est with the Countes sownde.

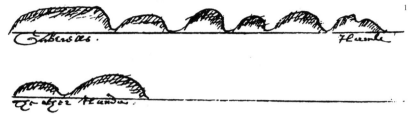

¹

The winde beinge upp the straites we were much hindred by the ize which were thick to gett by turninge, and at four of the clock in the morning it was litle winde south southest, were forced to towe with our boote to thestwardes and so contynued till the middaye with greate labour [37] yet therby gayninge 3 or 4L, towardes the Countess of Warwikes sownde which was 3L from us est and by southe.

20. Sonndaie the xxth daie, at Middaie we cam to ancour upon a greate ize, being verie calme & our men vtterlie wearied with towing, having used that exercise from 4 of the clock in the morning till middaie At that instante we were environed with much ize, being also verie thick to the shoorewardes, that we much feared we coulde not gett harbour for theim, otherwaies we had presentlie gayned harbour. But abowt 4 or 5 of the clock in the afternoone the ize were somewhat seperated that we might pass towardes the shoore and the Countess sownde, (where we labored and desiered be) Our men in respect of the greate daunger and continuall toyle they were in (having then a calme) entred a freshe their boote and towed the shipp, 1 or 2L nigh the shoore towardes the Countess sownde, being then within 4 or 5L of the same, bearing est and by south from us; contynewing towinge so till 10 or 11 of the clock in the night, The winde southerlie & south southest but very litle: and then beinge againe envyroned with ize, were constrayned to ancour againe of an other Ilande of ize which we had passed by almost a falconett shott, Spente there the rest of the night, till 3 or 4 of the clock in the morning at what time the weather bothe somewhat cleare and thize opened blowing a preetie gale of winde at the northwest we sett saile and bare with the Countess sownde, fynding not the waie so cleare for ize but that we abode some knockes (which were not daintie to us) And about 6 or 7 of the clock it fell somwhat calme, that we were gladd to towe afreshe with our boote, being then not farr from the shoore. Were by 9 or 10 of the clock within one L. of the [38] shoore, and 2 myles to the northwardes of the Countess

---

¹ Fenton's annotations (top): 'Gabriells Islande', (bottom): 'The other Islande'.

sownde. We then sowndinge fownde 26 fathoms of faire sande and shells, going in still were within 2 miles of the shoore founde the grownde still faire, cam there to ancour. The *Master* wente with the boote presentlie to the north pointe of the Countess sownde to view for ize which we much feared, but god be thanked fownde verie few there: and there he also sownded the more saffelie to bringe in our shipps there, the winde being at northwest. The sowth side of the sounde was so much pestred with ize that we coulde not well gett in there: But if we had attempted that waie, we must have goone 2L to the south, and 2L back againe to the northe, which by reason of thize, woulde have been performed with great difficultie, wheras the travaill of 1L gayned the other waie into the harbour, wherunto (god be praised) we passed saffelie, though finding some ize in the entraunce therof.

21. Monndaie the xxj[th] daie, at Middaie, we (thanked be god) ancored in the Countess of Warwikes sownde verie nigh to Winters furnace (an Ilande verie apte to ancour by) bothe for the faireness of the grownde and neareness of the shoore, being at a high water abowt 15 fathoms and at a low water 9. It doth high at a full sea, about 5 or 6 fathoms. And being thus ancored (gave hartie thankes to god for his gracious and mightie deliveraunce from so manie greate and daungerfull perills) wente to dynner, and in the afternoone, I tooke the *Master* with certein soldiours, and went to (Winters furnace)[1] as well to serche for the people (whome we founde not there) as to view the Straites for our Shipps which we coulde not see. But the Straites were very full of ize, and we right gladd we were delivered from theim. Then we wente to the Countess Ilande to view the same wherein our [39] judgmentes all things remayned at[2] we left them in so much as we founde divers osmondes which we lefte uncovered lying in their places untooched of the people. and we reatorned to our Shipp.[3]

22. Tewsdaie the xxij[th] daie: We did receave the Communion altogether, contynewing that daie in prayer and thankes givinge to god, aswell for the delivering of us from the daungers paste, as also for his greate goodnes in placinge us in so saffe an harbour. Desiering him of his mercie to contynue this his greate good favour towardes us. This daie it blew verie much winde at the northwest.

23. Wedensdaie the xxiij[th] daie, I marched with the *Master* and to the number of 26 soldiours to the Mayne on the north northwest side, aswell to view

---

[1] Newland Island.

[2] *Recte* 'as'.

[3] A lively modern debate has arisen as to the origin and nature of these 'osmondes', or iron blooms. It has been variously suggested that they were left by previous Norse visitors, traded by the Inuit from iron-producing societies, or abandoned there by Frobisher's previous expeditions and acquired subsequently by grateful Inuit scavengers (see Fitzhugh and Olin, *Archaeology*, pp. 232–4; Seaver, 'Baffin Island Walrus Mandibles and Iron Blooms', in Symons, *Meta Incognita*, II, pp. 563–73).

the nature of the grownde, as to serch for oare, and to finde (if I coulde) some dwellinges of the people, which I founde upon our first landing but newlie departed by sonndrie thinges they had new killed bothe fishe and deare: And marchinge 9 or 10 miles into the Countrey, founde the soyle therof most craggie and barraine, yelding no kinde of woode or fruite, neither any sorte of grasse but in some valies where the snow had covered the same, the soile was becomme marishe lik but of no depthe of earthe: therupon feedes the raine deere which we sawe to the nomber of viii, with some partriges, bigger than ours, ruffooted with white winges and the rest of their feathers like unto a graye plover. We killed one of theim. We also founde divers vaines of the same oare as in the Countess Ilande, wherof the vaines seame to lie northwest and by north and southest and by south;[1] And being thus at the furthest parte of our iorney for that time we sawe Gabriells Ilande thwart of us, and (as it seemed)[2] a goodlie sownde beneath us to the northwardes The lande seeming to us all brocken and full of Ilandes and sonke rockes upp into the Straites, so [40] that it appeares not navigable, aswell for the nomber of Ilandes, as sonke rockes lyinge from Gabriells Ilande into the Straites northwardes & to the Northwestwardes as on this side the same towardes the Countess sownde. In our reatorne home, we founde a greate freshe[3] betwixte twoe mountaynes, and some marishe grownde at the south ende therof, the water wherof had his course into the sea over against the place where we rode with our Shipps, and such a fall as is sufficiente to tourne twoo milnes: And wadinge over the ende thereof we passed upp an other hill, where below us we saw an other fresh growen by thabowndaunce of snoew distilling from the Mountaynes, at thende wherof, was some plaine grownde of better nature & soile then erst we had fownde before, not altogether marishelik but disposed to a better sorte and kinde of pasture, we departed thence, and reatorned to our Shipps againe, not finding any of the people. The winde was southerlie.

24. Thursdaie the xxiiii[th] daie, parte of our companie went on shoore to washe there lynnen, and in the afternoone I with the Master and certein soldiours went with our boote to Pembrookes Ilande,[4] to view the Manner of the Straites for ize which remayned therwith well replenished, but by reason the late northwest winde were fallen on the northest shoore We also cheiflie looked for our Generall and the fleete whom we coulde not see. In our

---

[1] Modern geological surveys have confirmed the accuracy of Fenton's assumption (see *HBM*, p. 113.).

[2] Editor's closing parenthesis.

[3] Outfall of water. This, and the earlier sighting of deer and partridges, were extremely important discoveries to men who assumed themselves still to constitute a colonial experiment. From his arrival at Countess of Warwick Sound, Fenton was assiduous in fulfilling his instructions to 'observe the nature of the ayre, and as moche as may be discover and knowe the state of the countrie'.

[4] The island has not been identified. Selman (document 9, p. 184), speaks of it as 'going into the Countess Sound', which indicates that it may be synonymous with Willows Island, immediately to the south of 'Winter's Furnace', or Newland Island. Cf. also Fenton's entry for September 1, which supports this.

travaill of that Ilande we fownde where the people had been after our departure the last yere, by certein sailes & fishe they had lefte there, & a piece of a hoggesheade which they had taken of ours, and heaped manie stones therupon, that the winde shoulde not blowe into the sea, and also founde there, the Stepp of the maste of the Pynass we sonke in the Countess sownde the laste yere, which (we supposed) to be splitt by some greate ize falling theron, and some parte thereof gotten by the people, We had serched for it before and coulde not finde it [41] We killed a hare there of a blew and white cooler and also iiii partriges, and so reatorned againe to our Shipp The winde southerlie.

25. Frydaie the xxvth daie. The winde was north west and by west, it blew much winde in the morninge and brought manie ize into the sownde abowt our shipps, but (god be thanked) they did us no hurte. The Master cutt owt Canvas and made therwith a forsaile and Bonett. we coulde do no other worke, for that our tooles were all (by thindescreccon of the purser) shipped in the Thomas Allin,[1] and noone in my shipp or any of the twoo Barkes, I went to winters fornace to looke for the fleete, but could not see theim.

26. Satterdaie the xxvith daie, the winde in the morninge eas esterlie, with a greate fogg snow and Raine till 4 of the clock in the afternone, the winde cam to the northwest with much winde and verie colde weather, that the sownde in the night was in effect frozen over of a preetie thicknes, by reason of the fowlenes of the weather we were not hable to go abrode.

27. Sonndaie the xxviith daie, the winde was at north west and blewe a greate gale and some times rownde abowt as at west southwest and southwest and west northwest, the weather notwithstanding reasonable faire, the Master and Master Wulfall wente to Winters fornace to looke for the Generalls cominge, but they could not see him or any of the Shipps where upon a point of that Ilande they founde some parte of the pynass sonke the last yere before, and also certein osmondes of iron caried thither by the people of the Countrey.[2]

28. Monnadye the xviiith daie the winde being at west southwest, it rayned in the morning, notwithstanding I marched with xxviii persons and ensigne displayed, upon the northest parte of the maine v or 6 leagues, aswell to serche for oare as to view the nature of that parte of the lande which I founde most craggie and full of stones, altogether [42] without earthe or any greensworde, and in my reatorne home, cam by a goulf we named the

[1] Yet another manifestation of a problem that dogged the expedition. The *Anne Frances*'s pinnace would be assembled inadequately, and Captains Best and Upcot risk their lives therein, for precisely the same reason (see document 11, p. 230).

[2] See p. 152, n. 3 above.

last yere Seate goulf,[1] to serche there for some apte place for habitacion, where I founde the soyle therof some what inclyned to grasse, and some twigges of birche growing there a handfull from the grownde, But by reason the place was subiect to twoo greate mountaines, from the which distended sonndrie freshes by thabondaunce of snowe falling theron, we founde it verie unfitt for our dwellinge and so departed to our Shipps. The same daie I sawe a crane, with deare in sonndrie places, but not above ii or iii in a place. We founde on the Maine a myne of the black oare trending southwest & by west and named the place Skipwith Mounte.[2]

29.   Tewesdaie the xxix[th] daie, I with my *Master* tooke our boote and rowed 3L to the southwardes to a low pointe of lande called (Corbettes point) where I entred with v other persons on lande and serched therin 4 or v miles for oare, and woulde have passed further into the land but that I was lett by a greate fresh of water, verie deepe to wade, and so forced to reatorne to my boote, findinge by the waie a myne of black oare which I named (fentons fortune) not much unlike thoare brought home by the Generall the firste yere: And within a league of the same northwardes, founde a hoole in a clif hable to containe 20 or 30 persons, of the substaunce of the black oare, which I named (Jackmans Cave).[3] The same hoole I verie well viewed, aswell for the nature of the oare, as to make a place there for habitacion (if neede shoulde require) being defendid from all weather but the west windes, but in thende I founde the place most unfitt for habitacion, being bothe brickle of it self, and also subject to water [43] distilling through divers vaines into the same: from thence I cam to an Ilande which I named Jones Ilande,[4] where in like sorte I founde of the black oare, and from thence I reatorned to the Shipps, by reason I harde a greate peice of ordinaunce discharged by theim, feared the people had betrayed some of my Companie washinge on the shoore, But it grew by occasion that i or ii of our companie supposed to see some of our Shipps, and for that cawse they shott of.

30.   Wedensdaie the xxx[th] daie, the *Master* and I with our boote wente to serche a sownde going a longe Jonas Mounte, and rowed to the ende therof which trended northest and by north, and northest 2L, from the Countess sownde.[5] We founde there where the people had latelie been by sondrie

---

[1] Probably Napoleon Bay. This reconnaissance in strength was doubtless intended to forestall any similarly aggressive display by the Inuit prior to the arrival of Frobisher with the bulk of the expedition. It had been Fenton's similar display in the previous year that had finally discouraged persistent Inuit attempts to take English hostages.

[2] Unidentified but presumably named after Lionel Skipwith, a gentleman-soldier in the *Judith* who, upon the evidence of Fenton's journal, was a trusted subordinate.

[3] Not identified. The ore from this location was not, apparently, assayed.

[4] *Recte* 'Jonas' (Fenton's *Judith* did not carry a crew member named Jones, after whom the feature might otherwise have be named). The feature itself has not been identified.

[5] ?Lincoln's Bay. If so, 'Jonas Mount' may have been a small island off Cape Russell.

thinges they had lefte behinde, amongest the which, Master Skipwith founde one of their dartes, the foreparte wherof, we judged to be the horne of one of the fyshes we brought home the last yere, which we preserved And in our waie homewardes we cam by (Jonas Mounte) where I serched for oare but coulde finde no certein vaine there, but some show of litle peices of thoare I founde there the laste yere: from thence cominge towardes our Shipps we discovered one of our shipps at the sea bearing with the Countess sownde, the winde beinge at south southwest, to whom we rowed with all dilligence and founde it the *Hopewell*, for she brought us newes of vi more of the fleete at hande, wherof some in our own view, for ymmediatlie the Generall cam aborde us with his pynass who cam in to the harbour by the northwest of whom we were right gladd; we (I)[1] presentlie dispatched my Master and the Master of the Michaell in the Generalls pynnass to bring in the rest of the Shipps with the Ayde into the Countess of Warwikes sounde, and after we had ancored the hopewell, the Generall supped & laie aborde with me that night.

[44] 31. Thursdaie the xxxi[th] daie, there cam into the Countess of Warwikes sownde thies shipps following viz. the Beare, the Fraunces of Foye, The Sailomon, The Armanell, The Busse of Bridgwater and the Ayde, who having ancored all night without the sounde by reason the winde skanted the night before; and in the waighing of their ancour the next morning, before they coulde fishe the same, and notwithstanding they rowed with their boote to towe the shipp on heade the winde at est northest and verie litle, she fell to Lee warde of a greate yze, and with the after bill of her ancour made a greate hoole in her,[2] so that they were in greate daunger, onlie they stopped the leeke with a peice of beif and with their pompes and Buckettes in thende freede the Shipp being commed with the winde at est into the Countess sownde, where the leeke was better amended and stopped, wherin the Generall used greate dilligence, and in the meane time I wente to Winters furnace to sett upp a tente, where we made triall of some oare;[3] it blew that daie much winde with greate Raine.

August 1. frydaie the firste daie of August, the winde was at north and by est with raine, notwithstandinge the Generall and I repaired to the Countess of Warwikes Ilande with divers Pyoners[4] to unbare & make readie the mynes, and there wrought that daie and began to make upp Lodginges for our pyoners and soldiours, making that night some assaies of the oare.

[1] 'we' inserted above the text, but 'I' not then erased.
[2] Cf. Selman's account of this (document 9, p. 185), and his implication of negligence.
[3] This, and subsequent references to assays, indicate that Fenton had responsibility for overseeing site-testing of ore deposits by Denham and his assistants, in keeping with the commissioners' strict instructions that all assays should be carefully supervised and recorded.
[4] Miners.

2. Satterdaie the ii[de] daie. The winde was at est northest with fogge but reasonable faire weather; verie erlie in the morninge the Generall with twoo litle Pynasses departed to Beares sownde to fetche some of the oare there and reatorned the same daie againe to us, bringing divers sorte of oare with him, which we made triall of that eveninge:[1] all that daie I followed the Pyoners in digging of oare. The Gabriell cam into the [45] Countesse of Warwikes sownde abowt xii of the clock in the night, Master hall being in her, and having lefte the Thomas Allin (wherof he was Pilott) in a harbour nigh Leicesters Cape.

3. Sonndaie the iii[de] daie the Generall and I wente erlie in the morning to (Winters furnace) to view the Mynes there, which we founde to lie so uncerteinlie and crabbedlie to gett, as we founde smale hoope of any good there, the winde all abowte and disposed to Raine. At after dynner he and I with Capten Carew and Capten Philpott in the presence of Christofer Hall Charles Iackman and Androo dyer, sett in consultacion aswell towching such instructions as we had receavid from the Lordes of her Maiesties counsaill; for the better order and government of this accion, as also to establishe certein necessarie rules meete for the good order of our people and disposing of the cawses as we had in hande; the manner wherof will appeare by (a booke)[2] of Register booke kept for that purpose.

4. Monndaie the iiii[th] daie, The winde was southwest and by west litle winde with some fogg. The Gabriell departed againe by the Generalls commaundmente towards Leicesters (pointe)[3] Cape to convoye the Thomas Allin to the Countesse sownde; Certein necessarie orders for government of the whole fleete was proclaymed,[4] and ymmediatlie after the Generall departed with divers soldiours to (Jonas Mounte) to seeke for the Myne there, he brought home divers sortes of oare wherof a triall was made. In the afternoone the winde was all abowt. I followed the pyoners on the Countesse Ilande. One of the soldiours killed a younge Foxe in cooller a duskie white or Russett.

5. Tewesdaie the vth daie. The winde was esterlie in the morninge with great Fogg but reasonable faire weather. My Generall and I departed to *fentons fortune* to view the myne there, where we founde great store of oare, black, mixed with a white stone like the flinte: the vaine wherof cometh from the Maine and lieth est and west. In our reatorne home we serched [46] dyers sownde for harbour for our shipping which we founde verie good, and by the waie sought in divers places for oares; but founde litle we liked of and so reatorned to the Countess Ilande.

---

[1] These were samples of ore mined in 1577 and stockpiled upon Sussex Island thereafter.
[2] Erased.
[3] Erased. Leicester's Point was a feature on the coast of 'Friesland'.
[4] Cf. Best, document 11, pp. 224–5.

6. Wedensdaie the vi^th daie. The winde in the morninge was southerlie with much fogg and a greate froste the Generall and I made upp a reckoning of certein oares wherof we had made triall, the valew wherof was regestred; and by reason the greatnes of the fogg we were forced to sett a drom to sownde to direct our bootes cominge from the shipps to the Countess Ilande, lest they hapned to miss therof, wherof some were in daunger to do and to row to the sea: albeit that some of our shipps ridd within one mile & less of the Ilande and the other but ii miles of: Towardes ix of the clock in the eveninge the winde cam at thest and blew much winde.

7. Thursdaie the vii^th daie. In the morninge the winde was at est and by north and blew verie much winde. The Generall notwithstanding with Capten Randoll and Capten Courtney departed in their pynnasses with divers pyoners and soldiours to (fentons fortune) to gett oare there, and I following with a new pynnas called the Serche with fyve or six and thirtie pyoners in her, had not sailed from the Countess Ilande above one mile and a half, but I bare my maste and sailes over borde, in casting abowte to meete the Generall, who was forced by the extreemitie of the winde to reatorne back againe, and Capten Courtney with his companie in great daunger of drowninge, who in the night dreamed he was sinking in the sea, and so troubled therwith in his sleepe, that he cried with such lowdnes, Iesus have mercie upon me, that we in the other tentes were awaked therwith, mistrusting a larom, yssued owt to understande the cawse Thus for this daie we were forced eftsones to ymploie our soldiours and pyoners in the Myne on the Countess Ilande, notwithstanding abowt 4 of the clock in the afternoone it began to Raine and the winde contynewed at est blowing all the night extreemelie with much Raine.

8. Frydaie the viii^th daie. In the morninge the winde was at est with muche winde and Raine till ix or x of the clock and then it began to ceasse, we [47] discovered the Thomas Allin and Gabriell, who cam to harbour in the Countess sownde abowte 2 of the clock in the afternoone; we tried sonndrie sortes of oare, the places and goodnes wherof remayneth in the Booke of Register provided for that purpose.

9. Satterdaie the ix^th daie, being verie calme and faire weather the winde at northwest, the Generall sente certein Pyoners and soldiours to (fentons fortune) to digg for oare, and provyded for an other companie to departe in the afternone to Beares sownde to digg for oare there. In the meane while we entred into consultacion for the disposinge of the habitacion and how the same might be performed, which after some conferrence had towching the same, it was founde a matter ympossible to be brought to pass, aswell by reason we had but xxvi daies to deale (their)[1] for the settinge upp of our howse (having then but ii partes therof in harbour) and

[1] Erased.

our carpenters not hable to builde the same under vi weik*es* if the Tim*ber* had been pute on lande, as also for wante of Beare and other necessaries w*hi*ch then remayned in three Shipps on the sea, viz. The Anne Fraunces, the Thom*as* of Ipswich and the Moone, in the w*hi*ch was one p*ar*te of *our* howse & 84 toons of Beare besides other victuall and necessaries for *our* buildinge. So that ev*er*y circumsta*u*nce well waighed it was not possible (w*i*thout supplie of those thinges) to have lefte there ten men, havinge at that instant not beare 24 toons sufficiente to convoye my self and com-panie into Englande being there 98 p*er*sons of the C. that were appointed to inhabitt there, neither could I be howsed for 60 men, with w*hi*ch nomber I made offer to abyde there, suche was the shortnes of time the wante of timb*er* and spoile of bordes (which)[1] amongest the Shipps in thextreemitie of yze, that there was not sufficient to have covered a pro-portion of dwelling for 40 p*er*sons.[2] In the afternoone the Gen*er*all dep*ar*ted w*i*th the Michaell and Gabriell and thing*es* to furnishe his com-panie appointed to worke in Beares sownde and founde the winde souther-lie and litle, so that he cam to anco*ur* nigh Corbett*es* pointe, where he bothe tooke in some Pyon*er*s working at (fentons fortune) and lefte some victualls for such as remayned there: thither in like manner I sente Capt*en* philpott w*i*th certein [48] of myne owne Companie so manie as the Gondelo[3] woulde convoye, and I remayned still at the Countess Ilande, bothe to oversee the companies there, and to p*ro*vide to sende more pyon-*er*s to (fentons fortune) in the mornin*g*.

10. Sonndaie the xth daie, The winde was at southwest in the mornin*g*e & faire weather, after prayer I with Capt*en* Yorke dep*ar*ted w*i*th certein of my Companie to *fentons fortune* to digg for oare, w*hi*ch companie I lefte under the charge of Capt*en* Philpott, whom I appointed to attende that s*ar*vice:[4] becawse I was to reatorne to the Countess Ilande to oversee such as remayned there and to dispose of other matters as occasion fell owt: Onlie I and M*aste*r denham viewed the manner of the Myne in (fentons fortune) and founde the same to proceede from the Maine lying est and west.

11. Monndaie the xi[th] daie, The winde was south and to the estwardes, in the mornin*g* foggie and disposed to raine. In the forenoone M*aste*r denham and I made proves of certeine black and redd oare founde the daie before by the M*aste*rs of the Ayde and Fraunces of Foye, w*hi*ch we founde answerable to some other oares we wrought upon, and therfor In the

---

[1] Erased.

[2] Cf. Lok's version of this meeting, document 5, p. 87.

[3] This may have been the newly-assembled vessel *Search* mentioned above. In contemporary and later parlance (particularly during the American War of Independence), a 'gundello' was a barge-like vessel car-rying a short lateen mast in the peak; useful for in-shore exploration and little else.

[4] All mining sites were guarded by ships' companies appointed to that purpose. Each flew their own ship's ensign to identify them from a distance (cf. Best's account of his sighting of the ensign of the *Beare Leicester* on 22 August: document 11, p. 232).

afternone Capt*en* Yorke my self and denham wente to view the same, *whi*ch lieth to the Northwardes from the Countes sownde 2L or there abowtes and adioyni*n*ge to the Maine; we liked the greatnes and goodnes therof so well, that I appointed Capt*en* Yorke w*i*th certein workmen to go thither in the morni*n*ge to uncover the vaine therof, whilest we made a new prooffe therof, My Gen*er*all wrote to me for denham to come to Beares sownde, whom I was forced to staie (a daie) ther longer by this occasion.

12. Tewesdaie the xii^th daie The winde litle but in the morni*n*ge southerlie and faire weather, having made prooffe of such oares as we brought from the Countess of Sussex Myne (for so at my requist the Gen*er*all named it)[1] the goodnes wherof remayneth in the booke of regester kept for that purpose, I sente denham [49] to Beares sownde to the Gen*er*all, and after dep*ar*ted my self to *fentons fortune* to view the workes there, and so reatorned late that night to the Countess Ilande, w*i*th some oare to make prooffe of w*i*th the Gondelo laden w*i*th oare for the Shipp.

13. Wedensdaie the xiii^th daie In the morni*n*ge faire weather w*i*th the winde southerlie. I wente to the Countess of Sussex myne to view the mann*er* therof and how the wrought in the same, where I founde sonndrie sort*es* of oare w*hi*ch I brought to the Countess Ilande to make prooffes of; cam from thence over lande against the place where o*ur* Shipps rode, being one league and better, the winde beinge then at north northwest and blew a greate gale and so contynewed all night.

14. Thursdaie the xiiii^th daie. In the morni*n*ge faire weather but it blew much winde at north northwest so that I coulde neither sende for the Compa-nies remayninge at *fentons fortune* whom I mente this daie to have sente for and placed theim in the Countess of Sussex Myne, nor yet gett well to the same: In the eveni*n*ge the weather calmed, all this daie I spente in making of prooffes of sonndrie sorts of oare gotten in the ( )[2] Myne, but by reason M*aste*r denham was absente coulde not devide the same, who then remayned w*i*th the Gen*er*all at Beares sownde.

15. Frydaie the xv^th daie In the morni*n*ge faire weather and litle winde wester-lie I dispatched pynnasses to *fentons fortune* to bring those companies awaie and to convoie theim to the Countes of Sussex Myne becawse the oare there rose as good and more plentifull then thother:[3] And I dep*ar*ted in the morni*n*ge to view the workes there where I spente all that daie, and abowte xii of the clock at middaie, we discovered a mile or ii from us twoo of the Countrey in their bootes, who made w*i*th the place where we wrought: I com*m*aunded all o*ur* companies there not make any showtes or

[1] These words inserted between the original text by Fenton.
[2] Left blank by Fenton; supply 'Countess of Sussex'.
[3] Being located upon the shore line at the base of shallow cliffs, the Countess of Sussex mine was the most accessible and easily worked of the various sites (see *HBM*, p. 113).

cries at them, neither yet to show theim selves to theim people, lest therby they should take cawse of feare and so retire theim selves *without* conferrence *with* us, and Cap*ten* Yorke [50] and I tooke *our* weapons, and went a mile from *our* myne to a place wher we thought they woulde Lande to trafique *with* theim, but they rowinge verie swiftlie and cloose under the shoore were com*m*ed almost to the Myne before we theim or they us: Onlie having viewed us neare at hande they retired themselves *without* any staie of conference we could devise, *which* by no meanes could allure them to staie, but so rowed from us into a sownde a league of. I reatorninge from the Myne abowt viii or ix of the clock in theven*in*ge to mak certein prooffes of oare discovered the Gabriell and Michaell com*in*g into the Countess sownde laden *with* oare from Beares sownde, the winde being then at south and to thestwardes.

16. Satterdaie the xvi[th] daie, In the morn*in*ge faire weather, litle winde south and by est My Gen*er*all cam to the Countess of Warwik*es* Ilande, (where)[1] and after the p*ar*ting of sonndrie assaies we had made, he dep*ar*ted to (Dyers sownde)[2] to view a Myne there *which* he named (Denhams Mounte) and I in like man*ner* repaired to the Countess of Sussex Myne to follow those companies there and in the even*in*ge repaired againe to the Countess of Warwik*es* Ilande *with* certein oare to make prooffe of, it blew a good gale of winde at est and by south, we had lyke to have been caste awaie upon a rock *which* the pynnass strooke upon laden *with* oare and at entring into the Countess of Warwik*es* sownde, the winde contynued all the night and blew extreemlie. This daie was buried owt of Thayde one Phillipp Ellarde a gent and one laborer, and one owt of the Armanell.

ayd that the Ayde had not for her prov*ici*on above 7 toones of beare being 115 persons.

17. Sonndaie the xvii[th] daie. In the morn*in*ge faire weather, but blew much winde at est and by south. The Gen*er*all cam in the morn*in*ge to me to the Countess of Warwik*es* Ilande, where (after prayers) we entred to make certein prooffes of such oare as had founde the daie before on (denhams Mounte) *which* falling not to be p*er*formed in such shortnes of time we looked for. In the afternoone the Gen*er*all and I dep*ar*ted to the Countess of Sussex Myne (where he desiered to be having not before seen the same) spente the afternoone there, and reatorned to [51] *our* shipps by lande, and by waie of marche fownde in a valey, the midwaie betwixte the Countess of Sussex myne and the Countess of Warwik*es* sownde, a peice of grownde rent and shaken in forme of an earth quake, the p*ro*portion or forme wherof standing firme seemed to be not unlike the shape of a wind milnes hill, But so shaken and rentt it was holowed like a vaunte the (earth)[3] substaunce wherof underneath was of massive and thick ize, thearth growing above (before the breaking therof) one foote and better

---

[1] Erased by Fenton.
[2] Editor's closing parenthesis.
[3] Erased by Fenton.

bedecked with sonndrie sortes of herbes such as the Countrey yeldeth, the circuit whereof (I judge) was 40 or 50 passes: to this place we were brought by (Capten Carew),[1] who had before fownde the same: I cam aborde Thayde with my Generall with whom I stayed for that night, not hable to recover the Countess of Warwikes Ilande for the greatness of winde.

Monndaie the xviii[th] daie. In the morninge foggie with some raine the winde at northest and to thest wardes: Being in our boote departe for the Countess of Warwikes Ilande where denham remayned making prooffes of the oare brought from his Mounte, he encowntred us with the same, putting from the Shipp side wherupon we entred aborde againe, and tooke view and prooffe therof and fownde iiii sortes therof to holde in goodnes equall in effect with any the other mynes before discovered.[2] And therfore we departed to the same Myne with sonndrie the Masters of the Shipps, aswell to make prooffe of the harbour where the shipps might ride there (being harde at hand the Myne) as also for expedicion of lading and plentie of oare which was like to fall owt there: and after view taken every waie therof, we reatorned back againe (having much raine) to the Countess of Warwikes Ilande to make a further prooffe of the oare they shoulde lade of, becawse the same rose in one sorte more plentifull then the rest.

ayd that this daie was not shipped nor gotten 300 toones of oare towardes 1000 & odd.

19. Tewesdaie the xix[th] daie, I departed erlie in the morninge aborde the Generall with certein prooffes made of the Countess of Sussex Myne of the wourst sortes of oare there which held bothe gould and silver not much inferiour to any of the [52] other mynes; afterwardes I departed to the Countess of Sussex Myne to southwest, to view and follow the workes there, the winde being at south Gabriell &·Michaell departed to Beares sownde to fetch oare from Sussex Ilande to lade the Ayde withall and the Salomon wente in like manner thither to 'take in her ladinge, and the hopewell into dyers sownde to lade of the oare of denhams Mounte. There dyed owt of the Fraunces of Foye one John Pope a sailour. It was Raynne with some slite and snowe.

ayde that thayde had not for her provicion but 3 firkins butter & half a kilderkin.

20. Wedensdaie the xx[th] daie, The winde was at est northest with fogg and some Raine I wente erlie in the morninge to the Countess of Sussex Myne to follow the workmen there and to see the lading of such oare as was brought from thence to the shipps. The Generall bestowing that daie in serching oare at denhams Mounte and making prooffe therof. Late in the eveninge I reatorned to the Countess of Warwikes Ilande to see the

---

[1] This is the only indication that patrols were made by ships' companies not specifically allocated to mining sites.

[2] It is not clear, either here or elsewhere, what distinguished the apparent 'sortes' of ore to contemporary assayers. Modern analysis of 123 samples of ore recovered from Dartford and Smerwick harbour have indicated five rock groups and 19 types of dominant mineral association (*HBM*, p. 122), with only hornblende providing a common constituent throughout. Other minerals present variously include diopside, enstatite, biotite, forsterite, spinel, almandine, plagioclase and cummingtonite.

ordringe of such provision of meale and other things as were to be
bestowed in the grownde there.[1]

21. Thursdaie the xxi[th] daie, reasonable faire and cleare weather in the
morninge, the winde at north northwest. The Generall departed to Beares
sownde and I to the Countess of Sussex Myne to follow the workmen
there. The Beare departed the Countess of Warwikes sownde to dyers
sownde to lade of dyers Mounte.[2]

22. Frydaie the xxii[th] daie, In the morninge some what clowdie with much
winde at north northwest. I departed from the Countess of Warwikes
Ilande to the Countess of Sussex Myne, and by the greatnes of the winde
had much to do to rowe on heade and to recover the Myne: and being owt
of the point of the Countess of Warwikes sownde, I might discrie a pynnass (towardes)[3] [53] up into the straites northwardes to Gabriells Ilande
and bare in towardes the Countess of Sussex myne wherat, I had for the
sodaine some marvaile to view a pynnass that waie: and entringe into
ymmaginacon what pynnass it shoulde be, in thende (I judged) the same to
be the (Anne Fraunces) pynnass and yet could not ymmagin how she
shoulde be putt together (knowing that the provision for that purpose
rested cheiflie with us) and then fearing the loss of their shipp, thought
that necessitie had forced theim to devise some waie to sett her together,
(judging withall that Capten Best was in her) And as I was thus ymma-
geninge therof with my self, might discerne them to be within a mile of the
Countess of Sussex Myne and withall might well discrie Capten Philpottes
Ensigne spredd upon the topp of the Myne, to give Capten Best tunder-
stand there being there, who presentlie upon the view of Thensigne and
show of our companies made to theim with his pynnass, and cam to lande
half an hower before me, where he was joyefullie receaved of Capten Yorke
Capten Philpott and their companies and lastelie of my self, who considering how mightelie god by his greate & wonderfull providence had bothe
delivered us owt of manie greate and sonndrie daungers, and also of his
spirituall favour & mercie given us sight one of an other: And conferring
with Capten Best for the state of his Shipp, he delivered unto me that she
rode in a sownde nigh Oxfordes Mounte where they were tryminge her
(sail)[4] and stopping a greate leake she had receavid being in greate daunger
to be caste awaie upon a rocke: There rode with her in like manner the
Mone, the Capten wherof (was)[5] whose name was (Master Upcoote) cam
in the Pynnass with Capten Best; who had made a verie daungerfull
attempte in serchinge for us in that sorte, the Pynnass being sett together

(marginal note:) ayd that thayde had not in fishe for her provicion but in poor John 240, & in stockfishe 250.

---

[1] Cf. Fenton's marginalia re: shortages of certain provisions.
[2] *Recte* Denham's Mount.
[3] Erased.
[4] Erased.
[5] Erased.

but with a few nailes wanting knees and all other matter that necessarlie shoulde have served for her strength and their saffeties: he brought with him certein black oare fownde nigh the Quenes forelande, wherof (afterw)[1] Master denham drew an assaie or twoo my Generall being then at Beares sownde, and the same night reatorned home to his Shipp and so did I from the Countess of Sussex Myne; Master denham showinge me what he had done with [54] sortes of oare Capten Best had brought. The assaies wherof I did not verie well like and therfore cawsed him to go in hande to make 4 prooffes more of the same sortes of oare.[2] The Gabriell cam from Sussex Ilande laded for the Ayde of the best Myne.

23. Satterdaie the xxiii[th] daie, It was a verie great froste, that the sownde where we rode was frozen with a thynn ize over, but the weather verie faire and calme The winde all abowtes. I in the morninge tooke order with Master denham to hasten those assaies he had in hande of the oare Capten Best had brought, and departed to the Ayde with Capten Best where we fownde my Generall aborde, with whom bothe I Capten Yorke and Capten Best remained that daie to consider, both of the goodnes of the oare brought by Capten Best and other cawses of ymportaunce towchinge the service in this accion and ordring of the same.[3] Abowt 4 of the clock in the afternone we discried a Shipp bearing into the Countess of Warwikes sownde, the winde being at north and to thest wardes; My Generall supposinge her to be the Thomas of Ipswich, sent his Master and a pynnass to meete her who founde her to be the Salamon which cam from Beares sownde, having taken in the moste parte of her lading from Sussex Ilande, and tolde the Master that there was good stoore of oare (there)[4] redie digged and that 4 or 5 of (bootes)[5] the greate bootes of the Countrey people used ther abowtes: my Generall therfor blamed Capten (Randal) his cominge awaie with the Shipp till an other had repaired thither for guarde of the Companies there. Master denham having made an ende of the prooffes of Capten Bestes oare brought the same aborde Thayde, wher my Generall and I sawe triall therof, the same holding bothe gould and silver, the valew wherof remaineth in the regester booke of (register)[6] kepte for that purpose. The Michaell cam laded with oare from Sussex Ilande of the best for the Ayde.

---

[1] Erased.

[2] Fenton's confidently expressed opinion of the results of the assay, and his subsequent employment, following the return of the voyage to England, in riding into the West Country to search for 'addittaments' (PRO SP/12/129, 2), suggests that he had some previous experience as an amateur metallurgist – a not uncommon accomplishment for educated gentlemen amongst whom the search for the philosopher's stone remained a popular, if occasional hobby.

[3] Best, as a leading 'colonist', would have been involved in decisions regarding the disposal of the abandoned colony's assets.

[4] Erased.

[5] Erased.

[6] Erased.

24. Sonndaie the xxiiii^th daie, In the morninge the weather was foggie and raynie and the winde northerlie. The Thomas Allin departed to Beares sownde to take in the rest of her lading she waited at Sussex Ilande, and so also did the Generall with his pynnasses, and Capten Best to his [55] Shipp, who had order to lade her and the Mone of the oare he had brought from the Quenes forelande, I bestowed this daie at the Countess of Warwikes Ilande to take order aswell for the providing of victuall for suche of my Companie as I was to bestowe in other Shipps, as also to hasten and view the ordring of suche provicion as we were forced to burie and leave behinde us there: and further to follow the (to)[1] finishing of a litle watche Tower I cawsed to be builded in the hight of the same Ilande with lyme and stone being xiiii foote in length and viii in bredthe with a litle rooffe covered with borde; this I did to prove what the vehemencie of winde and weather would do therwith this winter, to thende, that if the nexte yere habitacion shoulde be performed there, that then by this litle begynninge, a juste occasion and experiment should given how we shoulde deale in building greater howses.[2] In the afternoone it blew much winde at northest.

25. Monndaie the xxv^th daie. In the morninge reasonable faire weather with a litle froste, the winde west northwest. I wente erlie in the morninge to the Countess of Sussex Myne, to view the worke of suche as wrought there (which was then but my owne and Capten Courtneys companies) and that daie (I judged) there remayned (with that alreadie gotten) sufficient oare above grownde to lade and dispatch both our shipps, either of them wanting but 20 toones. I reatorned that night back againe to the Countess of Warwikes Ilande, aswell to provide bootes to fetch the oare awaie the next daie, as the gentlemen and others which remayned at that Myne.

26. ayde that this daie thayde had but a Butt &d. of Beif a hogeshead of marabones & a hogeshead of porke.

26. Tewesdaie the xxvi^th daie, In the morninge faire and cleare weather with some frost the winde at west southwest. I spente this daie on the countess of Warwikes Ilande, abowte the burying of tymber and other thinges there, and the furnishing of the Gabriell and Michaell of victualls and other thinges they wanted. In thevening the Generall reatorned from Beares sownde.

[56] 27. Wedensdaie the xxvii^th daie In the morninge frost with faire and cleare weather, the winde at west and by south, I with Thomas Morris Master of the Fraunces of Foye went on lande on the south side of (Jonas Mounte) directing our course est southest and having past 4 or 5 miles we in thende discovered the northe sea and made an Ilande therin being of this forme in

[1] Erased.

[2] This was probably the first stone structure erected in North America by Europeans. Modern excavations at the site of the house or watch-tower have indicated that the structure has been badly compromised by previous investigations (Hall 1864, Rawson McMillan 1927, McMillan 1929, Forbes 1942) – so much so that the original narratives of the voyage offer more data as to its form and purpose than archaeological activity can now supply.

the margent;[1] lying south est and by est from us, and in computacion an viii leagues from us, and at that instante we judged our selves within ii leagues of the north sea, which seemed to us to trende to the north est, having abowt this Ilande divers greate Mountaines of ize. And after we paste to dyers sownde to see how nigh the Shipps were laden riding there, finding the Beare departed with her lading to the Countess of Warwikes sownde, and the hoopewell and the Manuell riding there still not fullie laden, determyninge the nexte daie to comme from thence and go for beares sownde to take the rest of their lading at Sussex Ilande, I reatorned to the Countess of Warwikes Ilande, finding the Thomas Allin coming into the sownde there from Beares sownde laden: and Generall[2] departed into the straites towardes Gabriells Ilande to take some of the people if he coulde My companie having laded my Shipp cam from the Countess of Sussex Myne to the Ilande where I remayned. The winde towardes night at southest.

28. Thursdaie the xxviii[th] daie In the morning the weather was foggie and Rayne and blew much winde at est northest with snow haile & slite. In the morninge the Anne Fraunces cam to ancour in the Countess of Warwikes sownde, havinge bestowed the west parte of the howse in a sownde where they rode nigh the [57] Quenes forelande;[3] we well hooped to have receavid of her xxv toones of stronge beare which she had in charge to conveye for us that were to inhabitt (wherof we had greate need). But being commed to ancour the Master coulde not make accompte unto me of above vii toones & d. of our provicion and none remayninge of his owne, the reason wherof grew (as he saieth) by the evill casking of our Beare. But (I suppose)[4] rather by his owne necligence and the lewde abuse of his Manners (who without straight government) seeke the spoile of all thinges they have in charge, whose loosenesse of behaviour in this accion hath been well discovered, but sloolie punnished.[5] This daie in the eveninge the Generall reatorned owt of the straightes, without taking of any of the people, the weather being so fowle and tempestious that he was forced the rather speedelie to reatorne againe, having been vii leagues or thereabowtes, naming the sownde next the Countess of Sussex Myne, (Vincentes sownde)[6] and an Ilande in the mouthe therof (Essex Ilande) he sawe (in that mouth therof)[7] travaill but ii of the Country people.

Litlestone dyed.

---

[1] Fenton's sketch of this feature is too small to reproduce satisfactorily here. [2] *Sic.*

[3] This is the only clue as to the fate of that final portion of the great house in which the colony was to have dwelled.

[4] Editor's closing parenthesis.

[5] This is Fenton's only explicit complaint of the failures of discipline which marred the expedition, and in which his own authority had been so compromised. Despite Frobisher's antipathy towards his lieutenant-general, it is clear that Fenton – in 1578 – retained a strong sense of propriety regarding the exercise of authority. His subsequent behaviour during the 1582 Moluccas project may well have been a disproportionate response to the lessons of this, his earlier humiliation.

[6] Possibly named after Peter Vincent, one of the 'gentlemen' passengers in the *Ayde*.

[7] Erased by Fenton, though the sense of the sentence indicates that he intended to erase only the latter two words.

29.   (Satterdaie)[1] Frydaie the xxix[th] daie. The winde contynued at est northest tempestious with snow & raine. The Manuell[2] departed from dyers sownde erlie in the morninge to take in the rest of her lading at Sussex Ilande, And in like manner did the hopewell,[3] but she rode that daie before the mouth of dyers sownde and departed no further. In the morninge the Generall, Capten Yorke and Capten Best cam to the Countess of Warwikes Ilande to me, to view the thinges I was buryinge and the litle howse I had made being then in effect finished, which I named (fentons watche tower) This daie I disposed of the most parte of my companies into such Shipps as they were to reatorne home in, victuallinge every one of all thinges necessarie for ix weekes following. That night was verie tempestious with the winde as before and fell much snowe.

30.   Satterdaye the xxx[th] daie In the morninge verie tempestious weather with greate snowe and the winde at northest, so that the winde would not suffer my boote to come from the shipps to us: I [58] followed the despatch of all my thinges on the Countess Ilande in the forenone, preparing to go on borde. And my Generall cam to lande to me, and helped of my stuffe aborde with his pynnass, with whom I tooke order to sende more bootes ashoore for that purpose. And thus havinge dispatched all my busines I cam from the same Ilande late in the eveninge to my shipp. The winde being then at est northest somewhat calmed and reasonable cleare weather.

This daie at night John Graye Master mate of the Anne Fraunces reatorned from the seeking of the Thomas of Ipswich who was sente for that purpose abowt the quenes forelande and escaped in his Pynnass hardlie with his life back againe to the Quenes sownde.[4]

31.   Sonndaye the laste of Auguste, In the morninge faire & cleare weather, the winde westerlie, the sownde was frozen over with a preetie thick ize My Generall sett saile to Beares sownde to take in some oare at Sussex Ilande, and with him The Thomas Allin, the Gabriell, the Michaell, the Fraunces of Foye, the Armanell, the Salamon; The Anne Fraunces and my self with the Judith, stayinge till the (afternoone)[5] morninge for she was not readie by reason she had but new stopped her leeke, and manie of her thinges on shoore, and I for that I was forced to sende my Pynnass to the Countess of Sussex Myne to fetche a Bonnett of Thayde (lefte there)[6] and to burie divers thinges lefte there. And the weather beinge calme in the afternone, forced the shipps that departed with the Generall to ancour all night at Corbettes pointe.

September 1.   The first daie of September: We sett saile in the morninge from the Countess of Warwikes sownde to follow the fleete to Beares sownde (The fleete

---

[1] Erased by Fenton.

[2] *Hopewell* erased by Fenton.

[3] *Manuall* erased by Fenton.

[4] *recte* Countess Sound.

[5] Erased.

[6] Words erased. The *Ayde*'s bonnet, being canvas, may have been used as a tent for the miners there.

at that instaunce setting saile for the same place from Corbettes pointe)[1] the winde being at northwest and at middaie at north with litle winde and in effect calme, I tooke the proportion of Pembrookes Ilande being 4 leagues from it the same lying north and by est and on the west side of thentrie of the Countess sownde [59] rising in the forme conteyned in the margent with ii other Ilandes the one lyinge north northwest and the other north and by west, and one other clif called gulles clif lying north northest.

At night we cam to Beares sownde, and founde the fleete ancoring one league from the same; who waighed in the evening being 8 saile and departed thence, We did ancour there for that the tide of thebb was comme which setteth through Beares sownde & manie other places:[3] Besides that at viii or ix of the clock in the night it blew a good gale of winde at north northwest, and therefore woulde willinglie have waighed but coulde not without losse of ancour and cable, wherby we were forced to ride it owt till the fludd (at what time we purchazed our ancour) And as there sanke an olde Pynnass at our sterne, So blowing mutch winde in the morninge at north northwest we putt for the Quenes forelande.

2. The seconde daie of September Bearing over with the Quenes forelande it blew much winde at north northwest with some snow and sleete, woulde have taken in our boote, which being brought along the shipp side and in our tackles, by the greate rowling of the seas had a hoole brocken in her and did presently sinke with daunger also of the loss of our boteson and one of the quarter maisters. And thus setting saile with our forecourse before the sea, having a greate pynnass at our sterne, she followed the Shipp with such swiftnes, that she brake in her sterne three greate hooles & at the next encowntre strooke her self in ii peices and sanke, or otherwais she had commed into the shipp Thus having lost ii pynnasses and our boote (not without daunger of the looss of our shipp) abowt 4 or v of the clock in the afternoone we came [60] to the Quenes foreland, and there founde the Gabriell and the Generall aborde her, being commed that daie from Beares sownde with a Pynnass and 26 men in her like to be caste awaie; there was also in view iii other shipps; viz, the Michaell the Anne Fraunces, and the Moone, who for that she seemed to make saile awaie from the rest, the Generall sente his Pynnass to will her staie, but she past the faster awaie so that there was daunger to loose the Pynnass and men in her, wherupon the Generall willed us to make sail to save theim (if it were possible) which we willinge performed, But they being iii leagues before us (and the night drawing on) were forced to leave theim sailing nigh to the

[1] That is, those ships of the fleet that were fully laden and had not accompanied Frobisher to Beare sound the day before to 'top up' their allocations of ore.

[2] Fenton's annotations (from top): 'Pembrookes Ilande', 'the other ii Ilandes', 'gulles clif'.

[3] This entry appears to confirm the contemporary location of Beare Sound as being synonymous with the present-day feature of that name; being a confluence of several passages of water (Lupton Channel, Chapell Inlet and the Lefferts Island outfalls) the flow and direction of tides are difficult to establish precisely.

Moone (as we im*m*agyned) not farr from whom we might discrie v sailes more passing on there course to Englande:[1] and so we reatorned backe againe to the Gen*e*rall lying of and on of the Quenes foreland, attending for the Thayde and Tho*mas* Allin, w*h*ich we supposed to be behinde, spente all the night in this sorte before we mett w*i*th him.

3. Wednesdaie the iii^d daie of September. We mett w*i*th the Gen*e*rall erlie in the morni*n*ge, and told him what we had don*n*e, he sente unto us from the Gabriell a xi men wh*i*ch we receaved, becawse the Barke was neather hable to victuall nor conteyne theim, being over charged with other men besides her com*p*leme*n*te. And afterwardes we bare into the straites againe to see if we could meete the Ayde or any other of the shipps (wh*i*ch failing of) the Gen*e*rall determyned to passe home in the Gabriell [61] willing me, that if I mett with Thayde to entre into her and to take the charge of her; and in the meane time to pass home wardes if we failed that night of the shipps,[2] the winde was in the morni*n*ge at northwest and in the afternoone at southwest, We spente the daie of and on of the quenes forelande according to his appointme*n*te, and abowt vi of the clock in the afternoone it grew foggie with snowe good store, we caste abowte making o*u*r course southest and by south of from the quenes forelande, and so did also the Gabriell and Anne Fraunces, who in casting abow*t* were on the sterne of us, wh*i*ch was the best course we colde holde for 200 leagues to passe into a warmer climate.

ayds that if we had not receaved in xi of theire companie & as manie into the Anne Fraunces Bothe the Generall & reste in the ii Barkes had perished for want of victuall

4. Thursdaie the 4th daie of September we were 18 Leagues from the Quenes foreland at middaye southest and south from Halles Ilande, the winde southwest and by west with snow, we wente till 4 of the clock vi leagues southest and by south, having the Companies of the Gabriell, the Michaell and the Anne Frances, from 4 till 8, vii leagues, the winde southwest much winde, from 8 till 4 in the morni*n*ge 8 leagues and from 4 till 12, 8L, southest and by south.

s.e. b s.–47L

Altitude – 61–26.

5. Frydaie the vth daie we went at middaie southest and by south till 4 of the clock, 4 leagues, the winde west southwest, from 4 till 8, 6 leagues, the winde at northwest, from 8 of the clock till midnight, 8 leagues, from thence till 4, 8 leagues, from thence till 8, 8 leagues, it blew muche winde all daie so that we brake o*u*r mayne y*a*rde in the midle, and from 8 till middaie 8L, southest and by south.

s.e. b s.–L.42

6. Satterdaie the vi^th daie, At middaie it blewe much winde at the northwest, we wente till 4, 8L, from 4 till 8, 8L, from thence til midnight 6L, from

---

[1] The absence of comment upon this incident elsewhere suggests that the crew of the pinnace successfully overtook the *Moon of Foye* and were rescued.

[2] Absent any definitive explanation of his actions, Frobisher must be given much credit here for remaining with the dangerously overloaded *Gabriel*, rather than transferring into the larger – and faster – *Judith* to undertake the pursuit of the *Ayde*.

s.e. b e. 42L

thence till 4, [62] 6L., from 4 till 8, 7L., from 8 till 12 at middaye 7L, southest & by south.

Altitude 59–26.

s.e. b s.–40L

7. Sonndaye the vii^th daie. The winde was at northwest with manie gustes of snow and haile, from middaie till 4 of the clock, 6L, from 4 till 8, 7L, southest, from 8 till 12 at midnight, 6L, from 12 till 4 in the morninge, 6L, from 4 till 8, 7L, & from 8 till 12 at middaie, 7L, southest & by south.

Latitude 58–20.[1]

s.e. 45L

8. Monndaye the viii^th daie, At middaie & before in the morninge we lost the companies of the Anne Frances, Gabriell and Michaell, till 4 of the clock in the afternoone, we wente 8L, the winde southwest & by west, from 4 till 8, 8L, from 8 till 12 at midnight, 8L, from 12 till 4 in the morninge 8L, from 4 till 8, 7L, the winde west. from 8 till 12 at middaye 6L, the winde west northwest.

s.e. 44L

9. Tewesdaye the ix^th daie, At middaye the winde was west northwest and the weather somewhat thick we went till 4 of the clock in the afternoone 5L, from 4 till 8, 6L, from 8 till 12 at midnight, 8L, from 12 till 4, 8L, & from 4 till 8, 8L, from 8 till 12 at middaie 8L, southest.

s.e. 42L

10. Wedensdaie the xth daie at middaie the winde was southwest with much fogg and small raine[2], from thence till 4 of the clock in the afternoon 8L, from 4 till 8, 7L, from 8 till 12 at midnight 7L, from 12 till 4 in the morninge 7L, from 4 till 8, 7L, from 8 till 12 at middaie 6L southest.

s.e. 42L.

11. Thursdaie the xj^th daie. The winde was at middaie west northwest, from thence till 4 of the clock in the [63] afternoone, 8L, from 4 till 8, 8L, from 8 till 12 at midnight, 8L, from thence till 4 in the morninge, 8L, from 4 till 8, 6L, from 8 till 12 at middaye 4L.

Latitude – 55–15.

s.e.–18L

12. Frydaie the xii^th daie, At middaie the winde was at southwest, and faire weather, from thence till 4 of the clock in the afternoone, 4L, from 4 till 8, 6L, from 8 till 12 at midnight, 4L, from 12 till 4 in the morninge, 2L, from 4 till middaie it fell calme, 2L, southest, The winde southwest and by south.

13. Satterdaie the xiii^th daie. At middaie calme with thick and fogg and litle winde southest. we laye off northest from middaie till 4 of the clock in the afternoone, 1L, from 4 till 8 so calme that we knew not where the winde did bloo, from 8 till 12 the winde was southwest and by west, 3L, southest,

---

[1] It is not apparent why Fenton switches from his former references to 'Altitude', to the correct form 'Latitude' from this entry onwards, unless the error had been noticed and pointed out by the *Judith*'s master, Charles Jackman.

[2] Drizzle.

s.e.–7L

from thence till 4 in the morninge, 3L, from 4 till 8, calme. from 8 till 12 at middaie the winde was litle at southest, we did hull and mende our sailes.[1]

Latitude 54–26.

14.   Sonndaie the viiii[th] daie. At middaie the winde was est & by north with a freshe gale thick and foggie till 2 in the afternoone north and by est, 3L,

n. b e.–3L
s.e. b e.–3L
e.n.e.–4L
s.e.–5L

At 2 of the clock we Layde it about to the southwardes, Lying at southest and by south till 6 of the clock, 3L, And then it blew so much winde & raine that we were constrayned to Lye at hull till midnight, the winde west southwest, then the winde cam about to the west with such a monstrous winde, that we thought the maste woulde have blowen over borde, we did

s.e.–5L[2]

hull est northest [64] 4L, till i. in the morninge, And then the winde beinge at west did sett our fore course, we went southest, 5L.

Latitude 54–17.

15.   Monndaie the xv[th] daie. At middaie the winde was west southwest, sett our mayne corse and went till 4, 5L, southest. And then being faire weather putt on our bonnettes and went till 8, 4L southest. from 8 till 12 at mid-

e. b s.–6L.
s. & b e.–4.
e.s.e.–4.
s.e.–9L.

night we went 4L, south & by est, the winde southwest and by south, from thence till 4, 4L est southest, the winde south southwest and south and by west, from 4 till 8, 3L est and by south, the winde south, from 8 till 12 at middaie 3L, est & by south, the winde south with raine.

Latitude 53–55.

16.   Tewesdaie the xvi[th] daie. At middaie the winde south with reasonable faire weather and at two of the clock southest & besouth, till 4 of the clock in

n.n.e.–9L.
n.–3L.
s.e.b e.–10L.

the afternoone we wente north northest 3L, from 4 till 8, 3L, from 8 till 12 at midnight 3L on the same pointe, from 12 till 4 in the morninge, 3L, northe, and then the winde cam northest wente till 8, 4L, from 8 till 12 at middaye 6L southest and by est.

17.   Wedensdaie the xvii[th] daie At middaye the winde was north and by west,

e.s.e.–5L.
s.e.–4L.
s.–3L.
s.s.w.–4L.

faire and cleare weather. went till 4 of the clock in the afternoone 5L, est southest, from 4 till 8, 3L, southest, the winde northwest and but litle winde, from 8 till 12 at midnight 1L, southest it was almost calme, then the [65] winde was esterlie, we stoode to the south till 4 of the clock in the morninge 3L, from 4 till 9, 4L, south southwest, from 9 till 12 at middaie 1L, we tooke in our sailes to amende them and hulled, and saw a shipp to the weather of us.

18.   Thursdaye the xviii[th] daie At middaie the winde was est southest with thick

s.s.w.–2L.
s.w.–4L.

fogg and raine. went till 4 of the clock in the afternoone 2L, south south-west, from 4 till 8, 2L, southwest, from 8 till 12 at midnight 2L on the same

---

[1] Having made an *average* of more than six knots per hour in several of the previous few days (cf. Fenton's entries for 7–11 September), it is likely that the *Judith*'s sails and rigging were in dire need of repair.

[2] This margin note is a repetition of the previous note.

w.s.w.–4L.
w.–1L.

pointe, from 12 till 4 in the morninge 2L, west southwest, winde south southest. from 4 till 8, 2L, on the same pointe, from 8 till 11 we stayed our mayne maste and sett our shrowdes trying with our forecorse west 1L, faire weather.

Latitude 53–15.

19. Frydaie the xixth daie. At middaie the winde was south southest faire cleare weather. went till 4 of the clock in the afternoone 1L. do. from 4 till 8, 2L west southwest, from 8 till 12 at midnight 1L, from thence till 4 of the clock in the morninge calme, from 4 till 8 the winde was northest 2L, from 8 till 12 at middaie southest & by est 4L.

w.s.w.–5L.
s.e.b e.–6L.

Latitude 53–6.

20. Satterdaie the xxth daie. At middaie the winde was north northwest with faire weather but some fogg, wente till 4, 5L, from 4 till 8, 6L, from 8 till 12 at midnight, 6L, from thence till 4, 6L, the winde west, from 4 till 8, 7L, from 8 till 12 at middaie, 7L, all thies south & by est.

s.& b e.–37L.

21. Sonndaie the xxjth daie At middaie the weather foggie with raine. the winde south [66] west & by south, till 4 of the clocke in the afternoone we went 7L, from 4 till 8, 6L, from 8 till 12 at midnight 4L, southest and by est, the winde north northwest, from midnight till 4 in the morninge calme, 1L. do. from 4 till 8, 1L ditto. on the same pointe, from 8 till 12 at middaye 3L, southe. The winde beinge esterlie.

s.e.b.e.–16L.
s.–3L.

22. Monndaye the xxijth daie. At middaye the winde was at southest with verie faire weather. we did Lye south southwest till 5 of the clock in the after-noone 3L, southwest, from 5 till 8, 2L, southest and by est, the winde southwest, from 8 till 12 at midnight, 6L, from 12 till 4 in the morninge 7L, from 4 till 8, 8L, from 8 till 12 at middaye 8L, southest and by est, the winde verie greate and at west.

s.s.w.–5L.
s.e.b e.–31L.

Latitude 50–15.

23. Tewesdaie the xxiiith daie, At middaie it blew much winde at west north-west, till 4 of the clock we went 8L, est and by south, from 4 till 8, 6L, from 8 till 12 at midnight, 6L, on the same point, from 12 till 4 in the morninge 4L, from 4 till 8, 4L, from 8 till 12 at middaie ditto. L,[1] est with litle winde but a wrought sea. the winde southwest, Goinge hard with ii of the sailors in danger of drowninge abowt tryminge the sailes.

e.b s.–20L.
e.–10L.

24. Wedensdaye the xxiiiith daie. At middaie the winde was west northwest, from thence till 5 of the clock went est 6L, and sownded but fownde no grownde, from 5 till 12 at midnight 8L, on the same pointe, from thence till 4, 6L, est and by north and est northest to gett nil 50,[2] for that at mid-night we were fallen 5L to the south. It was stormie all night and blew

e.–14L.
e.b n. &

---

[1] Either this figure or the marginalia is incorrect; recte 2L.   [2] That is, Latitude 50°N precisely.

e.n.e.–14L

much winde at north [67] northwest, from 4 till 12 at middaie 8L, on the same pointe.

Latitude 49–50.

25. Thursdaie the xxv[th] daie. At middaie the winde was north northwest with much winde, so we went in our forecorse edging in for that till 4 of the clock in the afternoone we were not in 50 degrees, went 4L est and by north, from 4 till 6, jL do. from 6 till 6 of the clock in the morninge we tried in our

e.b n.–13L do.

forecorse with much winde north northwest, from 6 till 12 at middaie 8L, est and by north with the winde north and by west. reasonable weather.

Latitude 49–40.

26. Frydaie the xxvi[th] daie. At middaie the winde was north northwest, faire and cleare weather. till 6 of the clocke we wente est northest 6L, sownded and fownde 49 fathom, smale sande blacke Like oze.[1] from 6 till 12 at midnight 7L, on the same pointe, sownded and fownde 74 fathom faire sande with some smale eale thinges like branne, from 12 till 6 of the clock in the morninge est northest 6L, sounded and fownde 70 fathom oze sande, supposing Cillie to be est and by south from us, the winde cam to the north and north and by est and so we wente and some time est and by north as the winde woulde suffer us, from 7 in the morninge till 12 at middaye 7L, est, and soundinge fownde 67 fathom oze.

27. Satterdaie the xxvii[th] daie At middaie the winde was north northwest faire weather. went till 5 of the clock 7L est and by south but coulde see no lande.

e.b s.–7L.
e.b n.–3L.
e.–3L.

and sowndinge fownde 46 fathom sande of three cullers, the first and greatest part white, the seconde redishe brown, like branne the iii[d] being the lest part black, [68] We Layde it a hull (supposing)[2] Cillie to be est from us and litle winde & northerlie and so hulled till midnight, but having a whole ebb in hand were driven to the south and by west, the winde north and by west, sownded and fownde 65 fathom like to the sowndinges before, from thence till 5 of the clock in the morninge we drove esterly with our foresaile with litle winde, And discovered 2 lightes erlie in the morninge in twoo Shipps, viz, the Anne Frances and the Sallamon of Waymouth, sownding had 63 fathom oze and sande of divers culler, did then sett saile and had the companie of the Sallamon, who said we were abowt Cillie, but they were disceaved, they were going northest which course the Anne Frances helde But we parswaded them to go est and by north and est which they did, shootinge ii peices to hail the Anne Frances to have tackt with us, but she did not, from 5 of the clocke till 10 of the clock in the morninge, 3L, est and by north, sowndinge fownde 63 fathom oze sande divers as before, from 10 till 12 at middaie 3L, est, the winde south and by west.

Latitude 49–50.

---

[1] That is, they were now in the Soundings, off Scilly.
[2] Fenton's parenthesis.

28. Sonndaye the xxviii^th daie At middaie the winde was south and by west, wente till 3 of the clock est 4L, sawe Cillie est and by north from us 4L of. from 3 till 6 of the clock in the morninge 11L, est southest, from 6 till 7 did Lye by the Ley to tarie for the Sallamon, sowndinge fownde 56 fathom great bracken shelles, somwhat like skallop and Cockle shells, from 7 till 12 at middaie 7L, est northest, the winde southwest.

e.–4L
e.s.e.–11L.
e.n.e.–7L.

Latitude 49–50.

29. Monndaye the xxix^th daie, At middaie the winde was southwest, wente till 4 in the afternone 5L, est northest, and from thence till 2 of the clock in the morninge northest & by est 12L. And at vi of the clock we discovered the Baye betwixt the Start & Portlande, and then haled in northest & by north, harde aborde the point of the Lande becawse of thebb, and cam into the grass at middaye.

e.n.e.–5L.
n.e.b e.–12L.

30. Tewesdaie the xxx^th daie, At middaie the winde was at southwest, we cam to ancour in the grasse nigh waymouth, where I sett divers sick men on shoore, and others willing to departe to their frindes, the Shipp being personed with 67 men, the most parte wherof infected with the skirvie and other gingerfull diseases.[1] Rode at the pointe of the grasse for that daie till 3 or 4 of the clock next morninge, at what time the Master waighed (liking not to ride so nigh a Lee shoore) and cam and ancoured under the high pointe of the grasse nigh to the Castell Master Luson kepeth.[2] The winde then being at south and by est with raine & fogg.

October 1. Wedensdaie the first of October. The winde contynued at south & by est and south southest with much winde & raine. we ancoured at the place above saide.[3]

2. Thursdaie the ii^d daie. Contynued with the same winde at the place above said.

[70]

3. Frydaie the iii^d daie. Remayned there with the winde as aforesaid.

4. Satterdaye the iiii^th daie. Abowt vii of the clock in the morning we waighed and sett saile. The winde at southwest with reasonable faire weather but befor we had sailed 2 Leagues it calmed, so that till the next daie at noone we were but thwart the Nedells.

5. Sonndaie the vth daie. At middaie the winde was south and by west litle winde, we Laye of and on in the sea all that afternoone and all night to have doubled Beachie but the winde coming in the morning at vi of the clock to the south & by est and south southest we forced to putt for the Cow in

[1] This is one of the earliest known references to scurvy.
[2] Sandsfoot Castle.
[3] The *Judith* was embayed for three days by these contrary winds.

the wight[1] and coming for that place understoode of thaydes being at Portchmouth.

6. Monndaye the vi[th] daie. At middaie the winde was south & by est & at southest disposed to raine. we cam into Portchmouth at 2 of the clock in the afternoone where ancoured The Generall being then with Captain horsaye at the Ile of wight,[2] reatorned in the night & sente for me on the shoor to Portchmouth where I contynued all night and the next daie. at 12 he departed towardes the Court and I aborde my Shipp: he lefte me order to enter aborde the Ayde & to take charge of the whole fleet.

[71]

7. Tewesdaye the vii[th] daie. At middaie the winde was at south & by est and to the estwardes. The Generall departed towardes the Court, Leaving the charge to me of the Ayde & shippes there. went in the afternoone aborde myne owne Shipp to take order for thinges there, where I remayned all night being much raine and fowle weather, the winde as above said.

8. Wedensdaie the viii[th] daie, The winde was southerlie with raine & fogg, I wente aborde the Ayde, Leaving Master Skipwith as my deputie in the Judith,[3] the maine yarde of the Ayde was brought aborde about 5 of the clock in the afternoone, The winde being west southwest reasonable cleare weather.

9. Thursdaie the ix[th], In the morning faire weather the winde at southwest and so contynued all daie and the most part of the night. A boote was brought for the Ayde aborde abowt 6 of the clock in the evening, we then lacked sailors.[4]

10. Frydaie the xth daie. In the morninge raine with fogg. The winde at South, At middaie somwhat faire, the winde at southwest & by south with much winde. rode still at Portchmouthe.

11. Satterdaie the xj[th] daie. At abowt viii of the clock in the morninge we sett saile from Portchmouth with reasonable faire weather. the winde at northwest and by west, litle winde. At middaie the winde was at west. And upon Sonndaie at 8 of the clock in the morning we were thwart faire Lee,[5] the winde at west northwest. I sawe tholde man nigh Brittaine in France est from us.

[72]

12. Sonndaie the xii[th] daie. At middaie the winde was northwest and faire weather, were somwhat ahead Dover under the downes. And abowt 4 of

---

[1] Cowes, Isle of Wight.

[2] Edward Horsey, Captain of the Isle of Wight and an acquaintance since c. 1571. The reason for Frobisher's visit is not known, though it may have been connected with the participation in the venture of their mutual friend, Hugh Randall. Horsey may have partly financed Randall's *Salomon* in the voyage.

[3] Again, evidence that Lionel Skipwith was an intimate of Fenton's (cf. p. 155, n. 2. above).

[4] An indication that the discharge of diseased mariners (voluntary or otherwise), first noted in Fenton's journal entry for 30 September, had not abated.

[5] *Sic.*

the clock in the afternoone the winde skanting cam to anco*u*r thwart the south p*a*rte of the north forelande riding on thebb. where I tooke Tho*ma*s Halpenie in a litle Barke of 50 toones taken from a Brittaine w*i*th divers others of his companie: Sente of myne owne Companie to take charge of the Barke who by fowle and stormie weather was forced from us abowte vii of the clock, at what time we waighed anco*u*r and cam under the north forelande, anco*u*ring there till Monndaie at ix of the clock in the morni*n*ge, at what time we waighed and sett saile having the fends in hande, it blew much winde at north and by west.

13. Monndaye the xiii^th daie. At 2 of the clock in the afternone we were thwart M*a*rgerett Peare[1] the winde north northwest and reasonable faire weather. And betwixt 3 and 4 of the clock cam to Goore ende where we anco*u*red and fownde the Beare.[2]

14. Tewesdaie the xiiii^th daie. In the morni*n*ge faire clowdie weather, the winde at northwest and northwest and by north. And so contynued all the daie and night. Sent Le*tt*res to the Counsall about app*re*hending of Halpenie.

15. Wedensdaie the xv^th daie. In the morni*n*ge faire clowdie weather, the winde at northwest. abowt middaie The bark called (Halpenies doole) cam to Gore ende and anco*u*red by us and the Sallamon thwart Margarett. the m*a*st*e*r wente to shoore to p*r*ovide beare.

[73] 16. Thursdaye the xvi^th daie. In the morni*n*ge faire calme weather. The winde at southwest. The Beare dep*a*rted from us abowt ix of the clocke. The winde then cominge southest and by south, Waighed and sett saile comi*n*ge through the Quenes Channell, abowt middaie we were past the Landes ende entering the mouth of the Thamis having 3 foote sownding and 3 foote and better softer grownde. Cam to anco*u*r abowt 4 of the clock in the afternone in Tilberye hoope, where we remayned all night. Halpenye with iii others eskaped abowt 3 of the clock in the morni*n*ge by o*u*r owne boote, not without some suspicon that the watche was privie therunto, having good prooff that the Booteson sett on Lande ii of the p*r*isoners without my knowledg or the maisters.[3] I made presentlie hew and crie after the p*r*isoners eskaped.

17. Frydaie the xvii^th daie. At middaye we cam to anco*u*r in dartforde rode.

---

[1] Margate Pier.
[2] The *Beare Leicester*.
[3] The boatswain was the troublesome Alexander Creake, Frobisher's kinsman. Halfpenny may have been an acquaintance from their privateering days, thus qualifying for this illicit favour.

DOCUMENT 9

Edward Selman's 'official' account of the voyage.[1]

[166] **Edward Sellman** wrote this booke, and
he delivered yt to Michael Lok, the .2. of
October 1578. in London /

The .2. of May 1578. we departed from Bristoll with the Ayde & the Gabriell, Christopher
Hall, & Robert Davis Masters /

The .6. said we departed from Plymouth, with the Ayde, the Fraunces, and the Moone of
foy, the Arminell, & the Bark Denis, & arrived at the Downes the 20th said & the said at
midnight, we departed thence & arrived at Harwiche the 22. said to stay for the rest of the
fleete where we found the Thomas of Harwich /[2]

The 27. said, there arrived at Harwich, the Thomas Alin, the An fraunces, the Hopewell,
The Beare Lester, the Judith, the Gabriell & the Michael, the Salomon of Weymouth came
to us to Harwich, and the Emanuel of (blank)[3]

The .31. said the Aide with all the aboue named ships departed from Harwich with the winde
at N.E. making our passage towards the west coast & arrived at Plymouth the .3. of June /

The .3. of June .1578. at night we departed from Plymouth, with the winde next hand at
East, & the 4th said we had sight of the Lands end, from the which Lands end, we set of west
& west & by South, the winde next hand at South East /

The .6. said we had sight of *Cape cleere* & to the westwards of the Cape .7. leags we had
sight of a bark of Bristoll with whome after we had spoken, they declared that they came
out of Spayne & were robbed by .2. french men of war, & five of their company slayne, their
lading was oyle & sack, they spoiled them of all their victuall allso and left them nothing to
eate of but oyle beryes[4]. The Generall gaue them .3. sackes of bisket demi barrell of butter,
peason & chese to releve them withall, by which bark I wrote a letter & sent it to Master

---

[1] Document 11, p. 224: 'Maister Selman was appointed Notarie, to register the whole manner of proceeding in these affaires, that true relation thereof might be made, if it pleased hir Majestie to require it.' Again, the original manuscript (now lost) was copied by John Dee, possibly during 1580, when he also acquired Christopher Hall's log and the narrative attributed to Charles Jackman (documents 6 and 7 respectively).

[2] *Recte Thomas of Ipswich.* The second digit of the date upon which the ships arrived off the Downes is blotted in the manuscript. Stefannson & McCaskill took this to be 24th May (the 'th' alone is legible); however, given that the ships completed their journey to Harwich two days earlier, this cannot be the correct date.

[3] *Emanuel of Bridgewater.*   [4] Olives.

Kitchen to be conveyed to my *Master*, *Master* Michael Lock, advertising him of all the fleets arrivaile upon the coast of Ireland /

The .7. said we sailed N.W. & by W. the winde at S.E. a fyne bearing gale, with the winde sometimes at N.E. sometimes at E. sometimes at S.W. still keping *our* course (for the most part) N.W. & by W. & N.W. untill the .19. said at none, at w*hich* time we were in .60. degrees of Latitude, & to the Eastwards of *Friseland*, 30. leags, by the reckening of some .40. & .50. by others, & bearing N.W. & by W. & W.N.W. we fell with the land of *Friseland* bearing N.N.W. of us at the going down of the sunne, but at that time we had not made the land perfect, and so sayling untill mydnight, we came nerer unto yt & made yt perfectly At w*hich* tyme we shot of a pece of ordonance to geve the flete warning thereof. I judge this vyage is better to be attempted, followed & used by the West parts, then by the North parts, as well for the avoyding of much cold within the North passage we had, as allso redyer windes to follow *our* said vyage, as by the falling owt of this passage doth appere/[1]

The .20. of June, 1578. earely in the morning, the Gen*er*all caused a small pynnas to be hoysed owt of the Ayde, & w*ith* her he passed a boord the Gabriell, & did beare in with the land sayling alongst yt, untill he fownd asownd to enter in upon the Sowth side of the land, w*hich* sownd after he was entred, called yt *Lukes sound*, by reason of one *Luke Ward* that went with him a land.[2] In w*hich* sownd they fownd people & tents, but the people fled from them, and they entred their tents, finding thereby & by all things therein that they are a people like the people of *Meta incognita* with like boates of all sortes, but the Generall doth take them to be a more delicat people in lodging & feeding then the other. They fownd of their seals w*hich* they had taken [167] sundry,[3] & other victuaill w*hich* they could not tell what flesh or fish yt was.[4] At their said tent*es* they fownd allso .40. yong whelps, whereof .2. they brought away with them, they are allso like the dogs of the place afore named: Some of *our* men that were with the Gen*er*all aland did see in their tent*es* nayles like scupper nayles, & a tryvet of yron, but the Generall toke order with the company, that none shold bring any of their things away: The Generall hath named this Iland *West England*, and a certayn hedland upon the Sowth side, he hath called yt *Furbusher's foreland*, with other names he hath geven to particular places which I know not./

The ( )[5] said at night we departed thens with the winde N.E. & sayled W.N.W. towards the Streicts untill 9. or 10. a clock the 21. said./

The 21. said the winde N.W. we sayled N.E. & by E. towards the said *West England* to make better discovery of yt, bycause yt serued not us to procede of *our* pretended viage, & so sayling till 3. a clock, yt fell caulme, being 16. leags from yt: Abowt .6. a clock, the winde at N.N.E. we sayled N.W. & by W. towards the streicts./

---

[1] Margin note: 'We fell with friseland the .19. of June 1578.'

[2] Margin note: 'A very good Sound to harbour ships; and within yt clere of yse'.

[3] The wording here is obscure, and may have been intended as 'they found their (there) seals, of which they had taken sundry'.

[4] Margin note: 'Memo. That we found nothing so much yse uppon West Ingland as the last yere before we had, I meane not so many Ilands of yse'. The prevalence of ice off Meta Incognita was to be much greater than the previous year, however.

[5] Blank; ie. the same day as aforesaid.

The .22. the winde at E.S.E. we sayled N.W. & by W. untill none, & then we met with great store of yse, of broken Ilands in great peeces, which we judge to be the Ilands dissolued, that were there seene the last yere and driven upon the N.W coast, by reason of the Easterly windes which we had comming hitherwards, and for that we coveted to discover more of the Northwest coast by reason of clere weather which we had, we were the rather put amongst them, and thereby to clere our selves of them againe, to sayle Sowth S. & by W. & S.W. for the space of .3. or .4. howres with a great gale of winde.[1] And we feared the coast to lye owt more westerly then we could make yt by reason of foggy weather thereby might haue bin driven uppon a lee coast, but after we fownd our selves clere of the yse we sayled agayne N.W. & by W, with the winde at S.E. untill the 25. said, & then the winde came W. & we sailed N.N.W. untill the 27. said, at which time we came amongst as well great Ilandes of yse, as allso great quantity of broken yse of both sides of us being shot within channells of them, whereby yt was judged that we were open of the streicts, & we thereuppon did beare the bolder in amongst them, at which tyme we fownd our selves in the Latitude of 62. $^{2/3}$. & some 62.$^{1/2}$.[2] And the .28. said they observed the latitude by the sunne & found them in 62.$^{2/3}$ of latitude & afterwards had sight of 2. Ilands to the Northwards of *Warwicks foreland*,[3] & after had sight of the same foreland, we being to Northwards of yt .14. or .16. leags and the said day we lay to the ofwards Sowth East & Sowth Sowth East: And the 29. said sowth west, the winde at W.N.W. untill the 30. said, and then we sayled Sowth & by E. & S.S.E. untill we came in the latitude of 61$^{2/3}$ the first of July, at which tyme we had the winde at S.S.E. & then we sailed in W. And the 2. said we had sight of the *Queens foreland*[4] & sometimes did beare in N.W. & by W. & N.W. finding yse stragling over all the Streicts & after we did beare in furder uppon the Sowth side we fownd great quantity of yse, driving together, yet we had sundry chanells to pas betwene them, And after that we sent the pynnas from the ship to discover the best way our passage amongst them,[5] & so we followed with divers other of the fleete after the pynnas, untill she could not pas any farder, fynding the yse all closed abowt us, and afterward sent our boate & pynnases of divers [168] of the flete to breake a small neck of yse for passage into farder places that we did see clere, and at that tyme the winde began to blow very boystrous at the S.S.E. & caused the sea to heave & set very cruell; at that instant we were divers of the flete in a great channell indifferent free of yse, in which channell we determined to spend the night with bearing small sayles, being environed with yse. The bark Denis at that tyme plying up & down, did strike uppon a great yse, & there perished, so that the boates which were sent to breake the yse for passage, returned to her to saue the men & presently after the ship did sink down right;[6] divers of the flete notwithstanding with small sayles did ply up & down in the same channell, & other as they could fynd all that night, but we in the Ayde, & in the Thomas Alin did

[1] Margin note: 'The yse driven from the South coast adjudged to be 40 leags which to avoyd we did sale from some, and did bear rome from other some, the sea being full of peces dispersed of great bignes, being dangerous'.

[2] Margin note: 'Memo. That the 22 of June the Michael departed and kept a contrary course to us, as yt shold seme willfully don by the Master of her'.

[3] Margin note: 'Land by North'.

[4] Margin note: 'Sight of Queens foreland'.

[5] Cf. Hall's account of his attempted warning to the other ships not to enter the strait on 2 July (document 6, p. 115).

[6] Margin note: 'The bark Denis sunk'.

forsake yt, bearing no sayle, but lay adrift amongst the yse all the night, being terribly tormented therewith untill 11. of the clock,[1] the 3. of July, occupying our men with oares pikes & other powles to break the force of the yse from beating of the ship as much as we might, notwithstanding we had terrible blowes therewith & were preserved by the mighty power of *God* from perrishing, contrary unto our expectations: The winde afterward comming to the S.W. & having the eb with us, we did drive owt, sometyme setting sayle & sometimes a hull South East: And being allmost owt of the danger of the yse, we did discrye the most of the flete, which rejoyced us very muche: And the said .3. day abowt night, some of us talking with others did understand we were all in saffety, except onely the Michael of whome as yet we cannot understand where she ys,[2] we did arme the bowe of the ship with sundry planks of .3. inches thick & with capstayne bares & Junks, for that theyse stroke terribly against that place of her in so much that some of the plankes did perrish with the blowes; The rest of the flete except one or two more did not pas the like mysery, by reason they did kepe the channell betwene the yse with small sayles, which we could not do, for that our ship was long, & could not work with her as others did: And besides that yf we had kept that channell with sayle, where the rest did, we had burded one an other & thereby perished, as we had like to haue don by the ship of Weymouth (owner Hugh Randall),[3] in boording of us that night by drift & forcing upon us by yse, the boystrous winde that then did blow did cause us to unrig & take down both our topmasts for the ease of the ship, the which topmasts we did hang over boord allso to saue the ship from the yse /

The .4. said being in the morning clere withowt the Streicts & the winde at West, we did sayle S.S.W. bearing alongst the coast of *America*,[4] fynding yse driving from the coast, as though yt were long hedges into the sea to the Eastwards, we sayled as aforesaid untill .4. a clock at afternone, and then we layde yt a hull, untill .6. aclock the 5. said, & then we sailed Sowthwest alongst *America coast*, the winde at W. Northwest untill the 5. said at night abowt .6. aclock at which tyme we had sight of the coast, and very huge Ilands of yse, higher then ever we did see any, At which time we did cast abowt & did lye North of the Land, the winde as before untill the .6. said at night, at which time we were within the Streicts & did perfectly make the *Queens foreland*; to the Sowthwards of the *Queens foreland*, we had sight of a head of a land, being from yt about .20. leags,[5] which untill we had taken the latitude of yt we made yt to be the *Queens foreland* all, but **[169]** the *Master* Robert Davis onely, but he wold not agree to yt, nor so allow yt, aledging sundry reasons to prove the contrary by his marks when he saw yt a few dayes before/[6]

The .6. said being as aforesaid shot within the *Queens foreland* on the Sowth side, the winde came up to the S.S.E. & did blowe a great gale, & the weather waxed thick & foggy & therefore all the night we layde yt a hull, And upon the .7. said following we had sight of

---

[1] Margin note: 'The ships entred streicts in great danger of yse'. Presumably, the *Ayde* and *Thomas Allen*, the two largest vessels in the fleet, were too large to turn about in their narrow channel.

[2] The *Judith* was also missing.   [3] The *Salomon.*

[4] Margin note: 'owt of streicts'. Selman here is distinguishing the southern shore of Frobisher's imagined strait from the northern, which was then still thought to be part of Asia, in line with contemporary intelligence regarding the so-called 'Strait of Anian'.

[5] Margin note: 'A new land, Sowth'.

[6] Presumably, Selman mistook Davis for Christopher Hall here.

the North shore as we toke yt: And the 8. & 9. we did beare with yt, & alongst yt lying North & by West, but did not make yt perfectly, some imaginning rather that yt was the S. side of the *Queens foreland* (as afterward yt proved in dede,[1] & Master Hall of the same opinion, but yf yt fall owt so, they were deceyved with the setting of the tides The Generall & our Master could not be dissuaded,[2] but doth still make yt to be the North shore, the Generall assuring himself thereof to this present (the 10. said) that yt is so, and James Beare allso, but being foggy and darkened with mystes, they cannot yet make yt perfectly, I pray *God* send yt clere, that we may make yt perfectly: Alongst the said shore in sight and owt of sight by reason of fogs, we did runne in by the judgement of the *Master* &c. 35. leags bearing sayle & hulling, and there did remaine hulling being dark & foggy untill the .16. said, at which tyme we had yt somewhat clere, & thereuppon did beare towards the shore to make yt, at which time we did fall with the opening of a sownd, which we made for *Countes Sound* & did beare in with yt, all men that had sene it the yere before (except two, called Stobern & But)[3] allowed yt to be the same, which afterwards proved the contrary: The 17. said we toke the Altitude of the sunne & found us but in the Latitude of 62. & 10. minuts, and thereuppon found the error which we were in, then knowing that we were uppon the S. side of the S. shore called the *Queens foreland*, and with the winde at W. we did beare owt agayne, And the 18. said being shot owt so far as to the Masters judgement that we had sight of the Queens foreland being E. from us and then running alongst till we brought yt thwart of us the weather being foggy, notwithstanding we did alter our course more Northerly & brought us to be impatched with great quantity of yse and dark weather, being allso shot very nere the shore, still thinking that we had byn at the *Queens foreland*, alltering our course more Northerly, did bring our selves hard a boord the shore, at which tyme yt pleased *God* to geve us sight of yt, and thereby fownd yt did not lye as the *Queens foreland* did, fynding us deceyved and not so far shot as the said foreland, but being imbayed uppon a Lee coast & in sight of divers Ilands & rocks, not knowing how to escape with life, and in the depe of 50. faddoms of water, so that we could not well anker, but yet sometimes in mynde to anker yf we could haue set a poynt of an Iland which we made unto, and then fearing allso we shold haue had byn put from our anker, or greatly impatched with yse which we were allso amongst and then caulme, & could not get of from the rocks or Ilands which we did see, did strike all our sayles to anker, but before we were all ready to cast anker, the *Eternall God* (who delivereth all men being in perills) did send us a gale of winde to beare of from the said Ilands, but afterward we wished that we had ankred there, for that when we were of a small way from yt we sounded and fownd us in but .7. faddoms of water and hard roks, we lying under sayle towards the west which was our best way, for sure we were we could not dubble the land to the Eastwards, the winde being at S.S.E. [170] and the land

---

[1] No closing parenthesis.

[2] Margin note: 'The 9. Said Master Hall and 3. Of the other ships kept company together, Master Hall making the shore the S. side of the Queens foreland, and we the N. shore, so that we bearing into the streict and he owt of yt, lost company, the one of the other. The Generall condemned Master Hall, bycause he made yt not the land as he did, and Beares Sound was made to the Northwards of yt allso by the Generall, and all prooved contrary; yf the S. side of the S. shore had byn as the Generall did take to have byn the N. shore of his streicts, running up and so many leags as we did uppon the said S. side of the S. shore and in foggy wether (as we had no other) we had all perished'.

[3] *recte* Lunt.

lying E.S.E. & W.N.W., we after yt pleased *God* to send us .10. faddoms and then 17., and then 25. and so into 30. and 40., and allso did send us the winde at W.S.W. so that we did lye S.S.W. of into the sea untill we came into 120. faddoms with *our* sayling & towing owt with *our* boates, still having the eb with us untill night and then being caulme & little winde, we did strike *our* sayles, and did lye a hulling,[1] so, that the flud did port us in towards the shore againe untill we came into .80. faddoms, and then, we were forced to make a brude of cabells, & did anker untill the eb did come being the 19. day of July in the morning, at which tyme we did set sayle with a small gale of winde, the winde at S. & by E., and did sayle S.W. & by W. the weather still foggy / The .20. said the weather began to clere, the winde westerly, at which tyme we had sight of the ships that were before in *our* company and towards the afternone we came to speake with some of them, And they declared that some of *our* company were in 2. faddoms of water upon the less shore, being in great danger amongst the rocks & broken grownd, and delivered by Gods almighty power thus twise from perishing, towards night yt waxed somwhat foggy agayn, & a little before night we having sight of a point of land, bearing E.S.E. of us making yt the *Queens foreland*, we did beare with it in such sort as we thought to go clere of yt, and the land lying owt furder then we had sight of yt, we being not so far shot owt of the streicts that we were in by 20. Leages which 20. leags we were in furder then we made accownt of, being entred within yt at the least .60. leags, fell agayn in danger of that land in the night, but kept us of from yt, by *our* sownding lead: And in the morning the 21. said yt waxed clerer & then we made the land of the *Queens foreland* perfect and towards night opening a great bay at the wester end of the Sowthe parte of that lande, which we imagined to go throwgh into the Streicts of Frobusher, which to make triall thereof, the Gabriell was sent to discover, & we bearing abowt with the Easter end of yt the 22. towards night, had sight of the Gabriell comming into the Streicts through that sound passage at the *Cape of good hope*,[2] so that it is proved that the land of the *Queens foreland* to be an Iland;[3] the Gabriell having order to passe to the *Counteses sound*, did beare in towards yt, and we followed untill we could not passe any farder for yse lying so thick, and the Gabriell being within the yse, did still beare up into the streicts, & we forced to retire owtward agayn, being very much impatched therewith all the whole night /

The 23. said we had sight of the An fraunces whose company we lost as beforesaid, & when we came to the speche of the captayne & M*aster*, they declared, they had layn of & on open of the streicts .12. dayes & could not entre for fogs & yse, and was in danger before that uppon the lee shore of the S. side after she departed from us /

The 24. said the Generall being mynded to beare into the Streicts, bycause the Gabriell passed up in *our* sight, supposing allso the Th*omas* Allin, the Fraunces of foy, the Emanuell of Bridgewater, the Judith & the Michael to be above in the sownd, notwithstanding the great quantity of yse we were impatched withall the 23. Said and the winde at S.W. a good & reasonable gale, did mynde to beare up into the streicts agayne this present alledging that

---

[1] Margin note: 'The .18. said we did lose cumpany of all the flete that kept with us, being the Hopewell, the Thomas of Ipswich, the Mone, the Arminell, the Gabriell, the Beare, the ship Salomon'.

[2] Unidentified.

[3] Margin note: 'Queens foreland is an Ilande'. Fenton's *Judith* had made the same passage and confirmed this fact on the 4 July (doc. 7, p. 145).

the said wynde had brought owt all the yse, whereof great quantity we did see blown uppon the Lee coast; But yt pleased *God* to send us a **[171]** messinger owt of the Streicts called the fraunces of foy who did kepe company with the Tho*mas* Alin and the Emanuel of Bridgewater, & did enter into the Streicts the 19. said & the 20. said being shut up as far as *Jackmans sound* did put over with the *Countes sound* among very much yse & were environned therewith, frosen, & shut up therein, being marveylously tormented therewith, not onely with yse comming down, but allso with yse carried up with the winde & tyde:[1] This Fraunces of foy (I say) was a blessed messinger of God sent to us to warn us of the daungers that she & the others passed, who still did leave the Tho*mas* Alin, the Busse or Emanuel of Bridgewater & the Gabriel last come unto them in great danger being carried toward the lee coast in the frosen & thick yse as the winde did carry them: God deli*ver*ed them for his mercyes sake & for his blessed sonne *Jesus Christes* sake. The M*aste*r Tho*mas* Moris of the said ship the Fraunces of foy, before M*aste*r Hall & he with others entred the Streict was in a sownd uppon the N. side of the *Queens foreland* where they found very good owr by o*ur* judgements to the sight, & therefore the Generall is gone this morning a land to seke the same purposing to go into the said sownd with all our 9. ships now in company untill tyme may serve us to go furder & other o*ur* ports of lading /[2] The 25. at night we did beare into the Streicts & then had sight of the Emanuel of Bridgewater, And comming to the speche of them the M*aste*r of her affirmed that the yse did ly very thick over all the Streicts so that we could not attayn to the Countes Sound as yet; the Generall notwithstanding wold geve no credit thereunto, but did beare in with the Streicts to make triall thereof the 26. in the morning & finding great store of yse did retire back owt agayn with the winde at North and much yse following us, At that tyme (the 25. said) these ships did entre in with us, the Emanuel, the Armonell, the Hopewell and the Beare, and .5. others of the flete did put to sea, havinge the winde then at the S.E. and East *which* was a scant winde for them to dubble owt the foreland, being nere the land /[3]

The 26. at night we came back to the sea againe and brought the foreland of us Sowth West /

The .27. toward night, the winde at West we did beare in towards the foreland, and did lye of and on all the night /

The .28. in the morning we did beare agayn into the straight the winde westerly bearing inwards still untill we were repulsed and forced to put owt agayn by reason of much yse driving owt, but the Hopewell finding some clerer slade[4] then we could do did beare in, God send her good hap, And then we did seke to recover the wether shore *which* was the foreland, the winde at W.N.W. blowing somewhat boystrous /

The 29. in the morning we did beare into the streict agayn with the winde at W. a small leading gale, & sometimes at W.S.W. we lying up N.W. passing up amongst great quantity of yse, sometime thick, & sometime thinner, and so did still procede, bearing inwards untill

---

[1] Margin note: 'Memo that I do suppose the Easterly windes we had coming hither did not onely kepe the yse for coming owt of the Streicts, but allso filled the Streicts with yse of other places'.

[2] Margin note: 'A new sound North side of Queens foreland with new mynes'.

[3] Margin note: 'The 5. Ships that did put to sea, did break our company willinglly, and very willfully, to say, the An Frances, Thomas of Ipswich, Moone, Fraunces of foy, and the Salomon of Weymouth'.

[4] Slade: an open space or clearing.

the 30. said at none, keping about the middle of the streict,[1] And in the morning the .30. said we were thwart of *Yorks sound*, which I affirmed to the Generall to be so, but he denyed yt, saying that we were not shot up as high as *Jackmans sound* by .16. leags, at which instant, the Generall went up to the top, and descried *Gabriels Iland*,[2] making yt to be *Pembroke Iland* going into the *Countess sound*, and so directing his course with yt Christopher Iackson the trumpetter being in the top did [172] make yt playnly *Gabriels Iland* & allso made the *Countess sound* to the which the Generall yelded, & then presently did allter his course, and embarked him self in a pynnas with sayles & oares bycause yt did blow but little wynde for the ship, and gaue us tokens to follow him, & so signifyed to us thereby that yt was the right place or sownd as before is said: Into the which he entred with his pynnas, and being entred therein, fownd there the Judith, and the Michael, & caused them to shote of certayn peces of ordonance, to geve knowledge there were certayn of our flete, which comforted us very muche, but we imagined those ships to be the Thomas Alin & the Gabriel, for we did think verily the Judith & the Michael could not have escaped the dangers that they were in, being not of our company a month or more /

The .30. of July at night, we entred into the mowth of the Cowntesse sownd & there came to us sent from the Generall Charles Jackman to bring in the Ayde and for that yt fell caulme we came to an anker in the entring thereof, being ebbing water abowt .9. of the clock at night,[3] the Master his Mate & Charles Jackman going then to supper, gave charge to the company to looke well owt for yse driving towards the ship, willing them to prevent yt in tyme, & before the Master had half supped, one of the company came to the Master to know whether they shold watche half watche or quarter watche, the Master gaue order to watche half watche charging them to loke well owt for yse, but the watche neglecting their dutyes, there came driving thwart the halse of the ship a great pece of yse & the weather being caulme did ly uppon the cabell 1/4 of an howre before we could be clere of yt fretting the cable in suche sort, that yf yt had put us from our anker we had byn in danger of rockes lying not far from us, God be honored there chaunced no hurt of yt,[4] Notwithstanding I thought yt good & my duty therein to say somthing unto the watche of their negligence therein, bycause the charge of the vyage did depend upon the savegard of the Ayde being the Admirall, whereuppon I rebuked one Holmes a quarter Master, & Hill boteswayn mate charging them they shold aunswere their negligent loking to so great a charge, but they with one other called (   )[5] did will me to meddle with that I had to do, demaunding whether I had commission to speake or deale therein & this did Hill, and (   )[6] willed me to get me to my cabben, & wold not be checked at my hands, I aunswered them whither I had commyssion or not, I wold tell them their duties & go to my cabben when I did see cause, and thus

[1] Margin note: 'Entred into the Cowntesse sound'.
[2] Margin note: 'The Generall had no knowledge of Jackmans sound; nor Yorks sound no, nor yet of the Countess sound and yet had as fayre weather to make the land as any man might have had. He wold have sought the Countesse sound (yf others had not byn) at Gabriel Iland, and very hardly was perswaded to the contrary'.
[3] Margin note: 'The Ayde arrived in the Countesse sound'.
[4] Margin note: 'A great pece of yse thwart the halse at anker of Ayd by negligence'. Selman is the only authority for the detail of this incident.
[5] Blank.
[6] Blank.

with multiplying of woords, they abused me very much which I was fayn to put up at their hands: The Master can beare no rule amongst them bycause he is not cowntenanced by the Generall, & therefore all things hath fallen owt the worse with us, & that hath caused me to speake more earnestly in this cause, for neyther the boatswayn, nor any officer yet hitherto hath byn obedient to the Master, & the disobedience of the officers, doth cause the company allso to disobey and neglect their duties:[1] We had not byn aboue .2. howres at an anker, but that there came very muche yse driving inwards towardes us: at which tyme, I being still abrode, & the Masters mate allso, I said to him yt were good to way to way[2] our anker to prevent the danger of the yse and presently he called up [173] Charles Jackman and they caused the company to way the anker with the winde Easterly a smale gale, and after they had purchased home their said anker, there came yse upon us, but they setting sayle before the anker was catted,[3] the yse stroke the flok of the anker through the bow of the ship, that the water came in fercely, in so muche that we had water in hold .4. fote above the sealing within an howre or les,[4] And our pumps being unready could not free the ship of yt, but kept yt still at a stay, the leak being stopped as well as they could, with beffe & other provision, and thus we remayned pumping and freeing of the ship with buckets from 12. a clock at night, being the .30. of July untill 9. a clock in the morning the 31. said, at which tyme we were come into harbour. And then provision was made to beare the ship over of the one side, & the hole mended with lead untill we may come better to yt[5] / There came into the *Countesse Sound* in company with us and in our sight, the Hopewell, the Fraunces of foy, the Armonell, the Emanuell, the Salomon of Weymouth and the Bear: the Judith and the Michael came into this sownd the 21. of July, and for the space of .3. wekes before they continually were tormented (with yse)[6] up & down, within the Streicts amongst the yse and could not by any meanes get this place nor clere themselves of the yse, the Judith being bilged with yse in the bowes, having 2. great holes made in her, every howre loking when they shold perish therewith, but God delivered them, geving them fayre weather to work for their savegard /[7]

The first of August the Generall did take order to tents upon the Iland of the myne for the myners to succor them in their working there, & then began their work /

The second said the Generall with .2. pynnesses passed to Beares sownd, to bring prooffs of the owr there, & to vew what quantity there was to be had and returned agayn at night being distant from the Cowntesse Sound .9. leags.

The said at night the Gabriell came into the *Cowntess Sound* & Master Hall in her to vew whither the Streictes were clere of yse & left the Thomas Alin in a sownd nere *Oxford Mount* untill his return thither agayn /[8]

---

[1] Margin note: 'Variance betwene the Generall and the Master'. Cf. document 5, p. 88.
[2] *Sic.*
[3] Cat: to suspend the anchor off the deck, clear of the bow.
[4] Margin note: 'The anker thrust through the ships bow with yse'.
[5] Selman's use of the present tense here and elsewhere indicates the journal was written up every few days during the course of the expedition and not substantially altered subsequently.
[6] Erased.
[7] Margin note: 'The Judith arrived'.
[8] Margin note: 'By the way coming hither Master Hall entered into yorks sound and doth finde yt a very good road for many ships to ride in at the North part of the sound, land loked'.

The fyrst of August the Fraunces of foy toke in 2. pynnasses ladings of owre & the 2. day as much /

The 4. said Master Hall departed hence with the Gabriell toward the sownd nere *Oxford Mount* to bring hither the Thomas Alin /

The said the Generall with .4. pynnesses & boates with a iiii^{xx} men, soldiers & marriners & Denham with him went to Jonas Mownt, to seke for owr, & browght sundry samples, whereof as yet no assay is made, but of the riche owr that *Jonas* fownd the last yere, we could not light of any suche /

The .8. of August the Thomas Alin & the Gabriel arrived here towards night, by whome we could not here of the Thomas of Ipswiche the An fraunces & the Mone I pray God send us good newes of them /

The .9. said the Generall with the Gabriell & the Michael, with Mariners, Myners & soldiours departed towards *Bears Sound* to get owr, for that the myne in the *Countess Iland* fayled /

The said the most part of the myners & soldiours were removed to a place called *Fentons fortune* being [174] at the entrance of *Countesse Sound* to the Eastwards: And yt was reported that there were a 1000. tunnes to be had there, but Master Denham at his returne from thence this present at night sayth he can not see how 40. tunnes will there be had & that with great travayle to bring yt to the sea side.[1]

The .11. sayd the Master Robert Davis, Thomas Morace Master of the Fraunces of foy & I in company with them travayled with a pynnas to the Northwards of the *Countesse Sound* about .4. myles alongst the coast & there fownd a myne of black owr & allso an other of red & of sundry sortes of both, of which sorts we brought ensamples, whereof Denham made proof & the .13. said Capten Fenton & Denham passed thither liking the place very well, and aswell our Mariners as the Mariners of the said Fraunces were there set to work & by the .15. said we had gotten aboord the Ayde of the black sort & some of the red abowt .15. tunnes /[2]

The .15. said towards the evening, the Gabriell & the Michael came to the *Countesse Sound* both laden with owre from *Bears Sound*, & the .16. said discharged yt into the Ayde, there lading was adjudged to be abowt 50. tunnes of owr / The said all such Myners & soldiours as were sent from the *Countesse Sound* to *Fentons fortune* were removed to the myne that we found to the Northwards which was better liked, that yt of *Fentons fortune*, where, in the tyme they were there was gotten (with hard travayle of carriage to the sea side) but .60. or .70. tunnes of owre, they being myners and soldiours that wrought their .6. dayes lx. persons /

The .16. said the Generall & Denham with him is gon to a sownd *called Dyers passage*

---

[1] Presumably, the optimistic forecast had been that of the mine's discoverer and namesake, Edward Fenton (cf. document 8, p. 157).

[2] Margin note: 'The .13. said Denham was sent for to Beares sound, to make proofs of owr, & the .14. said he departed thitherwards and carried with him all the strong water that he should make the separations of Metalls'.

which is uppon the Souther land of the *Cowntess Sound* to vew a myne there fownd by Andrew Dyer & to make assayes thereof /

The said, God called to his mercy Philip ( )[1] who had who had charge of certayn apparell brought by the Generall for the marriners & myners, and allso one of the Bark Denys men called Trelos, one allso owt of the Armonell & an other owt of the Fraunces of foy all buryed uppon *Winters furnace* this present day /

The .18. sayd, the Gabriell and the Michael departed hence to *Beares Sound* to lade owr & to bring yt hither to the Ayde /

The .19. said the Solomon of Weymouth departed towards *Bears Sound* to take in her lading of owr /

The .20. said the Beare departed towards *Dyers passage* to lade there /

The .19. [2] said the Hopewell departed towards *Dyers passage* to lade there /

The .21. said the Busse of Bridgewater departed to *Dyers passage* to take her lading of owr there /

The .21. of August, the Fraunces of foy was full laden, part of the owr of the *Countesse Iland* & the rest of the owr of the myne to the Northwards of the *Cowntesse Sound* carrying in all tunnes by estimation .140. whereof .70. from the *Countesse Iland* and the rest as aforesaid /

The .19.[3] said Capten fenton came to make complaint to the Generall of the Boatswayn, and others of the Aydes mariners for disobeying him in certayn service to haue byn don for the furderance & dispatche of the ships lading at two severall tymes, his speches intending to due punishment for the same, & after long recitall of ther abuses, did loke that the Generall shold haue ayded him therein, & to haue commaunded due punishments for their defects, the Generall not taking order therefore *Master* fenton and he did grow to hoat speches by whome eche others credit did come, the Generall affirming that *Master* Fentons credit came by him, & he denying the same, left [175] their former matter, and fell to reason uppon the same with many hoat woords, in so muche that in the end, the Generall affirming he preferred *Master* Fenton to be the Queens servant & he denying, alledging that the Generall did not well to rob them that did prefer them both to that service, & then at *Master* Fenton's departure, he said he had offred him great disgrace in that he wold not punnish the offendours which he complayned of, but rather did animate them against him in neglecting of yt which he could not take in good part being his lieutenant generall, and commaunding them to do nothing but their duties in Her Maiesties service /[4]

---

[1] Blank: supply 'Ellarde'.

[2] *Sic.*

[3] *Sic.* The misplacing of entries for 19 August may indicate that they were written up several days after the events described therein.

[4] Margin note: 'Strife betwene Master Frobusher and Master Fenton / The Botswayne and divers of the marriners have byn all this vyage froward and untoward in their dealings toward the Master, not doying their duties, by reason the Master have byn discountenanced with the Generall, and therby he and his companions animated to do as they have don, and so doth still procede being still animated as here you have hard'. Cf. Lok's similar version of this confrontation (document 5, p. 88).

The .22. said the Gabriel arrived here at the *Countess Sound*, being laden with owr from *Bears Sound*, and discharged yt aboord the Ayde, bringing tunnes .25. by estimation /

The said, here at the *Countess Sound* arrived a pynnas of the An fraunces, wherein Captayn Best came, leaving the An Fraunces and the Mone of foy at anker in a sownd nere the *Queens Forelande*,[1] and they reported that they had not sene the Thomas of Ipswich this .14. dayes, with the said pynnas they came costing up alongst the Sowth coast to seke us, and did seke us in *Jackmans Sound* and *Yorks Sound* and passed up as far as *Gabriels Iland* & returned hither this present, bringing them samples of owres, much like that of *Winters Furnace*, & doth purpose that Denham shall make tryall thereof, & fynding yt good, they will lade of yt, having great plenty of yt as they report, they haue by report passed great troubles sins they departed from us, by dangers of yse, and rocks, I pray God send us good newes of the Thomas of Ipswich.

The .23. said the Generall, Captayn Fenton his lieutenant, Gilbert York, and George Beste gentlemen assembled themselves together, Christopher Hall, and Charles Jackman Masters with them, for causes touching their instructions, & amongst other matters, did call in question the abuses of the Boteswayne & one Robinson used towards the Generalls said lieutenant & after yt had byn argued of amongst the said Commissioners the Generall referred the punishment thereof to them to determyn, then they called the said offendours before them, who acknowledged their abuses, & uppon their submission, as allso affirming they did not know Capteyn Fenton to be the Generalls said lieutenant, they were pardoned & forgeven /[2]

The .23. said of August, the Michael arrived here laden with owr from *Bears Sound* bringing tunnes .25. by estimation & discharged yt aboord the Ayde /

The .24. said the Sollomon of Weymouth arrived here laden with owr of *Bears Sound* & with owr laden in her before her departure hence, all tunnes by estimation .130. tunnes, whereof *Bears Sound* tunnes .60. and of the Countesse Iland[3] & *Winters Furnace* tuns .10. The Generall departed this present towards *Bears Sound* in a pynnas & will return hither agayn before he go up into the Streicts.[4]

The said, Captayn Beste departed with his pynnas toward the *Queens Foreland* to a sownd where the An Fraunces and the Mone resteth and stayeth his coming The said Fraunces and Mone by their Marriners reports were allmost laden with owr before their coming hither, the samples thereof hath byn proved & ar reasonably well liked of Denham, and therefore I here order is taken, that the Moone shall discharge all her owr into the An Fraunces, & that the said Mone [176] shall take in all such bere as the An Fraunces hath discharged there aland which was provided for Capteyn Fenton & his company, and as wynde and weather shall serue to come hither with the same, and at *Bears Sound* she shall haue her lading of owr provided /[5]

---

[1] Margin note: 'Capteyn Best arrived at Countesse sound'.
[2] Margin note: 'Conferrence for offendors'.
[3] Inserted above text: Sussex myne .60. tunnes.
[4] Margin note: 'Salomon laden'. The clear inference in the final sentence of this passage is that Frobisher himself continued to regard the search for the western exit to his 'strait' as an active priority, and had stated so.
[5] Margin note: 'The An fraunces and the Mone laden'.

The said the Thomas Alin departed hens having having[1] taken in here .100. tunnes of owr had at the North Myne called the *Countesse of Sussex Myne* and the rest of her lading she is to take in at *Beares Sound* & to that end she is gon thither where she is to lade .60. tuns more /[2]

The .26. at night the Generall returned from *Bears Sound* with the pynnas that he departed from hens, And the .27. in the morning he passed with the same up into the Straict as well to discover mynes as allso to take of the people yf he may conveniently haue them /

The .27. said at night the Thomas Alin arrived here from *Bears Sound* being fully laden /

The .28. said in the morning the An Fraunces arrived here from a sownd called (   )[3] being nere the *Queens Foreland* & laden with owr of that place. The said at night, the Generall returned with fowle weather & the winde Easterly with rayne & snow and so continued till the .30. towards night /

The .31. said in the morning we wayed & made sayle from *Countesse of Warwik Sound* with the Ayde, the Thomas Alin, the Bear, the Salomon, the Armonell, & the two barks, & for that yt fell caulme, we ankered all that night at the mowth of the sownd, being all night caulme & the Fraunces of foy /[4]

The fyrst of September .1578. in the morning the Gabriell & the Michael did put into *Bears Sound* to lade there.

The said the Generall with a pynnas departed towards *Beares Sound* to provide .10. or .12. tunnes of lading more for the Ayde and to send yt owt to us with boats & pynnasses.

The said the Ayd & all the other ships aforesaid wayed the winde Northerly, bearing alongst towards *Beares Sound* with a small gale, & abowt none ankered thwart of *Beares Sound* /

The .28. of August before, God called to his mercy Roger Littlestonne, the Generalls servant, who by the Judgement of the surgian had the horrible disease of the pox.

The last of July[5] at night, God called to his mercy Anthony Sparrow, one of the quartermasters of the Ayde/ The Fraunces of foy, the Armonell, the Thomas Alin the Beare, the Salomon, came all laden owt of the *Countess Sound*, the Ayd lacked .10. or .12. tunnes, but laden of sundry mynes as before is said / The An fraunces, the Hopewell and the Judith arrived with us thwart of the said *Bears Sound* the fyrst of September & kept under sayle by us /

The fyrst of September said, we receyved ( )[6] tunns of owre into the Ayde, and all the myners this present at night were ready to come aboord from thens /

The said at night the winde chopping up to the N.W. a small gale and the sea growing thereby, forced us to way & made sayle, bearing of S.W. untill we came into 23. faddoms, &

---

[1] *Sic.*
[2] Margin note: 'The Thomas Alin laden'.
[3] Blank; unidentified.
[4] Margin note: 'Set saile homewards from Countess sound'.
[5] *Sic.*
[6] Blank.

then ankered agayn, staying for the coming of the Generall, & abowt .2. howres after, *our* ship did drive, *our* anker being broken, *which* caused us to set saile agayn & did beare of W. & W. & by S. & afterwards did lye a hull, staying for the Generall, the winde still growing of great force at N.N.W. caused us to set *our* foresaile agayn, bearing of Sowth towards the *foreland* the second day of September & towing *our* [177] Gondelo at starn, she did split therewith & so we were forced to cut her of from the ship & lost her & then we did strike *our* sayle & spooned before the sea S.E. untill the *Queens Foreland* did beare of us; The Generall is condemned of all men for bringing the flete in danger to anker there, thwart of *Beares Sound* onely for .2. boats of owre and in daungering himself allso, whome they judge will hardly recover to come aboord of us, but rather forced to go with the barks or the Emanuel of Bridgewater into England; of the whole flete, there is now in *our* company, or to be seen but .6. sailes /[1]

Master Hall went aland after the ship came first to an anker thwart the said Bears Sound, & did give him counsaill to make hast aboord before night; God send him well to recover us & all his company \

    The Ayde hath lading of owr in her as followeth.
        of *Bears Sound* tunnes by estimation – 110.
        of the *Countess of Sussex Myne* tunnes – 20.
    The Thomas Alin owr in her as followeth.
        of the *Countess of Sussex Myne*, tunnes – 100.
        of *Beares Sound*, owre tunnes – 80.
    The Hopewell owr in her as followeth.
        of *Dyers Passage* or *Sound*, tunnes – 140.
    The Fraunces of foy hath owr laden in her as followeth.
        of the *Cowntess of Warwiks myne* tun*n*s – 50.
        of the *Countess of Sussex myne*, tunnes – 80.
    The An fraunces hath owr in her as followeth.
        of the *Queens Foreland* tunnes – 130.
    The Mone of foy hath owr in her as followeth.
        of the *Queens Foreland*, tunnes – 100.
    The Beare Leycester hath owr laden in her
        of *Dyers Passage*, tunnes – 100.
    The Judith hath owr laden in her as followeth.
        of the *Countess of Sussex myne* tunnes – 80.
    The Gabriel hath owr laden in her as followeth.
    of *Beares Sound*, tunnes – 20.
    The Michael hath owr laden in her as followeth.
    of *Beares Sound*, tunnes – 20.
    The Armonell hath owr laden in her as followeth.
    of *Fentons fortune* tunnes – 5.
    of the *Countess of Warwicks myne*, tuns – 5.

[1] Margin note: 'How the Generall was left behinde his ship a land'.

of *Winters Furnace* tunnes – 5.
of the *Countess of Sussex myne*, tunnes – 85.
The Emanuel of Bridgewater hath owr laden in her as followeth.
of the *Countess of Sussex myne*, tunnes – 30.
of *Dyers Passage*, tunnes – 20.
of *Bears Sound*, tunnes – 60.
The Salomon hath owr laden in her as followeth.
of the *Countess of Warwicks myne*, tuns – 10.
of the *Countess of Sussex myne*, tunnes – 60.
of *Beares Sound*, tunnes – 60.

Forasmuch as the Countesse of Warwikes myne fayled being so hard stone to breke & by judgement *yelded not aboue a hundreth tunnes*,[1] we were driven to seke mynes as above named and having but a short tyme to tarry & some proofs made of the best owr fownd in those mynes abovesaid, men were willed to get there lading of them & every man so employed him self to have lading, that many symple men (I judge) toke good & bad together; so that amongst the fleets lading I think much bad owr will be found.[2]

If the owr now laden doth prove good, at the mynes & places abouesaid is plenty thereof, but gotten with hard labour & travayle upon the *Countesse of Warwicks Iland*. Capteyn Fenton hath hidden & covered in the place of the myne all the tymber that came hither for the howse, & divers other things to whose note I refer me /

Allso he hath caused to be buylded a little howse uppon the same Iland & covered yt with boords to prove how yt will abyde [178] or stand untill the next yere & hath left in yt sundry things.[3]

The second said of September, the *Queens Foreland* bearing from us N.W. and by North, there passed by us these ships bearing to seawards we lying a hull: the Hopewell the Fraunces of foy, the Beare leycester, the Armonell and the Salomon, the Armonell at that instant lost her boat & one man; The Salomon lost her boat before her comming by us. All which ships the .3. present in the morning was owt of our sightes homewards bound, lying to seawards S.S.E with the winde at N.W. a great gale of wynde /

The second said at night came unto us our pynnas with .8. mariners in her who came from *Bears Sound* that morning & bearing over with the S. coast with .18. mariners in her, landed uppon certayn Ilands to loke to seawards for us, and after them came the Generall in the Gabriell and in their company the Judith and the Michael, our men at that instant aland and loking for us, did scry .2. ships one under sayle & the other at hull, whereof we in the Ayde was one and the Armonell the other, she under sayle & we a hull, allso betwene us & them was the Mone of foy, our men which were landed as beforesaid enbarked them selves agayn in theyr pynnas & did beare after the Gabriell, the Michael & the Judith and did put aboord the Gabriell & Michael all the .18. mariners and then being somwhat nerer the Judith did

---

[1] Selman's emphasis.
[2] Margin note: 'Diversitie of owr laden'.
[3] Margin note: 'A house buylded'.

put a man allso aboord her:[1] And having order before of the Generall, the mariners remayning in the pynnas did beare from the Judith towards the Mone of Foy willing them to remayn with her, but they having a bold pynnas with sayles afterwards espying us a hull, but not knowing us to be the Ayde, did owt sayle the Mone of foy & at the closing up of the evening we made the said pynnas to be the Michael and the Moone to be the Gabriel & sometymes lying spooning before the sea & sometymes thwart remayning their cumming up at length we fownd yt the pynnas as abouesaid: then they bringing us newes that the Generall was comming in the bark abouesaid and in the company of the ships also aforesaid with the An fraunces allso, the said night we did ly a hull & did hang owt lights for them all night long to show him & burnt a pile of wylde fyre to the end they might the better fynde us we hoping to haue had them a boord long before day;[2] But when day was come we loking owt for them could not see any of them but the Mone of foy: then we judging they had overshot us did afterwards spone before the sea 3. or 4. howres, and the Thomas Alin then being to seawards & wyndwards of us came bearing toward us and after we had spoken with them, they allso judged them to be a hed of us & then we made our sayle with our corses and foretop saile, the winde at N.W. a great gale and we sayled S.S.E. towards night the winde came at W.S.W. & we sayled allso S.S.E. the winde somwhat slacked or lessor still keping company with the Thomas Alin & the Mone of foy /[3]

The second said allso our mariners of the pynnas declared that they at their comming over from *Bears Sound* did see the Emanuel of Bridgewater in great danger to be lost to the leewards of the sownd & did strike their sayles uppon the last of the flud to anker as they did judge amongst the rocks, And then yt was not likely they shold ride to escape all the next eb, the winde at N.N.W., & a very great gale: God be mercifull unto them/

The said allso they declared that the captayn of the An fraunces George Beste was with his pynnas in *Beares Sound* laden with owr & the number of myners & mariners in her abowt 30. persons: they rowed with the [179] said pynnas towards the Michael, but whither they boorded her, they cannot tell; and at that instant the Michael had the Thomas Alins pynnas at her starn which that Master[4] said he wold cut of yf she did hinder him his comming owt as yt was thought she wold be: And afterwards our said men did see the Michael withowt any pynnas at her starn, and thereby do judge that the An fraunces pynnas and her men remayned in the said sownd & are in dowt of their getting their ship/[5]

The .4. said still keping our course homewards S.S.E. the winde at N.W., a reasonable bearing gale: In the morning our company did hale up our pynnas which we towed at her starn to clere the water owt: the sea thrust her up with great force agaynst the starn of the ship whereby she perished, & so thay did cut of the tow ropes: she came up with such force,

[1] Margin note: 'The Armonells boat lost and a man'.
[2] Margin note: 'The Judith towing her boat, the Fraunces of foyes pynnas and the hopewells pynnas lost them all the .2. of this month'.
[3] Margin note: 'The Thomas Alin lost her Skyf and a man a cable and anker'.
[4] Bartholomew Bull.
[5] Margin note: 'The Thomas Alins Pynnas lost by the Michael as our men do judge'. In fact, the *Judith* and *Anne Frances* had already taken on miners and soldiers from these pinnaces. The *Michael*'s master had not made good his threat to abandon the pinnace he towed; however, as soon as Best and the others had managed to board the *Anne Frances*, it sank at the *Michael*'s stern.

that yf she had byn strong as she was but weak, she mought haue put the ship allso in danger striking in some plank, the blow was such that *our* company were commaunded to loke whether we had hurt thereby or not. but God be thanked we had none /[1]

The .5. said at night in a storme we lost the company of the Mone of foy.

The .6. said Thomas Batterby God called to his m*er*cy.[2]

The .10. said being in the Latitude of 53. $^{1/2}$ about .2. of the clock after midnight *our* mayn yard did break a sundre in the mydds w*h*ich to recover in we did beare rome with *our* fore-saile before the winde, the winde at S.W. and presently did put owt .2. lights & shot of a pece to geve the Thomas Alin knowledge of *our* mishap, but yt shold seme they loked not owt for our light nor pece, but still carry all their sailes & in the morning we could not see her: The sayd yard was peryshed 5. or 6. dayes before striking of yt tarrying for them at w*h*ich tyme yt gave a great crak, but we could not finde where yt was, nor what yt was that craked /[3]

The .11. said yt was amended & strengthened with a plank & anker stocks & moulded with ropes, and then we brought a new mayn saile to the yard: and about .7. of the clock at night we did set saile with yt with a reasonable gale of winde and immediatly yt being but weakly fisshed[4] gave a great clak & therewithall we stroke yt agayn & so rested with it all that night/

The 12. said yt fell caulme & then we fished the said yard & moulded yt with ropes in sundry other places and so strengthened yt very strong so that we had the use of yt agayne /

The 14. said at .3. of the clock at afternone, the winde at Sowth S.E. began very fiercely & so encreased all that night growing to a terrible storme contynuing untill the.15. said[5] to 8. a clock but altered uppon sundry point*e*s increasing that yt was not sayle worthy, whereupp-on we were forced to spone before the sea withowt sayle & at the end of the second watch, the seas was so terribly grown that one sea came so fast after the other, thone car-rying up her head & an other came with such force that yt brake in all the starn of the Gen-eralls cabben and did beare down with yt the cowbredge head of the said cabben, striking allso one Fraunces Austin from the helme, who called to the company for help fearing he shold haue perished, but withall spede yt was amended God by praysed, & we by his Godly providence wonderfully delivered /

The 17. said God called to his mercy George yong myner /

The .19. said being in the latitude of 52. degrees we encountred with the Hopewell being to the leewards of us they declared that the Beare & the Salomon were to weatherwards of us & that they were separated in the great storme from the Armonell & the Fraunces of foy: The Hopewell lost her boat & a cable & an anker at the comming from the Streict /

[180]   The 21. said we had sight of .3. sayles being in the latitude of 51. whereof .2. was to

---

[1] Margin note: 'The Ayds pynnas lost at her starn'.
[2] Cf. p. 124, n.1.
[3] Margin note: 'The weather was foggy in the morning & all the day'.
[4] Fish: a long piece of curved wood used to strengthen a mast.
[5] '13' erased.

leewards of us & one to weatherwards, we did suspect them to be men of war by their working and therefore we did hale close by the winde to speak with the weathermost ship, and being inough in the weather of the leaward ships did ly les in the winde untill the weathermost ship did come within *our* knowledge, and then we did fynde her to be the An fraunces at the shutting in of the evening & did lose sight of the other .2. sayles, but we judge them to be of *our* company, the winde was then at N.W. & by W. by the An Fraunces we had understanding the Generall to be in the Gabriell, and was separated from their company the 14. said in a storme, they judge them to be a head of us:[1] the Judith & the Michael they left in company together, w*h*ich they Judge to be a starn & allso the Mone, they spake with her & left her a starn allso. And the Busse of Bridgewater they left at an anker to leewards of *Beares Sound* amongst the rocks. God send good newes of her, she was left in great perill. Owt of the An Fraunces we received (   )[2] men of ours this instant 22. said /

The 23. said we lost the company of the Hopewell & the An Fraunces in a storme w*h*ich began the .22. at .6. a clock at night and continued till .8. of the clock the .24. in the morning, the winde at West and West N.W.

The .24. said God called to his mercy Water Krelle and Thomas Tort.

The said we sownded and had .70. faddoms oosy sand, whereby we judged us to the Northwards of Silly and afterwards sayled Sowth East all that night, the winde at North stormy weather /

The 25. said God called to his mercy Thomas Coningham /

The 27. in the morning we had sight of the *Start* .5. leags of *God* be praysed therefore & make us thankfull for delivering us.[3]

---

[1] It was during the same conversation that Christopher Hall learned of Frobisher's 'great coller' against him regarding his abandonment (document 6, p. 129).
[2] Blank.
[3] Margin note: 'At the Start in Cornwale'.

DOCUMENT 10

Thomas Ellis: A true reporte of the third and last voyage into Meta Incognita[1]

These are to let you knowe, that upon the 25. of Maie, The Thomas Alline, being the Viceadmerall, whose captain was M. Yorke, M. Gibbes Maister, Christopher Hall Pilot, accompanied with the Reareadmerall named The Hopewell, whose Capteine was Master Henrie Carewe, the Maister Andrew Dier, and certaine other shippes, came to Gravesend, where we anchored & abode the comming of certaine other of our fleete, which were not yet come.[2]

The 27. of the same Moneth, our fleete being nowe gone together, and all thinges prest in a redinesse, the winde favouring, and Tide serving, we being of sailes in number 8. waide anchors, and hoised our sailes toward Harwich, to meet with our Admerall, and the residue, which then and there abode our arrivall:[3] where we safely arrived, the 28. thereof, finding there our Admerall, where we, with the discharge of certeine peeces, saluted (according to order and dutie) and were welcomed with the like courtesie: which being finished, we landed: where our Generall continued mustring his Souldiers and Miners, and setting thinges in order apperteining to the voyage, untill the last of the saide Moneth of Maie, which day we hoised our sailes, and committing our selves to the conducting of almightie God, we set forward toward the West Countrie, in fine luckie wise, and good successe, that by the .5. of June, we passed the Dursies, being the utmost part of Ireland, to the Westward.[4]

And here it were not much amisse, nor farre from our purpose, if I shoulde a little discourse and speake of our adventures and chances by the way, at our landing at Plimmouth, as also the meeting of certeine poore men, which were robbed and spoiled of all that they had, by Pirates and Rovers: amongst whom was a man of Bristowe, on whom our Generall used his liberalitie, and sent him away with letters into England.[5]

---

[1] *A true report of the third and last voyage into Meta Incognita,: atchieved by the worthie Capteine, M. Martine Frobisher Esquire, Anno. 1578* by Thomas Ellis; published in London by Thomas Dawson at the sign of the Three Cranes, Vintry. Ellis claimed to be a sailor: 'more studied and used in my Charde and Compasse, and other thinges belonging to Navigation …' (in the preface of his *True Report*, not reproduced hereafter); however, his name does not appear in any of the wages lists for the voyage, which indicates that he sailed as a volunteer, and there is no hint of hydrographic ability in his narrative. This was the only published narrative of the voyage not to be dedicated to a noble patron.

[2] Margin note: 'M. Yorke. Christopher Hall. The Hopewell. Capteine Carew. Andrew Dier'.

[3] Margin note: 'Harwich'.

[4] Margin note: 'Dursies. Ireland'.

[5] Margin note: 'Bristowe. England'. This was the fortunate bark *Grechewinde* (see document 8, p. 138). The letters were for the attention of Michael Lok.

But because such thinges are impertinent to the matter, I will returne (without any more mentioning of the same) to that, from the which I have digressed, and swarved, I meane our shippes nowe sailing on the sourging seas, sometime passing at pleasure with a wished Easterne winde, sometime hindered of our course againe by the Western blastes, untill the .20. day of the foresaid Moneth of June, on which day in the morning we fell with Frizeland, which is a very high and cragged land, & being almost cleane covered with snowe, so that we might see nought but the craggie rockes, and the toppes of high and huge hilles, sometimes (and for the most part) all covered with foggie mistes. There we might also perceive the great Isles of yce lying on the seas, like mountaines, some small, some bigge, of sundrie kindes of shapes, and such a number of them, that we coulde not come neere the shoare for them.[1]

Thus sailing alongest the coast, at the last we sawe a place somewhat voyde of yce, where our Generall, (accompanied with certeine others) went a shoare, where they sawe certeine tentes made of beastes skinnes, and boates much like unto theirs of *Meta incognita*. The tentes were furnished with fleshe, fishe, skinnes, and other trifles: amongest the which was found a boxe of nailes: whereby we did conjecture, that they had either Artificers amongest them, or else a trafficke with some other nation. The menne ranne away, so that we could have no conferrence or communication with them. Our Generall (because he would have them no more to flee, but rather incouraged to stay through his courteous dealing) gave commaundement, that his men should take nothing away with them, saving onely a couple of white Dogges, for which he left pinnes, pointes, knives, and other trifling thinges, and departed, without taking or hurting any thing, and so came a boord, and hoised sailes, and passed forwardes.[2]

But beeing scarse out of the sight thereof, there fell such a fogge and hidious mist, that we coulde not see one another: wherupon we stroke our drummes, and sounded our trumpets, to the ende we might keepe together: and so continued all that day and night, till the next day, that the mist brake up: so that we might easily perceive all the shippes thus sailing together all that day, untill the next day, being the .22. of the same: on which day we sawe an infinite number of yce, from the which we cast about to shun the daunger thereof.

But one of our small barkes, named the Michael, whose Captein was Maister Kinderslie, the Master Bartholemew Bull, lost our companie, insomuche that we coulde not obteine the sight of her many days after, of whom I purpose to speake further anon, when occasion shalbe ministred, and opportunitie serve.[3] Thus we continued on our course, untill the .2. of Julie, on which day we fell with the Queenes foreland, where we sawe so much yce, that we thought it unpossible to get into the Streightes: yet at the last we gave the adventure, and entered the yce.

Being in amongst it, we saw the Michael, of whom I spake before, accompanied with the Judith, whose Captaine was Maister Fenton, the Maister Charles Jackman, bearing into the foresaid yce, farre distant from us, who in a storme that fell that present night, (whereof I will at large, God willing, discourse hereafter) were severed from us, & being in, wandered up and downe the Streightes, amongest the yce, many dayes in great perill, till at the last, (by the providence of GOD) they came safely to harbour in their wished port in the Countesse of Warwickes sound, the .20. of Julie aforesaid, 10. dayes before any of the other

---

[1] Margin note: 'Frizeland'.
[2] Margin note: 'The courtesie of our Generall'.
[3] Margin note: 'Master Kinderslie. Bartholemew Bull'.

shippes:[1] who going on shoare found where the people of the Countrie had bene, and had hid their provision in great heapes of stones, being both of fleshe and fishe, which they had killed: whereof we also found great store in other places after our arrivall. They found also divers engines: as bowes, slings & dartes. They found likewise certeine peeces of the Pinnisse which our Generall left there the yeare before, which Pinnisse he had soonke, minding to have him againe the next yeare.[2]

Now, seeing I have entreated so much of the Judith and the Michael: I will returne to the rest of the other shippes, and will speake a little of the storme which fell, with the missehappes that we had, the night that we put into the yce: whereof I made mention before.

At the first entrie into the yce, in the mouth of the Streightes, our passage was very narrowe, and difficult: but being once gotten in, we had a faire open place without any yce for the most part: being a league in compasse, the yce being round about us, and inclosing us, as it were within the pales of a Parke. In which place (because it was almost night) we minded to take in our sailes, and lie a hull all that nigh. But the storme so increased, and the waves began to mount aloft, which brought the yce so neere us, and comming on so fast upon us, that we were feigne to beare in and out, where we might espie an open place. Thus the yce coming on us so fast, we were in great danger, looking everie houre for death. And thus passed we on in that great danger, seeing both our selves, and the rest of our ships so troubled and tossed amongst the yce, that it woulde make the strongest heart to relent.

At the last, the Barke Dionyse, being but a weake shippe, & brused afore amongst the yce, being so leake that she no longer could tarrie above the water, sanke without saving any of the goodes which were within her: which sight so abashed the whole fleete, that we thought verily we should have tasted of the same sauce. But neverthelesse, we seeing them in such daunger, manned out our boates, and saved all the men, in such wise, that not one perished (God be thanked).[3]

The storme still increased, and the yce inclosed us, that we were faine to take downe toppe and toppe mastes: for the yce had so environed us, that we could see neither land, nor Sea, as farre as we could kenne: so that we were faine to cutte our cables, to hang over boorde for fenders, somewhat to ease the shippes sides from the great and drierie strokes of the yce: some Capstan barres, some fending off with Oares, some with planckes of 2. ynches thicke, which were broken immediately with the force of the yce, some going out uppon the yce to beare it off with their shoulders from the shippes. But the rigorousnesse of the tempest was suche, and the force of the yce so great, that not only they burst and spoiled the foresaid provision: but likewise so raced the sides of the shippes that it was pitifull to behold, and caused the heartes of many to faint.[4]

Thus continued we all that dismall and lamentable night, plunged in this perplexitie, looking for instant death: but our God (who never leaveth them destitute which faithfully call upon him) although he often punisheth, for amendments sake, in the morning he caused the windes to cease: and the fogge which all that night lay on the face of the water to cleare:

---

[1] Margin note: 'The Michael. The Judith. M. Fenton. Charles Jackman. The Countesse of Warwicks sound'.
[2] Cf. document 8, p. 154: these were Fenton's observations.
[3] Margin note: 'Barke Dionyse'.
[4] Margin note: 'Narowe shiftes for safetie'.

so that we might perceive, about a mile from us, a certeine place cleare from any yce, to the which with an easie breath of winde, which our God sent us, we bent our selves. And furthermore, he provided better for us than we deserved, or hoped for: for when we were in the foresaid cleare place, he sent us a fresh gale at West, or at West Southwest, which set us cleare without all the yce. And further, he added more: for he sent us a pleasant day, as the like we had not of a long time before, as after punishment, consolation.[1]

Thus we joyfull wightes, being at libertie, tooke in all our sailes, and lay a hull, praising God for our deliverance: and staide to gather together our fleete, which once being done, we seeing that none of them had any great hurt, neither any of them wanted, saving onely they of whom I spake before, & the shippe which was lost, then at the last we hoised our sailes, and lay bulting on and off,[2] till such time as it would please God to take away the yce, that we might get into the Streightes.

And as we thus lay off and on, we came by a marvellous huge mountaine of yce, which surpassed all the rest that ever we sawe: for we judged him to be neere a foure score fadams above water, and we thought him to be a ground for any thing that we could perceve, being there nine score fadams deepe, and of compasse about halfe a mile, of which Island I have, as neere as I could, drawne and here set downe the true proportion, as he appeared in diverse shapes passing alongest by him.[3]

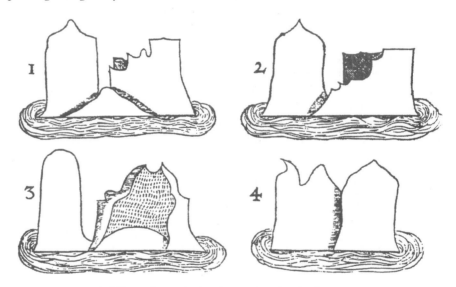

These foure being but one Island of yce,
and as we came neere unto it, and departed from it,
in so many shapes it appeared.[4]

[1] Margin note: 'Gods providence'.
[2] I.e., tacking.
[3] Margin note: 'A mounteine of yce appearing in sundrie figures'.
[4] Captions to Ellis's diagrams: '1. At the first sight of this great and monstruous peece of yce, it appeared in this waye. 2. In coming near unto it, it shewed after this shape. 3. I approaching right against it, it opened in shape like unto this, shewing hollow within. 4. In departing from it, it appeared in this shape'.

Also the .5. of Julie, there fell a hidious fogge and mist, that continued till the .19. of the same: so that one shippe could not see another.[1] Therefore, we were feigne to beare a small saile, and to observe the time: but there ranne such a current of a Tide, that it set us to the Northwest[2] of the Queenes forelande the backeside of all the Streightes: where (through the contagious fogge having no sight either of Sun or Starre) we scarse knewe where we were. In this fogge the .10. of Julie, we lost the companie of the Viceadmerall, the Anne Francis, the Busse of Bridgewater, and the Francis of Foy. The .16. day, one of our small barks, named the Gabriel, was sent by our Generall to beare in with the land, to descrie it, where being on lande, they mette with the people of the contrie, which seemed very humane and civil, and offered to trafficke with our men, profering them foules, and skinnes, for knives, and other trifles: whose courtesie caused us to thinke that they had small conversation with the others of the Streightes.[3]

Then we bare backe againe, to goe with the Queenes forelande: and the .18. day we came by .2.Islandes, whereon we went on shoare, and founde where the people had bene: but we sawe none of them. This day we were againe in the yce, and like to be in as great perill as wee were at the first. For through the darkenesse and obscuritie of the foggie mist, we were almost runne on rockes and Islandes before we sawe them: But God (even miraculously) provided for us, opening the fogges, that we might see clearely, both where, and in what daunger we presently were, and also the way to escape: or else, without saile, we had ruinously ranne upon the rockes.

When we knewe perfectly our instant case, we cast about, to get againe on Sea boorde, which (God be thanked) by night we obteined and praised God. The cleare continued scarse an houre, but the fogge fell againe as thicke as ever it was.

Then the Rearadmerall, and the Beare got themselves cleare without danger of yce and rockes, stroke their sailes, and lay at hull, staying to have the rest of the fleete come foorth: which as yet had not found the right way to cleare themselves, from the danger of rockes and yce, untill the next morning, at what time the Rearadmerall discharged certeine warning peeces to geve notice that she had escaped, and that the rest (by following of her) might set them selves free, which they did that day.[4]

Then having gathered our selves together, we proceeded on our purposed voyage, bearing off, and keeping our selves distant from the coast, till the .19. day of Julie: at which time the fogges brake up and dispersed, so that we might plainely and clearely beholde the pleasant aire, which so long had bene taken from us, by the obscuritie of the foggie mistes: and after that time, wee were not much encombred therewith, untill we had left the confines of the countrie.

Then we espying a faire sound, supposed it to go into the Streightes, betweene the Queenes forelande, and Jackemans sound, which proved as we imagined.[5] For our Generall sent forth again the Gabriel, to discover it, who passed through with much difficultie: for there ran such an extreme current of a Tide, with so horrible a gulfe, that with a fresh gale of

[1] Margin note: 'A fogge of long continuance'. Other accounts (Best, Hall), make it clear that the fog, though persistent, was intermittent.
[2] *Recte* southwest.
[3] Margin note: 'The people offer to trafficke with us'.
[4] Margin note: 'Warning peeces of safe passage discharged'.
[5] Margin note: 'A faire sounde betweene the Queenes foreland and Jackmans sounde'.

winde they were scarse able to stemme it: yet at the length with greate travell they passed it, and came to the Streights, where they met with the Thomas Alline, the Thomas of Ipsewich, and the Busse of Bridgwater: who all together adventured to beare into the yce againe, to see if they could obteine their wished port. But they were so encombred, that with muche difficultie they were able to get out againe, yet at the last they escaping, the Thomas Alline and the Gabriell bare in with the Western shore, where they founde harbour, and there mored their shippes, untill the .4. of August, at whiche time they came to us in the Countesse of warwiks sound. The Thomas of Ipsewich caught a great leake, which caused her to cast again to Sea boorde, and so was mended.

We sailed along still by the coast, untill wee came againe to the Queenes forelande, at the point wherof we met with part of the gulfe aforesaid, which place or gulfe (as some of our Masters do credibly report) doeth flowe .9. houres, and ebbes but 3. At that point we discovered certeine lands Southwarde, to the which neither time nor opportunitie would serve to serch.[1] Then being come to the mouth of the Streightes, we met with the Anne Francis, who had laine bulting up and downe ever since her departure alone, never finding any of her companie. Wee met then also the Francis of Foy, with whome againe wee intended to venter and get in: but the yce was yet so thicke, that we were compelled againe to retire and gett us on Sea boord.

There fell also the same day, being the .26. day of Julie, such an horrible snowe, that it laye a foote thicke upon the hatches, which frose as fast as it fell.[2]

We had also at other times, divers cruell stormes, both of snowe and haile, which manifestly declared the distemperature of the Countrie: yet for all that, we were so many times repulsed and put backe from our purpose, knowing that long lingering delay was not profitable to us, but hurtfull to our voyage, we mutually consented to our valiant Generall once againe, to geve the onset.

The .28. day therefore of the same Julie we assaid, and with little trouble (God be praised) we passed the dangers by day light. Then night falling on the face of the earth, we hull in the cleare, till the chearefull light of the day had chased away the noysome darkenesse of the night:[3] at which time wee set forward towards our wished port: by the .30. day we obtained our expected desire, where we found the Judith, and the Michael: which brought no small joy unto our Generall, and great consolation to the hevie heartes of those wearied wightes.[4]

The .30. day of Julie wee brought our shippes into the Countesse of Warwickes sounde, and mored them, namely these ships, the Admerall, the Rearadmerall, The Francis of Foy, the Beare, Armanell, the Salomon, & the Busse of Bridgwater which being done, our Generall commaunded us all to come a shore, upon the Countesse Island, where he set his miners to work upon the mine, geving charge with expedition to dispatche with their lading.

Our Generall himselfe, accompanied with his Gentlemen, diverse times made rodes into

---

[1] If the ships were indeed off the southern point of Resolution Island, the 'lands' could only have been the northernmost of the Button Islands; even so, the fleet must have been driven a considerable distance southwards by the 'Furious Outfall' to have made the sighting, even on a clear day.

[2] Margin note: 'An horrible snowe fell in Julie'.

[3] A good example of the worst of Ellis's laboured style, in which he merely reports that night fell and morning followed thereafter.

[4] Margin note: 'The time of our setting foreward &c'.

sundrie partes of the Countrie, as well to finde newe mines, as also to finde and see the people of the Countrie. He found out one mine, upon an Island by Beares sound, and named it the Countesse of Sussex Island.[1] One other was founde in Winters Fornace, with divers others, to which the shippes were sent sunderly, to be laden. In the same rodes he mette with diverse of the people of the Countrie, at sundrie times, as once at a place called Davids sound: who shotte at our men, and very desperately gave them the onset, being not above three or foure in number, there being of our Countrimen above a dozen: but seeing themselves not able to prevaile, they tooke themselves to flight: whom our men pursued, but being not used to suche craggie cliffes, they soone lost the sight of them, and so in vaine returned.[2]

We also sawe of them at Beares sounde, both by Sea and Land, in great companies: but they would at all times keepe the water betweene them and us.[3] And if any of our ships chaunced to bee in the sound (as they came divers times), because the harbour was not verie good, the ship laded and departed again, then so long as any ships were in sight, the people would not be seene. But when as they perceived the ships to be gone, they would not onely shew them selves standing uppon highe cliffes, and call us to come over unto them: but also would come in their botes, very neere to us, as it were to bragge at us: whereof our Generall having advertisement, sent for the Capteines and Gentlemen of the shippes, to accompanie and attende upon him, with the Capteine also of the Ann Francis, who was but the night before come unto us.[4] For they and the fleebote having lost us the .26. day, in the great snowe, put into an harbour in the Queenes foreland, where they found good oare, wherwith they laded them selves, and came to seeke the Generall: so that nowe we had all our shippes, saving one Barke, which was lost, and the Thomas of Ipsewiche, who compelled (by what furie I knowe not) forsooke our companie, and returned home without lading.

Our Generall acompanied with his Gentlemen (of whom I spake) came altogether to the Countesse of Sussex Island, neare to Beares sound, where he manned our certeine Pinnisses, and went over to the people: who perceiving his arrivall, fled away with all speede, and in hast left certeine dartes and other engines behind them, which we found: but the people we could not finde.[5]

The next morning, our Generall perceiving certeine of them in botes upon the Sea, gave chase to them in a Pinnisse under saile, with a fresh gale of wind, but could by no meanes come neere unto them: for the longer he sailed, the further off he was from them: which

---

[1] Margin note: 'The Countesse of Sussex Island'. It is not entirely clear whether this was in fact a new discovery, or the reopening of the site briefly worked by men of the *Gabriel* during the 1577 voyage.

[2] Margin note: 'Winters Fornace. Davides Sound' (the location of the latter – possibly 'Davis' – has not been identified). This encounter with the Inuit is Ellis's fiction. There was no hostile contact during the 1578 voyage; indeed, the only near-contact was that of Captains Fenton and Yorke on 15 August, when they vainly attempted to attract a nervous group of Inuit towards their own men. Presumably, Ellis believed his rather pedestrian account might benefit from a fight sequence.

[3] Margin note: 'The policie of the people for safetie of themselves'.

[4] Again, there is not the briefest mention of these supposed encounters in the other narratives. Best in particular, upon the evidence of his account of the second voyage, is hardly likely to have considered these incidents unworthy of mention, had they occurred.

[5] Margin note: 'Their speedie flight at our Generalles arrivall'.

well shewed their cunning & activitie. Thus time wearing away, and the day of our departure approching, our Generall commanded to lade with all expedition, that we might be againe on Sea boorde with our ship: for whilest we were in the countrie, we were in continuall danger of frising in: for often times we had stormes and tempests, often snow and haile, often the water was so much frosen and congeled in the night, that in the morning we could scarse rowe our botes or Pinnisses, especially in Diers sound, which is a calme and still water: which caused our Generall to make the more haste, so that by the .30. day of August we were all laden, and made all thinges readie to depart.

But before I proceed any further herein, to shewe what fortune befell at our departure, I will turne my penne a little to M. Capteine Fenton, and those Gentlemen which should have enhabited all the yeare in those countries, whose valiant mindes were much to be commended,[1] that neither feare of force, nor the cruell nipping stormes of the raging winter, neither the intemperature of so unhealthsome a Countrie, neither the savagenesse of the people, neither the sight and shewe of suche and so many straunge Meteores, neither the desire to returne to their native soile, neither regarde of friendes, neither care of possessions and inheritances: finally, not the love of life (a thing of all other most sweete) neither the terrour of dreadfull death it selfe, might seeme to bee of sufficient force, to withdrawe their prouesse, or to restraine from that purpose, thereby to have profited their countrie: but that with most willing heartes, venturous mindes, stoute stomachs, & singular manhod, they were content there to have tarried, and for the time (among a barbarous and uncivill people, Infidels and miscreantes) to have made their dwelling, not terrified with the manifolde and imminent daungers which they were like to runne into: & seeing before their eyes so many casualties, whereto their life was object, the least whereof would have made a milksoppe thereat astonished and utterly discomfited: being I say thus minded and purposed, they deserve speciall commendation: For doubtlesse, they had done as they intended, if lucke had not withstood their willingnesse, & if that fortune had not so frowned upon their intentes.[2]

For the Barck Dionyse, which was lost, had in her much of their house, which was prepared and should have bene builded for them, with many other implementes. Also the Thomas of Ipsewich, which had moste of their provision in her, came not into the Streightes at all: neither did we see her, since the day we were separated in the great snowe (of which I spake before). For these causes, having not their house, nor yet provision, they were disapointed of their pretence to tarie, and therefore laded their shippes, and so came away with us.

But before we toke shipping, we built a litle house in the Countesse of Warwickes Island, & garnished it with many kindes of trifles, as Pinnes, Pointes, Laces, Glasses, Kombes, Babes on horsebacke and on foote,[3] with innumerable other such fansies & toyes: thereby to allure & entice the people to some familiaritie against other yeares.[4]

Thus having finished all things, we departed the contrie (as I said before): but becase the Busse had not lading enough in her, she put into Beares sound to take in a litle more. In the

---

[1] Margin note: 'Gentlemen shoulde have enhabited the Countrie'.
[2] Margin note: 'Deserved praise and commendation'.
[3] Model soldiers.
[4] Margin note: 'An house erected and garnished with diverse trinkets'.

meane while, the Admerall, and the rest, without in the sea, stayed for her.[1] And that night fell such an outragious tempest, beating on our shipps, with such vehement rigor, that anchor and cable availed naught: for we were driven on rockes and Islandes of yce, insomuch that (had not the great goodnesse of God bene miraculously shewed to us), we had bene cast away every man. This daunger was more doubtfull and terrible, than any that preceded or went before: for there was not any one ship, (I thinke) that escaped without damage. Some lost anchor and also Cables, some botes, some Pinnisses: some anchor, Cables, botes, and Pinnisses.[2]

This boysterous storme so severed us, one from another, that one ship knewe not what was becom of another.[3] The Admerall knew not where to finde the Viceadmerall or Reareadmerall, or any other shippe of our companie. Our Generall being on lande in Beares sounde, coulde not come to his shippe, but was compelled to goe a boorde the Gabriel, where he continued al the way homewarde: for the boysterous blastes continued so extremely and so long a time, that it sent us homewarde: (which was Gods favour towardes us), will we, nill we,[4] in such hast, as not any one of us were able to keepe in companie of other, but were separated. And if by chaunce, any one shippe did overtake other, by swiftnesse of Saile, or mette (as they often did): yet was the rigour of the winde so hidious, that they could not continue companie together the space of one whole night.

Thus our journey outwarde was not so pleasant, but our coming thither, entering the coastes and countrie, by narrowe Streightes, perillous yce, and swift tides, out time of aboade there in snowe, and stormes, and our departure from thence, the .30. of August, with daungerous blustering windes and tempestes, whiche that night arose, was as uncomfortable: separating us so, as we sailed, that not any of us mette together, untill the .28. of September, whiche day we fell on The Englishe coastes, betweene Scylla and The landes ende, and passed the channell, untill our arrivall, &c.[5]

Thus having finished my purpose, and perfourmed my promise, I ende with these rude lines, compiled with the rusticall style of rurall God Pan, because I want Apollos skill: neither have I sucked the sugred sappe of eloquence, trusting that everie one, who is of good disposition, will accept my willing hart, and not despise my simple skill.[6] As for the other sort of men, which have bene fostered in Momus schole by Maister Zoilus: I weigh them as they doe deserve and yeelding thankes to God, beseech him (for Christ Jesus sake) to preserve our noble Queene, and graunt her Nestors long and happie yeares, with her noble Counsell, and Commons, in all her litle Islandes: and to our Generall long life, good health, and fortunate successe, in all his voyages, to the profite and commoditie of our native soile and Countrie. Amen.

---

[1] By the term 'Admerall', Ellis refers here to the *Ayde*, not to Frobisher himself, who had gone to Beare Sound to supervise the re-embarkation of the miners there.

[2] Margin note: 'An outragious tempest'.

[3] Margin note: 'Our shippes severed by a storme'.

[4] I.e., willy-nilly.

[5] Margin note: 'Our entring the coastes daungerous'.

[6] Ellis's assessment of his simple skill is, unfortunately, fully borne out by the poetical piece that forms the epilogue to this account.

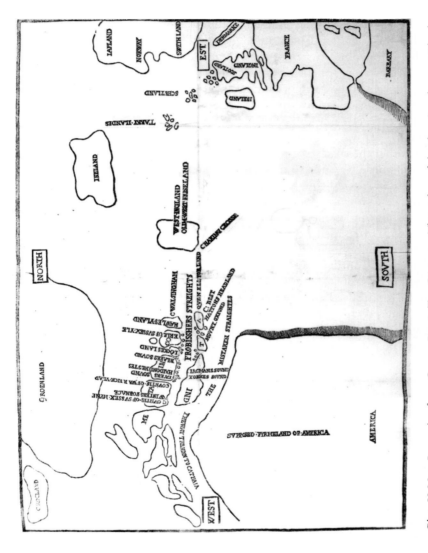

Plate V: Meta Incognita, from George Best's *True Discourse*. The author of the chart is unknown. Clearly its features are dissimilar from those of the world map that Best utilized. The northern shore of Frobisher's 'strait' is here represented as Greenland, rather than *Terra Septentrionalis*, the mythical northern continent. The author had access to detailed data secured during the voyages; however, whilst the nomenclature of features in Meta Incognita is comprehensive, their extremely inaccurate placement makes his presence in the voyage questionable.

By permission of the James Ford Bell Library, University of Minnesota.

DOCUMENT 11

George Best's *True Discourse*

The thirde voyage of *Captayne Frobisher,*
pretended for the discoverie of Cataya, by Meta Incognita, *Anno Do.* 1578.[1]

THE Generall beeing returned from from the second Voyage, immediatelye after hys arrival in Englande, repayred w*ithall* hast to the Court beeing the*n* at Windsore, to advertise hir Majesty of his prosperous proceeding, and good successe in this last voyage, and of the ple*n*ty of gold Ore, with other matters of importance which he hadde in these Septentrion-all partes discovered. He was courteously enterteyned, and hartily welcomed of many noble men, but especially for his great adventure, commended of hir Majestie, at whose hands he receyved great thankes, and most gratious countenance, according to his deserts.[2] Hir Highnesse also greatly commended the rest of the Gentlemen in this service, for their great forwardnes in this so da*n*gerous toyling and painefull attempte: but especiallye shee praysed and rejoiced, that among them there was so good order of governement, so good agree-ment, everye man so readye in his calling, to doe whatsoever the General should com-maunde, which due commendation gratiously of hir Majestie remembred, gave so greate encouragement to al the Captaines & Gentlemen, that they, to continue hir highnesse so good and honorable opinion of them, have since neither spared laboure, limme, nor life, to bring this matter (so well begon) to a happie and prosperous ende.[3] And finding, that the matter of the gold ore had appearance & made shew of great riches & profite, and the hope of *the* passage to CATAYA, by this last voyage greatly encreased, hir Majestie appointed special Commissioners, chosen for this purpose, Gentlemen of great judgemen, art, & skill, to looke thorowly into *the* cause, for *the* true trial & due examination therof, & for the full handling of al matters thereunto appertaining.[4] And bicause that place & country, hathe never heretofore bin discovered, and therefore had no speciall name, by which it might be

---

[1] The account of George Best, taken from *A True Discourse of the late voyages of discoverie, for the finding of a passage to Cathaya, by the Northweast, under the conduct of Martin Frobisher Generall.* First published in 1578 by Henry Bynnyman, it was reproduced subsequently, with certain omissions, by Richard Hakluyt in the 1598–1600 edition of his *Principal Navigations.*

[2] Margin note: 'Frobisher commended of hir Majestie'.

[3] Margin note: 'The Gentlemen commended'.

[4] Margin note: 'Commissioners appointed to examin the goodnesse of the Ore'. Best's chronology is misleading here. The commission had been established a year earlier, in March 1577, to examine Frobisher and others with the purpose of assessing the potential for a second voyage. With only minor changes in personnel to allow conflicting commitments, its composition remained constant between its inception and 1578, though it was reconstituted with new members early in 1579 to re-examine the work of Jonas Schutz (see document 5, page 98).

called & known, hir Majestie named it very properly Meta Incognita, as a marke and bounds utterly hitherto unknown.[1] The commissioners after sufficient triall & proofe made of the Ore, & having understood by sundrie reasons, & substanciall grounds, the possibilitie & likelihoode of the passage, advertised hir highnes, that the cause was of importance, & the voyage gretly worthy to be advanced again. Whereupon preparation was made of ships & al other things necessary, with such expedition, as the time of the yere then required. And bycause it was assuredly made accompt of, that the commoditie of Mines, there already discovered, wold at the least countervaile in all respects, the adventurers charge, & give further hope & likelihood of greter matters to follow: it was thought needful, both for the better guard of those parts alredy found & for further discovery of the Inland & secreats of those countries, & also for further search of the passage to Cataya (wherof the hope continually more & more encreaseth) that certain numbers of chosen soldiers & discreete men for those purposes should be assigned to inhabite there.[2] Wherupon there was a strong forte or house of timber, artificially framed, & cunningly devised by a notable learned men here at home, in ships to be carryed thither, wherby those men that were apointed there to winter & make their abode the whole yeare, might aswel be defended from the danger of the falling snow and colde ayre, as also be fortified from the force or offence of those Countrie people, which perhaps otherwise with too great companyes & multitudes might oppresse them.[3] And to this greate aventure & notable exploit, many wel minded and forward yong Gentlemen of our countrey willingly haue offered themselves. And firste Captaine Fenton Lieutenant Generall, for Captaine Frobysher, and in charge of the company with him there, Capitaine Best, & Captaine Filpot, unto whose good discretions the government of that service was chiefly commended, who, as men not regarding perill in respect of the profite and common wealth of their Countrie, were willing to abide the firste brunt and adventure of those daungers among a savage and brutishe kinde of people, in a place hitherto ever thoght for extreme cold not habitable.[4] The whole number of men whiche had offered, & were appointed to inhabite Meta Incognita al the yeare, were one hundreth persons, wherof .xl. shoulde be Marriners, for the use of ships .30. Miners, for gathering the golde Ore togyther for the nexte yeare, & .30. souldiers for the better guarde of the rest, within which last number are included the gentlemen, Goldfiners, Bakers, Carpenters, & all necessarye persons.[5] To eache of the Captaines was assigned one ship, as wel for the further searching

[1] Margin note: 'A name given to the place newe discovered'.

[2] Margin note: 'The hope of the passage to Cataya'.

[3] Margin note: 'A forte to be builte in Meta Incognita'. The identity of these 'notable learned men' is not known, but their design was given palpable form by the London carpenter, Thomas Townson, who constructed the frame of the great house for the considerable sum of £220 (HM 715, f. 12).

[4] This is the only account to clarify the command structure of the proposed colony, and offers further evidence of the high regard in which Richard Philpot, captain of the semi-officially hired vessel *Beare Leicester*, was held (he was also appointed to Frobisher's land-council in Meta Incognita). Unfortunately, little else is known of him. He had served as ensign in the *Ayde* in 1577, and was appointed to command the *Beare Leicester* in 1578 by the commissioners, rather than by Lok and her owner/master, Richard Fairweather the elder. Philpott is not known to have participated in any other contemporary overseas venture, though he may have been that 'Captain Philpott' who died of an unspecified sickness whilst commanding a company of foot in the 1589 Portuguese expedition (Wernham, *Expedition of Norreys and Drake*, pp. 213, 261).

[5] Margin note: 'A hundreth men appointed to inhabit there'.

of the coast & countrie there, as for to returne & bring backe their companies againe, if the necessitie of the place so urged, or by miscarying of the fleete in the yeare following, they mighte be disappointed of their further provision.

Being therefore thus furnished with all necessaries, there were ready to depart upon the said voyage .xv. Sayle of good Shippes, whereof the whole number was to returne agayne with their loading of gold Ore in the end of the Sommer, except those three Shippes, which should bee left for the use of those Captaynes whiche should inhabite there the whole yeare.[1] And being in so good readynesse, the Generall, with all the Captaynes came to the Court, then lying at Greenwich, to take their leave of hir Majestie, at whose hands they all receyved great encouragement, and gracious countenance. Hir Highnesse, besides other good giftes, and greater promises, bestowed on the Generall a faire Cheyne of Gold, and the rest of the Captaynes kissed hir hande, tooke their leaue, and departed euery man towardes their charge.[2]

The names of the Shippes with their severall Captaynes.

	In the Ayde being Admirall, was the Generall	Captayne Frobisher.
2	In the Tho*mas* Allen	Vice Admirall *Captayne* Yorke.
3	In the Judith	Lieuten*ant* General Fe*n*ton.
4	In the Anne Frances	Captayne Best.
5	In the Hopewell	Captayne Carew.
6	In the Beare	Captayne Filpot.
7	In the Thomas of Ispwich	Cap*tayne* Tanfield.
8	In the Emanuell of Exceter	*Ca*p*tayne* Courtney.
9	In the Frances of Foy	Captayne Moyles.
10	In the Moone	Captayne Upcot.
11	In the Ema*nuell* of Bridgewater	*Captayne* Newton.
12	In the Salomo*n* of Weymouth	*Captayne* Randal.
13	In the Barke Dennis	Captayne Kendall.
14	In the Gabriell	Captayne Harvey.
15	In the Michael	Captayne Kinnersley.

The sayd .xv. Sayle of Shippes arrived and mette together at Harwitch, the seaven and

---

[1] Margin note: 'Fifteene Sayle'.

[2] Margin note: 'A cheyne of gold given to Frobisher'. This episode, during which all the fleet's captains took their leave of the Queen in audience together, appears to be Best's dramatic creation. Michael Lok (document 5, p. 86) implied that the unofficial ships brought into the venture by Frobisher joined the other vessels of the fleet at Harwich. Given the extremely parlous state of the adventurers' finances at the despatch of the 1578 voyage, it is hardly likely that the Queen and Council would have permitted these ships – with their incremental costs – to join the enterprise, had they known in advance of their participation. It may be that some of the other ships' captains were indeed presented to the Queen on 24 May (several ships of the fleet departed from Gravesend the following day); but it seems significant that the accounts of Fenton, Jackman, Hall, Selman and Ellis do not mention what would have been a noteworthy occasion. In fact, Selman's account (document 9, p. 177) explicitly states that the ships *Ayde*, *Frances of Foy*, *Emmanuel of Exeter* and *Bark Denys* sailed directly from Plymouth to Harwich (with a brief pause in the Downs, probably on the afternoon of 20 May), reaching the latter on 22 May.

twentith day of May Anno .1578. where the Generall, and the other Captaynes made view, and mustered theyr companyes. And every severall Captayne receyved from the Generall certayne Articles of direction, for the better keeping of order and company togither in the way, which Articles are as followeth.

Articles and orders to be observed for the Fleete,
Set downe by *Captayne Frobisher* Generall,
And delivered in writing to every Captayne, as well for
Keeping company, as for the course, the 31. Of May.

In primis, to banishe swearing, dice, and cardplaying, and filthy communication, and to serve God twice a day, with the ordinarie service, usuall in Churches of England, and to cleare the glasse, according to the old order of England.

The Admirall shal carrie the light, and after his light be once put out, no man to go a head of him, but every man to fitte his Sayles to follow as neere as they may, without dangering one another.

That no man shall by day or by night depart further from the Admirall, than the distance of one English mile, and as neere as they may, withoute daunger one of another.

If it chance to growe thicke, and the wind contrary, eyther by daye, or by night, that the Admirall be forced to cast aboute, before hir casting aboute, she shal gyve warning, by shooting off a peece, and to him shall answere the Vizeadmirall, and the Rereadmirall, with every one of them a peece, if it be by nighte, or in a fogge, and that the Vizeadmirall shall aunswere firste, and the Rereadmirall last.

That no man in the Fleete descrying any Sayle or Sayles, give uppon anye occasion anye chace, before hee have spoken with the Admirall.

That everye evening, all the Fleete come uppe and speake with the Admirall, at seaven of the Clocke, or betweene that and eyght, and if weather will not serve them all to speake with the Admirall, then some shall come to the Vizeadmirall, and receyve your order of your course of Maister Hall, chiefe Pylot of the Fleete, as he shall direct you.

If to any man in the Fleete, there happen any mischance, they shall presently shoote off two peeces by day, and if it be by night, two peeces, and shew two lightes.

If any man in the Fleete come up in the night, and hale his fellow, knowing him not, he shal give him this watchword, Before the world was God. The other shall aunswer him, if he be one of our Fleete After God came Christe his Sonne. So that if anye be founde amongst us, not of oure owne company, he that firste descryeth anye such Sayle or Sayles, shall give warning to the Admirall by himselfe, or any other that he can speake to that Sailes better than he, being neerest unto him.

That every Ship in the Fleete, in the time of fogges, whiche continually happen with little windes, and moste parte calmes, shall keepe a reasonable noyse with Trumpet, Drumme, or otherwise to keepe themselves cleere one of another.

If it fall out thicke or misty that we lay it to Hull, the Admirall shall give warning by a peece, and putting out three lightes one over another, to the ende, that every man may take in his Sayles, and at his setting of Sayles agayne do the like, if it be not cleere.

If any man discover land by nighte, that he give the like warning, that he dothe for mischances, two lightes, and two peeces, if it be by day one peece, and putte out hys flagge, and strike all his Sayles he hath aboorde.

If any Shyppe shall happen to lose company by force of weather, then any suche Shippe or Shippes, shall gette hir into the Latitude of (erased) and so keepe that Latitude, untyll they gette Freeselande.[1] And after they be past the West partes of Freeselande, they shall getter them into the Latitude of (erased) and (erased) and not to the Northwarde of (erased) and beeing once entred within the straytes, all suche Shyppes shall everye watche shoote off a good peece, and looke out well for smoke and fire, whych those that gette in first, shall make every night, untill all the Fleete bee come togither.

That uppon the sight of an Ensigne in the Mast of the Admirall, a peece shotte of, the whole Fleete shall repaire to the Admirall, to understande such conference, as the Generall is to have with them.

If we chance to meete with any enimies, that foure Shyppes shall attend upon the Admirall, viz. The Frances of Foy, the Moone, the Barke Dennis, and the Gabriell: and foure upon my Lieutenant Generall in the Judith, viz. The Hopewell, the Armenall, the Beare, and the Salomon: and the other foure upon the Vizeadmirall, the Anne Frances, the Thomas of Ipswich, the Emanuell, and the Michaell.

If there happen any disordered person in the fleete, that he be taken and kept in safe custodie until he may conveniently by brought aboorde the Admirall, and there to receive such punishment as his or their offences shal deserve.

By me Martine Frobysher.

Oure departure from England.

Having received these articles of direction, we departed from Harwich the one and thirtith of May. And sayling alongest the South partes of England westward, wee at length came by the coaste of Ireland, at Cape Cleare the sixth of June, and gave chace there to a small barke which was supposed to be a Pyrat, or Rover on the Seas, but it fell out in deede that they were poore menne of Bristowe, who hadde mette with suche company of Frenchmen, as hadde spoyled and slayne manye of them, and left the rest so sore wounded, that they were lyke to perishe in the Sea, having neyther hande, nor foote hole, to helpe themselves withall, nor victuals to susteyne theyr hungrie bodyes. Oure Generall, who well understandeth the office of a Souldiore, and an Englishman, and knoweth well what the necessity of the sea meaneth, pitying much *the* miserie of the poore men, releived them with Surgerie and salves, to heale their hurtes, and with meate and drinke to comfort their pining hartes.[2] Some of them having neither eate nor drunck more than olives & stinking water in many dayes before (as they reported). And after this good deed done, having a large winde, we kept our course upon our sayde voyage withoute staying for the taking in of freshe water, or any other provision, whereof many of the fleete were not throughly furnished, and sayling towardes the Northwest partes, from Ireland, we mette with a greate currant from oute of the Southwest, which carryed us (by our reckning) one point to the Northestwardes of our said course, whiche current seemed to us to contnue it selfe towardes Norway, and other

---

[1] All references to latitude were omitted from the 1578 edition of the *Discourse*, and remained so in its reproduction in the 1598–1600 edition of Hakluyt's *Principal Navigations*.
[2] Margin note: 'A charitable deede'.

the Northeast partes of the World, whereby we may be induced to beleeve, that this is the same whiche the Portugalles meete at Capo d'buona speranza, where striking over from thence to the straytes of Magellanes, and finding no passage there for the narrownesse of the sayde straytes, runneth alongst into the greate Bay of Mexico, where also having a let of lande, it is forced to strike backe agayne towardes the Northeast, as we not only heere, but in another place also, further to the Northwardes, by good experience this yeare have founde, as shall heereafter in his place more at large declared.[1]

Nowe wee had sayled aboute foureteen dayes, without sight of any land, or any other living thing, except certayne Fowles, as Wylmots, Nodies, Gulles, &c. whiche there seeme only to live by Sea.

The twentith of June, at two of the clocke in the morning, the Generall desryed land, and found it to be Weast Freeseland, now named Weast England.[2] Heere the Generall, and other Gentlemen wente ashore, being the fyrste knowen Christians that we have true notice of, that ever set foote upon that ground: and therefore the Generall toke possession thereof to the use of our Soveraigne Lady the Queenes Majestie, and discovered heere a goodly harborough for the Shippes, where were also certaine little Boates of that Countrey. And being there landed, they espyed certayne tents and people of that Countrey, which were (as they judge) in all sorts, very like those of Meta Incognita, as by theyr apparell, and other things whych wee found in theyr tents, appeared.

The savage and simple people, so soone as they perceyved our men coming towards them (supposing there had bin no other worlde, but theirs) fledde fearefully away, as men muche amazed at so strange a sight, and creatures of humane shape, so farre in apparell, complexion, and other thinges different from themselves. They left in their tents all their furniture for haste behinde them, where amongst other things were founde a boxe of small nayles, and certayne redde Hearings, boordes of Fyrre tree well cutte, with dyvers other things artificially wroughte, whereby it appeareth, that they have trade with some civill people, or else are in deede themselves artificiall workemen.[3]

Oure menne broughte awaye wyth them, onelye twoo of theyr Dogges, leaving in recompence belles, looking-glasses, and dyvers of oure Countrey toyes behynde them.

This Countrie, no doubte, promiseth good hope of great commoditie and riches, if it maye be well discovered. The discription whereof you shall finde more at large in my seconde booke, Page .5.[4]

---

[1] Margin note: 'Marke thys Currant'. Despite Best's flawed understanding of its source, this passage appears to constitute the earliest extant English identification of the Gulf Stream.

[2] Margin note: 'Weast Englande'.

[3] The Inuit were not, of course, capable of metal refining. Selman (document 9, p. 178) mentions also an iron tryvet in one of the tents; it may be that Icelanders had visited the coast of southern Greenland in recent years to trade there without leaving any record of their coming.

[4] 'This Friseland sheweth a ragged and high lande, having the mountaines almost covered over with snow alongst the coast full of drift yce, and seemeth almost inaccessible, and is thought to be an Iland in bignesse not inferiour to England, and is called of some Authors, West Frislande, I thinke because it lyeth more West then any parte of Europe. It extendeth in latitude to the Northward very farre as seemed to us, and appeareth by a description set out by two brethren Venetians, Nicholaus and Antonius Zeni, who being driven off from Ireland with a violent tempest made shipwracke here, and were the first knowen Christians that discovered this land about two hundred yeares sithence, and they have in their Sea-cardes set out every

Some are of the opinion, that this weaste Englande is firme lande with the Northeast partes of Meta Incognita, or else with Groenlande. And their reason is, bicause the people, apparell, boates, and other thinges, are so like to theirs: and an other reason is, the multitude of Ilandes of Ise, whyche laye betweene it and Meta Incognita, doeth argue, that on the North side there is a bay, whych cannot be, but by conjoyning of these two lands togither.

And having a fayre and large winde, wee departed from thence towardes Frobyshers straites, the three and twentith of June. Bur fyrste we gave name to a hyghe clyffe in Weast England, the laste that was in oure sight, and for a certaine similitude, we called it Charing Crosse.[1] Then we bare Southerly towards the Sea, bycause to the Northwardes of this coaste wee mette wyth muche driving Ise, whyche by reason of the thicke mistes and weather might have bin some trouble unto us.

On Monday the laste of June, wee mette with manye great Whales, as they hadde beene Porposes.[2]

This same daye the Salamander[3] being under both hir corses and bonets, hapned to strike a greate Whale with hir full stemme, wyth suche a blow, that the ship stoode stil, and stirred neither forwarde nor backeward. The Whale thereat made a great and ugly noise, and caste up his body and tayle, and so went under water, and within twoo dayes after, there was founde a greate Whale dead swimming above water, which we supposed was that the Salamander stroke.[4]

The seconde daye of July early in the morning, wee hadde sighte of the Queenes forelande, and bare in with the lande all the daye, and passyng thorow great quantitie of Ise, by nighte were entered somewhat within the straites, perceiving no waye to passe further in, the whole place being frosen over from the one side to the other, and as it were with many walles, mountaines, and bulwarkes of yse, choaked uppe the passage, and denied us entraunce.[5] And yet doe I not thinke, that this passage or the Sea hereaboutes, is frosen over at anye time of the yeare: albeit it seemed so unto us, by the abundaunce of Ise gathered togyther, whyche occupyed the whole place. But I doe rather suppose these Ise to bee bredde in the hollowe sounds and freshets thereaboutes: whyche by the heate of the Sommers Sunne, beeyng loosed, doe emptie themselves wyth the ebbes into the Sea, and so gather in great abundaunce there togither.

And to speake somewhat here, of the auntiente opinion of the frosen Sea in these partes: I doe thinke it to be rather a bare conjecture of menne, than that ever enye manne hathe made experience of anye suche Sea. And that whiche they speake of Mare Glaciale, may be

---

part thereof and described the condition of the inhabitants, declaring them to be as civill and religious people as we. And for so much of this land as we have sayled alongst, comparing their Carde with the coast, we finde it very agreeable.' This apparent accuracy of the Zeno chart could hardly have been tested by Best, being far too imprecise to provide accurate representation of the features he observed at first-hand. It is probably rather the case that he could find no obvious contradictions between supposition and reality during the brief time the expedition lay off Greenland in 1577 and 1578.

[1] Margin note: 'Charing Crosse'. Presumably, this was a needle-shaped formation.

[2] From the location of this school, and the force of the collision of one of their number with the *Salomon*, it is likely that these were Right whales.

[3] *Recte* Salomon.

[4] Margin note: 'A Whale stroke a ship'.

[5] Margin note: 'Frobishers straites choaked up wyth Ise'.

truly thought to be spoken of these partes: for this maye well be called in deede the ysie Sea, but not the frosen Sea, for no sea consisting of salte water can be frosen, as I have more at large herein shewed my opinion in my seconde booke page .6. for it seemeth impossible for any Sea to be frosen, which hath his course of ebbing and flowing, especiallye in those places, where the tides doe ebbe and flowe above tenne fadome.[1] And also all these afore-saide Ise, which we sometime met a hundreth mile from lande, being gathered out of the salt Sea, are in taste fresh, and being dissolved, become sweet and holesome water.[2]

The cause why thys yeare we have beene more combred with Ise (than at other times before) may be by reason of the Easterly and Southerly windes, whyche brought us more timely thither now than wee looked for. Whiche blowing from the Sea directlye upon the place of our straites, hath kept in the Ise, and not suffered them to be caryed out by the ebbe to the maine Sea, where they woulde in more shorte time have beene dissolved. And all these fleeting Ise, are not onelye so daungerous, in that they winde and gather so neare tog-ither, that a man maye passe sometimes tenne or twelve myles as it were upon one firme Ilande of Ise: But also, for that they open and shutte togither againe in suche sorte wyth the tydes and Sea-gate, that whilest one Shyppe followeth the other with full sayles, the Ise whyche was open unto the foremoste, will joyne and close togyther, before the latter can come to followe the fyrste, whereby manye tymes oure Shippes were broughte into great daunger, as beeyng not able so sodainelye to take in oure sayles, or staye the swifte waye of oure Shippes.

Wee were forced manye tymes to stemme and strike great rockes of Ise, and so as it were make way through mightie mountaines. By which means some of the fleete, where they founde the yse to open, entred in, and passed so farre within the daunger thereof, with con-tinuall desire to recover their port, that it was the greatest wonder of the world, that they ever escaped safe, or were ever heard of againe. For even at this present, we missed two of the fleete, that is, the Judyth, wherein was the Lieutenant general Captaine Fenton, and the Michael, whome both wee supposed hadde bene utterlye lost, having not heard any tydings of them, in more than twentie dayes afore.

And one of our fleete named the Barke Dennys, being of an hundreth tunne burden, seeking way in amongst these Ise, received such a blowe with a rocke of Ise, that she sunke downe therewith, in the sighte of the whoale fleete. Howbeit having signified hir daunger by shooting of a peece of great ordinaunce, newe succour of other shippes came so readily unto them, that the men were al saved with boates.[3]

Within this shippe that was drowned, there was percell of our house, whiche was to be erected for them that shoulde staye all the Winter in Meta Incognita.[4]

---

[1] Margin note: 'Salte water cannot freese'. Contemporary Englishmen had very little experience of true polar conditions, though Best was right to assume that the ice which had so troubled the fleet in this voyage had indeed come from elsewhere – in this case, from the north-western coast of Greenland, being carried southwards thereafter on the Labrador current.

[2] Here, as earlier in his *True Discourse*, Best regarded the prevalence of salt-free ice at sea to indicate its origins in fresh water. It was not then understood that sea-water loses salt over time when frozen.

[3] Margin note: 'Bark Dennis sunke'. The fact that such a modest vessel was carrying a 'peece of great ordinaunce' gives further weight to the possibility that Frobisher had recruited more than the *Salomon* from among his prior acquaintances in the privateering industry.

[4] Margin note: 'Part of the house lost'.

Thys was a more fearefull spectacle for the Fleete to beholde, for that the outragious storme, which presentlye followed, threatened them the like fortune and daunger. For the Fleete being thus compassed (as aforesayde) on every side with Ise, having lefte muche behynde them, thorow which they had passed, & finding more before them, thorow whiche it was not possible to passe, there arose a sodaine and terrible tempest at the Southeast, which blowing from the mayne Sea, directlye upon the place of the straytes, broughte togither al the Ise aseaborde of us, upon our backes, and thereby debarde us of turning backe to recover sea roome againe: so that being thus compassed with daunger on every side, sundrye men with sundrie devises, sought the best waye to save themselves. Some of the Shippes, where they could not find a place more cleare of Ise, and get a little berth of sea roome, did take in their Sayles, and there lay adrift. Other some fastened and mored Ancker upon a great Iland of Ise, and roade under the Lee thereof, supposing to be better garded thereby, from the outrageous windes, and the daunger of the lesser fleeting Ise. And againe some were so fast shut up, and compassed in amongst an infinite number of great Countreys and Ilands of Ise, that they were fayne to submit themselves, & their Ships, to the mercie of the unmercifull Ise, and strengthned the sides of their Ships with junks of cables, beds, Mastes, planckes, and such like, which being hanged overboord, on the sides of their Shippes, mighte the better defende them from the outragious sway and strokes of the said Ise. But as in greatest distresse, men of best value are best to be discerned, so it is greatly worthy commendation and noting, with what invincible minde every Captayne encouraged his company, and with what incredible labour, the paynefull Mariners, and poore Miners (unaquainted with suche extremities) to the everlasting renowne of our nation, dyd overcome the brunt of these so great and extreame daungers: for some, even without boorde upon the Ise, and some within boorde, uppon the sides of their Shippes, having poles, pikes, peeces of timber, and Ores in their handes, stoode almost day and night, withoute any rest, bearing off the force, and breaking the sway of the Ise, with suche incredible payne and perill, that it was wonderful to behold, which otherwise no doubt had stricken quite through and through the sides of their Shippes, notwithstandyng our former provision: for planckes of timber, of more than three ynches thicke, and other things of greater force and bignesse, by the surging of the Sea, and billowe, with the Ise were shevered and cutte in sunder, at the sides of oure Shippes, that it will seeme more than credible to be reported of. And yet (that whiche is more) it is faythfully and playnely to be proved, and that by many substantiall witnesses, that our Shippes, even those of greatest burdens, with the meeting of contrary waves of the Sea, were heaved up betweene Ilandes of Ise, a foote welneere out of the Sea, above their watermarke, having their knees and timbers within boorde bothe bowed and broken therewith.

And amidst these extremes, whilest some laboured for defence of the Shippes, and fought to save their bodyes: othersome of the more mylder spirit, soughte to save the Soule by devoute Prayer and mediation to the Almightie, thinking indeede by no other meanes possible, than by a divine Miracle, to have their deliverance: so that there was none that were eyther ydle or not well occupyed, and hee that helde himselfe in best securitie had (God knoweth) but only bare hope remayning for his best safetie.

Thus all the gallant Fleete, and miserable men, without hope of ever getting forth agayne, distressed with these extremities, remayned heere all the whole night, and parte the next day, excepting foure Shippes, that is, the Anne Frances, the Moone, the Frances of Foy, and the Gabriell, which being somewhat a Seaboorde of the Fleete, and beeing fast Ships, by a winde having a more scope of cleere, tried it out all the time of the storme under Sayle, beeyng hardly able to beare a coast of each.[1]

And albeit, by reason of the fleeting Ise, whych were dispersed heere almost the whole sea over, they were brought manye times to the extreamest poynte of perill, Mountaynes of Ise tenne thousande tymes scaping them scarce one ynch, whiche to have stricken had bin theyr presente destruction, considering the swifte course and way of the Shippes, and the unwildyness of them to stay and turn as a *man* would wish. Yet they esteemed it their better safetie with such perill to seeke Searome, tha*n* without hope of ever getting libertie to lie striving against *the* streame, & beating amongst the Isie Mountaines, whose hugenesse and monstrous greatnesse was suche that no man would credite, but such as to their paynes sawe and felte it. And these foure Shippes by the nexte day at noone, got out to Sea, and were fyrste cleere of the Ise, who nowe enjoying theyr owne libertie, beganne a new to sorrowe and feare for their fellowes safeties. And devoutely kneeling aboute theyr mayne Mast, gave unto God humble thankes, not only for themselves, but besoughte him lykewise highly for theyr friends deliverance. And even nowe, whilest amiddest these extremities, thys gallant Fleete and valiant men were altogither overlaboured and forewatched with the long and fearefull continuance of the foresayde dangers, it pleased God with his eyes of mercie to looke downe from Heaven, to sende them help in good time, giving them the nexte daye a more favourable wind at the West Northweast, whiche did not only disperse and dryve forthe the Ise before them, but also gave them libertie of more scope and Sea roome, and were by night of the daye following perceyved of the other foure Shippes, where to their greatest comforte they enjoyed agayne the fellowship of one another. Some in mending of the sides of theyr Shyppes, some in setting vp theyr toppe Mastes, and mending theyr Sayles and tacklings. Agayne, some complayning of theyr false Stemme borne away, some in stopping their Leakes, some in recounting their daungers past, spent no small time and labour, that I dare well avouche there were never men more daungerously distressed, nor more mercifully by Gods Providence delivered. And heereof both the torne Shippes, and the foreweeryed bodyes of the men arrived, doe beare most evidente marke and witnesse. And now the whole Fleete plyed off to Seaward,[2] resolving there to abide, untill the Sunne might consume (or the force of wind disperse) these Ise from the place of theyr passage: and being a good berth off the shore, they toke in theyr Sayles, and lay adrift.

The seaventh of July, as men nothing yet dismayed, we cast about towards the inward, and had sight of lande, which rose in forme like the Northerland of the straytes, which some of the Fleete, and those not the worst Marriners, judged to be the North forlande:[3] howbeit, othersome were of contrary opinion. But the matter was not well to be discerned, by reason of the thicke fogge, whiche a long time hung uppon the coast, and the newe falling Snowe which yearely altereth the shape of the land, and taketh away oftentimes the Marriners markes.[4] And by reason of the darke mistes, whiche continued by the space of twenty dayes

---

[1] Best makes it clear here (if only implicitly) that his description of the fleet's peril was necessarily second-hand.

[2] Absent the *Judith* and *Michael*.

[3] Margin note: 'Another assault'.

[4] Margin note: 'Fogge, snow, and mistes hinder the Marriners markes'.

togither, this doubt grew the greater and the longer perillous. For wheras indeede we thought our selves to be upon the Northeast side of Frobishers straytes, we were now carried to the Southweastwards of the Queenes forlande, and being deceyved by a swift Currant coming from the Northeast, were broughte to the Southweastwardes of oure sayd course, many miles more than we dyd thinke possible could come to passe. The cause whereof we have since found, and shall be at large heereafter declared.

Heere we made a poynt of land, which some mistooke for a place in the straytes, called Mount Warwicke:[1] but howe we shoulde be so farre shotte up so soddaynely within the sayde straytes, the expertest Mariners began to marvell, thinking it a thing impossible, that they coulde be so farre overtaken in their accomptes, or that any Currant coulde so deceyve them heere, whiche they had not by former experience proved and found out.[2] Howbeit, many confessed that they founde a swifter course of floud than before time they had observed. And truly it was wonderfull to heare and see the rushling and noyse that the tydes do make in thys place with so violente a force, that oure Shippes lying ahull were turned sometimes rounde aboute even in a momente, after the manner of a whirlepoole, and the noyse of the streame no lesse to be hearde a farre off, than the waterfall of London Bridge.[3]

But whilest the Fleete lay thus doubtfull amongst great store of Ise in a place they knewe not, withoute sighte of sunne whereby to take the heigth, and so to know the true elevation of the pole, and withoute any cleare of lighte to make perfite the coast, the Generall with the Captaynes and Maysters of his Shippes beganne doubtfully to question of the matter, and sent his Pinnesse aboorde to heare each mans opinion, and specially of James Beare, Mayster of the Anne Frances, who was knowen to be a sufficiente and skilful Mariner, and having bin there the yeare before, had well observed the place, and drawne out Cardes of the coast.[4] But the rather this matter grew the more doubtful, for that Christopher Hall chiefe Pylot of the voyage, delivered a playne and publike opinion in the hearing of the whole Fleete, that he had never seene the foresayde coast before, and that he could not make it for any place of Frobishers straytes, as some of the Fleete supposed, and yet the lands do lye and trend so like, that the best Mariners therin may be deceyved.[5]

The tenth of July, the weather still continuing thicke and darke, some of the Shippes in the fogge lost sighte of the Admirall and the rest of the Fleete, and wandering too and fro, with doubtfull opinion whether it were best to seeke backe againe to seaward through great store of Ise, or to follow on a doubtfull course in a Sea, bay, or straytes they knew not, or alongst a coast, whereof by reason of the darke mistes they coulde not discerne the daungers, if by chance any Rocke or broken ground should lye of the place, as commonly in these partes it doth.

The Vizeadmirall Captayne Yorke considering the foresayd opinion of the Pylot Hall,

---

[1] The highest point of Hall's Island, at the northern entrance to Frobisher's 'strait'.

[2] Margin note: 'A Currant'.

[3] The wide starlings of old London Bridge compressed the flow of the Thames into narrow channels whose turbulence and rate of outfall proved extremely hazardous to boats during the ebb and surge of tides (cf. Pepys, *Diary*, iii, p. 160, x, p. 235).

[4] Margin note: 'James Beare a good Mariner'.

[5] Margin note: 'Christopher Hall chiefe Pylot'. Hall's own account (document 6, p. 116) is closely corroborated here, though without mention of Frobisher's ire against his chief pilot for expressing a contradictory opinion.

who was with him in the Thomas Allen, having lost sight of the Fleete, turned backe to sea agayne, having two other Shippes in company with him.[1]

Also the Captaine of the Anne Frances having likewise lost companye of the Fleete, and being all alone, helde it for best to turne it out to Sea agayne, untyll they mighte have cleere weather to take the Sunnes Altitude, and with incredible payne and perill got out of the doubtfull place, into the open Sea agayne, being so narrowly distressed by the way, by meanes of continuall fogge and Ise, that they were many times ready to leape upon an Ilande of Ise, to avoyde the present daunger, and so hopyng to prolong life awhile, meante rather to dye a pining death.

Some hoped to save themselves on chestes, and some determined to tye the Hatches of the Shippes fast together, and to bynde themselves wyth theyr furniture fast thereunto, and so to bee towed with the Shippeboate ashore, whyche meanes if happilie they hadde arrived, they shoulde eyther have perished for lacke of foode to eate, or else shoulde themselves have bene eaten of those ravenous, bloudye, and Maneating people.[2]

The rest of the Fleete following the course of the Generall whyche ledde them the way, passed up above .60. Leagues within the sayd doubtfull and supposed straytes, havyng alwayes a fayre continente upon their starreboorde syde, and a continuance still of an open Sea before them.[3]

The Generall albeit with the fyrste perchance he found out the error, and that this was not the old straytes, yet he persuaded the Fleete always that they were in theyr right course, and knowne straytes.[4] Howbeit I suppose he rather dissembled hys opinion therein that otherwyse, meaning by that policie (being himself ledde with an honorable desire of further discoverie) to enduce the fleete to follow him to see a further proofe of that place. And as some of the company reported, he hath since confessed, that if it had not bin for the charge and care he had of the Fleete, and fraughted Shippes, he both would and could have gone through to the South Sea, called Mare del Sur, and dissolved the long doubt of the passage which we seeke to find to the ritch Countrey of Cataya.[5]

1 Of which mistaken straytes, considering the circumstance, we have great cause to confirme oure opinion, to like and hope well of the passage in this place. For the foresaide bay

---

[1] These were the *Emanuel of Bridgewater* and the *Frances of Foy*.

[2] Margin note: 'Hard shiftes to save mens lives'. As so often in his account of the second, 1577 voyage, Best here displays a near-obsessive preoccupation with the Inuit's imagined taste for human flesh; indeed, his use of the term 'cannibals' as a descriptive is as frequent as the more circumspect 'country people'. His description of the plight of the *Anne Frances* is more sustainable; on 30 August, immediately before the fleet's departure from Meta Incognita, Hall (document 6, p. 122) reported that she had to be hauled aground and several great leaks in her hull repaired. However, the true extent of her tribulations immediately following her loss of the fleet on 10 July may have been exaggerated by Best to distract the reader from her – and, of course, his – implicit desertion.

[3] Interestingly, the version of Best's *True Discourse* published by Hakluyt (*PN* 1598–1600) contained two additional marginalia at this point which reflected the developing contemporary perception of Frobisher's discoveries. The first – 'The coast along the Southside of Gronland 60 leagues' – reflected the wholesale misplacement of Meta Incognita onto the coast of Greenland in contemporary charts and maps, beginning with its portrayal upon Emeric Molyneux's 1592 terrestrial globe (see p. 51); the second – 'Mistaken Straights which indeede are no straights' – stated the corollary of this misplacement.

[4] Margin note: 'Mistaken straytes.'

[5] Margin note: 'Frobisher could have passed to Cataya.'

or sea, the further we sayled therein, the wyder we found it, with great likelyhoode of end-lesse continuance.[1] And where in other places we were muche troubled wyth Ise, as in the entrance of the same, so after we had sayled 50. or 60. leagues therein, we had no lette of Ise, or other thing at all, as in other places we found.[2]

2 Also this place seemeth to have a marvellous greate indraft, and draweth unto it most of the drift yse, and other things, which do fleete in the sea, eyther to the North, or Eastwardes of the same, as by good experience we have founde.[3]

3 For heere also we mette with boordes, latthes, and divers other things driving in the Sea, which was of the wracke of the shippe called the Barke Dennys, which perished amongst the Ise, as beforesaid, being lost at the first attempt of the entrance overthwart the Queens foreland, in the mouth of Frobisher straytes, whiche coulde by no meanes have bin so brought thither, neyther by winde nor tide, being lost so many leagues off, if by force of the sayde Currant the same had not bin violently brought.[4] For if the same hadde bin brought thither by the tyde of fludde, looke how farre in the said fludde had caried it, the ebbe woulde have recaryed it as farre backe agayne, and by the winde it coulde not so come to passe, bycause it was then sometime calme, and most times contrary.

And some Marriners doe affyrme, that they haue diligently observed, *that* there runneth in this place nine houres floud to three ebbe, which may thus come to passe by force of the saide currant: for whereas the sea in most places of the world, doth more or lesse ordinarily ebbe and flow once every twelve houres, with six houres ebbe, and six houres floud, so also would it doe there, were it not for the violence of this hastning currant, which forceth the floud to make appearance to beginne before his ordinary time one houre and a halfe, and also to continue longer than his natural course by an other houre and a halfe, until the force of the ebbe be so greate, that it will no longer be resisted (according to the saying: *Naturam expellas furca licet tamen usque recurrit*, Although nature and naturall courses be forced and resisted never so muche, yet at laste it will have their own sway againe).[5]

Moreover, it is not possible, that so great course of flouds and currant, so highe swelling tides with continuaunce of so deepe waters, can be digested here without unburdening themselves into some open Sea beyonde this place, which argueth the more likelihood of the passage to be hereaboutes. Also we suppose these great indrafts do growe, and are made by the reverberation and reflection of that same Currant, whiche at oure coming by Ire-lande, mette and crossed us, of whiche in the firste parte of this discourse I spake, whyche coming from the bay of Mexico, passing by, and washing the Southweast parts of Ireland, rebou*n*deth over to the Northest parts of the world, as Norway, Islande, &c. where not finding any passage to an open Sea, but rather is there encreased by a new accesse, and another Currant meeting with it from *the* Scythian Sea, passing the bay of Saint Nicholas Westwarde, doeth once againe rebound backe, by the coasts of Groenland, and from thence uppon Frobishers straites being to the Southwestwardes of the same.[6]

---

[1] Margin note: 'Faire open way.' [2] Margin note: 'Reasons to proove a passage heere.'
[3] Margin note: 'Great indraftes. [4] Margin note: 'Currant'.
[5] Margin note: 'Nine houres floude to nine (*recte* three) houres ebbe'. The corresponding note in Hak-luyt's version corrected this.
[6] One cannot but suspect that Best's portrayal of the remarkable journey made by this supposed current was intended, in part at least, to discredit contemporary arguments for the feasibility of a north-eastern route to Cathay.

5 And if that principle of Philosophie be true, that *Inferiora corpora reguntur a superioribus*, that is, if inferior bodies be governed, ruled, and caried after the course of the superiors, then the water being an inferior Element, muste needes be governed after the superior Heaven, and so followe the course of *Primum mobile* from East to Weast.[1]

6 But everye man that hathe written or considered anye thing of this passage, hath more doubted the retourne by the same way, by reason of a greate downefall of water whyche they imagine to be thereaboutes (which we also by experience partly find) than any mistruste they have of the same passage at all.[2] For we find (as it were) a great downfall in this place, but yet not suche, but that we may return, althoughe with muche adoe. For we were easilyer caried in in one houre, than we coulde gette forth againe in three. Also by an other experience at an other time, we founde thys currant to deceive us in this sort: That whereas we supposed to bee 15. Leagues off, and lying a hull, we were brought within 2. leagues of the shoare, contrarie to al expectation.[3]

Oure menne that sayled furthest in the same mistaken straites, (having the maine lande uppon their starboorde side) affyrme, that they mette with the outlet or passage of water whiche commeth thorowe Frobyshers straites, and followeth as all one into this passage.

Some of oure companye also affyrme, that they hadde sighte of a continent upon their larbordside, being 60. leagues within the supposed straites: howbeit excepte certaine Ilandes in the entraunce hereof, we could make no part perfect thereof. All the foresaid tract of land seemeth to be more fruitful and better stored of Grasse, Deere, Wilde foule, as Partridges, Larkes, Seamews, Guls, Wilmots, Falcons and tassel Gentils,[4] Ravens, Beares, Hares, Foxes, and other things, than any other parte we have yet discovered, & is more populous. And here Luke Ward, a Gentleman of the Company, traded merchandise, & did exchange knives, bells, looking glasses, &c. with those countrey people, who brought him foule, fishe, beare skinnes, and suche like, as their countrey yeeldeth for the same.[5] Here also they saw of those greater boates of the Country, with twentie persons in apeece.

Nowe, after the Generall hadde bestowed these manye dayes here, not without many daungers, he returned backe againe. And by the way sayling alongest this coaste (being the backeside of the supposed continent of America) and the Queenes forelande, he perceived a great sounde to go thorowe into Frobyshers straites.[6] Wherevppon he sente the Gabriell the one and twentith of July, to prove whether they mighte go thorowe and meete againe with him in the straites, whiche they did, and as we imagined before, so the Queenes forelande proved an Ilande, as I thinke most of these supposed continentes will.[7] And so he departed towardes the straites, thinking it were highe time nowe to recover hys Porte, and to provide the fleete of their lading, wherof he was not a little carefull, as shall by the processe and his resolute attempts appeare. And in his returne with the rest of the fleete, he was so entangled,

---

[1] Margin note: 'The sea moveth from East to West continuallye'.   [2] Margin note: 'Authoritie'.

[3] Margin note: 'Harde, but yet possible turning back againe'.

[4] A repetition; a tassel-gentil (or tiersel-gentle) was a male falcon (from *tiercelet*, meaning third-part less – a reference to the smaller body of the male of the species).

[5] Margin note: 'Traffique'. Warde was one of only four men (including Frobisher himself) known to have sailed in all three northwest voyages.

[6] Margin note: 'Returne out of the mistaken straites'.

[7] See plate V. The fragmented representation of Meta Incognita which illustrated Best's *True Discourse* clearly reflects this perception.

by reason of the darke fogge, amongest a number of Ilandes and broken ground that lyeth ofthis coast, that many of the ships came over the top of rocks, which presently after they might perceive to ly a drie, havyng not halfe a foote water more than some of their ships did draw. And by reason they coulde not with a small gale of wind stem the force of *th*e floud, wherby to go cleare of *th*e rocks, they were faine to let an ancker fall with twoo bent of Cable togither, at a .C. and odde fadome deapth, where otherwise they hadde bin by the force of the tydes caried upon the rockes againe, & perished: so that if God in these fortunes, as a mercifull guyde (beyond *th*e expectati*o*n of man), had not caried us thorow, we had surely more than x.m. times perished amiddest these dangers.[1] For being many times driven harde aboorde the shoare withoute any sighte of lande, untill we were readye to make shipwracke thereon, beeyng forced commonlye with oure boates, to sounde before oure shippes, leaste we might light thereon before we coulde discerne the same. It pleased God to give us a cleare of Sunne and lighte for a shorte time, to see and avoide thereby the daunger, having bin continuallye darke before, and presently after. Manye times also by meanes of fogge and currants, being driven neare uppon the coaste, God lent us even at the very pintch one prosperous breath of winde or other, whereby to double the land, and avoyde the perill, and when that wee were all without hope of helpe, every man recommending himselfe to death, and crying out, Lorde nowe helpe or never: nowe Lorde looke downe from Heaven and save us sinners, or else oure safetie commeth too late: even then the mightie maker of Heaven, and our mercifull God, did deliver us: so that they who have bin partakers of these daungers, do even in their soules con-fesse, that God eve*n* by miracle hath soughte to save them, whose name be praised evermore.

Long tyme nowe the Anne Frances had layne beating off and on all alone, before the Queenes forelande, not beeyng able to recover their porte for Ise, albeit many times they daungerously attempted it, for yet the Ise choaked up the passage, and woulde not suffer them to enter. And haveng never seene any of the fleete since twentie dayes past, when by reason of the thicke mistes they were severed in the mistaken straites, did nowe this pre-sent three and twe*n*tith of July overthwart a place in the straites called Hattons Hedland, where they mette with seven shippes of the Fleete again, which good happe did not only rejoyce them, for themselves, in respect of the comforte which they received by suche good companye, but especiallye, that by this meanes they were put out of doubt of their deare friendes, whose safeties long time they did not a little suspecte and feare.[2]

At their meeting they haled the Admirall after the maner of the Sea, and with great joy welcomed one another with a thundring voly of shot. And now every man declared at large the fortune and dangers, which they hadde passed.

The four and twentith of July we mette with the Frances of Foy, who with much adoe soughte way backe againe thorowe the yse from out of the mistaken straites, where to their greate perill, they proved to recover their Porte.[3] They broughte the firste newes of the Vizeadmirall Capitaine Yorke, who manye dayes with themselves, and the Busse of Bridge-water was missing.[4] They reported that they lefte the Vizeadmiral reasonably cleare of the

---

[1] Margin note: 'Great daungers'.
[2] Margin note: 'Anne Fraunces met with some of the fleete'. Hatton's Headland was, and remains, the name of a small island off the south-easternmost tip of Resolution Island ('Queen Elizabeth's Foreland').
[3] Margin note: 'Fraunces of Foy'.
[4] Margin note: 'Bridgewater Shippe'.

Ise, but the other shippe they greatly feared, whom they could not come to helpe, being themselves so hardly distressed, as never men more. Also they tolde us of the Gabriel, who having gote thorow from the backside, and Wester point of the Queens forelande, into Frobyshers straites, fell into their companye about the Cape of Good hope.

And uppon the seaven and twentith of Julye, the ship of Bridgewater gote oute of the Ise, and met with the fleete whiche laye off and on under Hattons Hedland. They reported of their marvellous accidentes and daungers, declaring their Shyppe to be so leake, that they muste of necessitie seeke harborowe, having their stem beaten within theyr huddings, that they hadde muche adoe to keepe themselves above water. They had (as they say) five hundreth strokes at the pompe in lesse than halfe a watche, being scarce twoo houres. Their menne being so over-wearied therewith, and with the former dangers, that they desired helpe of menne from the other Shippes. Moreover, they declared, that ther was nothing but Ise and Daunger, where they hadde bin, and that the straites within was frosen uppe, and that it was the most impossible thyng of the worlde, to passe uppe unto the Countesse of Warwickes sounde, whiche was the place of oure Porte.[1]

The reporte of these daungers by these Shyppes thus published amongest the Fleete, wyth the remembraunce of the perilles paste, and those presente before their face, broughte no small feare and terror into the hartes of many considerate men.[2] So that some beganne privily to murmure against the Generall for this wilful maner of proceeding. Some desired to discover some harborowe thereaboutes, to refreshe themselves, and reforme their broken vesselles for a while, untill the North and Northwest winds might disperse the Ise, and make the place more free to passe. Other some forgetting themselves, spake more undutifully in this behalfe, saying: that they hadde as leeve be hanged when they came home, as without hope of safetie, to seeke to passe, and so perishe amongest the Ise.

The Generall not opening his eares to the peevishe passion of anye private person, but chiefly caryng for the publicke profite of his Countries cause, and nothyng at all regardyng hys owne ease, lyfe, or safetie, but especiallye respecting the accomplishement of the cause he hadde vndertaken (wherein the chiefe reputation and fame of a Generall and Capitaine consisteth), and calling to his remembraunce the shorte time he hadde in hande, to provide so great number of Shyppes their loading, determined with this resolution, to passe and recover hys Porte, or else there to bury himselfe with hys attempte, and if suche extremitie so befell him, that he muste needes perish amongest the Ise, when all helpe shoulde be paste, and all hope of safetie set aside, hauing all the ordinaunce within boorde well charged, resolued wyth pouder to burne and bury himselfe and all togyther with hir Maiesties Shyppes. And with this peale of ordinaunce, to receyve an honourable knell, in steede of a better buriall, esteeming it more happye so to ende hys lyfe, rather than hymselfe, or anye of hys companye or anye one of hir Majesties Shyppes shoulde become a praye or spectacle to those base bloudye and man eating people.[3]

Notwithstandyng, somewhat to appease the feeble passions of the fearefuller sorte, and the better to entertaine time for a season, whilest the Ise might the better be dissolved, hee

---

[1] Margin note: 'Straightes frosen over'.
[2] I.e., thoughtful men.
[3] Margin note: 'A valiaunt mynde of Frobisher'.

haled on the Fleete, wyth beleefe, that he woulde putte into harborowe: thereuppon whilest the Shippes laye off and on under Hattons Hedlande, hee soughte in wyth hys Pynnesses amongest the Ilandes there, as thoughe hee meant to searche for harborowe, where in deede, hee meant nothing lesse, but rather sought if anye Ore mighte be found in that place, as by the sequele appeared.

In the meanetime, whilest the Fleete laye thus doubtfull wythoute anye certaine resolution what to doe, beeing harde aboorde the leeshoare, there arose a sodaine and terrible tempest at the Southsouthest, whereby the Ise began marvellouslye to gather aboute us.

Whereuppon everye manne, as in suche case of extreamitie hee thoughte beste, soughte the wisest waye for hys owne safetie. The moste parte of the Fleete whych were further shotte uppe within the straites, and so farre to the leewarde, as that they coulde not double the lande, following the course of the Generall, who led the*n* the waye, tooke in their Sayles, and laide it a hull amongest the Ise, and so passed over the storme, and hadde no extreamitie at all, but for a shorte time in the same place.

Howbeit the other Shyppes whiche plyed oute to Sea-warde, hadde an extreme storme for a longer season. And the nature of the place is suche, that it is subject diversly to divers windes, according to the sundrie situation of the greate Alpes and mountaynes here, everye mountaine causing a severall blaste, and pirrie, after the manner of a Levant.[1]

In this storme being the six and twentith of July, there fell so much snow, with such bitter cold ayre, that wee coulde not scarce see one another for the same, nor open oure eyes to handle our ropes and sayles, the snow being above halfe a foote deepe uppon the hatches of our shippe, which did so wette thorowe our poore Marriners clothes, that he that hadde five or six shifte of apparell, hadde scarce one drie threede to his backe, whiche kinde of wette and coldenesse, togither with the over-labouring of the poore menne amiddest the Ise,[2] bred no small sickenesse amongest the Fleete, whyche somewhat discouraged some of the poore men, who hadde not experience of the like before, everye man perswading himselfe, that the wynter there must needs be extreme, where they founde so unseasonable a Sommer.[3]

And yet notwythstandyng this cold ayre, the Sunne many times hath a marvellous force of heate amongest those mountaines, insomuche, that when ther is no breth of wind to bring *th*e cold ayre from *th*e dispersed Ise uppon us, we shall be weary of the bloming heate,[4] & then sodainly with a perry of wind whiche commeth down from *th*e hollownes of *th*e hilles, we shal have such a breth of heate brought upon our face, as though we were entred within some bastow or hote-house, & when the first of the pirry & blast is past, we shall have the winde sodainly anew blow cold againe.[5]

In this storme the Anne Fraunces, the Moone, and the Thomas of Ispwich, who founde themselves able to holde it uppe with a Sayle, and coulde double aboute the Cape of the Queenes forelande, plyed oute to Sea-warde, holding it for better policie and safetie, to seeke Sea roome, than to hazarde the continuaunce of the storme, the daunger of the Ise

---

[1] Pirrie: a squall.
[2] Margin note: 'Snowe in July'.
[3] Margin note: 'Extreame Winter'.
[4] Margin note: 'Greate heate in Meta Incognita'.
[5] Margin note: 'Unconstant weather'.

and the leeshoare. And being uncertaine at this time of the Generalles private determinations, the weather being so darke, that they coulde not discerne one another, nor perceive whiche waye he wrought, betooke themselves this course for best and safest.

The Generall notwithstanding the greate storme, following his owne former resolution, soughte by all meanes possible, by a shorter way, to recover his Port, and where he saw the Ise never so little open, he gat in at one gappe, and out at another, and so himselfe valiantly ledde the way through before, to induce *the* Fleete to followe after, & with incredible payne & perill, at length gat through the Ise, and upon the one and thirtith of July recovered his long wished Porte after many attempts, and sundry times being put backe, and came to Ancker in the Countesse of Warwickes sound, in the entrance whereof, when he thoughte all perill past, he encountred a great Iland of Ise, whyche gave the Ayde suche a blow, having alittle before wayed hir Ancker a cocke bill, that it stroke the Ancker flouke through the Shippes bowes under the water, whych caused so great a leake, that with muche adoe they preserved the Shippe from sincking.[1]

At theyr arivall heere, they perceyved two Shyppes at Ancker within the harborough, whereat they beganne muche to marvell, and greately to rejoyce, for those they knewe to bee the Michaell, wherein was the Lieutenante generall Captayne Fenton, and the small Barke called the Gabriell, who so long tyme were missing, and never hearde of before, whome every man made the last reckning, never to heare of agayne.[2]

Heere every man greatly rejoysed of their happie meeting, and welcomed one another after the Sea manner, with their great Ordinance, and when eache partie hadde reaped up their sundry fortunes and perils past, they highlye praysed God, and altogither uppon their knees gave hym due, humble and harty thanckes, and Mayster Wolfall a learned man, appoynted by hir Majesties Councell to bee theyr Minister and Preacher, made unto them a godly Sermon, exhorting them especially to be thankefull to God for theyr strange and miraculous deliverance in those so dangerous places, and putting them in mynde of the uncertainetie of mans life, willed them to make themselves always ready, as resolute men, to enjoy and accept thankefully whatsoever adventure his divine Providence should appoynt.[3] This Mayster Wolfall being well seated and setled at home in his owne Countrey, with a good and large living, having a good honest woman to wife, and verie towardly Children, being of good reputation among the best, refused not to take in hand this paynefull voyage, for the only care he had to save Soules, and to reforme those Infidels, if it were possible, to Christianitie: and also partle for the great desire he hadde, that this notable voyage so well begunne, might be brought to perfection: and therfore he was contented to stay there the whole yeare, if occasion had served, being in every necessarie action as forward, as the resolutest men of all. Wherfore in this behalfe he may rightly be called a true Pastor and minister of Gods word, which for the profite of his flocke, spared not to venture his owne life.

But to returne agayne to Captayne Fentons company, and to speake somewhat of their dangers (albeit they bee more than by writing can be expressed). They reported that from the night of the first storme, whiche was aboute the first day of July,[4] untill seaven dayes

---

[1] Margin note: 'The Generall recovereth his port'.
[2] Recte *Judith* and *Michael*. Best's error was repeated by Hakluyt.
[3] Margin note: 'Mayster Wolfall Preacher'.
[4] *Recte* 2 July.

before the Generalls arrivall, which was the sixe and twentith of the same,[1] they never sawe any one day or houre, wherein they were not troubled with continuall daunger and feare of deathe, and were twentie dayes almost togither fast amongst the Ise.[2] They had their Shippe stricken through and through on both sides, their false stemme borne quite away, and could go from their Shippes in some places upon the Ise very many miles, and might easilie have passed from one Iland of Ise to another, even to the shore, and if God had not wonderfully provided for them, and theyr necessitie, and time had not made them more cunning & wise to seeke strange remedies for strange kinds of dangers, it had bin impossible for them ever to have escaped: for among other devises, wheresoever they founde any Iland of Ise of greater bignesse than the rest (as there be some of more than halfe a mile compasse about, and almost .40. fadome high) they commonly coveted to recover the same, and thereof to make a bulwarke for their defence, wheron having mored Ancker, they roade under the lee thereof for a time, beeyng therby garded from the danger of the lesser driving Ise.[3] But when they must needes forgoe this newe founde forte, by meanes of other Ise, whiche at length woulde undermine and compasse them round about, and when that by heaving of the billow they were therwith like to be brused in peces, they used to make fast the Ship unto the most firme and broad peece of Ise they could find, and binding hir nose fast thereunto, would fill all their Sayles, whereon the winde having great power, would force forward the Ship, and so the Ship bearing before hir the yse, & so one yse driving forward another, should at length get scope & sea-roome.[4] And having by this meanes at length put their enimies to flight, occupyed the cleere place for a prettie season, among sundry Mountaynes, and Alpes of Ise. One there was founde by measure to be .65. fadome above water, which for a kind of similitude, was called Salomons porch. Some thinke those Ilands eight times so muche under water, as they are above, bycause of their monstrous weight. But now I remember I saw very strange wonders, men walking, running, leaping & shoting upon the maine seas .40. miles from any land, without any Shippe or other vessell under them.[5] Also I saw fresh Rivers running amidst the salt Sea a hundred myle from land, which if any man will not beleeve, let him know that many of our company lept out of their Shippe uppon Ilandes of Ise, and running there uppe and downe, did shoote at buttes upon the Ise, and with their Calivers did kill greate Ceales, which use to lye and sleepe upon the Ise, and this Ise melting above at the toppe by reflection of the Sunne, came downe in sundrye streames, whyche uniting togither, made a prettie brooke able to drive a Mill.

The sayd Captayne Fenton recovered his Porte tenne dayes before any man, and spente good time in searchyng for mine, and found good store thereof, which bycause it proved good, was after called Fentons Fortune. He also discovered aboute tenne Miles up the Countrey, where he perceyved neyther Towne, Village, nor likelyhoode of habitation, but seemeth (as he sayth) barrennous as the other parts which as yet we have entred upon: but their victuals and provision went so scante with them, that they had determined to returne homeward within seaven dayes after, if the Fleete had not then arrived.

---

[1] *Recte* 21 July.
[2] Margin note: 'The adventures of captayne Fenton and his company'.
[3] Margin note: 'Extremitie causeth men to devise new artes and remedies'.
[4] Margin note: 'Hard shiftes'. Fenton himself made no reference to such tactics; his lashing of the *Judith* to icebergs appears rather to have been a recourse of desperate exhaustion.
[5] Margin note: 'Strange wonders'.

The Generall after his arrival in the Countesses sound, spent no time in vayne, but immediately at his first landing, called the chiefe Captaynes of his Councell togither, and consulted with them for the speedier execution of such things as then they had in hand. As first, for searching and finding out good Minerall for the Miners to be occupied on. Then to give good orders to be observed of the whole company on shore. And lastly, to consider for the erecting up the Forte and House for the use of them whiche were to abide there the whole yeare. For the better handling of these, and all other like important causes in this service, it was ordeined from hir Majestie and the Councell, that the Generall should call unto him certayne of the chiefe Captaynes and Gentlemen in councell, to conferre, consult, and determine of al occurrents in this service, whose names are here as folow.

Captayne Fenton.   Captayne Carew.
Captayne Yorke.   Captayne Philpot.
Captayne Best.

And in Sea causes to have as assistants, Christopher Hal, and Charles Jackman, being both very good Pylots, and sufficient Mariners, whereof the one was chiefe Pylot of the voyage, and the other for the discoverie. From the place of our habitation weastward, Maister Selman was appointed Notarie, to register the whole manner of proceeding in these affaires, that true relation thereof might be made, if it pleased hir Majestie to require it.

The first of August every Captaine, by order from the General & his councell, was commaunded to bring ashore unto the Countesses Iland, al such gentlemen, souldiors, and Myners, as were under their charge, with suche provision as they had of victuals, tents, and things necessarie for the speedie getting togither of Mine, and fraight for the Shippes.

The Muster of the men being taken, and the victuals with all other things viewed and considered, every man was set to his charge, as his place and office required. The Myners were appointed where to worke, and Mariners discharged their shippes.

Uppon the seconde of August, was published and proclaymed, uppon the Countesse of Warwickes Iland, with sound of Trumpet, certain orders by the general and hys counsel, appointed to be observed of the companye, during the time of their abiding there. The copie whereof here followeth.[1]

Orders set down by *M. Frobisher* Esquire,

Captaine Generall for the voyage to *Cataya*, to be observed
of the companie, during the time of their abode in *Meta Incognita*.
Published the second day of August. Anno .1578.

1 *In primis*, the Generall in hir Majesties name, straightly chargeth and commaundeth, that no person or persons, with Boate nor Pinnesse, shall go ashoare, for any cause, but to the Countesse of Warwickes Ilande, and Winters Fornace, without licence of the general, or his deputies. And if they fortune at anye time, having licence, to meete with any of the Countrey people, that they shall not enter into any conference or armes wyth them, untyl they have given intelligence thereof to the Generall or hys Lieutenaunt.

---

[1] These orders were omitted from the version reproduced by Hakluyt.

1 Item, that no person of what calling soever he bee, shal make an assay of any maner of mettal, matter, or ore, in *th*e partes nowe called Meta Incognita, but only suche as shal be appointed by the General, or in his absence by his Lieutenaunt, to doe the same: nor that anye person shall take up and kepe to his private use, anye parte or parcel of Ore, pretious stone, or other matter of commoditie to be had or founde in that lande, but he the sayde person, so seased of such Ore, stone, or other matter of commoditie, shall with al speede, as soone as he can, detect the same, and make deliverie thereof to the Generall, or his Lieutenaunt Generall, uppon paine to forfaite for everye suche ounce thereof, the value treble of anye wages he is to receive, after the daye of such offence committed: And further, to receyve suche punishmente as to hyr Majestie shall seeme good.

3 Item that no shippe or shippes, shall take uppon them to loade any manner of Ore, without licence of the General, or he that shal be appointed deputie for him, for *th*e view of the same.

4 Item that all the Maisters of everye shippe or shippes within the Fleete, shal upon Mundaye next coming, by foure of the clock in the morning, wyth all the moste parte of theyr companies, make theyr repayre to the Countesses Ilande aforesayde, there to viewe and make suche places, for loading and unloading of Ore and other thyngs, as shall be moste commodious and meete for that purpose.

5 Item that no person or persons within this service, by sea or lande, shall use anye discovered speeches, swearyng, brauling, or cursing, uppon payne of imprysonmente.

6 Item that no person or persons, eyther by Sea of lande, shal drawe his or theyr weapons in quarrellyng manner, to the intente to offende or disturbe the quiete of anye person or persons wythin thys service, uppon paine that being so taken, he or they whatsoever, immediately loose his right hande.

7 Item that no person or persons shall washe their handes or anye other things, in the Spring uppon the Countesses Ilande, where the water is used, and preserved for the dressing of their victuals, upon paine to receive such punishmente as shall be thought good by the generall or his Lieutenaunte for the same. And for the better preservation and healthe of everye manne, that no person or persons shall doe his easemente but under the cliffes where the Sea maye washe the same awaye upon paine that everye one so offending, for the first time shall be imprisoned in the billow fourteene houres, and for the second time being so taken by the provost Martiall, to pay twelve pens.[1]

8 Item that no person or persons, of what nature or condition soever, shall cast out of their shippe or shippes anye ballast or rubbish into the roade where these shippes now rydeth, or may conveniently ryde, within this sounde, that thereby the same sounde or roade steade maye be impared, but shall carrie the same and lay it where it may not offe*n*d. Upon paine that every man so offending, the owner of such shippe or shippes shall forfaite the fraight of one tunne.

By me Martyn Frobisher

In the meane time, whylest the Mariners plyed their work, *th*e Captaines sought out new Mynes, the Goldfiners made tryall of the Ore, the Mariners discharged their shippes, the

---

[1] In the absence of corroborating evidence of measures enacted in other contemporary voyages, it is difficult to judge the prevalence of such concern for general hygiene. Nevertheless, these orders indicate that the link between dirt and infection were well understood, even by relatively untutored men.

Gentlemen for example sake laboured hartily and honestlye encouraged the inferiour sorte to worke. So that small time of that little leasure that was lefte to tarrie was spent in vaine.

The second of August, the Gabriel arrived, who came from the Vizeadmirall, and being distressed sore with yse, put into harborrow neere unto Mount Oxford. And now was the whoale Fleet arrived safely at their port, excepting foure, besides the shippe that was loste: that is, the Thomas Allen, the Anne Frances, the Thomas of Ipswich, and the Moone, whose absence was some let unto the works and other proceedings, aswell for that these shippes were furnished with the better sort of Myners and other provision for the habitation.

The ninth of August, the Generall with the Captaynes of his councell assembled togither, beganne to consider and take order for the erecting up of the house or forte, for them that were to inhabite there the whole yeare, and that presently the Masons and Carpenters might go in hande therewith.[1] First therefore they perused the Bils of ladyng, what every man received into his shippe, and founde that there was arrived only the eastside and the South-side of *the* house, and yet not that perfecte and intier, for many peeces thereof were used for fenders in many shippes, and so broken in peeces, whylest they were distressed in the Ise. Also after due examination had, & true accompt taken, there was founde want of drinke and fuel, to serve one hundreth men, which was the number appointed firste to inhabite there, bycause their greatest store was in the ships which were not yet arrived. Then Cap-taine Fenton seeing the scarcity of *the* necessarie things aforesayde was contented, and offred himselfe to inhabite there, with sixtie men. Wherupon they caused the Carpenters and Masons to come before them, and demaunded in what time they woulde take upon them to erect up a lesse house for sixtie men. They required eight or nine weekes, if there were Tymber sufficient, whereas now they had but six and twentie dayes in al to remayne in that Countrey. Wherefore it was fully agreed uppon, & resolved by the General and his councell, that no habitation shoulde be there this yeare. And therefore they willed Maister Selman the Register, to set downe this decree, with all their consentes, for the better satis-fying of hir Majestie, the Lords of the Counsel, and the adventurers.[2]

The Anne Frances, since she was parted from the Fleete, in the last storme before spoken of, could never recover above five leagues within the straightes, the wind being sometyme contrarie, and moste times the Ise compassing them round about. And from that time, being aboute the seaven and twentith of July, coulde neyther heare nor have sight of any of the Fleete, untill the third of August, when they descried a sayle nere unto Mount Oxford, with whome when they had spoken, they could understande no newes of any of the fleete at all. And this was the Thomas of Ipswich, who hadde layne beating off and on at sea, with very foule weather, and contrarye winds, ever since that foresaide storme, without sight of any man. They kepte company not long togyther, but were forced to lose one another again, the Moone being consort always with the Anne Fraunces, and keping verie good company plyed up togither into the straites, with desire to recover their long wished port: and atempted as often, as passed as far as possible the winde, weather, and Ise gave leave, whyche

---

[1] Margin note: 'Consultation for inhabiting Meta Incognita'.

[2] Margin note: 'No habitation on this yere'. Best here refutes Lok's claim (document 5, p. 87) that Fro-bisher alone was responsible for preventing the establishment of the colony in 1578. Nor does Fenton him-self (document 8, pp. 158–9) infer that the decision was other than fully agreed by all the members of the land-council who were present (that is, those other than Best himself and Yorke, who remained at sea).

commonly they found very contrary. For when the weather was cleare, and without fogge, then commonly *the* wind was contrarie. And when it was eyther easterly or southerly, whiche woulde serve their turnes, then they had so great a fogge, and darke miste therewith, that eyther they could not discerne way thorow the Ise, or else the Ise laye so thicke togither, that it was impossible for them to passe. And on the other side, when it was calme, the Tydes hadde force to bryng the Ise so sodaynelye about them that commonlye then they were moste therewyth distressed, having no Winde to carry them from the daunger therof.

And by the sixte of August, being with much adoe, got up as high as Leicester point, they had good hope to find the Souther shore cleare, and so to passe uppe towardes their porte. But being there becaulmed and lying a hull openly upon the great Bay which commethe oute of the mystaken straites before spoken of, they were so sodainlye compassed with Ise rounde about, by meanes of the swifte Tydes whiche runne in that place, that they were never afore so hardly beset as nowe. And in seeking to avoyde these dangers in the darke weather, the Anne Frances lost sighte of the other two ships, who being likewise hardly distressed, signifyed their daunger, as they since reported, by shooting off their ordinaunce, whiche the other coulde not heare, nor if they had been hearde coulde have given them no remedie, being so busily occupied to winde themselves out of their owne troubles.

The Fleeboate called the Moone was here heaved above the water with the force of the Ise, and received a great leake therby.[1] Likewise the Thomas of Ipswich and the Anne Frances were sore brused at that instant, havyng their false stemme borne away, and their shippe sides stroken quite through.

Now considering the continuall daungers and contraries, and the little leasure that they had lefte to tarrie in these partes, besides that every night the roapes of theyr shippes were so frosen that a man coulde not handle them without cutting his handes, togither with the great doubt they had of the Fleetes safety, thinking it an impossibilitie for them to passe unto their port, as well for that they saw themselves as for that they harde by the former reporte of the shippes whiche had proved before, who affirmed that the straites were al frosen over within: They thought it now very hie time to consider of their estates and safeties that were yet left togither. And herevppon the Captaines and maisters of these shippes desired the Captaine of the Anne Frances to enter into consideration with th*em* of these matters, wherfore Captaine Tanfield of the Thomas of Ipswich, with his Pylot Richard Coxe, and Captaine Upcote of the Moone, with his maister John Lakes came aboorde the Anne Frances the eight of August to consult of these causes.[2] And being assembled togither in the Captaynes Cabin, sundrie doubtes were there alleaged. For the fearefuller sorte of Mariners, being overtyred with the contuinuall labour of the former daungers, coveted to returne homewarde, saying that they woulde not againe tempte God so muche, who hadde given them so manye warnings, and delivered them from so wonderfull daungers: that they rather desired to loose wages fraighte and all, than to continewe and followe such desperate fortunes. Again their shippes were so leake, and the men so wearie, that to amende the one, and refresh the other, they muste of necessitie seeke into harborough.

---

[1] Margin note: 'The Moone'. This is one of the rare clues to the type of vessels employed as freight ships in the expedition. If Best's term is accurate, the *Moon* was a probably a flat-bottomed, broad-waisted coaster that was parlously unsuitable for trans-oceanic voyaging, even in relatively fair conditions

[2] Margin note: 'The Anne Frances the Thomas of Ipswich and the Moone consult'.

But on the other side it was argued againe, to the contrarie, that to seeke into harborow thereaboutes was but to subject themselves to double daungers, for if happilye they escape the daungers of rockes in their entring, yet being in they were neverthelesse subject there to the daunger of the Ise, which with the swift tydes and currantes is caried in and out in most harborowes thereaboutes, and may thereby gaule their Cables asunder, drive them uppon *th*e shoare, and bring them to muche trouble. Also the coast is so much subject to broken ground & rockes, especially in the mouth and entraunce of everye harborow, that albeit the channell be sounded over and over againe, yet are you never the neare to discerne the daungers. For the bottome of the sea, holding like shape and forme as the lande, beyng full of hilles, dales and ragged rockes, suffereth you not, by your soundings, to knowe and keepe a true gesse of *th*e depth. For you shall sounde upon the side or hollownesse of one hil or rocke under water, and have a hundreth, fiftie, or fourtie fadome depth: and before the next cast, ere you shal bee able to have your leade againe, you shall be uppon the toppe thereof, and come agrounde, to your utter confusion.

Another reason against going to harborowe was, that the colde ayre did threaten a sodaine freesing uppe of the sounds, seeing *that* every night there was new congealed Ise, even of that water which remayned within their shippes. And therefore it should seeme to be more safe to lye off and on at sea, than for lacke of winde to being them forth of harborow, to hazard by sodaine frostes to be shut uppe the whole yeare.

After many such daungers and reasons alleaged, & large debating of these causes on both sides, the Captayne of the Anne Frances delivered his opinion unto the company to this effect. First con*c*erning the question of returning home, he thought it so much dishonorable as not to grow in any farther question: and agayne to returne home at length (as at length they must needes) and not be able to bring a certayne report of the Fleete, whether they were living or lost, or whether any of them had recovered their porte, or not, in the Countesses sounde (as it was to be thoughte the most part would if they were living) he sayd that it would be so great an argume*n*t, eyther for wante of courage or discretion in them, as he resolved rather to fall into any daunger, than so shamefully to consent to returne home, protesting that it should never be spoken of him, that he woulde ever returne, withoute doing his endeavour to finde the Fleete, and knowe the certaynetie of the Generals safetie.[1] He put his company in remembrance of a pinnesse of five tunne burthen, which he had within his Ship, whiche was caryed in peeces, and unmade up for the use of those whiche shoulde inhabite there the whole yeare, the whiche if they coulde fynde meanes to joyne togither, hee offered himselfe to prove before therewith, whether it were possible for anye Boate to passe for Ise, whereby the Shippe myghte bee broughte in after, and mighte also thereby gyve true notice if any of the Fleete were arrived at theyr porte or not.

But notwithstanding, for that he well perceyved that the most parte of hys companye were addicted to put into harborough, he was willing the rather for these causes somewhat to encline thereunto. As first, to search alongst the same coast, and the soundes thereaboutes, he thoughte it to be to good purpose, for that it was likely to fynd some of the

---

[1] Margin note: 'Captayne Bestes resolution'. The somewhat self-serving tenor of Best's recalled speech requires that it be treated with caution; nevertheless, the fact that the ships – absent the *Thomas of Ipswich* – subsequently pressed on to search for Frobisher in the face of these dangers undoubtedly gives some credence to his version of this meeting.

Fleete there, whiche beeing leake, and sore brused with the Ise, was the rather thought lykely to be put into an yll harborough, beyng distressed with foule weather in the last storme, than to hazarde theyr uncertayne safeties amongst the Ise: for about this place they lost them, and lefte the Fleete then doubtfully questioning of harborough.

It was lykely also, that they mighte fynde some fitte harborough thereaboutes, whiche myghte bee behovefull for them againste another tyme. It was not likewise impossible to fynde some Ore or Myne thereaboutes, wherewithall to fraighte theyr Shyppes, whiche woulde bee more commodious in this place, for the neerenesse to Seawarde, and for a better outlette, than further within the straytes, beeyng lykely heere alwayes to loade in a shorter tyme, howsoever the strayte shoulde be pestered wyth Ise within, so that it myghte come to passe, that thereby they mighte eyther fynd the Fleete, Mine, or convenient harborough, any of these three woulde well serve theyr present turnes, and gyve some hope and comforte unto theyr companyes, whiche nowe were altogyther comfortlesse. But if that all fortune shoulde fall out so contrarye, that they could neyther recover theyr Porte, nor anye of these aforesayde helpes, that yet they woulde not departe the coast, as long as it was possible for them to tarrie there, but woulde lye off and on at Sea athwart the place. Therefore hys finall conclusion was sette down thus, Firste, that the Thomas of Ipswiche and the Moone, shoulde consorte and keepe companye togyther carefully wyth the Anne Frances as neere as they could, and as true Englishmen and faythfull friends should supplye one anothers want in all fortunes and dangers. In the morning following, every Shippe to sende of hys Boate, with a sufficient Pylot, to searche out and sounde the harboroughes for the safe bringing in of theyr Shippes. And beeyng arrived in harborough, where they mighte finde convenient place for the purpose, they resolved forthwith to joyne and set togyther the Pinnesse, wherewythall the Captayne of the Anne Frances might accordyng to his former determination, discover up into the straytes.

After these determinations thus sette downe, the Thomas of Ipswiche the nyghte following lost the company of the other Shyppes, and afterwarde shaped a contrarye course homewarde, whyche fell out as it manyfestlie appeared, very muche agaynste theyr Captayne Mayster Tanfieldes mynde, as by due examination before the Lordes of hir Majesties most Honorable privie Counsell, it hathe since bin proved, to the greate discredite of the Pilot Coxe, who specially persuaded his company, against the opinion of hys sayde Captayne, to returne home.

And as the Captayne of the Anne Frances dothe witnesse, even at theyr conference togither, Captayne Tanfield tolde hym, that hee did not alittle suspect the sayde Pylot Coxe, saying, that he had neyther opinion in the man of honest duetie, manhoode or constancie.[1] Notwythstanding the sayde Shippes departure, the Captayne of the Anne Frances beeyng desirous to putte in execution hys former resolutions, went with hys Shyppe-boate (beeyng accompanied also wyth the Moones Skyffe) to prove amongst the Ilandes whiche lye under Hattons headland, if anye good Ore was there to be founde. The Shyppes lying off and on at Sea the whyle under Sayle, and searching through manye soundes, they saw them all full of

---

[1] The judgement seems a little harsh. Cox had proved an excellent seaman in the previous voyage, when the *Ayde* was caught in a tempest as Frobisher and the leading officers explored Hall's Island. Then, Cox, with Andrew Diar and Charles Jackman, had handled the ship with great skill, causing Settle (Hakluyt, *PN* 1589, p. 624) to recall him as being: 'expert both in Navigation and other good qualities'. Cox's poor performance this year may have been influenced in part by his rejection for service in one of the four 'company ships' (HM715, fo. 20).

manye dangers, and broken grounde, yet one there was, which seemed an indifferent place to harborough in, and whiche they did very diligently sounde over, and searched agayne.

Heere the sayde Captayne founde a great blacke Iland, wherunto he had good liking, & certifying the company therof, they were somewhat comforted, & with the good hope of his words rowed cheerefully unto the place, where when they arrived they found such plentie of blacke Ore of the same sorte whiche was broughte into Englande thys last yeare, that if the goodnesse myghte aunswere the greate plentye thereof, it was to be thoughte that it might reasonably suffice all the golde gluttons of the worlde. Thys Ilande the Captayne for cause of his good happe, called after his owne name, Bestes blessing, and wyth these good tydings returning aboorde hys Shyppe the ninth of August, about tenne of the Clocke at nighte, he was joyfully welcomed of hys companye, who were before discomforted, and greatelie expected some better fortune at hys handes.[1]

The nexte daye beeyng the tenth of August, the weather reasonably fayre, they put into the foresayde harborough, having their Boate for theyr better securitie sounding before theyr Ship. But for all the care and diligence that coulde be taken, in soundyng the Channell over and over agayne, the Anne Frances came agrounde uppon a suncken Rocke within the Harborough, and lay thereon more than halfe drye untill the nexte floud, when by Gods Almighty providence, contrarye almost to all expectation, they came afloate agayne, beeyng forced all that tyme to undersette theyr Shyppe wyth their mayne yarde, whyche otherwyse was lykely to oversette and putte thereby in daunger the whole companye.[2] They hadde above two thousande strokes at the Pumpe, before they coulde make theyr Shyppe free of the water agayne, so sore shee was brused by lying upon the Rockes. The Moone came safely, and roade at Ancker by the Anne Fraunces, whose helpe in theyr necessitie they coulde not well have missed.[3]

Nowe, whilest the Marriners were romaging theyr Shyppes, & mending that whiche was amisse, the Miners followed their laboure, for getting togither of sufficient quantitie of Ore, and the Carpenters endevoured to doe theyr beste, for the making uppe of the boate or pinnesse, whiche to bring to passe, they wanted two speciall and moste necessary things, that is, certaine principal timbers that are called Knees, whiche are the chiefest strength of any boate, & also nayles, wherwithall to joyne the plancks togither. Whereupon having by chance a Smyth amongest them (and yet unfurnished of his necessarie tooles to worke and make nayles withall), they were faine of a gunne chamber to make an anvile to worke uppon, and to use a pickaxe in steede of a sledge to beate withall, and also to occupy two small bellowes in steede of one payre of greater Smiths bellowes. And for lacke of small Iron, for the easier making of the nayles, were forced to breake their tongs, grydiern, and fiershovell in peeces.

The eleaventh of August, the Captaine of the Anne Fraunces, taking the Maister of hys Ship with hym, went up to the toppe of Hattons Hedland, whych is the highest lande of all the straites, to the ende to descry the situation of the Country underneath, and to take a true plot of the place,, whereby also to see what store of Ise was yet lefte in the straites, as also to searche what Mine matter or fruite that soyle might yeelde.[4] And the rather for the

---

[1] Margin note: 'Bestes blessing'. [2] Margin note: 'Anne Fraunces in daunger'.
[3] Margin note: 'The Moone in harborough'.
[4] Margin note: 'Hattons Hedlande'. Best's topographical observations are wildly inaccurate here; perhaps a reflection of his prudent, if ingratiating, respect to his patron, Christopher Hatton. At an elevation of some eight hundred feet, Hatton's Headland is far from being the highest point of Resolution Island, much less of Frobisher Bay as a whole.

honor *the* said Captaine doth owe to that Honorable name which himselfe gave thereunto the laste yeare, in the highest parte of this Hedlande, he caused his companye to make a Columne or Crosse of stone, in token of Christian possession. In this place there is plentie of blacke Ore, and divers preatie stones.

The seaventeenth of Auguste, the Captaines wyth their companies chaced and killed a greate white Beare, whiche adventured and gave a fierce assaulte upon twentie men being weaponed. And he served them for good meat many dayes after.

The eighteenth of August, the Pinnesse with muche adoe, being set togyther, the saide Captaine Beste determined to departe uppe the straites, to prove and make trial, as before was pretended,[1] some of his companye greatlye persuading him to the contrarie, and specially the Carpenter that set the same togither, who saide that he would not adventure himselfe therein, for five hundreth poundes, for that the boate hung togither but onelye by the strength of the nayles, and lacked some of hir principall knees and tymbers.[2]

These wordes somewhat discouraged some of the company which should have gone therin. Whereupon the Captaine, as one not altogether addicted to his own self-wil, but somewhat foreseeing how it might be afterwards spoken, if contrarye fortune shoulde happen upon him (Lo he hathe followed his own opinion and desperate resolutions, and so thereafter it is befallen him), calling the Maister Marriners of beste judgement togyther, declared unto them howe muche the cause imported him in his credite, to seeke out the Generall, as wel to conferre with him of some causes of waight, as otherwise to make due examination and triall of the goodnesse of the Ore, wherof they had no assuraunce but by gesse of the eye, and was wel like the other: which so to cary home, not knowing the goodnesse thereof, might be asmuch as if they should bring so many stones. And therefore hee desired them to delyver their plaine and honest opinion, whether the Pinnesse were sufficient for him to so adventure in or no. It was aunswered, that by carefull heede taking thereunto amongest the Ise, and the foule weather, the Pinnesse might suffise. And hereuppon the Maisters mate of the Anne Frances called John Gray, manfully and honestly offering himselfe unto his Captain in this adventure and service, gave cause to others of hys Marriners to follow the attempt.

And upon the ninteenth of August, the said Captain being accompanied with Captayne Upcot of the Moone, & xviii. persons in the small Pinnesse, having convenient portion of victualles & thinges necessary, departed upon the said pretended voyage, leaving their shippe at ancker in a good readinesse for the taking in of their fraight. And having little winde to saile withall, they plyed alongest the Souther shoare, and passed above 30. leagues, having the onely helpe of mans labour with Ores, and so entendyng to keepe that shoare aboorde untill they were gote up to the farthest and narrowest of *the* straites, minded there to crosse over, & to search likewise alongest the Northerland, unto the Countesses sound, & from thence to passe all that coaste along, where by if any of the Fleete hadde been distressed by wracke of rocke or Ise, by that meanes they might be perceived of them, and so they thereby to give them such helpe and reliefe as they could. They did greatly feare, and ever suspecte that some of the Fleete were surely caste awaye, & driven to seeke sowre sallets amongest the colde cliffes.[3]

And being shot up about 40. leagues within *the* straites, they put over towards *the*

---

[1] I.e., intended.
[2] Margin note: 'A Pinnesse there builte'.
[3] 'Sower sallets': bitter desserts.

Norther shore, whiche was not a little daungerous for theyr small boates. And by meanes of a sodaine flawe,[1] were driven, and faine to seeke harboroughe in the night amongest all the rockes and broken grounde of Gabriels Ilande, a place so named within the straites above the Countesse of Warwickes sounde.[2] And by the way where they landed, they did find certaine great stones sette uppe by the Countrie people, as it seemed for markes, where they also made manye Crosses of stone, in token that Christians had bin there. The xxii. Of August, they hadde sighte of the Countesses sounde, and made the place perfecte from the toppe of a hill, and keepyng along the Norther shoare, perceived the smoake of a fyre under a hylles side. Whereof they diverslye deemed, when they came nearer the place, they perceyved people whiche wafted unto them, as it seemed, with a flagge or auntient. And bycause the Caniballes and countrie people had used to doe the like when they perceived any of our boats to passe by, they suspected them to be the same. And comming somewhat nearer, they might perceyve certaine tents, and discerne this auntient to be of mingled coloures, black and white, after the Englishe fashion. But bycause they coulde see no shippe, nor likelihoode of harborowe within five or six leagues aboute, and knewe that none of oure men were wonte to frequent those partes, they coulde not tell what to judge thereof, but imagined that some of the Shyppes being carried so highe wyth the storme and mistes, had made shipwracke amongest the Ise or the broken Ilandes there, and were spoyled by the Countrey people, who might use the sundrye coloured flagge for a policie, to bring them likewise within their daunger. Wherupon the saide Captaine wyth his companies, resolved to recover the same Auntient, if it were so, from those base, cruell, and man eating people, or else to lose their lives, & all togither. One promised himselfe a payre of garters, an other a scarffe, the third, a lace to tye hys Whistle withal, of the same. In the ende, they discerned them to be theyr Countreymen, and then they deemed them to have loste theyr Shyppes, and so to be gathered togyther for theyr better strength. On the other side, the companye a shoare feared that the Capitayne, having loste his shippe, came to seeke forth the fleete for his reliefe, in hys poore pinnesse, so that their extremities caused eache parte to suspecte the worste.

The Captaine nowe with his pinnesse being come neere the shoare, commaunded his Boate carefully to be kepte aflote, least in their necessitie, they might winne the same from hym, and seeke firste to save themselves (for everye manne in that case is nexte himselfe).[3] They haled one another according to the manner of the Sea, and demaunded what cheare: & either partie answered the other, that all was well: whereuppon there was a sodaine and joyfull outeshoote, with greate flinging up of cappes, and a brave voly of shotte to welcome one an other. And truelye it was a moste straunge case, to see howe joyfull and gladde everye partie was to see themselves meete in safetie againe, after so straunge and incredible daungers: Yet to be shorte, as their daungers were greate, so their God was greater.

And here the companye were workyng uppon newe Mines, whych Captayn Yorke being here arrived not long before, hadde founde out in this place, and it is named the Countesse of Sussex Mine.[4]

After some conference wyth oure friends here, the Captaine of the Anne Fraunces

---

[1] *Recte* flow.
[2] Margin note: 'Gabriels Ilande'.
[3] Margin note: 'Proximus sum egomet mihi'.
[4] Margin note: 'Captaine York arrived'.

departed towardes the Countesse of Warwickes sounde, to speake with the Generall, & to have triall made of suche mettall as he hadde broughte thither, by the Goldfiners. And so determined to dispatche againe towardes his shippe. And having spoke wyth the Generall, hee received order for all causes, and direction as well for the bringing uppe of his Shippe to the Countesses sounde, as also to fraight his Shippe with the same Ore he himselfe hadde found, which upon triall made, proved to be very good.

The thirteenth of Auguste, the saide Captaine mette togither with the other Captaines (Commissioners in counsell with the Generall) aboorde the Ayde, where they considered and consulted of sundrie causes, whiche particularly registred by the Notarie, were appointed, where and howe to be done againste an other yeare.

The fourteenth of August, the Generall with two Pinnesses and good numbers of men, wente to Beares sounde, commaunding the saide Captaine with his Pinnesse, to attend the service, to see if he could encounter or apprehend any of the Caniballes, for sundry tymes they shewed themselves busy thereaboutes, sometimes with 7. or 8. boates in one company, as though they minded to encounter with our company, whiche were working there at the mines, in no greate numbers. But when they perceived anye of oure shippes to ride in that roade (being belike more amazed at the countenaunce of a shippe, and a more number of men) didde never shewe themselves againe there at all. Wherfore oure men soughte with their Pinnesses to compasse aboute the Iland, where they did use, supposing there sodainely to intercept some of them. But before oure men coulde come neare, having belike some watch in the toppe of the mountaines, they conveyed themselves privily away, and lefte (as it shoulde seeme) one of their great dartes behinde them for haste, whiche we founde neare to a place of their caves and housing. Therefore, though our Generall were very desirous to have taken some of them to have brought into Englande, they being nowe growen more wary by their former losses, woulde not at any time come within our daungers.[1] About midnight of the same day the Captaine of the Anne Fraunces departed thence & set his course over the straites towards Hattons Hedland, being about fifteene leagues, and returned aboord his ship the five and twentith of Auguste, to the great comforte of his company, who long expected hys coming, where hee founde hys shippes ready rigged and loaden. Wherfore he departed from thence agayne the next morning towards the Countesses sounde, where he arrived the eight and twentith of the same. By the waye he sette hys Miners ashoare at Beares sounde, for the better dispatche and gathering of the Ore togither, for that some of the ships were behinde hande with their fraighte, the time of the yeare passyng speedily away.

The thirtith of August, the Anne Frances was brought aground, & had .viii. great leakes mended, whiche she had received by meanes of the rockes and Ise. This daye the Masons finished a house whiche Captaine Fenton caused to be made of lyme and stone upon the Countesse of Warwickes Ilande, to the ende we might prove againste the nexte yere, whether the snowe coulde overwhelme it, the frosts breake uppe, or the people dismember the same.[2] And the better to allure those brutish & uncivill people to courtesie, againste other times of oure coming, we left therein dyvers of oure countrie toyes, as belles, and knives, wherein they specially delight, one for the necessarie use, and the other for the great pleasure thereof. Also pictures of men & women in lead, men a horsebacke, lookinglasses,

---

[1] Margin note: 'None of the people wil be taken'.
[2] Margin note: 'A house builded and lefte there'.

whistles, and pipes. Also in the house was made an oven, and breade lefte baked therein, for them to see and taste.

We buryed the timber of our pretended fort, with manye barrels of meale, pease, griste, and sundrie other good things, which was of the provision of those whych should inhabite, if occasion served. And insteede therof we fraighted oure ships full of Ore, whiche we holde of farre greater price.[1] Also here we sowed pease, corne, and other graine, to prove the fruitfulnesse of the soyle against the next yeare.

Maister Wolfall on Winter's Fornace preached a godly Sermon, whiche being ended, he celebrated also a Communion upon the lande, at the pertaking whereof, was the Capitaine of the Anne Fraunces, and manye other Gentlemen & soldiors, Marriners, & Miners wyth hym. The celebration of divine mistery was *the* first signe, seale, & confirmation of Christes name death & passion ever knowen in all these quarters. The said M. Wolfall made sermons, & celebrated the Communion at sundrie other times, in severall and sundrie Ships, bicause the whole company could never meet togither at any one place. The fleet now being in some good readinesse for their lading, *the* General calling togither the Gentlemen & Captains to consult, told them that he was very desirous *that* some further discovery should be attempted, & *that* he woulde not only by Gods help bring home his Shippes laden with golde Ore, but also meant to bring some certificat of a further discoverie of *the* Countrie, which thing to bring to passe (having sometime therein consulted) they founde verye harde, and almost invincible. And considering, that alreadie they hadde spente some time in searching out the trending and fashion of the mistaken straites, and hadde entred verye farre therein, therefore it coulde not be saide, but that by thys voyage they have notice of a further discovery, and that the hope of the passage thereby is muche furthered and encreased, as appeared before in the discourse thereof. Yet notwithstandyng, if anye meanes mighte be further devised, the Capitaynes were contented and willing as the Generall shoulde appointe and commaunde, to take anye enterprise in hande. Whiche after long debating, was found a thing verye impossible, & that rather consultation was to bee had of returning homewarde, especiallye for these causes followyng. First, the darke foggy mistes, the continuall fallyng Snowe and stormy weather which they commonly were vexed with, and nowe dalye ever more and more increased, have no small argument of the Winters drawing neare. And also the froste everye nighte was so harde congealed within the sounde, that if by evill happe they shoulde be long kepte in wyth contrarye windes, it was greatlye to be feared, that they should be shutte uppe there faste the whole yeare, whyche being utterly unprovided, woulde be their utter destruction. Againe, drincke was so scant throughout al the Fleete, by meanes of the greate leakage, that not onely the provision wiche was layde in for the habitation was wanting and wasted, but also eache Shippes severall provision spent and lost, which many of oure companye, to their greate griefe, founde in their returne since, for al the way homewards they dranke nothing but water.[2] And the great cause of this lekage and wasting was for that *the* great timber & seacole, which lay so waighty upon *the* barrels, brake, brused, & rotted *the* hoopes in sunder. Yet notwithstanding these reasons alledged, *the* Generall himselfe (willing the rest of the Gentlemen & Captains every man to looke to his severall charge and lading, that against a day appoynted, they shoulde be all in a readinesse to sette homeward) went in his Pinnesse, and discovered further Northward in

---

[1] Predictably, this entire sentence was omitted from the version later produced by Hakluyt.
[2] That Best mentions this indicates something of the horror with which mariners regarded a beer-less ship.

the straytes, and found that by Beares sound and Halles Iland, the land was not firme, as it was first supposed, but all broken Ilandes in manner of an Archipelagus, and so with other secret intelligence to himselfe, he returned to the Fleete.[1] Where presentlye upon his arrivall at the Countesses sound, he began to take order for their returning homeward, and first caused certayne Articles to be proclaymed, for the better keeping order and courses in their returne, which Articles were delivered to every Captayne, and are these that follow.

Articles sette downe by *Martin Frobisher* Esquier,
Captayne Generall of the whole Fleete, appoynted
For the Northweast discoveries of *Cataya*, published
And made knowen to the Fleete, for the better observing
Certayne orders and course in their returne homewarde.[2]

1 Firste and principallie he doth straytely charge and commaunde, by vertue of hir Majesties commission which he hath, and in hir Majesties name, that every Captayne and Captaynes, Mayster and Maysters of the sayde Fleete, do vigilently and carefully keepe company with the Admirall, and by no maner of meanes breake companye willingly now in our returne homewards, yppon payne of forfeture of his or their whole frayte, that shall be founf culpable therein, and further, to receyve suche punishment, as to hir Majestie shal seeme good therein, and also to answere all suche damages or losses as may happen or growe by dispersing and breaking from the Fleete. And therefore for the better keeping of companye, the Generall straytely chargeth and commaundeth all the Maysters of these Shippes, and every one of them, that they repayre to speake with the Admirall once every day, if he or they may convenientlye doe it, uppon payne of forfeting of one tunne fraighte to hir Majestie, for every daye neglecting the same.

2 Item, that every Mayster in the sayde Fleete, observe and keepe orderly and vigilantly, all such Articles as were outwardes bounde drawen and published by the Generall in hir Majesties name, whereof there was delyvered to every Shippe a copie.

3 Item, that all Captaynes and Maysters of everye Ship and Shippes, do proclyame, and make it knowen to their company, that no person or persons within the sayde Fleete, of what condition soever, doe take or keepe to their use or uses any Ore, or stones, of what quantitie soever it be, but forthwith upon publication hereof, to delyver them and yeelde them to the custodie of the Captayne, to deliver unto the Generall his officers, that shall be appoynted to call for them, upon payne or losse of his or their wages, and treble the value, of them or him that shall be founde giltie, the one halfe thereof to be given unto him that shal apprehand any suche person, and the other halfe at hir Majesties appoyntment, and the partie found guiltie therein to be apprehended as a fellon.

4 Item, that no person or persons convey or carrie, out of any Ship or Shippes, any Ore or stone, or other commoditie whatsoever were had or found in the land called Meta Incognita, before they come in the place appoynted, which is against Dartford creeke in *the* River

---

[1] Best's narrative is slightly misleading here; Frobisher may indeed have reconnoitred further to the north; but to have made a further examination of the Hall's Island/Beare Sound area, he would have had to turn about and pass considerably to the south-east of the Countess of Warwick's Sound.

[2] These articles were omitted from the version reproduced by Hakluyt.

of Thames, and then and there to deliver none to anye person or persons, but such as shall be appoynted by hir Highnesses most honorable privie Counsell, upon the payne and danger abovesayd.

5 Item, forasmuche as in my voyage hither bounde, I landed uppon Freeseland, and divers other of the said Fleete, which land I named West England, from which land some brought stones, Ore, and other commodities, whereby hereafter they might use coulorable meanes to convey as well Ore, stones, and other things found in the abovesayd land, I do therefore charge every person and persons in the sayd Fleete, to deliver, or cause to be delivered, al maner of Ore, stones and other commodities, founde as well there as heere, to the Captaynes of every Shippe or Shippes, to be redelivered by him or them to the Generall, upon payne and danger abovesayd.

6 Item, that if any Shippe or Shippes by force of weather shall be separated from the Admirall, and afterwards happen to fall, or shall be in danger to fall into the handes of their enimies, that then all and every suche Shippe or Shippes shall have speciall regard before his falling into theyr handes, to convey away, and cast into the Seas all soche plattes or Cardes, as shall be in suche Shippe ot Shippes, of the abovesayde discovered lande, and all other knowledges thereof.

7 Item, that if any such Shippe or Shippes by force of weather shall be separated from the Fleete or Admirall, and shall afterwardes arrive at any Port in England, that then in suche case he shall not depart from that Porte, but shall give order and advertisemente to Michaell Locke, Treasourer of the companye, by whome hee or they shall have order from the Lordes of the privie Councell, what they shall do.

8 Item, forasmuch as sundry of the Fleetes companies have had lent them Crowes of Iron, sledges, pikeaxes, shovels, spades, hatchets, axes and divers other instrumentes for Mines, and mining used, and also dyvers of the sayde kind of instrumentes above named was lefte at the Countesse of Sussex Mine by the Aydes companye, and are yet kept from their knowledge by such as wrought at the sayd Myne, which instruments do apperteyne to the righte honorable and worshipfull company of the abovesayde discoverie, I do therefore charge all Captaynes and Maysters of every Shippe or Shippes, to make it knowen to his or their companyes, to the end that all such instrumentes, as well those lente as those that are otherwise deteyned and kept away, may be agayne restored and broughte aboord the Admirall ypon payne and danger expressed in the third Article.

By me *Martin Frobisher.*

The Fleetes returning homeward.

Having nowe receyved Articles and direction for oure returne homewardes, all other things being in forwardnesse and in good order, the last day of August the Fleete departed from the Countesse sound, excepting the Judith, and the Anne Frances, who stayed for the taking in of fresh water, and came forth the next daye, and mette the Fleete lying off and on, athwart Beares sounde, who stayed for the Generall, which was then gone ashore to dispatch the two Barkes, and the Busse of Bridewater, for their loading, whereby to get the companyes and other things aboorde.[1] The Captayne of the Anne Frances having most part of his company ashore, the first of September went also to Beares sound in his Pinnesse, to fetch hys men aboorde, but the winde grew so great immediatelye uppon their landing, that the Shippes at Sea were in great danger, and some of them hardly put from their Anckers, and greately feared to be utterly lost, as the Hopewell, wherein was Captayne Carew and others, who could not tell on which side their danger was most, for having mightie Rockes threatning on the one side, and driving Ilands of cutting Ise on the other side, they greatly feared to make shipwrack, *the* Ise driving so neare the*m*, that it touched their borde sprete. And by meanes of *the* sea, that was growne so hie, they were not able to put to sea with their smal Pynnesses, to recover their shippes.[2] And againe, the ships were not able to tarrie or lye athwarte for them, by meanes of the outrageous windes & swelling seas. The General willed the Captaine of the Anne Frances with his companye, for that nighte to lodge aboorde the Busse of Bridgewater, & went himself with the rest of his men aborde the barkes. But their numbers were so great, and the provision of the Barkes so scant, that they pestered one another exceedingly. They had good hope, that the nexte morning the weather woulde be fayre, wherby they might recover their shippes. But in the morning following it was farre worse, for the storme continued greater, the sea being more swollen, & the Fleete gone quite out of sighte. So that now their doubts beganne to growe great, for the ship of Bridgewater which was of greatest receit, and wherof they had best hope and made most accompt, roade so far to leewarde of the harborow mouth, that they were not able for the rockes (that lay betweene the winde and them) to leade it out to sea with a sayle. And the Barkes were alreadie so pestered with me*n*, and so slenderly furnished of provision, that they had scarce meate for six dayes, for such numbers.

The Generall in the morning departed to sea in the Gabriel, to seke for the Fleete, leaving the Busse of Bridgewater, and the Michael, behinde in Beare sound. The Busse set sayle, and thought by turning in the narrowe channell within the harborow, to get to windewarde: but being put to leewarde more, by that meanes was fayne to come to Ancker for hir better safetie, amongst a number of rockes, and there left in great danger of ever getting forth againe. The Michaell set sayle to follow the Generall, and could give *the* Busse no reliefe, although they earnestly desired the same. And the Captaine of the Anne Frances was lefte in harde election of two evils: either to abide his fortune with the Busse of Bridgewater, which was doubtfull of ever getting forthe, or else to be towed in his smal Pinnesse at the sterne of the Michae thorow the raging seas, for that the Barke was not able to receive or releeve halfe his company, wherin his daunger was not a little perillous.

So after, resolved to committee himselfe, withall his company, unto that fortune of God and sea, hee was daungerously towed at the sterne of the Barke for many myles, untill at length they espyed the Anne Frances under sayle, harde under their Lee, which was no smal comforte unto them. For no doubt both those and a great number more had perished for lacke of victuals and conveniente roome in the Barkes, without the helpe of the sayde ships. But the honest care that the Maister of the Anne Frances had of his Captaine, and the good regarde of dutie towards his General, suffered him not to depart, but honestly abode to hazarde a daungerous roade all the night long, notwithstanding all the stormy weather, when all

---

[1] Margin note: 'Returne homeward'.
[2] This final sentence refers once more to the men onshore at Sussex Island.

the Fleete besides departed. And the Pinnesse came no sooner aborde the shippe, and the men entred, but she presently sheavered and fel to peeces, and sunke at the ships sterne, with al the poore mens furniture: so weake was the boate with towing, and so forcible was the sea to bruse her in peeces. But (as God woulde) the men were all saved.

And at this presente in this storme, manye of the fleete were daungerously distressed, and were severed almost asunder. And there were lost in the whole Fleete well neere .xx. boates and Pinnesses in this storme, and some men stroken over boorde into the sea, and utterly lost. Manye also spente their mayne yardes and mastes, and with the continuall frostes, and deawe, the roapes of our shippes were nowe growen so rotten, that they went all asunder. Yet thankes be to God, all the fleete arrived safely in Englande aboute the firste of October, some in one place, and some in another. But amongst other it was most marvellous, how *the* Busse of Bridgewater got away, who being left behinde the fleete in great daunger of never getting forth, was forced to seeke a way northwarde, thorowe an unknowen channel full of rockes, upon the backe side of Beares sounde, and there by good hap found out a way, into the North sea (a very daungerous attempte) save that necessitie, which hath no lawe, forced them to trie masteries.[1] This foresayde North sea is the same which lyeth upon the backe side of all the North lande of Frobishers straites, where first *the* General himself in his Pinnesses, and some other of our company, have discovered (as they affirme) a great foreland, where they would have also a greate likelyhoode of the greatest passage towardes the South Sea, or *Mare del Sur*.[2]

The Busse of Bridgewater, as she came homeward, to *the* Southeast warde of Freseland, discovered a great Ilande in the latitude of (erased) Degrees, which was never yet founde before, and sayled three days alongst the coast, the land seeming to be fruitful, full of woods, and a champion countrie.[3]

There dyed in the whole Fleete in all this voyage not above fortie persons, whiche number is not great, considering howe many ships were in the Fleete, and how strange Fortunes wee passed.

A generall and briefe Description of the Countrey,
And condition of the people, which are found in Meta Incognita.

Having now sufficiently and truly set forth *the* whole circumstance, and particular handling of every occurrente in the three Voyages of our worthy Generall, Captayne Frobisher, it shal not be from the purpose to speake somewhat in generall, of the nature of this Countrey called *Meta Incognita*, and the condition of the savage people there inhabiting.

---

[1] It seems, therefore, that the *Busse of Bridgewater* was the first known European vessel to navigate Lupton Channel.

[2] If indeed Frobisher had passed north of Lok's Land (which could only have occurred during the 1576 voyage, when, according to Best, he 'met with store of exceeding great yse al this coast along, & coveting still to continue his course to the Northwardes, was alwayes by contrarie winde deteyned overthwarte these straytes, and could not get beyond'), the brevity of his reconnaissance – being of a few hours' duration only – indicates that he passed no further than the mouth of Cyrus Field Bay: a far less promising 'passage' even than Frobisher Bay.

[3] Margin note: 'A fruiteful new Iland discovered'.

First therefore concerning the Topographicall description of the place. It is nowe found in the last voyage, that Queene Elizabethes Cape, being scituate in Latitude at (erased) Degrees and a halfe, which before was supposed to be parte of the firme land of America, and also all the rest of the South side of Frobishers straytes, are all severall Ilands and broken land, and likewise so will all the North side of the said straytes fall out to be, as I thinke.[1]

These broken landes and Ilandes, being very many in number, do seeme to make there an Archipelagus, which as they all differ in greatnesse, forme, and fashion one from another, so are they in goodnesse, couloure, and soyle muche unlike. They all are very high lands, Moun-taynes, and in the most parts covered with Snow, even all the Sommer long. The Norther lands have lesse store of Snow, more grasse, and are more playne Countreys, the cause may be, for that the Souther Ilands receive all the Snow, *that* the cold winds and percing ayre bring out of the North. And contrarily, the Norther partes receive more warme blastes of milder aire from the South, whereupon may grow the cause why the people covet and inhabit more upon the North partes, than the South, as farre as we can yet by our experience perceive they doe. These people I judge to be a kinde of Tartar, or rather a kind of Samowey, of the same sort and condition of life *that* the Samoweides be to the Northeastwards, beyond Moscovy, who are called Samoweydes, which is as much to say in the Moscovy tong, as eaters of them-selves, and so the Russians their borderers doe name them.[2] And by late conference with a friend of mine (with whom I did sometime travell in the parts of Muscovy) who hath great experience of these Samoweides & people of *the* Northeast, I finde, that in all their maner of living, those people of the Northeast, and these of the Northweast, are like. They are of the couloure of a ripe Olive, which how it may come to passe, being borne in so cold a climate, I referre to *the* judgement of others, for they are naturally borne children of the same couloure & complexion as all the the Americans are, which dwell under the Equinoctiall line.

They are men very active and nimble. They are a strong people, and very warlike, for in our sighte, uppon the toppes of the hilles, they would often muster themselves, and after the maner of a skirmish, trace their ground very nimbly, and mannage their bowes and dartes with great dexteritie. They goe clad in coates made of the skinnes of beastes, as of Ceales, Dere, Beares, Foxes, and Hares. They have also some garments of feathers, being made of the cases of Foules, finely sowed and compact togither. Of all which sortes, we broughte home some with us into England, whiche we found in their tents. In Sommer,

---

[1] Best's error regarding the southern shore of Meta Incognita, first promulgated upon the map which accompanied his *True Discourse*, was no doubt influenced by the fleet's experiences in Hudson Strait. Fog had hidden much of the coastline during its westward passage therein, but on the returned passage, the dis-covery of the Annapolis and Gabriel straits seemed to suggest that the coastline was formed by a series of islands rather than a continuous landmass. Cf. plate V and Lok's comment (doc. 5, p. 72) on the region's topography, both of which appear to have been influenced by this perception.

[2] Best had first-hand experience of Muscovy, but in making this comparison, he may also have been recalling the letter recently sent to Elizabeth by the Russian tsar, Ivan IV, in which he had demanded the return of the three Inuit taken by Frobisher in the second voyage, claiming they were Samoyeds from the Iugra region in the far north-east of European Russia (PRO SP/91/1, 1a; 26 January 1578). The Russian word 'samoed', lit. 'self-eater' is probably a popular etymology from a Lappish word, and was applied by the Russians to several peoples of the Russian and Siberian north. Since the Iugra region is mentioned in the letter, Ivan's 'samoedy' were presumably the Nentsy. The reputation for cannibalism, for which there is no evidence (but which so profoundly influenced Best's narrative), seems to have arisen simply from the Russian name of the people.

they use to weare the hearie side of their coates outwarde, and sometime go naked for too much heate. And in Winter (as by signes thay have declared) they weare foure or five folde upon their bodies with *the* heare (for warmth) turned inward. Hereby it appeareth, that the ayre there is not indifferente, but eyther it is fervent hote, or else extreeme colde, and far more excessive in both qualities, than the reason of the clymate shoulde yeelde. For there it is colder, being under (erased) Degrees in Latitude, than it is at Warhins in the voyage to Saint Nicholas in Moscovie, being at above 70. degrees in latitude.[1] The reason hereof perhappes maye be, that thys Meta Incognita is much frequented and vexed with eastern and Northeasterne windes, whiche from the sea and Ise bringeth often an intollerable colde ayre, whiche was also the cause that this yere our straites were so long shutte up. But there is great hope and likely-hoode, that further within the straightes it will be more constant and temperate weather.

These people are in nature verye subtil, and sharpe witted, readie to conceive our meaning by signes, and to make answere, well to be understoode againe. As if they have not seene the thing whereof you aske them, they wyll winck, or cover their eyes with their hands, as who would say, it hath bene hyd from their sighte. If they understande you not, wherof you aske them, they wil stoppe their eares. They will teache us the names of eache thing in their language, which we desire to learne, and are apt to learne any thing of us. They delight in Musicke above measure, and will kepe time and stroke to any tune which you shal sing, both with their voyce, heade, hande, and feete, and will syng the same tune aptlye after you. They will rowe with our Ores in our boates, and kepe a true stroke with oure Mariners, and seeme to take great delight therein. They live in Caves of the Earth, and hunte for their dinners or praye, even as the Beare, or other wilde beastes do. They eate rawe fleshe and fishe, and refuse no meate, howsoever it be stincking. They are desperate in their fighte, sullen of nature, and ravenous in their manner of feeding.

Their sullen and desperate nature doth herein manifestlye appeare, that a companie of them being environed of our men on the toppe of a hie cliffe, so that they coulde by no meanes escape our handes, finding themselves in this case distressed, chose rather to cast themselves headlong downe the rockes into the sea, and so to be brused and drowned, rather than to yeelde themselves to our mens mercies.[2]

For their weapons, to offende their enimies, or kill their pray withal, they have Dartes, slings, bowes, and arrows headed with sharp stones, bones, and some with yron. They are exceedingly friendly and kinde harted, one to the other, & mourne greatly at the losse or

---

[1] 'Warhins': Vardö. Warhins appears to be a corruption of 'Wardhuis', the contemporary Dutch variant of the English 'Wardhouse', or Vardö, and may be the error of the original publisher. If Best used a bastard secretary script (which is almost certainly the case), 'ui' would appear near-identical to 'in'. The missing 'd' is more problematical, though it is by no means unlikely that the word was badly, or ambiguously written by Best. The context of the sentence – particularly Best's placement of the town at 70 degrees North – further supports its identification as Vardö.

[2] Best refers here to the incident during the 1577 voyage, when a number of gentlemen, led by Gilbert Yorke and Best himself, fell upon a small Inuit camp on the southern shore of Frobisher Bay, west of Jackman Sound. The Inuit fled to their boats, but, finding their escape blocked by an English pinnace which had tracked the march of the advancing land party, threw themselves into the sea thereafter rather than surrender. As the attack had been entirely unprovoked (this had been the first contact between Englishmen and the Inuit of the southern shore), it is hardly to be wondered at that the Inuit put little faith in their opponents' 'mercies'.

harme of their fellowes, and expresse their griefe of minde, when they part one from an other, with a mournefull song, and Dirges. They are very shamefast in betraying the secretes of nature, and verye chaste in *the* maner of their living: for whe*n* the ma*n* which we brought fro*m* thence into England (*the* last voyage) should put of his coat,or discover his whole body for cha*n*ge, he would not suffer the woman to be present, but put hir forth of hys Cabyn. And in all the space of two or three monethes, while the man lived in companie of the woman, there was never any thing seene or perceived betweene them, more than might have passed betweene brother and sister: but the woman was in all things very serviceable for the man, attending him carefully, when he was sicke,and he likewise in al the meates whiche they did eate togither, would carve unto hir of the sweetest, fattest, and best morsels they had. They wondred muche at all our things, and were afraide of our horses, and other beastes, out of measure. They beganne to growe more civill, familiar, pleasaunt, and docible amongst us in a verye shorte time.[1]

They have boates made of leather, and covered cleane over, saving one place in the middle to sit in, pla*n*cked within with timber, and they use to rowe therein with one Ore, more swiftly a great deale, than we in our boates can doe with twentie. They have one sort of greater boates wherin they can carrie above twentie persons, and have a Mast with a Sayle thereon, whiche Sayle is made of thinne Skinnes or bladders, sowed togither with the sinewes of fishes.

They are good fishermen, and in their small Boates, beeing disguised with their coates of Ceales skinnes, they deceyve the Fishe, who take them rather for their fellow Ceales, than for deceyving men.

They are good marke men. With their dart or arrowe they will commonly kill Ducke, or any other foule, in the head, and commonly in the eye.

When they shoote at a great fishe with anye of theyr Dartes, they use to tye a bladder thereunto, whereby they may the better finde them agayne, and the fishe not able to carrie it so easily away, for that the bladder dothe boy the darte, will at length be weerie, and dye therewith.

They use to traffike and exchange their commodities with some other people, of whome they have such things, as their miserable Countrey, and ignorance of arte to make, denyeth them to have, as barres of iron, heads of iron for their dartes, needles to make fouresquare, certayne buttons of copper, whiche they use to weare uppon theyr forheads for ornament, as our Ladyes in the Court of England do use great pearle.[2]

Also they have made signes unto us, that they have sene gold, and such bright plates of met-tals, whiche are used for ornaments amongst some people, with whome they have conference.

We fou*n*d also in their tents a Guinney Beane, of redde couloure, the which dothe usually grow in the hote Countreys: whereby it appeareth they trade with other Nations whiche dwell farre off, or else themselves are greate travellers.

They have nothing in use among them to make fyre withall, saving a kind of Heath and Mosse which groweth there.

---

[1] This is perhaps the most remarkable passage of Best's *True Discourse*. Having remorselessly attributed the worst habits and characteristics to the race (including wanton cruelty, treachery, cannibalism and, in his final comments, devil-worship), these, his only close-hand observations of individual Inuit, are ungrudgingly positive. There is no indication that Best was aware of the inconsistency of which he was strikingly guilty.

[2] Cf. p. 210, n.3.

And they kindle their fyre with continuall rubbing and fretting one sticke againste an other, as we do with flints.[1] They drawe with dogges in sleads upon the Ise, and remove their tents therwithal, wherein they dwel, in sommer, when they goe a hunting for their praye and provision againste Winter. They do sometime parboyle their meate a little and seeth the same in kettles made of beasts skins: they also have pannes cutte and made of stone very artificially: they use preaty ginnes wherewith they take foule.[2] The women carry their suck-ing children at their backes, and do feed them with raw flesh, which first they do a little chawe in their owne mouths.

The women have their faces marked or painted over with small blewe spottes: they have blacke and long haire on their heades, and trimme the same in a decent order. The men have but little hair on their faces, and very thinne beardes. For their common drincke, they eate Ise to quench their thirst withal. Their earth yeeldeth no graine or fruite of sustenaunce for man, or almost for beast to live uppon: and thepeople will eate grasse or shrubs of the grounde, even as our Kine doe.[3] They have no woodde growing in theyr countrey thereaboutes, and yet wee finde they have some timber among them, whiche we thinke doth grow farre off to the Southwardes of this place, about Canada, or some other part of the newe founde land: for there belike, the trees standing on the cliffes of the Sea side, by the waight of Ise and snowe in Winter overcharging them with waighte, when the Sommers thawe commeth above, and also the Sea underfretting them beneath, whiche winneth daylye of the land, they are undermined and fall down from those cliffes into the Sea, and with the tydes and currants are driven to and fro upon the coastes further off, and by conjecture are taken uppe here by these countrie people, to serve them to plancke and strengthen their boates withall, and to make dartes, bowes, and arrowes, and suche other things necessarie for their use. And of this kind of drift woodde wee finde all the Seas over, great store, whiche being cutte or sawed asunder, by reason of long driving in the Sea, is eaten of wormes, and full of hoales, of whych sorte theirs is founde to be.[4]

We have not yet founde anye venemous Serpent or other hurtefull thing in these partes, but there is a kinde of small flye or gnat that stingeth and offendeth sorelye, leaving many red spots in the face, & other places, where she stingeth. They have snowe and hayle in the beste time of their Sommer, and the ground frosen three fadome deepe.

These people are greate inchaunters, and use manye charmes of Witchcraft: for when their heads do ake, they tye a great stone with a string unto a sticke, and with certaine prayers & wordes done to the sticke, they lift up the stone from ground, which sometimes wyth all a mans force they cannot stir, & sometime againe they lifte as easily as a feather, and hope thereby with certaine ceremonious words to have ease and helpe. And they made us by signes to understand, lying groveling with their faces upon the grounde, and making a noise downeward, that they worshippe the Divell under them.

---

[1] Margin note: 'Howe they make fyre'.
[2] Margin note: 'Their Kettles and Pannes'.
[3] Margin note: 'The people eate grasse & shrubbes'.
[4] The strong south-westerly currents prevalent off Baffin Island makes it unlikely that such driftwood had moved north from Labrador. It is more likely that most, if not all, had originated as tree-falls in Hudson Bay and had been salvaged subsequently by the Inuit from inlets on the southern shores of the Meta Incognita peninsula.

They have great store of Deere, Beares, Hares, Foxes, and innumerable numbers of sundry sortes of wilde Foule, as Seamews, Gulles, Wilmotes, Duckes, &c. wherof our men killed in one day fifteene hundred.

They have also store of Hawkes, as Falcons, Tassels, &c. whereof two alighted upon one of our Shippes at theyr returne, & were brought into England, which some thinke will prove very good.

There are also great store of Ravens, Larkes, and Partridges, whereof the Countrey people feede.

All these Fowles are farre thicker clothed with downe and feathers, and have thicker skinnes than any in England have: for as that Countrey is colder, so nature hathe provided a remedie thereunto.

Our men have eaten of their Beares, Hares, Partriches, Larkes, and of their wilde Fowle, and find them reasonable good meate, but not so delectable as ours.

Their wilde Fowle must all be fleyne, their skinnes are so thicke: and they tast best fryed in pannes.

The Countrie seemeth to be muche subjecte to Earthquakes.

The ayre is very subtile, piercing and searching, so that if any corrupted or infected body, especially with the disease called Morbus Gallicus come there, it will presentlye breake forth and shewe it selfe, and cannot there by anye kinde of salve or medicine be cured.

Their longest Sommers day is of greate length, without any darke night, so that in July all the night long, we might perfitely and easilie wright & reade whatsoever had pleased us, which lightsome nightes were very beneficiall unto us, being so distressed with abundance of Ise as wee were.

The Sunne setteth to them in the Evening at a quarter of an houre after tenne of the clocke, and riseth agayne in the morning at three quarters of an houre after one of the clocke, so that in Sommer, theyr Sunne shineth to them twentie houres and a halfe, and in the nighte is absent three houres and a halfe.[1] And although the Sunne bee absent these 3½ houres, yet it is not darke that time, for that the Sunne is never above three or four degrees under the edge of their Horizon: the cause is, that the Tropicke Cancer doth cutte their Horizon at very uneaven and oblique Angles. But the Moone at any time of the yeare beeing in Cancer, having North Latitude, doth make a full revolution, so that sometimes they see the Moone above 24. houres togither.[2] Some of oure companie, of the more ignorant sort, thought we mighte continuallye have seen the Sunne and the Moone, had it not bin for two of three high Mountaynes.

The people are nowe become so warye, and so circumspecte, by reason of their former losses, that by no meanes can we apprehend any of them, althoughe we attempted often in this laste voyage. But to saye truth, we could not bestowe any great time in pursuing them, bycause of oure greate businesse in lading, and other things.[3]

To conclude, I finde in all the Countrie nothing, that maye be to delite in, either of pleasure or of accompte, only the shewe of Mine, bothe of golde, silver, steele, yron and blacke lead, with divers preaty stones, as blewe Saphyre, very perfect and others, whereof we

---

[1] Margin note: 'The length of their daye'.

[2] Margin note: 'The Moone maketh a revolution above ground'.

[3] Again, Hakluyt reflected the subsequent disappointment of hopes for the commodities of the new lands in ending Best's narrative at this point in the 1598–1600 edition of the *Principal Navigations*.

founde great plentie, maye give encouragement for men to seeke thyther.[1] And there is no doubt, but being well looked unto and thorowly discovered, it wyll make our Countrie both rich and happye, and of these prosperous beginnings will growe hereafter (I hope) moste happye endings. Whiche GOD of hys goodnesse graunte, to whom be all Prayse and Glorie, Amen.

[1] Margin note: 'Commodities of Meta Incognita'.

Plate VI: The elusive island of Busse, as represented in John Seller's *English Pilot* (2nd edn, 1673). Prudently, Seller named its features after several of his prominent contemporaries, and even included detailed soundings (which, of course, were never taken) for the hazardous 'Duke of Yorke's Sands'. The decorative embellishments indicate that Englishmen had as high hopes of the area's ivory and whale oil resources as they had of finding the island.

Editor's collection.

DOCUMENT 12

Thomas Wiars's *Relation*

The report of Thomas Wiars, passenger in the Emanuel, otherwise
called the Busse of Bridgewater, wherein James Leeche was Master,
one of the shippes in the last voyage of Master Martin Frobisher, 1578.
Concerning the discoverie of a great Island in their way homeward
the 12. of September.[1]

The Busse of Bridgewater, was left in Bears sounde at *Meta Incognita*, the second day of September behinde the fleete, in some distresse, through much winde ryding neere the Lee shoare, and forced there to ride it out upon the hazard of her cables and ankers, which were all aground but two. The thirde of September being fayre weather, and the wind North northwest she set sayle,[2] and departed thence and fell with *Frisland*, on the 8. day of September, at 6. of the clocke at night, and then they set off from the Southwest poynt of *Frisland*, the winde being at East, and East southeast, but that night the winde beared Southerly, and shifted oftentimes that night: but on the tenth day in the morning, the wind at west northwest fayre weather, they steered southeast, and by south, and continued that course untill the 12. day of September, when about 11. a clocke before noone, they descryed a lande, which was from them about five leagues, and the Southermost part of it was Southeast by East from them, and the Northermost next, North Northeast, or Northeast. The master accompted that *Frisland*, the Southeast poynt of it, was from him at that instant, when hee first descryed this newe Island, Northwest by North, 50. leagues.[3] They account this Island to be 25. leagues long, and the longest way of it Southeast, and Northwest. The Southerne part of it is in the latitude of 57. degrees and 1. second part, or thereabout.[4] They continued in sight of it, from the 12. day at 11. of the clocke, till the 13. day three of the clocke in the after noone, when they left it: and the last part they saw of it, bare from them, Northwest by North. There appeared two harboroughs upon that coast: the greatest of

---

[1] Originally published in the 1589 edition of Hakluyt's *Principall Navigations*.

[2] Cf. Best's contradictory account (document 11, p. 237), which claimed that the *Emmanuel* sailed northwards through a previously unknown strait (probably Lupton Channel) into the ocean. Had the wind been at west northwest, such a maneouvre would have been extremely difficult, and, more pertinently, pointless, given that setting a more straightforward south-easterly course would have delivered them directly from the lee-shore.

[3] If this was an accurate estimation of the *Emanuel*'s position in relation to the southern tip of Greenland (we have no way to verify the point), she would have been over the mid-Atlantic abyssal plain at this point.

[4] Margin note: 'The Island in length 25. leagues. This Island is in the latitude of 57. degrees and 1. second part'.

them seven leagues to the Northwardes of the Southermost poynt, the other but foure leagues.[1] There was verie much yce neere the same lande, and also twentie or thirtie leagues from it, for they were not cleare of yce, till the 15. day of September, after noone. They plied their voyage homewards, and fell with the west part of Ireland about *Galway*, and had first sight of it on the 25. day of September.

---

[1] It would appear that this comment provided the spur for later representations of 'Rupert's Harbour' and 'Shaftesbury Harbour' on the map of Busse Island included in Sellers' *English Pilot*.

DOCUMENT 13

Correspondence of Don Bernadino de Mendoza to Philip II, 15 November 1578.[1]

Since I wrote to your Majesty on the seventh ultimo, the minerals and duplicate text were sent to France on the twenty-sixth of the same.[2] I saw the arrival of Frobisher and the fleet that carried him, with that which was sent in it, as the ships had arrived at this river from the voyage to which I referred when I spoke to Your Majesty.

Frobisher sailed for Ireland with the 15 ships, conforming to the order of the Queen, left with his armada on the night of 6 June and passed a small island off Cape Durcey in western Ireland. He headed northwest and on the twentieth touched the Island of Frisland, wich they call West Frisland, described thus on map 17 of Ptolemy: In 1380, the brothers Nicolo and Antonio Genius (i.e., Zeni) were shipwrecked, during a severe storm, off the island of Frisland, where Zichmus was ruler. His customs were those of the Christians.

At this island, they entered a very large bay or branch of the sea, capable of accommodating 100 ships. Frobisher, with 14 men in a small boat, in a place which he has not been able to reach in the previous years, found two tents and a ship furnished with wood and covered with skins of seal and fish. Inside were some of their people, who, according to other observers, numbered about 20.[3] Their costume and manner were those of the land the English call Cathay or Meta Incognita. At 10 in the morning, in this inlet, a ship, in which was stored part of the wood with which they intended to build the houses and shelters that the Queen had requested and the beer to drink, was lost after having weathered a storm. The same day, at three in the afternoon, in order to have the most favourable winds, they sailed towards the northwest, in order to see the cape. The second of July they espied the land of the Queen's Foreland and Meta Incognita. Here they encountered an abundance of ice and at night, because of the force of the west[4] wind, all the ships found themselves ice-bound and in a great danger. They lost one vessel which was wrecked by the ice, for having full sails; the others travelled at half sail during the following day at sea.

The third (of July), they wished to enter into one of the two mouths which could be

---

[1] Archivo General de Simancas, Sección Estado, L831, ff. 266–7. We are indebted to Dr Bernard Allaire for the discovery and translation of this piece. Whilst broadly accurate upon general events and nomenclature, it contains several notable errors of detail (for example, the multiple sinkings of the bark *Denys*) which suggest that his spy's 'debriefing' had been a cursory one, or that he was being given deliberately misleading information.

[2] October.

[3] In fact, all other accounts state that the Inuit had fled upon seeing Frobisher's boat approach the shore (cf. docs 6, p. 112; 8, pp. 140).

[4] *Recte* east. Like many landsmen, Mendoza probably confused the correct statement of current and wind directions.

accomplished because the wind had grown so much stronger in the strait where they had been in the previous year. Land 12 leagues away was inaccessible, due to wind, which kept the ice from going out to the open sea, and the extremely foggy weather, which prevented them from recognizing the two capes[1] and being able to take to sea. With the force of the tides, the ships headed for the western part of the strait where they seemed more secure from stormy weather and mists that were at the entrance. Then they travelled 14 days and 50 leagues into a strait towards the western region, where they found a calm sea, finally arriving at a cape or island, which they called St George's and where they set off in a bark to reconnoitre.[2] They found many islands, all of which were small and on which they were unable to land any boat due to surrounding ice. Clear weather permitted these discoveries, they having been unable to enter this bay or strait the preceding year. For this reason they took a route along the coast of Labrador, heading southwest for more than 40 leagues without seeing land but, on 22 July, sailed towards the strait and cape which he had explored earlier.[3] They encountered much ice and a severe storm, which stormy and windy conditions never changed and kept the ice and high tide from escaping. Thus the tide of the strait constrained the sea in it with such fury that they were lifted to a great height by the waves and their sails became entangled, one with the other.[4] Because of this, when they arrived at their destination, they were in temporary ruin; the sailors were soaked. Now that the wind had grown so much stronger, on 26 July Frobisher resolved to enter with five ships, the largest of the two entrances.[5] This took place (on) 30 July in an arm of the sea or sound, named the previous year the Countess of Warwick sound.

Now the remaining five ships of the eight, were outside the entrances to the strait, where they spent 12 days and, being delayed, entered in good weather into the same sound, where they found the others. This was off a small island. Here, at the very location where they had mined last year, they extracted three kinds of ore from two places. they found similar ore, in the area surrounding, to be less rich.[6] Here was a stone like white sapphire, though not as hard, and another like ruby, but with a depth of colour inferior to jacinth. All of this land is very austere and sterile.

From this sound, they travelled five leagues into the land. A mountain appeared where

[1] Possibly Hatton's Headland and Cape Oxford, Resolution Island.

[2] Possibly in the latter-day North Bay area.

[3] Mendoza's report is confused here. Clearly, the English fleet did not sail southwestwards, otherwise, it would have entered Hudson Bay proper. The cape that he imagined the Englishmen to have sighted on 21 July was the Queen's Foreland, the fleet having retraced its passage eastwards in the three days following their observation of latitude. 'Labrador' was, of course, a contemporary catch-all term for the poorly-understood coast of North America above c. 55 degrees.

[4] Again, Mendoza appears to be confusing several occasions upon which the fleet encountered foul weather. His description here of the ships' predicament is more appropriate to the night of 2/3 July.

[5] But only because the other vessels had temporarily deserted the fleet. This, and the earlier reference to two 'entrances' or 'mouths', is confusing. Mendoza may have misunderstood the significance of the *Gabriel*'s discovery of the passage of water now known as Gabriel Strait, and assumed that it was regarded as a viable passage into Frobisher's 'strait' by members of the 1578 expedition, which it certainly was not.

[6] In fact, the reverse was true. The Reservoir trench on Countess of Warwick Island was only mined when poor weather prevented Frobisher's miners from travelling to the more productive outer workings.

they observed the sea on the opposite side. They distinguished a separate island, but were unable to discern what lay in the land beyond it.[1]

They men and women they saw were tiny and fled to the mountains. The land is very sterile and no trees can be seen, nor can it be said to be well inhabited. The men are small and of bad colour; the women wear lines on their faces like Indians. They are clothed in seal skins in the manner of the savages of the land of Labrador. They[2] put mirrors, little knives and other things on the ground in order to bring them to trade. They took them and left, in exchange at the same place, skins and other things of little value. then they departed in their small barks of leather with which they fish.

While they loaded their ships, they built a small stone house, where they left a quantity of gifts and little candles, buried the wood with which they intended to build houses, and 30 barrels of flour and salted meat, dry cod and pork, the provisions which 100 men, during eighteen months, were supposed to consume.[3] This plan was cancelled after they lost the ship which carried the beer, brought as drink for the colony, and part of the wood for their houses.

The salt they had buried the year before was found in ice, because the land is so frigid that it was snowing and Freezing on Santiago Day, so that they had to be diligent in removing the snow from ropes and ships, to prevent it from freezing in place.

The 13 charged ships sailed at low tide from their port, the beginning of September, although one of them could not leave with the others and remain behind; the crescent moon, which was thinly curled, came and they waited for the (next) tide. This tide changed every six hours, and six hours later most of the ships were en route. By 28 September they had returned to England, without receiving any news of the one that stayed behind with ore.[4]

Four miles from here, they discharged ore from the 12 ships into a house, which the Queen had ordered built for the purpose. The bulk of this rock (of which I sent your Majesty a sample)[5] resembles marcasite, with the other two types containing either white sapphire or mediocre ruby.

There is no one capable or reliable and I am therefore not at present sending Your Majesty the navigation chart, which shows the disposition of the newly discovered territory and island.[6]

He (?the spy) made an assay of the rocks, which does not agree, in the manner that one

---

[1] This description conforms to that of Fenton (doc. 8, pp. 165–6), regarding his reconnaissance with Thomas Morris on 27 August.

[2] I.e. the Englishmen.

[3] Cf. Fenton's claim that 'all thinges necessarie' of the colony's victuals were distributed throughout the fleet on 29 August for the return voyage. On 26 August, the day that he had buried some unspecified food-stuffs (probably meal and peas), the *Ayde* was down to a butt and a half of beef and a hogshead each of marow bones and pork (doc. 8, p. 166: marginalia). Under the circumstances, it is hardly likely that precious stocks of these commodities would have been interred.

[4] The *Emanuel of Bridgewater*.

[5] Philip's assayers had swiftly concluded the sample to be so worthless that Mendoza's spy's cover was suspected to have been compromised and a piece of false ore deliberately supplied (Philip II to Mendoza, 13 June 1578; *CSPS*, 1568–1579; 595).

[6] The provenance of this chart is not known. Clearly, it was more than a broad representation of the region of the type prepared for Best's *True Discourse* (plate V); but the only navigator's chart taken in the voyages that is known to us was that prepared by William Borough in 1576, and subsequently annotated by Christopher Hall to record variation of the compass. No copy of this is known to have been made (on this chart, see Waters, *Art of Navigation*, appendix 10a).

man had taken from it, from which they claimed they could subtract the cost from the profit. Now, it appears that the expense will exceed even that of the navigation.[1] This makes me wonder why someone who took part in this venture, a gentleman and a scholar, should sell that which they returned and then suggest that they could extract gold profitably.[2] It is incomprehensible that a land so cold as this can produce anything, though Frobisher has supported it as much as possible. Though fearful of discovery, they augmented assay results of the previous years, in order to encourage interested parties,[3] who maintain that it is the will and within the power of the Queen to make a return voyage next year. It would be useful to learn, at no cost, which of the ships, in particular, remains behind in the summer.[4] Under threat of pain of death and confiscation of goods, no one dares write about the navigation chart, about the voyages, the assays, nor anything about the new metallurgical plant because, according to Frobisher, the French with six ships went this summer to discover the land but due to ice, they did not advance sufficiently far. Then they sailed to Newfoundland, where they fought with an Englishman.[5]

[the remainder of the letter relates news of the failure of Humphrey Gilbert's 1578 voyage, the status of Drake's voyage ('now among the Camarrones') and a forthcoming Muscovy voyage]

[1] This appears to be a reference to the freight costs due to the owners of the hired ships. With over twelve hundred tons of ore returned in the voyage, they were owed almost fifty per cent more than had been envisaged at the despatch of the voyage.

[2] Presumably this was Michael Lok; though his transfer of £1000 of his stock in the enterprise to the Earl of Oxford was less than one half of his total commitment.

[3] A reference to Burchard Kranich's deliberate salting of his assays with silver-bearing 'antimonies' (PRO SP/12/122, 62; Collinson, p. 178), though this had certainly not been done with the knowledge of the adventurers, who stood to be (and were) the greatest losers from the despatch of a new, expensive voyage.

[4] I.e., in 1579, during a fourth voyage to Meta Incognita.

[5] Cf. Lok on Frobisher's revelation of this voyage to the commissioners (document 5, p. 84) Dr Allaire speculates that Mendoza referred to Troilus de la Roche's 1578 expedition, which encountered and fought with four English vessels. Clearly, there was no contact between this and the Frobisher voyages, though Mendoza's error is understandable.

BIBLIOGRAPHY

MANUSCRIPT SOURCES

CAMBRIDGE, Magdalene College, Pepys MSS 2133: Edward Fenton's 1578 ship's log of the ship *Judith*.

KEW, Public Record Office:

—— Exchequer King's Remembrancer (EKR) E164/ 35, 36: Michael Lok and others, financial accounts for the north-west enterprise.

—— E351/2195, 2215, 2216, 2219, 2200, 2203, 2204, 2235: Declared accounts of the Treasurer of the Navy.

—— State Papers, domestic, Elizabeth (SP/12 series): Too numerous to list in full here (see references in the footnote texts); many of those relating to the 1578 voyage were presented by Jones and Collinson; these were later reproduced, without additions, by Stefansson & McCaskill.

—— State Papers, Colonial: CO1/93, 156.

LONDON, British Library:

—— Additional MSS: 5664; 35831.

—— Cotton MSS: Otho E VIII, ff. 40-57.

—— Harleian MSS: 167/40, 41, 42 (respectively, Edward Selman's account of the 1578 voyage, Charles Jackman's 1578 ship's log for the *Judith* (fragment) and Christopher Hall's ship's 1578 log for the *Thomas Allen* and – on the return passage – *Ayde*);168; 541; 4630.

—— Lansdowne MSS: 100/1: 'The doynges of Captayne Furbusher Amongest the Companyes busynes' (Michael Lok's detailed and damning critique of Frobisher's activities during the course of the north-west enterprise); 100/4.

—— Sloane MS 2442

LONDON, Mercers' Hall, Ironmonger Lane, London: *List of Members of the Mercers Company from 1347*: Biographical card index of livery members.

OXFORD, Bodleian Library, Oxford: Rawlinson MS A200, 201.

SAN MARINO, California, Henry E. Huntington Library: HM MS 715 (Lok's accounts for the outfitting of the 1578 voyage. These pages were separated from the main body of accounts sometime before 1821, when Craven Ord, secondary of the King's Remembrancer Office, acquired and paginated the material now preserved in the PRO).

PRIMARY PRINTED SOURCES
Place of publication London unless stated otherwise

Anon, *A prayse, and reporte of Maister Martyne Forboishers voyage to Meta Incognita*, 1578.

Best, G., *A True Discourse of the Late Voyages of Discoverie ... under the Conduct of Martin Frobisher General*, 1578.

Billingsley, H., *The Elements of Geometrie of the most auncient Philosopher Evclide*, 1570.

Calendar of Letter books of the City of London, 1899.

Calendar of Patent Rolls, Elizabeth I, 1939–60.

Calendar of State Papers, Colonial Series, 1513–1616, 1862.

Calendar of State Papers relating to English affairs ... in the archives of Simancas, 4 vols, 1892–9.

Camden, W., *History of the Most Renowned and Victorious Princess Elizabeth, Late Queen of England*, edn of 1688.

Churchyard, T., *A prayse, and reporte of Maister Martyne Forboisher's Voyage*, 1578.

Collingwood, W., *Elizabethan Keswick: Extracts from the Original Account Books, 1564-1577, of the German Miners, in the Archives of Augsburg*, Whitehaven, 1987.

Collinson, R., *The Three Voyages of Martin Frobisher*, Hakluyt Society, 1st ser., 38, 1867.

Croft, P., *The Spanish Company*, London Record Society, 9, 1973.

Culpepper, N., *The Physicall Directory, or a Translation of the London Dispensatory*, 1649.

Dasent, J. R., ed., *Acts of the Privy Council of England*, new ser., 1890–1902.

Donno, E. S., ed., *An Elizabethan in 1582. The Diary of Richard Madox, Fellow of All Souls*, Hakluyt Society, 2nd ser., 147, 1976.

Ellis, T., *A true report of the third and last voyage into Meta Incognita atchieved by the worthie Capteine M. Martine Frobisher, Esquire. Anno 1578*, 1578.

Fleming, A., *Rythme Decasyllabicall, upon this last luckie voyage of worthie Capteine Frobisher*, 1577.

Fry, G. S., ed., *Inquisitiones Post Mortem Relating to the City of London, Tudor Period*, 3 vols, Index Library, 1896, 1898, 1901.

Hakluyt, R., *Discourse of Western Planting*, ed. by D. B. & A. M. Quinn, Hakluyt Society, extra ser., 45, 1993.

——, *The principall navigations, voiages and discoveries of the English nation by Richard Hakluyt* (facsimile of 1589 edn), ed. by Skelton, R. A. and Quinn, D. B. and A. M., 2 vols, Hakluyt Society, extra ser., 39a and 39b, 1965.

——, *The Principal Navigations, Voyages, Traffiques and Discoveries of the English Nation, etc.*, 12 vols, Glasgow, 1903–5.

Halliwell, J. O., *The Private Diary of John Dee*, Camden Society, 1842.

Hughes P. L. and Larkin, J. F., eds, *Tudor Royal Proclamations*, vol. 3; New Haven, 1969.

Kinder, A. G., 'The Protestant Pastor as Intelligencer: Casiodoro de Reina's Letters to Wilhelm IV, Landgrave of Hesse-Cassel, 1577–1582'; *Bibliothèque d'humanisme et renaissance*, 58, 1, 1996, pp. 105–18.

Markham, A. H., *The Voyages and Works of John Davis the Navigator*, Hakluyt Society, 1st ser., 59a, 1880.

Marsden, R. G., ed., *Select Pleas in the Court of Admiralty*, Selden Society, 6, 1894; 9, 1897.

——, *Documents Relating to the Law and Custom of the Sea*, Navy Records Society, I, 1915.

Martin, C. T., 'The Diary of Francis Walsingham, 1570–83', *Camden Society Miscellanies*, 6, 1871, pp. 1–104.

McDermott, J., *The Account Books of Michael Lok, relating to the North-West Voyages of Martin Frobisher, 1576–1578: Text and Analysis* (with transcriptions of PRO E164/35, 36 and HM 715), unpublished M.Phil. thesis, University of Hull, 1984.

Murdin, W., ed., *Collection of State Papers … of Lord Burghley*, 2 vols, 1740, 1759.

Purchas, S., *Hakluytus Posthumus, or Purchas his Pilgrims, etc*, London, 1625–6.

Quinn, D. B., ed., *The Hakluyt Handbook*, 2 vols, Hakluyt Society, 2nd ser., 144–5, 1974.

——, *The Roanoke Voyages 1584–1590*, 2 vols, Hakluyt Society, 2nd ser., 104–5, 1955.

——, *The Voyages and Colonising Enterprises of Sir Humphrey Gilbert*, 2 vols, Hakluyt Society, 2nd ser., 83–4, 1940.

——, *Richard Hakluyt, Editor: A Study Introductory to the Facsimile Edition of Richard Hakluyt's Divers Voyages, 1582*, 2 vols, Amsterdam, 1967.

——, *New American World*, 5 vols, New York, 1979.

Read, C., 'Despatches of Castelnau de la Mauvissière, 1577–81', *American Historical Review*, 31, 1926, pp. 285–96.

Rundall, T., *Narrative of Voyages Towards the North-west in search of a Passage to Cathay and India, 1496 to 1631*, Hakluyt Society, 1st ser., 5, 1849.

Stefansson, V. and McCaskill, E., *The Three Voyages of Martin Frobisher*, 2 vols, 1938.

Stow, J., *Annales, or, a Generall Chronicle of England, etc*, edn of 1615.

Tawney, R. H., *Tudor Economic Documents*, 3 vols, 1924.

Taylor, E. G. R., ed., *A Regiment for the Sea*, Hakluyt Society, 2nd ser., 121, 1963.

——, *The Troublesome Voyage of Captain Edward Fenton, 1582–3*, Hakluyt Society, 2nd ser., 113, 1959.

——, *The Original Writings and Correspondence of the two Richard Hakluyts*, 2 vols, Hakluyt Society, 2nd ser., 76–7, 1935.

Temple, R. C., ed., *The World Encompassed and Analogous Contemporary Documents Concerning Sir Francis Drake's Circumnavigation of the World*, Amsterdam, 1971.

SECONDARY WORKS

Allaire, B., 'French Reactions to the North-West Voyages and the Assays of the Frobisher Ore by Geoffrey Le Brumen, 1576–1584', in Symons, *Meta Incognita*, II, pp. 589–606.

——, 'Martin Frobisher, the Spaniards and a Sixteenth Century Northern Spy', in Symons, *Meta Incognita*, II, pp. 575–88.

Alsford, S., ed., *The Meta Incognita Project: Contributions to Field Studies*, Hull, Quebec, 1993.

Andrews, K. R., *Elizabethan Privateering*, Cambridge, 1964.

——, *Drake's Voyages: a Re-assessment of their Place in Elizabethan Maritime Expansion…*, New York, 1967.

——, 'The Elizabethan Seaman', *Mariner's Mirror*, 68, 1982, pp. 245–62.

Babcock, W. H., *Legendary Islands of the Atlantic: A Study in Medieval Geography*, New York, 1922.

Baldwin, R., 'Speculative Ambitions and the Reputations of Frobisher's Metallurgists', in Symons, *Meta Incognita*, II, pp. 401–76.

Boas, F. S., *Sir Philip Sidney: Representative Elizabethan*, Rochester, 1955.

Bramston, Sir John, *The Autobiography of Sir John Bramston*, Camden Society, 1845.

Burwash, M., *English Merchant Shipping 1460–1540*, Toronto, 1947.

Carus-Wilson, E. M., *Medieval Merchant Venturers*, 1954.

Cawley, R. R., *Unpathed Waters: Studies in the Influence of the Voyagers on Elizabethan Literature*, New York, 1967.

Cheshire, N., Waldron, T. and Quinn, A. and D. B., 'Frobisher's Eskimos in England', *Archivaria*, 10, 1980, pp. 23–50.

Cipolla, C. M., *Guns and Sails in the Early Phase of European Expansion, 1400–1700*, 1965.

Clay, C. G. A., *Economic Expansion and Social Change: England 1500–1700*, 2 vols, Cambridge, 1984.

Connell-Smith, G., *Forerunners of Drake*, Plymouth, 1954.

Davis, R., *The Rise of the English Shipping Industry*, 1962.

Dickens, A. G., *The English Reformation*, 1964.

Dictionary of National Biography, 1895–1900.

Donald, M. B., 'Burchard Kranich', *Annals of Science*, 6, 1950, pp. 308–22.

—— , *Elizabethan Copper: The History of the Company of the Mines Royal, 1565–1603*, Whitehaven, 1955.

Elliott, J. H., *The Old World and the New: 1492–1650*, Cambridge, 1970.

Elliot, K. M., 'The First Voyages of Martin Frobisher', *English Historical Review*, 32, 1917, pp. 89–92.

Fitzhugh, W. W. and Olin, J. S., eds, *Archeology of the Frobisher Voyages*, Smithsonian Institution, 1993.

Foster, F. F., *The Politics of Stability: A Portrait of the Rulers in Elizabethan London*, 1977.

Friel, I., *The Good Ship: Ships, Shipbuilding and Technology in England, 1200–1520*, 1995.

—— , 'Frobisher's Ships: the Ships of the North-West Atlantic Voyages, 1576–1578', in Symons, *Meta Incognita*, II, pp. 299–352.

Fuller, T., *The History of the Worthies of England*, 3 vols, edn of 1840.

Fury, C. A., 'Training and Education in the Elizabethan Maritime Community, 1585–1603', *Mariner's Mirror*, 85, 1999, pp. 147–61.

Gad, F., *History of Greenland*, I, Montreal, 1971.

Hall, C. F., *Arctic Researches and Life Among the Esquimaux*, New York, 1865.

Herbert, W., *The History of the Twelve Great Livery companies of London*, 2 vols, 1834–7.

Hill, C., *Intellectual Origins of the English Revolution*, Oxford, 1965.

Hogarth, D. D., Boreham, P. W. and Mitchell, J. G., *Mines, Minerals, Metallurgy: Martin Frobisher's North-west Venture, 1576–1581*, Hull, Quebec, 1994.

Hutchinson, G., *Medieval Ships and Shipping*, Leicester, 1994.

Jones, F. *The Life of Sir Martin Frobisher, knight, containing a Narrative of the Spanish Armada*, 1878.

L'Estrange-Ewen, C., 'Organized Piracy round England in the Sixteenth Century', *Mariner's Mirror*, 35, 1949, pp. 29–42.

Lloyd, R., *Dorset Elizabethans at Home and Abroad*, 1967.

Loades, D., *The Tudor Navy*, Cambridge, 1992.

MacCaffrey, W.T., *Queen Elizabeth and the Making of Policy, 1572–1588*, Princeton, 1981.

Manhart, G. B., 'The English Search for a North-west Passage in the Time of Queen Elizabeth', in Rowland, A. L. and Manhart, G. B., *Studies in English Commerce and Exploration in the Reign of Elizabeth*, University of Philadelphia, 1924, pp. 1–179.

Marcus, G. J., 'The First English Voyages to Iceland', *Mariner's Mirror*, 42, 1956, pp. 313–18.

Marsden, R. G., 'Early Career of Sir Martin Frobisher', *English Historical Review*, 21, 1906, pp. 538–44.

Mathew, D., 'The Cornish and Welsh Pirates in the Reign of Elizabeth', *English Historical Review*, 39, 1924, pp. 337–48.

McDermott, J. and Waters, D. W., 'Cathay and the Way Thither: the Navigation of the Frobisher Voyages', in Symons, *Meta Incognita*, II, pp. 353–400.

McDermott, J., *Elizabethan Privateer: Sir Martin Frobisher*, Yale, 2001.

——— , 'The Company of Cathay: the Financing and Organization of the Frobisher Voyages', in Symons, *Meta Incognita*, I, pp. 147–78.

——— , 'Michael Lok, Mercer and Merchant Adventurer'; in Symons, *Meta Incognita*, I, pp. 119–46.

——— , 'A right Heroicall Heart: the Life of Sir Martin Frobisher', in Symons, *Meta Incognita*, I, pp. 55–118.

——— , 'The Construction of the Dartford Furnaces'; in Symons, *Meta Incognita*, II, pp. 505–22.

——— , 'Frobisher's 1578 Voyage: Early Eyewitness Accounts of English Ships in Arctic Seas', *Polar Record*, 32, 183, 1996, pp. 325–34.

——— , 'Humphrey Cole and the Frobisher Voyages', in Ackermann, S., ed., *Humphrey Cole: Mint, Measurement and Maps in Elizabethan England*, British Museum Occasional Paper no. 126, 1998, pp. 15–19.

McFee, W., *The Life of Sir Martin Frobisher*, New York, 1928.

Morrison, S. E., *The European Discovery of America: The Northern Voyages A.D. 500–1600*, New York, 1971.

Oppenheim, M., *A History of the Administration of the Royal Navy, and of Merchant Shipping in Relation to the Navy from 1509 to 1660*, 1896.

Parker, J., *Books to Build an Empire*, Amsterdam, 1965.

Parks, G. B., *Richard Hakluyt and the English Voyages*, New York, 1928.

Pulman, M. B., *The Elizabethan Privy Council in the Fifteen-Seventies*, Berkeley, 1971.

Quinn, D. B. and Ryan, A. N., *England's Sea Empire*, 1983.

Quinn, D. B., 'The Context of English North-west Exploration', in Symons, *Meta Incognita*, I, pp. 7–18.

——— , 'Renaissance Influences in English Colonization', *Royal Historical Society Transactions*, fifth ser., 26, 1976, pp. 73–93.

——— , *Sebastian Cabot and Bristol Exploration*, Bristol, 1993.

Rabb, T., *Enterprise and Empire, Merchant and Gentry Investment in the Expansion of England, 1575–1630*, Cambridge, Mass., 1967.

Ramsay, G. D., *English Overseas Trade during the Centuries of Emergence*, 1957.

Read, C., *Bibliography of British History, Tudor Period*, Oxford, 1959.

——, *Lord Burghley and Queen Elizabeth*, New York, 1960.

Rowley, S., 'Inuit Oral History: The Voyages of Sir Martin Frobisher, 1576–1578', in Alsford, S. ed., *The Meta Incognita Project: Contributions to Field Studies*, Canadian Museum of Civilization, Mercury Series, Directorate Paper no. 6, 1993, pp. 211–19.

Rowse, A. L., *Tudor Cornwall*, 1941.

Ruggles, R. I., 'The Cartography of the Frobisher Voyages', in Symons, *Meta Incognita*, I, pp. 179–256.

Scammell, G. V., 'The Sinews of War: Manning and Provisioning English Fighting Ships', *Mariner's Mirror*, 73, 1987, pp. 351–67.

Scott, W.R., *The Constitution and Finance of English, Scottish and Irish Joint-Stock Companies to 1720*, 3 vols, Cambridge, 1910.

Senior, W., 'Judges of the High Court of Admiralty', *Mariner's Mirror*, 13, 1927, pp. 335–7.

Shammas, C., 'The "Invisible Merchant" and Property Rights'; *Business History*, 17, 1975, pp. 95–108.

Sherman, W. H., 'John Dee's Role in Martin Frobisher's North-west Enterprise', in Symons, *Meta Incognita*, I, pp. 283–98.

Shirley, R. W., *The Mapping of the World: Early Printed World Maps, 1472–1700*, 1984.

Skeat, W. W. and Mayhew, A. L., *A Glossary of Tudor and Stuart words*, Oxford, 1914.

Smith, J. C. C., ed., *Index of Wills proved in the Prerogative Court of Canterbury, 1383–1558*, II, 1895.

Sturtevant, W. C. and Quinn, D. B., 'This New Prey: Eskimos in Europe in 1567, 1576 and 1577'; in Feest, C., ed., *Indians and Europe: an Interdisciplinary Collection of Essays*, Aachen, 1987, pp. 61–140.

Symons, T. H. B., *Meta Incognita: A Discourse of Discovery. Martin Frobisher's Arctic Expeditions, 1576–1578*, 2 vols, Hull, Quebec, 1999.

Taylor, E. G. R., *Tudor Geography, 1485–1583*, 1930.

——, *Late Tudor and Early Stuart Geography*, 1934.

——, 'Voyages of Martin Frobisher', *Geographical Journal*, 91, 1938, pp. 360–63.

——, *The Haven-Finding Art*, 1956.

Tillyard, E. M. W., *The Elizabethan World Picture*, 1943.

Unwin, G., *The Gilds and Companies of London*, 1908.

Waters, D. W., *The Art of Navigation in England in Elizabethan and Early Stuart Times*, 1958.

Watt, J. and Savours, A., 'The Captured "Countrey People": Their Depiction and Medical History', in Symons, *Meta Incognita*, II, pp. 553–62.

Watt, J., 'The Medical Climate of Frobisher's England: Maritime Influences', in Symons, *Meta Incognita*, I, pp. 257–82.

——, 'The Frobisher Voyages of 1576, 1577 and 1578: The Medical Record', in Symons, *Meta Incognita*, II, pp. 607–32.

Wernham, R. B., *Before the Armada: the Growth of English Foreign Policy, 1485–1588*, 1966.

Willan, T. S., *The Muscovy Merchants of 1555*, Manchester, 1953.
——, *The Early History of the Russia Company*, Manchester, 1956.
——, *Studies in Elizabethan Foreign Trade*, Manchester, 1959.
——, *A Tudor Book of Rates*, Manchester, 1962.
Williamson, J. A., 'Michael Lok', *Blackwoods Magazine*, 196, 1914, pp. 58–72.

INDEX

Contemporary place-names which have not survived are shown in italics. Numbers in italics refer either to the depiction of the subjects in illustration or, in the case of documents, to the page numbers in which they are reproduced. Ship names are listed under 'ships'.